Women of America

Women of America
A History

Carol Ruth Berkin
Baruch College, City University of New York

Mary Beth Norton
Cornell University

Houghton Mifflin Company • Boston

Dallas   Geneva, Illinois   Hopewell, New Jersey
Palo Alto   London

Library of Congress Catalog Card Number: 78-69589
ISBN: 0-395-27067-7

We dedicate this book jointly to the women who taught us and the women we teach, in the hope that it may prove a fitting tribute to the former and an encouragement for the latter.

Contents

List of Documents

Preface

This volume of original essays and documents has been carefully planned to present a chronologically and topically balanced picture of the lives of American women throughout the history of European settlement on the North American continent. It presents systematic analyses of major aspects of the American female experience, though it does not attempt to be comprehensive.

The articles, all written specifically for this book, are grouped into three chronological sections, with the exception of an opening essay that examines demographic influences on the lives of American women over the past 370 years. Within the chronological divisions, articles touch on four topical areas of crucial significance: education, economic status, legal status, and ideology.

Each part begins with an introductory essay containing an overview of women's status during that period and a preview of the articles to follow. The first essay in each of the chronological divisions is the biography of a woman who is not necessarily well known or "representative," but whose life illuminates especially well the status of women in her own day. Most of the authors have selected documents to accompany their articles, so that students may become acquainted with the wide variety of sources that can be used for the study of women's lives. The women represented in the volume range from colonial Quakers, Chinese in California, and a black union organizer to a businesswoman, an educator, World War II workers, and a writer.

The editors express their thanks to the editors at Houghton Mifflin, whose advice and guidance have been instrumental in bringing the project to fruition. We are also grateful to those who read the manuscript before publication: Carroll Smith-Rosenberg, University of Pennsylvania; Mary P. Ryan, State University of New York at Binghamton; and Sudie Duncan Sides, San Francisco State University.

C. R. B.
M. B. N.

Part One
Introduction

Women and American History

Mary Beth Norton and Carol Ruth Berkin

It is singularly appropriate that Virginia Dare, the earliest American woman whose name is familiar to the general public, vanished without a trace shortly after her birth, along with all the other members of the Roanoke colony. For like her, successive generations of American women have vanished from the historical record, leaving not even their names for their descendants to recognize and revere. The United States had founding mothers of various races and ethnic backgrounds, but on the whole our history celebrates only the white founding fathers whose names appear again and again in standard textbooks.

Within the past ten years this situation has started changing, for younger scholars of both sexes are trying to recapture the lost history of American women. Their work, coupled with other studies of the women of Africa, Asia, and Europe, represents the beginnings of the new discipline of women's history. Although few people today would question the validity of studies investigating the role of racial and ethnic minorities in the American past, many still doubt the value of inquiries into the history of the American majority: females. Yet the growing number of women's history courses and the publication of books like this one testify to increasing interest in the field and to its intellectual vitality.

Each year new discoveries in the history of women illuminate shadowy corners of the lives of white, red, yellow, and black people on the American continent, and it seems clear that such findings will soon force the rewriting of the standard accounts of our nation's past. Just as recent studies of Native Americans have changed our view of European-Indian contacts and examinations of life in the slave quarters have altered our picture of the "peculiar institution," so scholarly work on women also promises to reshape our understanding of American history, perhaps more dramatically than anyone can predict today.

When women, who have until now been seen as peripheral to the study of the past, are placed at the center of our inquiry, historical commonplaces are frequently turned inside out and even upside down. Furthermore, topics that once received no attention from scholars—such as the experience of childbirth, changing household technology, and female friendships—suddenly come to the fore. It is as though, like Columbus, historians have found a whole new hemisphere crying out for exploration, the existence of which will eventually change their comprehension of the previously known world.

The potential impact of the new scholarship becomes impressively clear when the recent work on women's history is placed beside the mainstream studies that have centered, and continue to focus, on men, even though their titles contain sexually neutral words like *family, children, youth,* or *people.* Ironically, despite many years of male-oriented research and thousands of books written about the male experience in America, scholars have rarely asked questions about men that parallel those now being asked about women. Thus, students of the female experience have opened up new realms of inquiry that should greatly increase our understanding of the lives of American men in the past; male friendships, the paternal role, men's self-perceptions, and the functions of men's organizations should now come under renewed and more sophisticated scrutiny.

Of course, the primary justification for the study of women's history does not come from its creation of new insights for the history of men. Rather, the examination of the history of women as a distinct group has two purposes: to rescue that past from obscurity and identify those parts pertaining exclusively to females; and to contribute to the rewriting of American history so that the experience of women may be encompassed within a synthetic overview of the development of our nation.

The essays in this volume, all composed specifically for publication here, represent the latest scholarship in the field. The authors have adopted different approaches to their subjects, and taken as a whole the articles not only provide a great deal of new information about the history of American women, but they also illustrate the myriad ways in which women's history can be studied. Before we can examine the contributions of this book in the context of current scholarship, however, we must briefly survey the history of American women's history, an endeavor known as *historiography.*

THE HISTORIOGRAPHY OF AMERICAN WOMEN

Although the discipline of women's history is new, the first book examining the role of women in the American past appeared in

1848, when Elizabeth Fries Lummis Ellet, author of numerous books and magazine articles, published her two-volume work, *The Women of the American Revolution.* (She subsequently added a third volume.) Elizabeth Ellet, dismayed by the lack of attention to women's contributions to the war effort found in standard histories of the time—a flaw that continues to our own day— carefully researched her study by talking to the children and grandchildren of her subjects and by gaining access to private family correspondence. She confined her study to the "great women" of the late eighteenth century, such as Martha Washington and Abigail Adams, and did not even mention female Loyalists. Although she did not present a comprehensive picture of revolutionary women, her work nevertheless set enviable standards for authenticity and accuracy in an era when male historians tended to be careless in their use of sources.

It is perhaps a coincidence that Elizabeth Ellet's first book on the history of American women (she eventually wrote several others) appeared in 1848, the year of the first women's rights conference at Seneca Falls, New York. Although the precise timing was possibly fortuitous, the general conjunction between the women's rights movement and the writing of women's history was not, just as it was not by chance that the civil rights movement and the burgeoning of interest in black history occurred in close proximity in the 1950s and 1960s. When a group that views itself as oppressed or discriminated against seeks to gain a more secure status in the present, that group often tries to recapture its collective past. A minority hitherto deprived of power and status, and perhaps even of a mutual heritage, attempts to better its position not only by winning current political and economic battles, but also by separating its history from that of the controlling faction, which in the United States is composed of white males.

These observations should make it apparent that the same historical forces that led Elizabeth Ellet and her immediate successors to write about the history of American women in the mid-nineteenth century apply also to the scholars of the 1970s. Only with the rebirth of feminism in our own era has women's history acquired recognition as a valuable field of study. But in the intervening years, other scholars labored to recover the female past, and their work also deserves recognition.

The leaders of the women's rights movement—Elizabeth Cady Stanton, Susan B. Anthony, and their associates—understood the importance of their enterprise; beginning in the late nineteenth century, they collaborated on the multivolume *History*

of Woman Suffrage (completed in 1922 after the long-sought
goal had at last been won), which remains the standard source
for the study of the early women's movement. In subsequent
years, biographies of the suffragists and of other prominent American women of the seventeenth, eighteenth, and nineteenth
centuries gained a large popular audience, but few books were
published that would today be termed substantial scholarly
contributions. An exception was Elisabeth Anthony Dexter's
Colonial Women of Affairs (1924), which examined the role of
ordinary eighteenth-century women in business enterprises. By
carefully culling colonial newspapers for advertisements placed
by businesswomen, Dexter showed that female colonists participated
in a wide variety of occupations outside the home. Interestingly,
Dexter, like many current historians of women, had an explicit
ideological purpose in mind when she wrote her book: she
wanted to prove to the people of the twentieth century that in the
past some American women had been more than wives and
mothers, working at very "unfeminine" occupations outside the
home, and she succeeded admirably.

Other historians interested in defining women's role in the
American past began to examine not the reality of their lives,
as Dexter had done, but rather the ideology behind the common
dictum that "woman's place is in the home." Mary Sumner
Benson's *Women in Eighteenth-Century America: A Study in
Opinion and Social Usage* presented an exhaustive discussion of
English, French, and American writings on the subject of women's
place in society. Her work, published in the 1930s, stood alone
for some years, but then in 1966 Barbara Welter's influential article,
"The Cult of True Womanhood," appeared, which analyzed in
detail the characteristics of the "true woman" described at length
in the many nineteenth-century books advising young ladies on
their behavior. Several years later Gerda Lerner supplied a
necessary corrective to Welter's work when she pointed out in
another major article, "The Lady and the Mill Girl," that the
ideal of the lady was just that—an ideal—and that many nineteenth-century American women were factory workers who had
neither the time, the money, nor the inclination to become "true
women." Unfortunately, in recent years some scholars have
forgotten Lerner's warning and have overemphasized the importance of prescriptive literature in determining the conditions
of women's lives.

Space will not permit a more extended discussion of historiography at this point, but the broad outlines of American
women's history as written before 1970 should be clear. For the
most part, scholars studied the lives of great women, nearly all

of them white, and focused their attention almost exclusively on two aspects of the American female past: the woman suffrage movement (the most important examination of which was Eleanor Flexner's *Century of Struggle,* published in 1959) and nineteenth-century definitions of woman's place written mainly by men.

A CONCEPTUAL BACKGROUND FOR CURRENT SCHOLARSHIP

A summary of the common view of women's history that could be drawn from the works just discussed would read something like this. In the colonial period, women were active partners in the effort of each household to earn its living in a harsh, trying environment. Working alongside their husbands and toiling at difficult tasks, they made vital economic contributions to society and enjoyed the respect of their families. After the process of industrialization began in the nineteenth century, by contrast, women became "ladies of leisure" because of the development of mass production of cloth and large-scale food processing. Having lost their economic function, they also lost status and gained a reputation for weakness and delicacy. They retreated into the home, concentrating their energies on childbearing, wearing fashionable clothing, and reading genteel novels. In the early twentieth century, so the account continues, women finally won the vote, and the slow but inexorable emancipation from the confines of the home began. Women in the United States today, it is often argued, find themselves better off than any of their female predecessors with the exception of those who lived in the early colonies.

This schema is neat; it is also satisfyingly filled with a nostalgic vision of past egalitarianism, a fall from that perfection, and a recounting of women's attempts to regain what had been lost. It has both heroines (the leaders of the women's rights movement) and villains (those who opposed suffrage). It is, furthermore, morally uplifting, suggesting that things are getting better and that improvements have come largely through the efforts of hard-working women. The theory has many attractions, but is it accurate? The newest scholarly work in the field, including the essays in this book, suggests that it is not. Upon examination, the notion that women's lives were better in the colonial era, grew worse in the nineteenth century, and are currently becoming better again proves to be seriously flawed and simplistic. Recent books and articles not only dispute the facts and interpretations that form the foundation of the synthesis just outlined but also raise questions about the basis of the analysis itself, the attempt to judge women's experiences in terms of whether they were good or bad.

The problem is caused by scholars' inability to agree on the components of a better or worse life. A variety of conclusions can be reached from the same evidence or from different sorts of evidence that address the same point. How, for example, should we interpret the introduction of the mass production of cloth in the early nineteenth century in terms of its impact on women's daily lives? On the most direct level, it replaced the laborious process of the home manufacture of cloth—involving the lengthy tasks of carding wool or hatcheling flax, spinning, weaving, and then sewing—with a simple trip to the local store to buy finished, machine-made cloth and eventually ready-made clothing. If the women who lived through the transition had been asked what they thought of the new circumstances, they would undoubtedly have been pleased to be freed from the monotonous and time-consuming chore. But historians have largely interpreted the same development as bad for women because it removed a vital economic function from the home and thus apparently reduced women's importance in the household. Whom are we to believe? Can historians, in their assessment of the past, ignore the attitudes of the women they study? On the other hand, must we entirely accept our subjects' view of themselves? Or, perhaps, is the argument over this value judgment a smokescreen that has prevented scholars from fully examining the implications of changes in the female role in America over time?

Increasingly, it appears that the answer to this last question is yes. Attempting to measure the position of women in American society over the past 370 years by an absolute standard of good or bad (as defined by current feminist thinking) can trap women's history in a maze in which polemics dominate conceptual schemes. Instead of maintaining the mental distance from their sources that would facilitate an objective analysis, historians sometimes allow themselves to become swept up in the same arguments that engrossed their subjects, taking sides in the age-old conflict concerning women's role in society. To contend that such an anachronistic mode of conceptualizing women's history is faulty and should be discarded is not to say that historians should avoid all value judgments in assessing the circumstances of women's lives in the American past. But it is to argue that scholarly work organized around a determination to prove that women in a particular era were better or worse off than those in another time or place leads ultimately to an interpretive dead end.

Fortunately many scholars, including those whose work is published in this book, have now recognized the failings of the value-laden approach and have started to study women in the American past with an open mind. They have challenged the earlier synthesis by asking new questions and by looking at previously untapped sources. In reassessing the status of women in America they have ventured into novel fields of inquiry, interesting themselves in issues never before considered. Among the questions that intrigue contemporary historians of female Americans are the following: How did family context shape the lives of women from different economic classes and various racial and ethnic backgrounds? How did they relate to their husbands and children, especially their daughters? What sorts of relationships (informal or organized) did they have with other women? What did they think about the conditions of their existence, and did they act on their conclusions? Were their lives changed in any way as they gained increasing access to higher education? What role did religion play in their lives? How were they affected by the law and by public institutions? And, finally, in what ways does the history of women mesh with or deviate from the history of men in America?

RECENT SCHOLARLY TRENDS

Paradoxically, the new research has simultaneously demonstrated the validity of two seemingly contradictory propositions: writing the history of "women" as such is impossible; yet women must be seen precisely as women to be fully understood.

Just as mainstream historians have started learning to modify their statements about men by using adjectives like *middle class, white, northern, urban,* and so forth, so historians of women now also recognize that females cannot be defined solely by their sexual identity. The circumstances governing the lives of white middle-class urban northern women, for example, would be very different from those influencing the existence of poor black rural southern women of the same time. A common womanhood might be the most significant aspect of the self-perception of today's feminists, but modern working-class housewives might instead identify themselves primarily with their class, their ethnic origins, or their families. Nevertheless, it cannot be asserted that females have nothing in common, for they share nearly universal experiences alien to men, most notably childbirth, housekeeping responsibilities, and wage discrimination on account of sex. It is this common background that emerges with full force from current scholarship. A woman can neither be categorized solely as a female nor be treated as just another factory worker, or just another child with a career decision to make, or just another businessperson, for in all such instances a woman's circumstances are indelibly affected by her sex.

␫ ␫

THE FAMILY CONTEXT

Advances in computer technology now allow historians to examine family patterns in a detail and with a precision not possible 20 years ago, but most of these studies are, and remain, male-oriented, concerning themselves most directly with the effects of familial relationships on men. Historians who study European women have been more willing than Americanists to question the impact of varying family structures and work experiences on women's lives. Yet what can be accomplished when a woman-centered demographic inquiry is undertaken is demonstrated by the first essay in this book, "Women's Lives Transformed," by Robert V. Wells. In a survey covering the period 1600-1970, Wells shows how women's lives have changed because of alterations in basic demographic patterns, such as age at marriage, number of children, and life expectancy. Although there are other ways of creating an overview of women's experience in the American past, demography helps us to understand how the ordinary givens of our existence determine our lives in ways that most of us never consider.

Other articles in this volume examine internal family relationships in order to cast new light on the roles of females within this institution so central to all our lives. We can gain a much better sense of how girls were *socialized* (that is, introduced to adult roles) in eighteenth-century America by learning about how Elizabeth Murray Smith Inman (the subject of the first biography) raised her nieces than we can obtain by reading the formal works on child rearing written in the period. The goals that Elizabeth Inman set for her nieces were clearly determined by her own experience, not by any advice from books she may have read. By the same token, a recognition of Mary Lyon's close relationship with her mother (as outlined by Kathryn Kish Sklar in her study of the founding of Mount Holyoke College) suggests a reason for Miss Lyon's lifelong commitment to improving the lot of other women, just as our understanding of Charlotte Perkins Gilman is heightened by a comprehension of her family life, as Carol Berkin makes clear in the second biography.

WOMEN AS WORKERS

Women in America have always worked, both inside and outside the home, but only in recent years has the phenomenon of women's work, and women workers, drawn much systematic attention from historians. This collection contains five distinct examinations of women workers drawn from all the chronological periods, each with a different focus. Mary Beth Norton's biography of Elizabeth Murray Inman looks in detail at one of the women whose existence was first noted by Elisabeth Anthony Dexter. Elizabeth Inman was that relatively rare creature, a colonial businesswoman, and the care with which she protected her financial interests in her successive marriages indicates how deeply committed she was to independent enterprise. The collar laundry workers of nineteenth-century Troy, New York, studied by Carole Turbin, similarly demonstrated their determination to acquire financial well-being by using all the weapons at their disposal. On the West Coast, the Chinese prostitutes discussed in Lucie Cheng Hirata's essay were held in virtual slavery, but many nonetheless attempted to better their circumstances by running away or finding a marital partner. And in the twentieth century the black union organizer Lillian Roberts, who shared her life story with Susan Reverby, displayed the same motivations and the same tenacity in fighting for her rights. In all these cases the women involved were recognized by society as more or less permanent parts of the work force—Elizabeth Inman because for much of her early life she was either single or widowed and had to support herself, the Troy workers, the Chinese prostitutes and seamstresses, and Lillian Roberts because they were from ethnic minorities not subject to the role constraints imposed on native-born American middle-class females (that is, the employers who thought it would be "unladylike" for their own wives and daughters to work outside the home felt no such compunction about hiring black, Asian, and Irish women).

The fifth essay pertinent to work, Leila Rupp's examination of the ambiguous attitude of the American and the German governments toward mobilizing housewives into the labor force during World War II, vividly illustrates the ideological conflicts over working women that have arisen in our own day. As Rupp

demonstrates, men refused to believe the evidence they themselves
had gathered about working women's motivations and goals,
and continued to adhere to the stereotype that women had
joined the paid work force only temporarily. But twentieth-century
women, like their predecessors, proved reluctant to retreat into
the home once they had participated in paid productive labor.
Women who entered the labor force, regardless of the century in
which they lived, clearly gained a different understanding of
their own identity from their experience.

FEMALE FRIENDSHIPS AND ORGANIZATIONS

Much scholarly work in recent years has focused on women's
reform societies and informal female friendship networks. Articles
and books by a number of authors have demonstrated that
throughout American history women have drawn great strength
from their associations with other women. Evidence from essays
in this volume points in the same direction. Two pieces—by
Carole Turbin and by Jacquelyn Dowd Hall—center explicitly on
women's organizations. Hall's examination of the antilynching
league founded by white southerners shows how women could
use their shared feminine identity as a rallying point from
which to attack social ills—a conclusion that also emerges
from studies of nineteenth-century women's groups. But, even
more strikingly, the importance of female networks is revealed in
essays whose major focus is quite different. Mary Lyon turned
to women's religious groups when she needed contributions for
Mount Holyoke; Elizabeth Murray Inman assisted a number of
female friends; the academic women studied by Rosalind Rosenberg
had a strong sense of kinship with each other, as did the female
civil rights workers interviewed by Sara Evans; and the Quaker
women's meetings, run by the women themselves, gave female
members of that sect an extraordinary amount of control over
their own religious affairs.

RELIGION

The history of women in religion, a topic neglected in past years,
has come to the fore because of a new awareness that American
women have always been religious activists. Scholars like Mary
Dunn—author of the pioneering examination of the roles of
women in the Society of Friends included in this volume—are now

arriving at the realization that religion provided an outlet for female talent denied access to political or economic leadership. Especially within the Quaker sect, but also in evangelical movements in general, women could assume positions of power and prestige, influencing not only children and other women but men as well. And women's ties to each other through religious organizations provided them with some of their most dependable allies. Mary Lyon and Jessie Daniel Ames (organizer of the antilynching league) turned to female religious groups for assistance; and Lillian Roberts speaks movingly of the meaning religion had for her when she was a black child growing up in the Midwest.

WOMEN AND THE LAW

For the most part, American legal historians have failed to analyze the status of women under the law or even to consider somewhat more generally the relationship of women, who have been shut out of the formal lawmaking process, to the law and legal reform efforts. Even today there is only a trickle of work in the field, but within the next few years that small rivulet may become a flood because of the significance of the undertaking. The five essays in this volume that concern themselves with legal questions make that fact abundantly clear.

Marylynn Salmon's "Equality or Submersion? Feme Covert Status in Early Pennsylvania" is the first systematic examination in more than 40 years of the legal status of colonial women. Her findings raise questions about the previously accepted "truth" that the colonial failure to follow strict common law procedures brought uniform benefits to American women. Furthermore, her research challenges Mary R. Beard's contention that married women were able to use equity to soften the common-law restrictions on their actions. Interestingly enough, Elizabeth Murray Inman's successive marriage settlements provide a case study of the way in which a knowledgeable woman could protect her financial independence by using equity to her own advantage, but Salmon shows that women like Elizabeth Inman were few and far between, at least in colonial Pennsylvania.

John Harper's examination of the campaign against planned parenthood in the nineteenth-century United States shows how the law could be used in another way to lessen a woman's independence—in this case, her attempts to limit her own fertility through a variety of means. Harper's essay illustrates the truism that the law can become a weapon to advance particular points of view and raises key questions about the objectivity of the law and of male lawmakers.

In sharp contrast to these analyses of eighteenth- and nineteenth-century American law, in which women were the more or less passive objects of regulation, the twentieth-century women examined by Jacquelyn Dowd Hall and Sara Evans actively worked to change the law—not as it applied to them, but as it applied to southern blacks oppressed by generations of segregation and discrimination. Even though the women of the anti-lynching league and the 1960s' civil rights movement could not themselves revise the law, they effectively reached the same end through organization and active effort. Thus, it ironically becomes clear that suffrage did not alter the way in which American women have most effectively exerted political power. Even with the vote, modern American women have had to achieve many of their goals by working outside the political establishment.

WOMEN'S EDUCATION

The history of education, like many other fields, has been dominated almost exclusively by studies of boys. Literally hundreds of books and articles whose titles promise discussion of the education of children refer only to male children. In recent years, however, there has been some reversal of that trend. As historians of women become more and more convinced of the vital role of education in people's lives, they are beginning to look systematically at the ways in which women have been educated over the past 370 years in America, and particularly at the beginnings of higher education for women.

Until the 1780s, American girls received the sort of training provided by Elizabeth Murray Inman for her nieces: girls were educated largely at home by their mothers, with perhaps only a few months of formal schooling. The founding of the Philadelphia Young Ladies Academy in 1787, the subject of Ann Gordon's essay, changed the situation by making higher education available to girls for the first time. As Gordon demonstrates, the rationale for the school was confused and contradictory, and once the girls were educated they had no way to use that education. But in subsequent generations women like Mary Lyon pushed women's education still further by creating colleges designed specifically for females. Throughout the nineteenth century, institutions like Mount Holyoke prepared young women for careers in teaching and other professions, until in the twentieth century, with the women studied by Rosalind Rosenberg, there developed a group of highly educated female professionals. They were the direct fore-runners of the young women who are today entering law, medicine, college teaching, and business in unprecedented numbers, thus fulfilling at last the hopes of the Philadelphia girls in the 1780s.

CONCLUSION

It is appropriate to end the introduction with a reference to education, for this book is, above all, intended as an educational tool. The various approaches taken to the history of women in this volume—through biography, legal analysis, quantitative data, organizational studies, examinations of role prescriptions, and the like—illustrate only a few of the possible ways Americans today can learn about the women of the past. Once thought to have been unrecoverable because of a lack of sources, the history of American women of all races and ethnic backgrounds proves upon examination to have been there all along. Historians just had to know where, and how, to look.

1 Women's Lives Transformed: Demographic and Family Patterns in America, 1600–1970

Robert V. Wells

A cotton mill widow and her family. Courtesy of International Museum of Photography/George Eastman House.

Even the most cursory comparison of the lives of seventeenth-century women with those of women today produces an extraordinary array of contrasts. Important changes have occurred in legal and political power, in economic activity, and in the roles of women in society. Yet no changes are of greater importance than those involving basic patterns of birth, death, marriage, and migration, for people's experiences with and expectations of these demographic phenomena are critical in forming the fundamental rhythms of their lives.

A few contrasts show the importance of the changes that we shall examine in greater detail. Before 1800, women who married at the normal age and whose marriages were uninterrupted by early death of either spouse might expect to bear six or seven children. Today, a reasonable expectation is two children for such marriages. Colonial women who married, and the vast majority did, seldom remarried after their husbands died. In the twentieth century, divorce and remarriage have combined with a recent tendency to delay or avoid marriage, thereby greatly complicating the picture. Life expectancy at birth has approximately doubled since the eighteenth century; thus, a girl born today has as good a chance of living to the age of 65 as her counterpart born in the eighteenth century had of living to her *first* birthday! In addition to these contrasts, women have been profoundly affected by their involvement in the three great migrations that dominate American history: the influx of immigrants from Europe, Africa, and to a lesser degree Asia; the expansion westward across North America (or contraction for the Native Americans); and the move from country to city that changed the population from 95 percent rural to over 70 percent urban.

To understand the transformations in the lives of American women, we will trace these changes in detail. When, why, and how rapidly the shifts occurred are subjects of considerable interest. Of equal importance, however, is the question of how these changes altered basic family patterns in America, because, for better or for worse, most women have had much of their lives centered in the family. All the important changes in American families that have occurred over the past three centuries cannot be covered here; therefore, we shall focus on a few general observations about shifts in life cycles and in living arrangements (households).

Because the United States is a continental country encompassing a variety of geographic regions and peopled by individuals of widely divergent origins, we must recognize that there was no one typical American woman. For example, black women in the South, daughters and wives of New England patriarchs, and Norwegian women who helped settle the Dakotas differed in significant ways. Therefore, we will occasionally examine factors other than their sex that shaped the experiences American women had with basic demographic events and family patterns. It is impossible to provide a complete survey of the literature, but a few examples can remind us how important race, ethnicity, religion, class, and geography were in determining such things as how long women might live, how many children they might have, and what kinds of households they might live in.

Three additional comments will put what follows into its proper context. The focus of this book and this chapter is on American women; however, many patterns described here apply equally well to women who live in other developed countries. Similarly, males have been involved in one way or another in virtually all the changes described; in some instances the basic experiences of men and women have been different enough to warrant comment and they shall be duly noted. Finally, a word on chronology is in order. Although the scope of this essay involves over three and one-half centuries, the period between 1770 and 1920— when the major shifts occurred—will receive the greatest attention.

DEMOGRAPHIC REVOLUTIONS

We could begin to examine the basic patterns of birth, death, marriage, and migration with any of these subjects because all are important, and all interact extensively. We shall begin by looking at changes in childbearing patterns, if only because in this area, more than any other, women's lives have been affected more directly than those of male Americans.

Because records of populations have evolved almost as dramatically as the patterns they seek to describe, we have no one single measure of reproduction running from the seventeenth century to the present. However, information from church records, censuses, genealogies, and current surveys points to the same conclusion: Childbearing in America has been dramatically reduced since 1800. For example, estimates and calculations of trends in the white birthrate indicate a steady reduction from about 50 births per year for each 1,000 people in the population before 1800, to 28.5 per 1,000 in 1900, and 16.7 per 1,000 in 1933. After 1933, the birthrate leveled off for a few years before experiencing a temporary surge in the 1940s and 1950s. Since 1958, the birthrate has resumed its downward trend. Similarly, the number of children a married woman who lived with her husband until the end of her childbearing period (approximately age 45) might expect to bear has fallen from about 7 in eighteenth-century America to about 2 today. This process was well under way in the nineteenth century, for several studies show that native-born wives were averaging only about 3 children in the second half of the nineteenth century.[1]

[1] Ansley J. Coale and Melvin Zelnik, *New Estimates of Fertility and Population in the United States,* Princeton University Press, Princeton, 1963, pp. 21–41; Bureau of the Census, "Vital Statistics," *Historical Statistics of the United States, Colonial Times to*

In general, the trends in childbearing followed a pattern like this. After some initial years of adjustment to the New World environment (a period taking longer in the South than in the North), colonial women, both black and white, came to have rather large families, especially compared to European families of the time. By 1800, a few groups in America began to have smaller families, and this practice continued throughout the nineteenth and twentieth centuries and spread until childbearing reached an all-time low in the 1930s. Almost all American women eventually were affected by this change, even though some groups, such as blacks, did not begin to have smaller families until the last half of the nineteenth century. Since the 1930s the pattern of childbearing has been somewhat irregular, largely because of the baby boom of the post–World War II era, but since 1958 the long-term trend toward having fewer children has reasserted itself.

At least two alternatives are possible explanations for this change. The first reason might be that the health of American parents deteriorated, reducing their capacities to conceive and bear children. But in fact, as we shall see, trends in health improved and could have encouraged rather than inhibited reproduction. So the birthrate fell in spite of, not because of, changes in life expectancy. A second possible alternative might be that women married at an older age and more remained single, so fewer children were born. When we look at marriage patterns, we see that some change did occur, though not great enough to explain a decline in childbearing of the magnitude described here. Thus, we are forced by the elimination of alternatives and by evidence that childbearing declined among *married* women to conclude that families were limited by choice, not by chance.

The fact that American women and their husbands were able to control reproduction successfully in the nineteenth century is indicative of a tremendous desire on their part to do so. Margaret Sanger and her colleagues did not popularize birth control clinics or make public discussion of such matters acceptable until the 1920s. Modern birth control devices, such as pills and IUDs, are the result of technological improvements since *1950*. Only when we consider the techniques available in the nineteenth century, such as unreliable mechanical devices (condoms or diaphragms) or unpleasant physical options (abortion, abstinence, withdrawal), can we truly understand the strong motives needed to limit childbearing. Both women and men sacrificed sexual pleasure to achieve this goal. Perhaps it is safe to say that the recent revolution in birth-control techniques and in public discussion of these matters has had greater impact on human sexuality than on the rate of reproduction.

1957, U.S. Government Printing Office, Washington, D.C., 1960; Bureau of the Census, "Vital Statistics," *Statistical Abstract of the United States, 1976*, U.S. Government Printing Office, Washington, D.C., 1976; Carl E. Jones, "A Genealogical Study of Population," American Statistical Association, *Journal*, 16 (1918–1919), 209.

Any discussion of childbearing in our society leads to a consideration of marriage, for illegitimacy has been relatively uncommon except at the end of the eighteenth century and during the last 25 years.[2] Any consideration of the marriage patterns of American women divides into areas of remarkable stability and areas of dramatic change.

By and large, the patterns of women marrying for the first time have stayed stable over the three centuries that concern us.[3] Except for the seventeenth century when an unusually high ratio of males to females put pressure on young women (that is, under 18) to marry early, the tendency has been for American women to marry, on average, between the ages of 20 and 23. The age range of American women at their first marriage is rather small when compared with the average age for women in other populations, which has varied from about 15 to over 30. Likewise, with few exceptions, about 9 of every 10 females who lived to a marriageable age eventually took a spouse, regardless of the century we might choose to examine. Data for the nineteenth century suggest that women married later and less often than they did at any other time in American history, but viewed in the context of other demographic changes and compared to the history of other peoples, the shifts in marriage patterns among American women are hardly worth mentioning.

For men, the situation has not been as stable. Throughout much of the first three hundred years of American history, men took wives at relatively late ages (25 to 28 on average), following patterns common in Europe at the time. In the twentieth century, American men began to marry at ages closer to those of their wives. By 1950, American men on the average were seldom more than two years older than their wives (23 versus 21), whereas in the late eighteenth and early nineteenth centuries the difference was about four years (25 versus 21).

When we turn to the questions of how long marriages last and what brings them to an end, quite a different picture emerges. The dissolution of marriage has never attracted as much attention as its formation. The result is that we do not have extensive knowledge about how and why unions dissolved, but the general patterns seem clear.

Before 1800, most marriages ended with the death of one spouse. Despite the rigors of childbearing, it appears that wives outlived their husbands about as often as husbands survived their wives. Frequently,

[2] Daniel Scott Smith and Michael S. Hindus, "Premarital Pregnancy in America, 1640–1971: An Overview and Interpretation," *Journal of Interdisciplinary History*, 5 (Spring 1975), 537–570.

[3] The Bureau of the Census publications listed in note 1 provide data for the twentieth century. For earlier periods, see Thomas P. Monahan, *The Pattern of Age at Marriage in the United States*, Stephenson-Brothers, Philadelphia, 1951; Robert V. Wells, "Quaker Marriage Patterns in a Colonial Perspective," *William and Mary Quarterly*, 3rd Ser., 29 (1972), 415–442.

marriages ended before all the children had left home. Divorce was rare, as can be seen from one recent study of Massachusetts's records, which discovered only 229 divorce petitions between 1692 and 1786. Of these, only 143 were actually granted.[4] Some historians have suggested that separation and abandonment were common in early America, though supporting evidence is necessarily scarce.

The first three-quarters of the nineteenth century brought little change to this pattern. Divorce was legally easier to obtain than in the colonial period, but only slightly so. Beginning about 1880, two trends emerged that profoundly altered marital stability. Life expectancy began to rise rapidly, leading to a longer life together for couples. This development, along with smaller families, led to fewer women becoming widows with dependent children. But at the same time that changing health conditions improved the chances for marital stability, the divorce rate began to increase rapidly. Between 1890 and 1970, the number of divorces per 1,000 existing marriages rose from 1.2 to 15.2 each year. In 1890, divorce accounted for only 3.5 percent of all marriages ended in that year; the comparable figure for 1970 was 44.0 percent. Interestingly, the rise in divorces almost exactly balanced out improvements in life expectancy, so that the proportion of marriages being ended in any year was almost the same in 1970 as in 1890.[5]

It is tempting to interpret the rise of divorce as a sign of dissatisfaction with marriage. However, the evidence shows that divorced people remarry rapidly, suggesting that most Americans still feel that marriage is desirable, even though they may no longer find their particular partner appealing. From this perspective, the rise in divorce rates suggests an increased concern for personal satisfaction within marriage, coupled with the realization that death can no longer be counted on to bring quick release.

We should note here that the preceding comments are based primarily on the experience of white females. Black American women have never enjoyed the same levels of marriage stability. Under slavery, black unions had no standing in a court of law, which left them vulnerable to forced separations by the sale of one spouse. Despite this fact, recent study has shown that black women formed and maintained stable unions whenever possible. After the abolition of slavery, many blacks hurried to legalize their marriages. But the desire to maintain a permanent union could not offset the higher mortality among blacks, which generally led

4 Nancy F. Cott, "Divorce and the Changing Status of Women in Eighteenth-Century Massachusetts," *William and Mary Quarterly*, 3rd Ser., 33 (1976), 586–614.
5 Kingsley Davis, "The American Family in Relation to Demographic Change," in the Commission on Population Growth and the American Future, *Research Reports*, Vol. I, *Demographic and Social Aspects of Population Growth*, U.S. Government Printing Office, Washington, D.C., 1972, pp. 239–265, but especially Table 8, p. 256.

to shorter marriages and more widows with dependent children than among whites.

Although we alluded earlier to the rapid rise in life expectancy experienced by American women after 1880, we will now consider the change in greater detail. Because our information is more complete for the experience of white women, we will look at them first.

In the early years of settlement, high rates of death of colonial women were frequent, partly because of primitive living conditions, but also because of new diseases in the New World. First in New England and later in the South, the initial drastic rate of loss of life disappeared due to living conditions that were among the most favorable to long life of any found during the eighteenth century. Taking into account some major geographic variations, we can estimate that life expectancy at birth was probably about 40 years for white women living in the continental colonies in the eighteenth century. When we compare that figure with white female life expectancy now, which is over 76 years at birth, we see that a major change occurred. After a gradual gain in health throughout most of the nineteenth century that increased the life chances of women by 2 or 3 years over those of their colonial counterparts, health improved notably after 1880, so that life expectancy passed 50 years at birth by 1900. By 1930 the figure was 63.5, and by 1950 life expectancy for white women was 72.2 years.[6]

The full meaning of these changes is difficult to convey. We can note that along with living longer, American women lived better, for a major cause of the change was preventive rather than curative medicine —that is, American women found their lives improved both by getting sick less often and by increased chances of survival when they fell ill. A second way to demonstrate the remarkable improvement in life expectancy is to look at the chances a girl baby had of surviving from birth to certain critical ages under various mortality conditions. For example, when life expectancy at birth was about 40, only about 82 of every 100 girls would reach their first birthday; today the figure is over 98. The number living to age 20, when marriage might occur, has increased from 66 to 98. Of the same 100 girl babies, 49 could expect to live to age 45 (the end of childbearing) before 1850, whereas 95 will reach that age today. Finally, if we define old age as 65, then the numbers who reached old age are 30 and 83 out of 100 for these two groups. Truly the change has been dramatic.

Improvement in health has been more striking for white women than for any other group in the American population. Until 1880, white

6 "Vital Statistics," *Historical Statistics,* Series B92–100; "Vital Statistics," *Statistical Abstract, 1976;* Louis I. Dublin, A. J. Lotka, and M. Spiegelman, *Length of Life: A Study of the Life Table,* rev. ed., Ronald Press, New York, 1949, pp. 3–79.

men and women had relatively even life chances. Today, women have an advantage of over seven years' life expectancy at birth. The reasons for this change are not clear, but they appear to include a greater biological hardiness, the elimination of childbirth and tuberculosis as highly sex-selective killers, and a greater tendency for men to kill themselves via tobacco, alcohol, and automobiles. Black women have never had as favorable life chances as their white counterparts, but they, too, have experienced remarkable improvements in health since 1900. In fact, by 1960, black women could expect to outlive white men by a small margin, even though white males had had an advantage of 13 years over black women in 1900. The difference in life expectancy between male and female blacks is about the same as among whites.

The women who have suffered the most are, of course, the Native Americans. Both male and female Indians died at extraordinary rates as they were exposed to new diseases from Europe and Africa. Frequently, as many as 90 percent of a tribe would die in less than a decade when first exposed to such Old World diseases as smallpox, measles, malaria, and yellow fever. Thus, Indian women also found their lives transformed by shifts in the death rate, but in this instance the change was catastrophic. Only recently have they too had better health.

The causes for increased life expectancy are many, and the interrelationships are too complex to describe fully here. But perhaps the most important cause was better public health via clean water, waste disposal, inoculations, and other forms of preventive medicine; an improved standard of living brought better diet, better clothing and housing, and purer foods and drugs. Only after 1920 did medicine contribute to this change by any significant ability to cure disease once contracted.

The final transformation experienced by American women is related to where they lived. During the nineteenth century, three great migration streams altered the face of America: the great international migrations, which brought over thirty million people to the United States between 1820 and 1930; the move west, which created a continental nation out of the original colonies along the Atlantic coast; and the move from country to city, which changed the proportion of women living in urban environments from about 5 percent in 1790 to over 70 percent today.

As we can only touch on the most important points of this very complex story, this discussion will be limited to some observations on how women were involved in these movements, ignoring in the process many matters of significance relating either to men or to the overall numbers of migrants regardless of sex.

First, although little work has been done on the subject, it seems safe to say that many women moved involuntarily, once a husband or father made a decision to go. No doubt a number of women found such decisions acceptable, if not agreeable. On the other hand, a common theme in American literature (ranging from O. E. Rolvaag's *Giants in the Earth,* Hamlin Garland's *Son of the Middle Border,* and Sinclair Lewis's *Main Street* to Laura Ingalls Wilder's *Little House* stories) is that of women suffering from the isolation and instability of migration to communities selected by their men, who decided to move with little concern for their wives and daughters. Willa Cather's portrait of Antonia stands out as an exception to this rule.

A second major point is that women were generally in a minority in two of the three migrations. For example, over the century between 1820 and 1920 the proportion of women among all immigrants was 40 percent or less in 66 years. The year 1857 had the highest proportion of women immigrants, when females accounted for 46.1 percent of the total.[7] The same pattern is clearly visible in the move west. Only the movement to the cities was different. Urban opportunities offered enough attraction to single women and widows so their numbers offset the influx of single males. But the numerical advantage of women over men was not large. Surveys of eight major cities in 1860 and 1900 show that the ratio of men to women in both years was 98 to 100. For the country as a whole, the comparable figures were 105 and 104 men respectively per 100 women.[8]

In many ways, the rural–urban migration has probably had a greater effect on women's lives than either of the other patterns. Moving from one farming region to another was unsettling, but it did not call for a dramatic reorganization of life although it involved crossing the Atlantic Ocean. In contrast, the move to the city frequently changed such basic social arrangements as family contacts, housing possibilities, diet, language, and the extent of joint economic activity between husbands and wives.

In the twentieth century, the move to the suburbs further altered the lives of many women, especially those in the white middle class. If nothing else, this shift enhanced a trend to separate the lives of men and women, as the former commuted between bedroom and boardroom, leaving the women at home with their washers, freezers, and children. Unfortunately, we know less than we should about this change, for male scholars have been more concerned with the "bedroom" aspect of the suburbs, and have frequently overlooked the women and children whose lives are centered in these communities.

[7] "Migration," *Historical Statistics,* Series C133–138.
[8] Bureau of the Census, *Population of the United States in 1860; Compiled from the Original Returns of the Eighth Census,* U.S. Government Printing Office, Washington, D.C., 1864, pp. 608–615; Bureau of the Census, *Abstract of the Twelfth Census of the United States, 1900,* U.S. Government Printing Office, Washington, D.C., 1902, pp. 103–105. The eight cities selected by the author were Boston, New York, Philadelphia, Baltimore, Cincinnati, Chicago, St. Louis, and New Orleans.

A beggar, New York City, 1910. Photo by Lewis Hine, courtesy of International Museum of Photography/George Eastman House.

DEMOGRAPHIC CHANGE AND WOMEN'S LIFE CYCLES

Each change outlined so far has had a major impact on women's lives. However, women have found their situations equally affected by inter-actions among the various demographic factors. There are, of course, numerous women's roles in American society that have changed because of demographic shifts. But in the remainder of this essay we will con-centrate on how the life cycle of women from birth to death has been altered and on the changes that have occurred in the living arrangements (that is, the household) in which women have found themselves. These factors, the life cycle and the household, show the most immediate effects of altered demographic behavior. The remaining essays should present ample opportunities to explore additional connections.

The idea of the life cycle is one of the most useful concepts that historians have adopted from other disciplines in recent years. By fol-lowing an individual from birth, through growth and maturation, the adult years, and finally to death, we can observe the basic rhythms of life, including the times that major changes occur and the length of time that particular stages last. The same approach can be applied to the cycle of family growth and development with equally beneficial results. In exploring the life cycles of American women over the last several centuries, the most useful approach is to contrast current experience with that of women born before the major changes began. This contrast allows us to understand just how different our world is from that of the colonists. Of course, such an approach eliminates consideration of the varied experiences of American women and obscures the fact that the changes have occurred over several generations. But our main purpose is to emphasize the extraordinary transformation in women's lives, and we must sacrifice attention to individual cases.

The life cycle obviously begins with birth, so the first question becomes: How does the experience of twentieth-century daughters differ from that of their counterparts who lived before 1800? Perhaps the most important change in this regard stems from the fact that fewer children in families has meant far fewer sisters and brothers in families today than in the past. In addition, as control over fertility has grown more precise so that the timing as well as the number of babies can be determined, children find a greater age difference between themselves and their siblings today than they did two centuries ago. In such a situation, modern-day daughters can expect greater attention from their parents, especially in the younger years when personality and learning skills are being developed. Along with this, longer life expectancy has reduced the chances of a child losing either a parent or a sibling. Thus, current daughters find their development less frequently disturbed by the addition or subtraction of other family members than was the case in the colonial period. To some extent, increased stability from lower birth and death rates has been offset by the rise in divorce. But by and large it seems safe to say that young women today have a more stable family environment in which to grow than did the daughters of early America.

Because the age at which women marry has remained remarkably constant over time, we could argue that no great change has occurred with regard to this major turning point in a woman's life. On reflection, however, marriage appears less important as a transition today. Before 1800, opportunities for single women were scarce, and few girls received much education outside the home. The change from daughter to wife (and soon after to mother) marked a major step in the life cycle of a woman. Today, however, many women leave home for work, school, and travel several years before they think about marrying. Ties with the family in which they were raised are gradually broken, and women often have had a period of relative independence before marrying. Recent data suggest that increasing numbers of women may never marry at all, thus bypassing what was once an almost universal step in the female life cycle, although it is too soon to tell how permanent this trend may be.

For women who do marry (and the vast majority still do), lower fertility and mortality have significantly altered the meaning of marriage.

Before 1800, women who married could expect their first child within a year or two of the wedding. The same is true today. But with the larger colonial families, a woman could expect to spend most of the next 20 years of her life bearing children. In contrast, today childbearing is spread over less than the first 10 years of a woman's married life. Similarly, the amount of time a woman has children at home in need of attention has also decreased partly because of smaller families, but also because children leave home earlier as part of the educational process. Mothers begin to feel some relief from the demands of child rearing 5 years after their last child is born, and as college education or work becomes more common (especially for females), mothers find themselves with no youngsters at home at far younger ages than before. Almost 40 years elapsed before a woman born in the eighteenth century might expect to see all her children gone. Although precise figures are not available for the 1970s, a reasonable guess would suggest that with smaller families (2 children) and the tendency to leave home before marriage, women are free of their child-rearing duties within 25 years of their marriage. And the process of achieving their independence from this task begins on average perhaps 10 or 15 years after marriage. The advent of day care may well reduce this even more.

The impact of greater life expectancy is important to mention, too. Before 1800, wives and husbands could expect that their unions would be broken by death *before* all the children had left home. Widows and widowers generally did not have a long life alone (perhaps 3 or 4 years). Today, companionship has been added to child rearing as a main component of marriage, for women can expect a significant period of time (perhaps 12 to 15 years) alone with their husbands before death breaks the union. It is interesting to speculate whether the increase in divorce in this century is related to this change.

The last stage of the life cycle for many modern women is widowhood. Because of better life chances and a slightly younger age at marriage, women have increasingly tended to outlive their husbands. For example, in 1974 among those 65 or older, there were only 70 men for every 100 women in the United States. (Under age 65, the ratio of men to women was 99 to 100.) Thus, a significant period of life as a widow with no children around has become a part of the life cycle of modern American women. Previous generations of women found this a far rarer situation. Although the evidence from before 1800 is scanty, it suggests that marriages were broken by the death of a wife about as often as by the death of a husband. If we consider the fact that the proportion of the total population over the age of 65 has tripled (from 4 to 5 percent to over 13 percent) over the last two centuries, it should be clear that one of the major changes in women's lives has been in the older years, with a potential for loneliness and isolation today that earlier women seldom had to confront.

DEMOGRAPHIC CHANGE AND HOUSEHOLDS

Just as women's life cycles have been transformed by shifts in basic demographic patterns, so too have the households in which they lived. We will now focus on the contrasts that can be observed here and try to describe some of the variety of households in nineteenth-century America, in part to emphasize that the transformation did not occur to all women simultaneously, and also to illustrate that a woman's cultural and ethnic background, as well as her place of residence, frequently had a profound effect on her life.

The first point of interest is that women today have less than half as many people living with them as they did in 1790. From an average of 7.0 persons (5.7 free persons) in the United States in 1790, the mean number of persons per household declined to 3.1 in 1970, and to 2.9 by 1975.[9] Looking at the timing of this change, we find that it has occurred more rapidly in recent years. If we exclude slaves from the calculations, we find that during the 70 years between 1790 and 1860, mean household size fell by 0.4 person. The last 40 years of the nineteenth century saw a corresponding decline of 0.5 person. During the first half of the twentieth century the decline continued as households in 1950 averaged 1.3 persons less than in 1900, while between 1950 and 1975 an additional 0.6 person was lost from the average household. Thus, we find not only that households have decreased in size from the eighteenth century to the present, but also that the rate of decline has increased remarkably.

Another way to examine what this has meant for American women is to look at shifts in the proportions of households that might be considered either very large or very small. In 1790 only 3.7 percent of all households had one person, while 62.7 percent had five or more. By 1975 the proportion of single-person households had risen to 19.6 percent of the total, about 3 percent more than the proportion of households with five or more persons. Once again, much of the change occurred relatively recently, as single-person households accounted for only 5.1 percent of the total in 1900, and 10.9 percent in 1950. As a result of these changes, most Americans now live in households of between two and four persons. By 1975, 63.6 percent of all households fell within this range, about twice the proportion in 1790.

A few brief comments should demonstrate how the demographic shifts we have already examined helped change the households women lived in. But we must also look at other factors, such as social arrangements, attitudes, and economic prosperity, for they have also had an influence.

---

[9] Except where otherwise noted, the data on households are from Bureau of the Census, *A Century of Population Growth*, U.S. Government Printing Office, Washington, D.C., 1909, pp. 96–110; "Population," *Historical Statistics*, Series A255–263; and "Population," *Statistical Abstract, 1976*, pp. 1–48.

The remarkable reduction in fertility that the American population has achieved over the past two centuries is, perhaps, the most obvious cause for the decline in mean household size. As the birthrate fell, the proportion of childless households increased from about 20 percent in 1790 to 48.3 percent in 1950. The effects of the postwar baby boom temporarily reversed this trend, so that only 43.0 percent of all households were childless in 1960. But with the recent decline in fertility, childless households have once again started to increase, accounting for 46.0 percent of the total in 1975.

Increased life expectancy may also have helped to lower the average size of the household. We have seen how the combination of lower fertility and longer life meant that twentieth-century couples were among the first in history who could expect to have a significant number of years together after their children left home. Thus, an increase in childless households and households with one or two children reflects not only lower levels of childbearing, but also more older couples whose children have grown up and left home. For example, in 1970, fully 82.2 percent of all married couples in which the husband's age was between 55 and 64 had no children in their household, a remarkable contrast to the 11.7 percent of couples without children when the husband was 35 to 44.

One other interesting change is the increasing tendency for women to head the households. In part this is directly related to improved life expectancy, although it seems likely that alterations in social attitudes are also involved. If we assume that data for Rhode Island in 1774 are not dramatically different from those for the other colonies (and there is no reason to expect that they are), then we can see a gradual increase in the proportion of households headed by women, from about 9 percent before 1800 to about 14 percent by 1950.[10] It seems probable that this change reflects the fact that between the middle of the nineteenth century and the middle of the twentieth century the advantage of females over males in life expectancy at birth rose from about 2.5 to 7 years. As more wives outlived their husbands by a considerable length of time, we should expect to find more female household heads.

Since 1950, the proportions of households headed by women have greatly increased. By 1975, women headed fully 21.8 percent of white households and 37.6 percent of black households (23.5 percent of all households). To some extent this is still part of the long-term improvement of life chances, because about one-third of the women who head households today are widows. The fact that approximately three of every four widows live alone helps explain part of the increase in single-person

---

[10] Data for Rhode Island in 1774, and for households headed by women in other colonies are in Robert V. Wells, *The Population of the British Colonies in America before 1776: A Survey of Census Data,* Princeton University Press, Princeton, 1975, pp. 317–319.

households. But when we consider that widows accounted for most of the women heads of households before 1800, it becomes clear that social changes involving the rising divorce rate and the willingness of young single women to leave home have contributed in significant ways to reducing the average household size and to increasing the proportion of households headed by women.

These changes in households over two centuries have not only altered the lives of American women; they also reflect new roles that women have assumed in recent years. The contrasts over time are indeed striking. But it is important to remember that factors such as geography, cultural heritage, economic necessity, and migration patterns had major impacts on the living arrangements of American women. Undoubtedly, individual households varied considerably in any period, but we will focus on the nineteenth century, when the variety was extraordinary.

Because scholars have frequently suggested that changes in household size and composition occurred as people moved off the farms and into the cities during the nineteenth century, let us look first at urban families. Women in nineteenth-century American cities experienced a considerable variety in living arrangements. This is to be expected, because different groups were exposed to different aspects of the city; hence flexibility in responding to a new environment was important in ensuring the successful adaptation of some families to city life.

It is relatively easy to show that not all urban households were alike.[11] For example, one group of middle-class Chicago women lived in households averaging 3.0 persons in 1880. This figure is only slightly below the 3.8 persons per black family in New Orleans in the same year, but the New Orleans families were forced to double up often enough so that there were 6.0 persons living in each "Negro family dwelling." This congestion among black families in New Orleans is similar to that experienced by women immigrants in Boston in the 1840s, where the influx of Irish raised the average number of persons per dwelling to over 10 in 1840 and 1845. In New York City in 1875, the average number of persons per dwelling went from a low of 6.2 persons in the Twenty-fourth Ward to a high of 25.9 persons in the Sixth Ward. In Albany the range was not as great, but the number of persons per dwelling averaged from 5.5 to 10.4 persons. Poverty forced many women and their families into tenements, which is one reason for the high number of persons per dwelling.

[11] Data for the following paragraph are from Richard Sennett, *Families Against the City*, Vintage Press, New York, 1970, pp. 71–83; John W. Blassingame, *Black New Orleans, 1860–1880*, University of Chicago Press, Chicago, 1973, pp. 79–105, 236–240; Oscar Handlin, *Boston's Immigrants*, rev. ed., Atheneum, New York, 1969, pp. 88–123, 329; New York Secretary of State, *Census of the State of New York for 1875*, Weed, Parsons, and Co., Albany, 1877, pp. 254–262; John Modell and Tamara Hareven, "Urbanization and the Malleable Household: An Examination of Boarding and Lodging in American Families," *Journal of Marriage and the Family*, 35 (1973), 467–492.

Also, many lower-class women began to accept boarders into their homes in the late nineteenth century, just when the practice seems to have begun to disappear among middle-class families.

It is easy to interpret crowding, boarders, and female heads of households as evidence of family disorganization. In practice, many of the more "unusual" household arrangements proved beneficial to the people involved, at least in the short run. Among the middle-class Chicagoans mentioned earlier, those families who maintained or developed some form of extended family relationship often adjusted more successfully to city life than did the majority of people who lived in the supposedly more efficient nuclear families. Recent work on eastern New England immigrant families has shown that the maintenance of complex family ties was helpful in bringing extra income into the household and in aiding immigrants newly arrived in the community.

One of the most interesting examples of the beneficial aspects of a form of family life often presumed to be undesirable is found in Cohoes, New York. This particular community had a high proportion of households headed by women, a situation that has often been seen as evidence of severe social disorder in a community or among a particular social group. But in Cohoes, a large number of textile mills offered widows a chance to keep their families together by providing employment for both women and children. Thus, a close examination of these unusual circumstances reveals families preserving ties they valued, which they might otherwise have had to abandon.

Any effort to explore how American women were affected by the move into the cities naturally raises a comparable question about what happened to the households of their sisters who participated in the westward expansion. Although it is logical to assume that the very act of migrating produced a certain amount of household dislocation (whether the move was to the city or to the west), it does not necessarily follow that different destinations produced similar stresses on families, thus evoking similar patterns.

As was the case in urban areas, women who moved west found themselves in a variety of living arrangements, if only because of the differences among various western frontiers. California illustrates this well. For example, women living in Los Angeles in 1850 confronted complex household patterns related to the relatively recent American conquest of that territory. The older Hispano families frequently lived either in nuclear households or, when wealth permitted, in rather complex units of parents, children, relatives, and laborers. The more recently arrived Anglo residents of Los Angeles lived either in arrangements not familial in form or else in nuclear families with boarders. Both household forms reflect recent arrival, relative youth, and lack of money among the Anglos. (This contrast between Hispano and Anglo households is of some interest because it suggests that in agricultural areas, wealth and permanence of residence may allow larger households, whereas in the city, poverty and recent arrival seem to be related to larger, complex households.)

The inhabitants of Butte County, California, a mining frontier in 1850, were composed of 3,463 males and 104 females. Although 87.5 percent of the females lived in what appear to have been relatively stable households, it is clear that in mining regions women and family life were remarkably rare. A third experience also comes from California, toward the end of the nineteenth century. Between 1870 and 1900, people who sought to cure tuberculosis by moving to California appear frequently to have brought their families and seem to have settled down as relatively permanent inhabitants with stable habits.

A look at midwestern agricultural frontiers stretching from Indiana and Iowa down to Texas suggests another main point—namely that, within a year or two after a territory was opened for settlement, women participated fully in establishing pioneer farms.[12] In the initial years of settlement, a region might well experience some demographic abnormalities. For example, Nueces County, Texas, in 1850 was characterized by high sex ratios (177 men for every 100 women) and low fertility. In this instance, we find a situation much like Los Angeles in the same year, where the more normal household and demographic patterns of the older Hispano residents moderated the effects of young, single, Anglo male immigrants on the characteristics of the population. The settlement of the Peters Colony in Texas from 1845 to 1850 involves much the same story. During that 5-year period, 896 couples moved into the region, each with an average of 3.3 children. In addition came 698 single males, 97 single men who married after migrating, 45 widowers, 41 widows, and 10 remarried widows. Although we cannot be sure, it seems probable that the 896 couples with children soon came to dominate, for their family pattern of 2 adults living with slightly over 3 children on average is remarkably similar to patterns found in Indiana in 1820, in Iowa in 1850, and in Michigan in 1850.

WOMEN'S LIVES TRANSFORMED—WHAT DOES IT MEAN?

This brief look at households on the urban and agricultural frontiers should make it clear that women's lives were affected not only by the demographic transitions of the nineteenth century, but also by their

[12] For agricultural regions, see Susan Bloomberg, et al., "A Census Probe into Nineteenth Century Family History: Southern Michigan, 1850–1870," *Journal of Social History*, 5 (Fall 1971), 26–45; Seymour V. Connor, "A Statistical Review of the Settlement of the Peters Colony, 1841–1848," *Southwestern Historical Quarterly*, 57 (1953–1954), 38–64; John Modell, "Family and Fertility on the Indiana Frontier, 1820," *American*

cultural background, their class, and where they lived. Sex was (and is) only one of a variety of factors that has helped to determine the patterns of a woman's life in America. As a result, diversity must remain a constant theme in any effort to understand women's roles in the American past.

But we cannot forget the profound changes in most women's lives during the last two centuries. Between 1800 and the present, major trans-formations have occurred in terms of how many children a woman could expect to have, how long she might live, where she might live, and in what kind of household she might live. The basic rhythms of twentieth-century life are new, not only for American women, but also in terms of human history in general.

Obviously, the changes we have considered here are important in themselves, but they take on added interest in view of social, political, and economic developments that have occurred over the same time span. To explore possible ties is beyond the scope of this essay. As readers go through the rest of this book, it is hoped they will ask how the stories told here relate to these fundamental transformations. In particular, three questions come to mind. Did demographic shifts make it possible for women to change other aspects of their lives? Or did women attempt to reduce childbearing, improve their health, and so on, as they sought out new roles in American society? Finally we must ask, is it possible that the demographic transformations and new social, economic, and political patterns are all part of some broader movement that distinguishes our world from that of the eighteenth century?

Quarterly, 23 (1971), 615–634; Sherman L. Ricards and George M. Blackburn, "A Demographic History of the West: Nueces County, Texas, 1850," *Prologue,* 4 (1972), 3–20; Mildred Throne, "A Population Study of an Iowa County in 1850," *Iowa Journal of History,* 57 (1959), 305–330.

Part Two
Colonial America to 1800

The Myth of the Golden Age

Mary Beth Norton

HOUSEHOLD PATTERNS

When discussing colonial women, we must focus on the household, for that was where most of their lives were spent. As daughters as well as wives and mothers, white women were expected to devote their chief energies to housekeeping and to the care of children, just as their husbands were expected to support them by raising crops or working for wages. Household tasks were not easily or lightly accomplished, although their exact nature varied according to the wealth and size of the family and its place of residence. In addition to the common chores still done today—cooking, cleaning, and washing—colonial women had the primary responsibility for food preservation and cloth production.

On farms women raised chickens, tended vegetable gardens, and ran the dairy, making cheese and butter for family use. When hogs and cattle were butchered in the fall, women supervised the salting and smoking of the meat so that the family would have an adequate supply for the winter. They also gathered and dried fruits, vegetables, and berries and occasionally oversaw the making of hard cider, the standard drink in the colonies. In towns and cities women also performed many of these chores, though on a lesser scale: They raised a few chickens and a cow or two, cultivated a kitchen garden, and preserved the beef and pork purchased at the local market. Only the wealthiest women with numerous servants could escape tiring physical labor, and as mistresses of the household they too had to understand the processes involved, for otherwise they could not ensure that the jobs were done correctly.

The task of making cloth by hand was tedious and time consuming. If women lived in towns and could afford to do so, they would usually purchase English cloth rather than manufacture their own. On remote farms or in poorer households, however, females had no choice: If the family was to have clothes, they had to spin the wool or flax threads, then weave those threads into material that could be used for dresses, shirts, and trousers. Usually girls were taught to spin at the early age of 7 or 8 so that they could relieve their mothers of that chore. Weaving demanded more technical skill, not to mention a large, bulky loom, and so not all women in an area would learn to weave. Instead neighbors would cooperate, "changing work," and the woman who wove the cloth for her friends would be paid in cash or by barter.

Native American women had similar work roles. They did not spin or weave, but they did make clothing for the family by tanning and processing the hides of animals killed by their husbands and fathers. They had greater responsibilities for the cultivation of plants than did their white counterparts; the men of many tribes devoted most of their time to hunting, leaving their wives with the major share of the burden of raising the corn, squash, and beans that formed the staples of their diet. But like the whites, Native American cultures drew a division between the domestic labors of women and the public realm of men. Only in rare instances—as when the older women of the matrilineal Iroquois society named the chief of the tribe—did Indian women intrude upon that male realm.

The patterns for African women were somewhat more complex, but their lives too were largely determined by the type of household in which they lived. A female slave in a northern urban home—and there were many such by the mid-eighteenth century—would probably have been a cook or a maid. On small farms slave women would have been expected to work in both field and house. On large southern tobacco or rice plantations, however, black women might specialize in certain tasks, devoting themselves exclusively to spinning, cooking, childcare, dairy work, or poultry keeping, or they might be assigned to the fields. Black women were therefore more likely than whites to engage in labor out of doors. Significantly, the household in which they lived was not theirs: Their interests and wishes, and those of their husbands and children, always had to be subordinated to the interests of their white masters and mistresses. White women's lives, we might say, were governed by the whims of men, legally and in reality; but black women's lives were governed by white men and white women, and perhaps even by white children.

WOMEN'S LIVES OUTSIDE THE HOME

For female whites or blacks living on isolated farms or plantations, opportunities for contacts with persons outside their immediate families were extremely rare. Thus, farm and plantation women took advantage of every excuse they could to see friends and neighbors: Quilting bees and spinning frolics were common in the North, barbecues were prevalent in the South. Church attendance provided a rural woman not only with the solace of religion, but also with a chance to greet acquaintances and exchange news. Literate women kept in touch with each other by writing letters, many of them carried not by the rudimentary colonial mail service but by passing travelers, usually men.

Because there were few colonial newspapers, and those were published exclusively in cities like Boston or Philadelphia, most farm areas were a part of what has been termed an *oral culture.* Much of the important information about local and regional developments was passed on by person-to-person contact, which generally occurred at the local tavern or the county courthouse, both of which were male bastions. As a result, white farm women tended to be excluded from men's communication networks and to rely for news on exchanges with each other or with their husbands.

Urban women were not nearly so isolated. Close to their friends, they could visit every day. Their attendance at church was not limited to infrequent occasions, and so they could become more active in religious affairs than their rural sisters. They had greater opportunities to receive an education, since the few girls' schools were located in or near colonial cities. For the most part their education consisted of elementary reading, writing, and arithmetic, with perhaps some needlework or musical training thrown in for good measure. Once women knew how to read, they had newspapers and books at their disposal. Moreover, because their household tasks were less demanding than those of their rural counterparts, they had more time to take advantage of all these amenities of the urban setting.

If this account makes it seem as though colonial women's lives lacked variety, that impression is correct. Their environment was both limited and limiting: limited, because of the small sphere of activity open to them; limiting, because they could not realistically aspire to leave that sphere. Faced with a paucity of alternatives, colonial women made the best of their situation. What evidence is available suggests that both white and black women often married for love, and that they cared a great deal for their children. Their female friends provided support in moments of crisis—such as childbirth or the death of a family member—and women could take some satisfaction from knowing that they were active contributors to their families' well-being.

THE MYTH ANALYZED

Historians of American women have traditionally regarded the
seventeenth and eighteenth centuries as a "golden age" in which
women were better off than their English female contemporaries
or their descendants of the succeeding Victorian era. Elisabeth
Anthony Dexter explicitly asserted as much; other authors have
accepted the same argument implicitly by contending that female
Americans "lost status" in the nineteenth century. But even leaving
aside the troublesome (and infrequently addressed) issue of how
status is measured, there are a number of difficulties with the
standard interpretation. Evaluation of women's position depends
on what aspects of their experience are relevant to an understanding of their social and economic position, for no one would
claim that colonial females exerted much political power.

Three basic assertions support the traditional interpretation.
First, historians have noted the imbalanced sex ratio in all the
colonies before 1700 and in some parts thereof during later years.
Hypothesizing that the absence of sufficient numbers of women
to provide wives for all male colonists would lead men to compete
vigorously for mates, they have concluded that women could
wield a good deal of power through their choice of a spouse.
Second, scholars have commonly pointed to the economic contributions women made to the colonial household through their
work in food processing and cloth production. They have correctly
noted that it was practically impossible for a man to run a colonial
household properly without a wife, for a woman's labor was
essential to the survival of the family. They presume, then, that
husbands recognized their wives' vital contributions to the household by according them a voice in decision making, and that a
woman's economic role translated itself into a position of power
within the home. Third and finally, historians argue that sex
roles in early America were far more fluid and less well defined
than they were in the nineteenth and twentieth centuries. They
quote both foreign travelers' accounts and newspaper advertisements to show that in many instances women labored at tasks
later considered masculine and frequently ran their own businesses.

In assessing these common contentions, we must look closely
at their component parts in light of recent scholarship. When
we do so, all are rendered suspect. The first argument asserts that
a scarcity of women works to their advantage in the marriage
market and assumes that the choice of a husband was entirely
within a seventeenth-century colonial woman's discretion. Yet
demographic studies have clearly demonstrated that, when women

are scarce, the average female age at first marriage drops, sometimes precipitously. Even in New England, where the sex ratio was closer to being balanced than anywhere else in the early settlements, the average marriage age for women seems to have fallen into the high teens during the first years of colonization, in sharp contrast to England, where the nuptial age for women remained near the mid-20s.

These figures have several implications. Initially, they suggest that first marriages were not long delayed by women's searches for spouses who met exacting criteria. Furthermore, since seventeenth-century brides were often teenagers, even more frequently so in the Chesapeake Bay area than in New England, one wonders just how much power they could have wielded. Immature themselves, legally the wards of their parents, it is highly unlikely that they had much to say about the choice of a spouse.

A possible counter-argument might assert that the advantages of the imbalanced sex ratio are more applicable to a woman's second or third marriage than to her first, because then she would be older and in addition would have control of her first husband's property. Although studies of remarriage patterns in the early years of the colonies are not completely satisfactory, they nevertheless appear to challenge even this claim. In New England, life expectancy in the seventeenth century was sufficiently great that few marriages seem to have been broken early by death. Therefore, relatively few persons married more than once. In the Chesapeake area, where mortality was much higher, the frequency of remarriage was similarly high, but analyses of wills demonstrate that widows were rarely given much control over their dead husbands' estates. The property was usually held in trust for the decedent's minor children, with the widow receiving only a life interest in part of it. Sometimes even that income was to cease upon her remarriage.

Taken as a whole, then, the evidence indicates that seventeenth-century English women transplanted to American shores might not find the imbalanced sex ratio to be beneficial. After all, a scarce resource can be as easily exploited as it is cherished, an observation dramatically proved in the third section of this book by Lucie Hirata's examination of the exploitation of scarce Chinese women in sexually imbalanced nineteenth-century California. Also, by approximately 1720 the sex ratio had evened out in the Chesapeake, having already reached that point to the northward, so that whatever advantages women may have derived from the situation were negated and cannot be used to characterize the entire colonial period.

Turning next to the assertion that women's economic role gave them a powerful position in the household, we can discern problems with both the evidence and the reasoning that support it. Historians have not systematically examined the conditions under which women wield familial power, assuming instead that an essential economic contribution would almost automatically lead to such a result. Anthropologists who have investigated the question, however, have discovered that the mere fact that a woman's economic contribution to the household is significant is not sufficient to give her a voice in matters that might otherwise be deemed to fall within the masculine sphere. Rather, what is important is a woman's ability to control the distribution of familial resources. Thus, African women who not only cultivate crops but also sell that produce to others are more likely to wield power in their households than are their counterparts in other tribes whose husbands take on the trading role, or who live in a subsistence economy that does not allow for the sale of surplus goods.

That this analogy is indeed appropriate, despite the wide difference in time and space between twentieth-century Africa and colonial America, is suggested by a recent study of female Loyalist exiles in England after the American Revolution. In order to win compensation from the British government for the losses their families suffered as a result of their political sympathies, the women had to submit descriptions of the property confiscated from them by the rebels. In the process, they revealed their basic ignorance of family landholdings and income, in turn demonstrating that their husbands had not regularly discussed financial affairs with them. If the Loyalist women refugees, who were drawn from all ranks of society, had actively participated in economic decision making, then they would have been far better able to estimate their losses than they proved to be. Thus, the second foundation of the traditional interpretations is shown to be questionable.

The third standard contention, that colonial sex roles were relatively fluid, is rendered at least partially doubtful by other aspects of the same study of Loyalist exiles. The wide variations in the contents of men's and women's Loyalist claims, and the inability or the unwillingness of men to describe household furnishings in the same detail adopted by women, appear to indicate that a fairly rigid line separated masculine and feminine spheres in the colonies. Indeed, the fact that men did not talk about finances with their wives suggests that both sexes had a strong sense of the proper roles of women and men; women did not meddle with politics or economics, which were their husbands'

provinces, and men did not interfere with their wives' overseeing
of domestic affairs, excluding child rearing, where they did take
an active role. Moreover, even though the claims show that some
women did engage in business activities, their number was
relatively small (fewer than 10 percent of the claimants), and most
of them worked in their husbands' enterprises rather than running their own.

That the number of Loyalist women working in masculine
areas was not uniquely limited has been suggested by a recent
study of Baltimore women in the 1790s, which concludes that
only about 5 percent of the female urban population worked
outside the home. Thus, it seems likely that eighteenth-century
Americans made quite distinct divisions between male and female
roles, as reflected in the small numbers of women engaging in
masculine occupations and in the fact that men did not normally
interfere in the female sphere.

NEW ISSUES

Recent scholarship has considered a number of issues not even
raised by earlier authors. Interest in these different areas of inquiry
owes a great deal to current trends in the study of the history of
the American family, of minority groups, and of ordinary people.
Although this work has just begun, it is nevertheless already
casting innovative light on the subject of colonial women's role
in society.

In the first place, it is important to point out that published
studies of the lives of colonial women have, with but one or two
exceptions, centered wholly on whites. Even though at the time
of the Revolution blacks constituted almost 20 percent of the
American population, a higher percentage than at any time
thereafter, historians have completely neglected the study of female
slaves in the colonial era. Therefore, all the statements that
women had a relatively good position in the colonies must be
immediately qualified to exclude blacks. No one could seriously
argue that enslavement was preferable to freedom, especially
since female slaves were highly vulnerable to sexual as well as
economic exploitation by their masters. Intriguingly, recent work
has shown that the sexual imbalance among the earliest African
slaves in the South was just as pronounced as that among whites,
so that female blacks probably found themselves in a demographic
situation comparable to that of their white mistresses. The sex-role
definitions applied to whites, though, were never used with respect

to blacks. The labor of slave women was too valuable for their masters to pay attention to the niceties of sex; thus, many of them spent their lives laboring in tobacco fields or on sugar plantations alongside their husbands, although others were indeed used as house servants performing typically feminine tasks.

The one concession wise colonial masters made to the sex of female slaves was a recognition of their importance as child-bearers. Since under the law any child of a slave woman was also a slave, masters could greatly increase their human property simply by encouraging their female slaves' fertility. For example, Thomas Jefferson, whose solvency for some years depended on the discreet sale of young blacks, ordered his overseers to allow pregnant and nursing women special privileges, including lighter work loads and separate houses. Since colonial slave women normally bore their first children at the age of 17 or 18, they would experience perhaps 10 or 11 pregnancies (not all of which would result in live births) during their fertile years, which may be contrasted to the standard pattern among white eighteenth-century women, who married perhaps 4 to 6 years later and thus bore fewer children (the average being 6 offspring who lived).

This attention to childbearing patterns has led to a major challenge to the "golden age" theory. As Robert V. Wells pointed out in the first article in this book, colonial women were either pregnant or nursing during most of their mature years. Such a pattern of constant childbearing was debilitating, even if it was not fatal to as many women as we once thought; the diaries of white female colonists are filled with references to their continued poor health, and the records of planters show similar consequences among female slaves. Furthermore, the care of so many children must have been exhausting, especially when combined with the extraordinary household demands made on women: production of clothing and time-consuming attention to food preservation and preparation, not to mention candle- and soap-making and doing laundry in heavy iron pots over open fires, with all the water carried by hand from the nearest well or stream. It is questionable how much household power could have been wielded by a woman constantly occupied with such work, even if she was in good health.

It is instructive to stress once again the lack of options in colonial women's lives. Until late in the eighteenth century, mar-riage was a near-universal experience for women; in an over-whelmingly agricultural society, most female whites ended up as farm wives and most female blacks were farm laborers. For black women burdened with small children, running away was not even the remote chance it was for young unattached male slaves. (In any case, until the Revolution there was no safe place to go, except Spanish Florida, because all the colonies, north and south, allowed slaveholding.)

It might be contended that since most white men were farmers, white women's lack of opportunities was not unique to them. But boys like John Adams, Richard Cranch, and John Shaw had opportunities to gain an education that were closed to their wives, the sisters Abigail, Mary, and Elizabeth Smith. All were exceptionally intelligent and well-informed women, but none received other than a rudimentary formal education, despite the fact that their father was a minister. Since the ability to write a good letter—defined as one that was neat, intelligently constructed, properly grammatical, and carefully spelled—was the mark of a person of substance and standing in colonial America, it is easy to discern the source of the distress Abigail Adams constantly expressed about her inability to write and spell well.

If a white woman did not want to be a farm wife, assuming she had a choice in the matter, then she had only a narrow range of alternatives. In order to take advantage of those alternatives she had to be located in an urban area, where she could support herself in one of three ways: by running a small school in her home; by opening a shop, usually but not always one that sold dry goods; or by in some manner using the household skills she had learned from her mother as a means of making money. This might involve hiring out as a servant, doing sewing, spinning, or weaving for wealthy families, or, if she had some capital, setting up a boardinghouse or inn. There were no other choices, and women who selected one of these occupations—or were compelled by adverse economic circumstances to do so—were frequently regarded as anomalous by their contemporaries.

A major component of the traditional view of American women's history is the assertion that the 40-year period centering on 1800 was a time of retrogression. Joan Hoff Wilson, the most recent proponent of this interpretation, links the setbacks she discerns in women's position explicitly to consequences of the American Revolution. But other work published in the last few years points to an exactly opposite conclusion: It has been suggested (if not yet fully proved) by a number of scholars that the late eighteenth century witnessed a series of advances for women, in some respects at least.

An examination of all extant Massachusetts divorce records seems to indicate, for example, that at the end of the century women seeking divorces were more likely to have their complaints judged fairly and were less likely to be oppressed by application of a sexual double standard than their predecessors had been.

In a different area, it has been noted that women's educational opportunities improved dramatically after the mid-1780s, an observation that is supported by evidence presented in the essays by Ann Gordon and Kathryn Kish Sklar included in this volume. Finally, extensive research into the patterns of first marriage in one New England town has uncovered changes in marital alliances that can be interpreted as evidence of a greater exercise of independent judgment by girls. Analysis of the records of Hingham, Massachusetts, has shown that in the latter years of the century more daughters married out of birth order and chose spouses whose economic status differed from that of their own parents than had previously been the case. If we assume that both sorts of actions would be contrary to parents' wishes, and couple that assumption with the knowledge that in the same town the premarital conception rate (judged by a comparison of wedding dates with the timing of births of first children) simultaneously jumped to more than 30 percent, we receive the clear impression that parental control of sons and daughters was at a low ebb.

Paradoxically, that last piece of evidence can also be read as suggesting a greater exploitation of women by men. The rise in premarital conception rates, which stretched over the entire eighteenth century and peaked in its last two decades, does not necessarily mean that all the women involved were willing participants seeking what would today be termed sexual fulfillment. On this issue, as on others discussed in this essay, a great deal more research is needed in order to allow historians to gain a fuller picture of the female experience in colonial America.

✿✿✿

In many ways, the woman whose biography begins this section was an anomaly. Elizabeth Murray Campbell Smith Inman married three times, when most eighteenth-century women married only once. She lived in a city at a time when the vast majority of American men and women were farm dwellers. She had no children in an era when women normally bore many. Moreover, she ran her own business, unlike most female Americans of her time. Consequently, her life shows us the outer limits of an eighteenth-century white woman's aspirations. Her experience demonstrates what could be won if a woman was independent, hard-working, tenacious in the defense of her interests, and exceptionally perceptive. But what was typical about Elizabeth Inman's life should not escape notice: She raised five surrogate daughters though she had none of her own, she at least attempted to depend on a husband's guidance, and like the other Americans who survived the Revolutionary War, her life was changed by it and by the years of agitation that preceded the actual fighting. Thus, despite the unique character of certain parts of her career, other aspects of it link her experience to her female contemporaries.

This is nowhere clearer than if one considers her circumstances in light of the analysis presented in Marylynn Salmon's article, "Equality or Submersion? Feme Covert Status in Early Pennsylvania." Salmon demonstrates how the common law practice of subsuming a wife's legal identity into that of her husband worked against women, and how only a very few extraordinary women like Elizabeth Inman were able to use the equity system to protect themselves. Although the law pertaining to femes coverts was extremely complex, its study repays one's efforts at comprehension, for only then can we fully understand the legal disabilities that were a part of every married colonial woman's life.

In contrast to the law, which conferred few benefits on women, education and religion brought them some hope for the future. As Ann Gordon shows in her essay on the Young Ladies Academy of Philadelphia and its students, young women there learned to think about their role in ways their mothers never had. The Young Ladies Academy was the first institution of higher learning for women in the United States, and even if its curriculum only approximated that used for teenage boys, it still provided girls from well-to-do backgrounds with a better formal education than had been received by any female Americans to that time. As such, the founding of the academy marked a major turning point in women's education in this country, even if one can point to few concrete results of the schooling girls obtained there. The existence of such schools formed a necessary prelude to the founding of women's colleges in the next century.

Mary Dunn's "Women of Light" illustrates the impact that religious affiliation could have on colonial women's lives. The Society of Friends was not the only sect in which women assumed leadership roles, but it was the sole group in which those roles were formalized. No other sect organized women's meetings or regularly used female preachers. Accordingly, just as Elizabeth Murray Smith Inman illustrates the outer limits on colonial women's secular lives, Dunn's essay reveals the utmost possibilities of women's religious lives. Quaker women had greater opportunities to develop their capacity for leadership than did their female contemporaries, a fact reflected in the major roles they eventually assumed in the reform movements of the nineteenth century, most notably that which sought women's rights.

2 A Cherished Spirit of Independence: The Life of an Eighteenth-Century Boston Businesswoman

Mary Beth Norton

Mrs. James Smith (Elizabeth Murray) by John Singleton Copley. Courtesy, Museum of Fine Arts, Boston.

The John Singleton Copley portrait of Mrs. James Smith, painted in 1769 when his subject was 43 years old, shows a stout, mature woman of strong character. With only the faintest trace of a smile, she stands rigidly erect in the lavish gown and the conventional pose dictated by contemporary standards of genteel portraiture. She seems above all to be intensely uncomfortable as she holds several pieces of fruit awkwardly before her in an apron. And no wonder. For this woman, appearing here in the guise of an idle, wealthy matron, was in fact a successful Boston businesswoman who had won the unqualified praise of both male and female friends. Married three times, widowed twice, she was accustomed to relying on her own abilities, and in later years she attributed her material well-being to a unique "spirit of independence" that had led her to a way of life from which she received "the greatest advantages & satisfaction." Although childless herself, she was devoted to the five nieces she helped to raise, and she consciously inculcated in them the same respect for self-reliance that guided her all her life. Much admired in her own day—a friend once wrote that "never was a woman Better Beloved in New England"—she has since slipped into the obscurity that history reserves for women who are not members of prominent families.[1]

Elizabeth Murray (for that was her birth name) was by no means a typical eighteenth-century American woman. Most of her female contemporaries, taught from their earliest years that their greatest glory consisted in being properly submissive to their husbands, lacked her sense of initiative and her independent spirit. Because so little is known of her youth, it is impossible to locate the origins of her remarkable personality. But the themes of her mature life may be readily identified: She took pride in aiding other women, especially those who were self-supporting like herself; she was determined that her nieces would not grow up to be what she called "fine delicate creatures of the age"; and she despised weakness and incompetence wherever they appeared. By examining her beliefs and experiences, we of the twentieth century can learn much about what it was like to be a self-reliant woman in the eighteenth century, when female Americans had far fewer options than they do today and when their lives were constrained by sharp, seemingly impenetrable boundaries.

Independence in Business and Marriage

Born in 1726 in Scotland, Elizabeth Murray was 13 when she first went to America to serve as housekeeper for her bachelor older brother James, who had established himself as a planter in North Carolina. After living

---

[1] The major collection of documents pertinent to Elizabeth Murray is the J. M. Robbins Papers, Massachusetts Historical Society, Boston. Unless otherwise identified, all quotations in this article come from that collection.

at Cape Fear for four years, they returned to Scotland in 1744 to settle some business affairs. By the time they once again sailed for America five years later, James had acquired a wife and daughter and Elizabeth had obtained a stock of dry goods: Not for her was the permanent role of spinster dependent in a married sibling's household.

Evidently she originally intended to open a shop in North Carolina, but instead of re-embarking with her brother after their vessel made an unscheduled stop at Boston, Elizabeth remained in the northern city to start her business there, thus demonstrating at the age of 23 the self-reliance that was to be the hallmark of her later years. In addition to selling millinery, cloth, and sewing supplies, she taught needlework to young ladies. By 1754, although she commented ruefully that others tended to "laugh" at her business practices, she had an inventory worth £700, had hired an assistant, and was able to afford a voyage to England, where she learned "a short method of bookkeeping" from a helpful London merchant and purchased a stock of fashionable goods that she knew would suit the Boston market.[2]

The following year, after she returned to Massachusetts, Elizabeth married Thomas Campbell, a Boston merchant and ship captain who also came from a Scottish background. James Murray told their brother John, who still lived in Scotland, that Elizabeth had dutifully asked his approval of the match, "which I gave, not doubting of her having accepted the best that offer'd & considering she had not much time to wait for further Choice." Then 29, she apparently did not continue her mercantile business during her brief marriage, for under the common law a married woman was forbidden to own property or to make contracts unless she had reached an antenuptial agreement to that effect with her intended spouse. There is no evidence that she and Thomas made such an arrangement.[3]

A widow by early 1760, Elizabeth soon married again. In the spring of that year, when she was 34, she took as her second husband the wealthy 70-year-old Boston distiller, James Smith. Their antenuptial agreement guaranteed her a settlement of £10,000 in lieu of all dower rights and allowed her to manage the property she had brought to the marriage, in itself a fairly substantial estate. In addition, she was granted the right to make a will (normally denied to a wife) disposing of her property and of any sum up to £2,000. It was further provided that if she predeceased her husband without writing a will, her property would be distributed

[2] The biographical information is drawn from Nina M. Tiffany, ed., *The Letters of James Murray Loyalist*, printed: not published, Boston, 1901, pp. 9, 29, 47, 67, 103. For her advertisements as a teacher of needlework, see, for example, *Boston Evening Post*, April 1 and 22, 1751.

[3] Tiffany, ed., *Murray Letters*, p. 105. For a summary of the legal rights of women in the colonial period, see the article by Marylynn Salmon, this volume.

to her heirs as if "she had died sole and unmarried." She named two male friends as trustees charged with carrying out the intent of the agreement and with ensuring that her wishes were not "frustrated" by any legal technicalities.

Given the fact that Elizabeth Campbell was so obviously a gainer by this second marriage to a man she greatly respected, the scope of the antenuptial agreement is both striking and suggestive. Despite the promise of a settlement that would make her a wealthy woman upon her husband's death—which, judging by his age, could not be far off—she still wanted to control her own property during coverture. Although she nowhere said so explicitly, it is clear that she had learned an indelible lesson from her union with Campbell: She realized that before she married she had to secure her right to dispose of her property as she wished and to carry on her own business enterprises.

CREATING "USEFUL MEMBERS OF SOCIETY"

The independent ethic that led Elizabeth to insist upon maintaining her legal identity during marriage affected every aspect of her existence. Enabled "to live & act as I please" through the generosity of her second husband and her own prudence, Elizabeth Smith now devoted herself to helping other women become self-supporting and to overseeing the education of her nieces. When two Boston girls, Anne and Betsy Cuming, were orphaned by the death of their mother, Elizabeth Smith set them up in a small shop, and they also began to teach fancy needlework to the daughters of well-to-do Bostonians. In 1769 Anne effusively thanked her "kind adviser": "you . . . directed us in the way that would most Contribut to our Mutual Happiness, without Considring how much your intrest might suffer in trusting your property in the hands of two young unexperienced Girls," she wrote; "so much was we united, we must have been unhappy asunder you kindly contrived to keep us together and made us independent of evry one but your self. . . . what should we have been without such a friend."

Similar testimony to Elizabeth Smith's benevolence came from Jannette Day Barclay, who had borne an illegitimate daughter in Rhode Island and thereafter found herself "Helpless Friendless almost reduced to want" and so "sunk in my Opinion" that "I had nothing to Support me." It was Elizabeth Smith's "Acts of Benificence" in helping her to establish a school, she later declared, that "seemed to give me a Merit in my own Eyes, and in those of the World." Through her friend she discovered "that Internal Satisfaction I had lost by my own folly" and gained the confidence she needed to return to Britain, marry, and introduce her daughter Jackie to her natural father's initially hostile relatives.

Despite such activities, Elizabeth Smith devoted the major portion of her time to her own family, and primarily to her nieces. As she repeatedly told her friends, she believed that young women should have "an usefull education" so that each could "improve her mind time & fortune." She did not like to see "young people being brought up in idleness and entering the world with all its gaietys, triffling away the most active part of their life or marrying imprudently." Instead, a young woman should be placed in a situation that would "rouse her facultys and make her industrious." "I prefer an usefull member of society to all the fine delicate creatures of the age," [4] she remarked decisively, and from the time that she began to direct the education of her oldest niece, Dorothy (Dolly) Murray, in 1755, she put these principles into practice.

Dolly, who was then 10 years old, was sent north by her father James so that she could have the advantages of a Boston education. Her aunt saw to it that she attended classes in reading, writing, dancing, and sewing; "I try'd her to sew att home," Elizabeth explained to her brother in late 1756, "but people coming out & in so much to the shop took her of[f] so much she made nothing of it." In the education of her niece, Elizabeth Smith emphasized skills in writing and accounting: Become a "perfect mrs of your pen," she told Dolly in 1762, and perhaps "your papa will let you keep his Books the learning of it as they doe at school is nothing without the practice. how many familys are ruined by the women not understanding accounts."

James Murray's wife died in 1758, and two years later he took his niece Anne Clark and his other surviving daughter Elizabeth (called Betsy) to Boston to be educated by their aunt. Although Betsy's progress is not recorded in as much detail as that of her older sister, in 1762—when she was 6—Elizabeth Smith called her "a very good Schollar" who "knets well [and] reads better." Anne Clark was similarly described as a good reader who by 1764 had "learn'd the first principles of Geography." According to Jannette Barclay, Betsy's only problem was the fact that she "was always Sensible Above her years, but at one time she was told too much of it" and had therefore acquired "the most dangerous sort of Vanity." Evidence of the truth of this observation was provided by Christian Barnes, another of Elizabeth's friends, who had a "little Skirmish" with Betsy when she refused to iron her dress while on a visit to the Barnes home in Marlborough in 1768.[5] Accordingly, when Elizabeth Smith went to Great Britain in 1769 following the death of her husband, she insisted that Betsy accompany her so that she could be placed in an

[4] Elizabeth Smith to Christian Barnes, April 24, 1770, Murray Family Papers, box 4, New-York Historical Society.

[5] Christian Barnes to [Elizabeth Smith], Aug. 20, 1768, Christian Barnes Letterbook, Library of Congress Manuscript Division, Washington, D.C.

Edinburgh boarding school that stressed discipline as well as educational achievement.

At this juncture it seems appropriate to comment on the subsequent history of the three girls discussed so far. Dolly married John Forbes, a clergyman from St. Augustine, even before Elizabeth Smith left for Europe. Elizabeth parted with her favorite niece reluctantly, telling her that "whenever I have thought of your settling in the world, it has been the height of my ambition to have you near me. It is ordered otherwise and I must submit." As it happened, though, Dolly Forbes was visiting her aunt when the American Revolution began in 1775 and consequently remained with her throughout the war, being prevented from rejoining her husband, who continued to reside in British-controlled East Florida until his death in 1783.

Anne Clark had also married by 1769, moving back to North Carolina with her husband, William Hooper. Although James Murray strongly disapproved of the young man, Hooper went on to become a lawyer, a leader of the Revolution, and a signer of the Declaration of Independence. More important in this context is the fact that his marriage to Anne appears to have been both highly successful and unusually egalitarian for the eighteenth century. A surviving joint letter to Dolly Forbes dated 1771 reveals the Hoopers' affectionate regard for one another, as William complained good-humoredly that Anne had "disciplined me into the humble, inoffensive—submissive—Apron-string Husband" with "no Opinion of my own," while Anne retorted that he was "still as saucy as ever," claiming that it was highly unlikely "his unruly Spirit will ever be brought under subjection." On Anne's distinctiveness there is also the testimony of that prominent North Carolina lawyer, James Iredell, who visited her in 1778. Anne Hooper had "really charmed" him, he told his wife Hannah; though she was not beautiful, "her mind appears to be highly cultivated; she has read much; her sentiments are just and noble; she speaks with great correctness and elegance, as well as with care; her conversation is extremely interesting, and equal to high subjects." [6]

Betsy Murray also proved in her maturity to be a woman of whom her aunt could be proud and whose talents likewise served as a tribute to her upbringing. Betsy's granddaughter Susan Lesley praised her ability to run a large household smoothly and vividly recalled her grandmother's "strong family feeling," her "stately air and manner, her vigorous mind," and—interestingly enough, in light of the comments by Christian Barnes and Jannette Barclay—her "high spirit." [7] Evidently, Betsy Murray also

[6] Tiffany, ed., *Murray Letters*, pp. 118, 117; James Iredell to Hannah Iredell, June 4, 1778, in Don Higginbotham, ed., *The Papers of James Iredell*, vol. 2, galley proofs, N.C. Department of Archives and History, Raleigh, N.C.

[7] Susan I. Lesley, *Recollections of My Mother*, printed: not published, Boston, 1886, pp. 39, 25.

learned from her older sister's and cousin's mistakes; both of them, it appears, were "often at a Loss about cookery" after their early marriages. Elizabeth Smith told Dolly Forbes in 1769 that Betsy "rather than be laughed at as Cousin Anny is . . . will go in to the kitchen & take derections about Cooking," adding in an admonitory tone that "I am afraid Anny & you will repent not attending a little more to family affairs I dare say you were both afronted when I used to say how necessery it was."

Elizabeth Smith took responsibility not only for these daughters of her brother James and her sister Barbara Clark, but also for two daughters of her brother John. Mary (Polly) Murray, John's eldest child, was in her teens when Elizabeth visited the family in England from 1769 to 1771. She immediately interested herself in the welfare of this niece, who had been in a boarding school since the age of 10, and who, Elizabeth feared, "must enter the gay seens of life & become a fine Lady" if she remained in her Norwich home. "In my opinion," she told her brother James, "that will enervet her so much that business will ever be irksome to her." Consequently, although regretting the fact that she proposed separating the girl from her parents, Elizabeth urged that Polly, whom she regarded as "very capable," be sent to Boston where she could board with the Cuming sisters and "gain experience by attending to their selling things."

In accordance with her aunt's wishes, Polly sailed for America in the spring of 1770, taking with her £300 worth of goods supplied by Elizabeth's London correspondents. Elizabeth asked James, who had moved to Boston, to see that Polly's business was established on a sound footing and that she was taught proper accounting methods. But the uncertain political situation in the aftermath of the Boston Massacre made it impossible for her to open a shop at that time. Thus, it was not until Elizabeth herself returned from England the following year with Polly's younger sister Ann and Jackie Day (Jannette Barclay's now-orphaned daughter) that the project to start the girls off in business got fully under way.

With financial help from Elizabeth, the three girls formed a successful partnership. Jackie had learned to be a mantua maker in England; she and Ann made hats and other items while Polly tended the shop and kept the accounts. The latter proved herself to be just as "Notable dilligent, & Cleaver" a businesswoman as her aunt had predicted, but Ann and Jackie did not adapt so readily to their new lives. Jackie, it appears, saw herself as being "greatly above her bussness" and was accordingly "much Disliked by her Customers"; and Ann, although "very industerous," depended so heavily on her older sister that when Polly returned to England on a visit in mid-1774 she became increasingly depressed. Describing her melancholy mood to her cousin Betsy Murray, she wrote in

August, "since her absence, I . . . have met with more disagreeable Sensations than I would have done had she been here—I have at times been so chagrin'd that I have thought my resolution would not hold me up." A year later, with Polly trapped in England by the war, Ann married William Powell, a young Loyalist, and sailed with him to London.

Despite the fact that the business enterprise Elizabeth so carefully planned for her nieces had thereby collapsed, something did survive from the obvious wreckage. Christian Barnes found in the girls' early success a source of pride in her own sex: "who shall say we have not equal abilitys with the Men," she asked, "when Girls of 18 years of age discover such great capacitys"? And Polly Murray, who in 1779 found it "humiliating" that "I have no money but what my Dear Father gives me," told her aunt plaintively from England in 1783 that "that spirit of independence you cherished in me, is not yet extinct." [8]

THE IMPACT OF THE AMERICAN REVOLUTION

While Elizabeth Smith was in Great Britain from 1769 to 1771, her Boston friends kept her fully informed of the "Broils and animositys" and the "Spirit of discord and confusion" that prevailed in Massachusetts in the aftermath of the Townshend Acts. Most of her correspondents were merchants, and most ran afoul of the committees attempting to enforce the nonimportation agreements adopted in major American port cities in late 1769. Christian Barnes's husband, Henry, was a prime target; after one of his many confrontations with a local committee, Christian told her friend that "these dareing Sons of Libberty are now at the tip top of their Power and to transact any thing contrary to their Sentiments . . . is a Crime equal to high Treason." [9]

Even the young Cuming sisters with their tiny shop did not escape surveillance. In November 1769, three days after they had imported some English goods, they were visited by a merchants' committee that charged them with breaking the nonimportation pact. Betsy Cuming angrily retorted that their business was "verry trifling," that "we have never antred into eney agreement," and that she was amazed they would "try to inger two industrious Girls who ware Striving in an honest way to Get there Bread." In retaliation, the committee published their names in the paper as "Enimys to their Country," but both Betsy and Anne assured Elizabeth that "it has not hurt us at all in our Business," for it "Spirits up our Friends to purchas from us" and as a result "we have mor custom then before."

[8] Christian Barnes to [Elizabeth Inman], March 6, 1774, Barnes Letterbook; Mary (Polly) Murray to James Murray, March 10, 1779, Murray Papers, box 3.
[9] Christian Barnes to Elizabeth Smith, May 11, 1770; July 6, 1770; [c. Dec. 1769]; Dec. 23, 1769, all in Barnes Letterbook.

Despite a plethora of such accounts of her friends' troubles, Elizabeth Smith initially supported the New Englanders' resistance to British measures. She told her brother James in May 1770 that it was the Bostonians' "duty to stand up for so valuable a Country & not to be tax'd to feed the worst set of men that ever lived if I was in Boston I wou'd drink no tea and advise all my friends to sign." Her position rested securely on her admiration for hard work and her detestation of idleness: If James disagreed with her, she declared, he should come to England "& see what a vile set of Placemen & pentioners lives upon our industery." Later that year, however, she changed her mind after she received a long letter from Christian Barnes describing how some of the Barnes's possessions had been vandalized, her husband Henry hung in effigy, and their lives threatened with such vehemence that they now slept every night with five loaded guns at their side. The men who perpetrated such acts were "deluded," Elizabeth commented; "surely Indieans could not have invented more barbarity." She warmly sympathized with her friend's situation, praising her "resolution" in the face of danger. Although Elizabeth never became as vocal a Loyalist as her brother James Murray—who was forced into exile at the evacuation of Boston in 1776—from this time on she opposed the trend of American resistance.

In the personal as well as the political realm, Elizabeth retreated from her previous commitment to independence. Shortly after her return from England in the summer of 1771, with the heartfelt approval of Christian Barnes (who had told her, "you must fix upon some worthy Person who will releve you from the fetigues and cares of life"),[10] Elizabeth Smith married for the third time. Her new husband, Ralph Inman, was a retired merchant of substantial means, although his fortune did not compare to hers. Inman had courted her assiduously before she left for Europe, and his name had figured prominently in her friends' speculations on whom she would choose as her next spouse. In late 1771 Elizabeth explained to her brother John that on her return to America she had "found things in a Situation that was very disagreeable to me," for her late husband's estate had been reduced in value by £1,200 sterling during her absence. Inman was "an honest generous Man" who would manage the property for her and who "will render a faithful Account [of his] Stewardship." Furthermore, and perhaps more important, Inman had agreed to a marriage settlement that guaranteed her financial security: She would have the benefit of her large estate but not have to cope with the problems of running it.

Some months after the wedding, Elizabeth Inman told an English relative that "if I am not a happy wife it is my own fault no one has more of their own Will & few so much as I have." This was indeed an

[10] Christian Barnes to [Elizabeth Smith], Aug. 5, 1771, Barnes Letterbook.

accurate characterization of her antenuptial accord with Inman, which was even more tightly drawn than the one she had signed with James Smith in 1760. The agreement, dated September 24, 1771, reserved to herself and her heirs all her considerable real estate, while allowing Inman to use "the income, interest and profits of the same" during their marriage, with the proviso that he pay her £200 sterling a year for her "separate use and benefit." Inman was to have no claim whatsoever on her personal property; if he predeceased her she would have lifetime rent-free tenancy of his home in Cambridge; he promised to abide by any decision she might make to sell her real estate holdings (the proceeds would be added to her personal property, which he could not touch); and she was granted the same right to make a will, with the same intestacy clause, that had been contained in her agreement with Smith. Finally, to make the accord even more ironclad, in a separate bond Inman declared himself liable for a payment of £1,000 sterling if he failed to meet these obligations.

These extraordinary precautions might seem unnecessary, but such was not the case. Whether it was prescience, her normal prudence, or simply a continuing desire for financial independence that led Elizabeth to insist upon the carefully worded settlement, she was later to bless the day it had been signed. Ralph Inman turned out to be exactly the sort of idle, avaricious, and weak person that his wife so heartily detested.

She first fully realized his failings in the crisis following the battles at Lexington and Concord. He had been in Boston on April 19, 1775, and was trapped in the city by the subsequent American siege. Elizabeth remained at their Cambridge farm with her nieces Betsy Murray and Dolly Forbes, all three of them being regarded as "wonders" because most other women quickly abandoned Cambridge, which was the headquarters of the rebel army. For several weeks the Inmans exchanged letters about possible courses of action. Elizabeth, who initially proposed that the entire family consider leaving Massachusetts, had by mid-June adapted to the situation with her usual resilience: "I throw my anxiety off with a laugh, go about and order things as if I was to stay here for years," she informed Ralph. When warned she was living in the midst of danger, she retorted, "we could die but once, and I was a predestinarian, therefore [had] no personal fear." With her normal practicality, she decided that she could harvest and sell that summer's crop, thereby salvaging something from the catastrophe. "As we have sown it is a pitty not to reap," she told her husband when he urged her to "leave the Farm to take its Chance" and come to join him in Boston.

Because matters were so well under control and she was anticipating a handsome profit from hay sales, Elizabeth Inman was astonished when she learned from the panicked Ralph at the end of July that he planned to sail for London as soon as possible. This is hardly a proper return "for the many anxious and fatigueing days I have had," she told him angrily. Since his letter had said he lacked money, she sent him an order for £100, writing sarcastically: "Now, Sir, you have received this valuable treasure I beg you'll cast off your cares. Anxiety is very bad for the health." Finding his arrangements for her support in his absence entirely inadequate, she fumed, "Believe me, Mr. Inman, I am not anxious about a mentinence. Experience has taught me, water-gruel and salt for supper and breakfast, with a bit of meat, a few greens or roots, are enough for me." And finally, reacting to his accusation that she was consorting with the rebels, she wrote, "Be assured, Dear Sir, I will with pleasure account for every action that I remember since the year seventeen hundred and twenty-six (the year of my birth)."

Although James Murray tried to smooth over the rift between his sister and her husband by asserting that "1726 was at distance enough to learn to make allowance for the vexation the times give to one quite put out of his usual mode of life," the damage was done. Elizabeth Inman never forgave her husband for his weakness in time of crisis. Unlike Ralph, she thrived under adversity. In the spring of 1776 one of her young female admirers correctly described her as "in her proper element" when she aided those with "neither Spirits or ability to do for themselves." No other woman behaved as she did, the girl continued, for Mrs. Inman "is above the little fears and weaknesses which are the inseparable companions of most of our sex." [11]

In the end, Ralph Inman did not go to England but instead was reunited with his wife after the British evacuated Boston in the spring of 1776. During the rest of the war Elizabeth remained as fearless as ever: "no Disguiser of her Sentiments," she and her nieces openly assisted British prisoners of war by supplying them with books, candles, food, and rum, disregarding the "Calumny" they had to endure as a result. Despite their poor financial circumstances—Elizabeth later told her brother John that they had lived on £50 sterling a year while the war continued—and the strained relationship with the husband she no longer respected, Elizabeth declared herself content with her lot in 1778. "When I feel dull or disapointed," she told a friend, "I do not upbraid I compose myself with the Flowers of the forest when the slumber is over I rouse & tune up Life is but a Passage &c this method I find good for health & spirits."

It would be pleasant to believe that Elizabeth Inman ended her days in such quiet contentment, but, according to her devoted niece Betsy, that did not happen. After her aunt's death in 1785 Betsy informed her cousin Polly that Ralph had given Elizabeth "more trouble than her friends are aware of & his failings were dayly increasing. his avarice & excesses was a source of real misfortune to her & persued her even to a

[11] All quotations in the three preceding paragraphs come from Tiffany, ed., *Murray Letters*, pp. 184, 208, 211, 210, 215–216, 219, 246.

bed of sickness." On her deathbed in May 1785, Elizabeth drew up the will she had been authorized to make in her marriage settlement. To her "esteemed Friend" Ralph Inman she left only a yearly annuity of £100 for life, while she made bequests of £500 or £1,000 to each of her nieces and also remembered many female friends with smaller amounts. She further demonstrated her mistrust of her husband by providing that his annuity would begin only after he had turned over to her executors "all the Goods, Chattels & Estate of which at my Decease he shall be possessed in my right" and all the records pertaining to the estate.[12] Once again she had read her husband correctly: Betsy told Polly in June that Ralph "alternately curses your family [John Murray's children were the residuary legatees], our, & even his own Children. . . . Because he has not got the whole of the estate or such part of it as he requested, he has as yet declined giving up the Papers." It was not until February 1786 that John Innes Clark, executor of his aunt's estate, certified that Ralph Inman had in fact complied with the terms of the will and the original marriage settlement, thereby authorizing the annuity payments and releasing him from his obligations.

The Legacy of Elizabeth Murray

During her life, Elizabeth Murray's friends and relatives had attested to her intelligence, her unique abilities, and her forceful personality. In 1769 Betsy Cuming told her, "all I can say fals short of your deserts." Two years later an English cousin wrote, "I know not her equal, generosity truth & Noble Sentiments wholy Possess her Breast"; and John Clark, her nephew and eventual executor, in 1783 called her "my more than Parent," telling his wife that he was "under the greatest obligations and owe all that I have in the World [to her]." In recognizing the strength of her character, contemporaries also realized that she was especially able to influence young women. Christian Barnes, for example, commented after one of Elizabeth's visits that her niece Caty now took Elizabeth as her "Oracle." "She has adopted all your sentiments," Christian told her friend ruefully, "and it is sufficient for her to affirm a thing must be so because it was your opinion." [13]

Accordingly, it is to the women in whose upbringing Elizabeth Murray had a hand that we must look for her legacy. And that legacy is noticeably there: The same "spirit of independence" that Elizabeth nurtured in herself she transmitted to her surrogate daughters. The effects

12 Elizabeth Inman, will, May 14, 1785, Murray Papers, box 3.
13 John Innes Clark to Lydia Clark, July 10, 1783, John Clark Papers, Rhode Island Historical Society, Providence; Christian Barnes to [Elizabeth Inman], March 6, 1774, Barnes Letterbook.

of her education can be found in Anne Clark Hooper's egalitarian relationship with her husband, in Dolly Murray Forbes's influence on younger women (as recorded by her grandniece Susan Lesley), in Betsy Murray Robbins's notable housewifery skills and unquenchable high spirits, in Ann Murray Powell's ability to cope with the problems of life as a Loyalist exile in Canada, and in Polly Murray's proud memories of a time when she had been a self-supporting Boston shopkeeper. Moreover, Elizabeth Murray's influence by no means stopped with the first generation: Her nephew John Clark, for instance, gave his daughters Anne and Harriet an education far in advance of that received by most of their contemporaries. Further, one can be certain that Elizabeth would have been proud of her grandniece and namesake, Elizabeth Murray Robbins, a woman of "discriminating intellect" who never married but who had devoted 30 years of her life to abolitionism, prison reform, and writing schoolbooks for children by the time she died in 1853.[14]

Even though Elizabeth Murray was admittedly an extraordinary woman, this study of her life suggests that historians have neglected to make a number of important and revealing inquiries about the feminine experience in colonial America. Many researchers have been content simply to identify the types of businesses in which eighteenth-century women engaged, never bothering to investigate the impact of the process of running an enterprise upon the woman involved. Yet it is clear that Elizabeth Murray's economic endeavors, and the conclusions she drew from them, affected almost every aspect of her life.

Furthermore, although some authors, like Page Smith in *Daughters of the Promised Land* (Little, Brown, Boston, 1970), have focused on *father*-daughter relationships, scholars have rarely turned their attention to the influence of *mothers* on daughters. Elizabeth Murray had no daughters of her own, but her five nieces were surely her daughters in spirit. Her enormous impact on them, attested to by themselves and their descendants, indicates that historians should examine in detail the succession of feminine, as well as masculine, generational ties.

Finally, the obvious affinity of mind and purpose that would have existed between Elizabeth Murray, born in 1726, and her nineteenth-century grandniece, Elizabeth Murray Robbins, suggests that perhaps scholars have too easily accepted the common dictum that the personal experiences of women in nineteenth-century America were vastly different from those of their colonial female ancestors. It is therefore important to look beyond the prescriptive literature, beyond the attitudes of men toward women, to actual female lives, in order to recapture the essence of the feminine past.

[14] On these points, see Tiffany, ed., *Murray Letters*, p. 306; Lesley, *Recollections*, pp. 438, 468–469; Ann Powell's letters from Canada in the late 1780s in Robbins Papers, VI; and Clark Papers, *passim*, 1780s and 1790s, on the education of his daughters.

Documents

Antenuptial Agreement of Elizabeth Murray Smith and Ralph Inman, September 24, 1771

This Indenture tripartite made this twenty fourth—day of September Anno Domini one thousand seven hundred and seventy one,* in the eleventh year of his Majestys Reign. Between Ralph Inman of Cambridge in the County of Middlesex Esq. of the first part, Elizabeth Smith of Milton in the County of Suffolk Relict Widow of James Smith late of said Milton Merchant deceased on the second part and Ezekiel Goldthwait of Boston in said County of Suffolk Esq. and John Innes Clark of Providence in the County of Providence and Colony of Rhode Island and providence plantations Merchant as Trustees for the said Elizabeth Smith on the third part.

Whereas a Marriage by Gods permission is intended shortly to be had and solemnized between the said Ralph Inman and Elizabeth Smith and the said Elizabeth being seized in her own absolute right of a very considerable Estate both Real and personal, the greatest part whereof was given and bequeathed to her by her late husband the said James Smith deceased in and by his last will and Testament, she the said Elizabeth is desirous to reserve to herself the whole thereof excepting the income, interest and profits of the same during such time as they shall continue to live together, which the said Ralph is to receive and apply to his own use, paying out of said Income Interest and profits the sum of Two hundred pounds sterling yearly and every year and in the same proportion for part of a year unto the said Ezekiel Goldthwait and John Innes Clark Trustees as aforesaid or either of them during such time as said Ralph and Elizabeth shall live together to and for the separate use and benefit of said Elizabeth Smith and in case said Marriage therefore takes place, certain Marriage Articles and Covenants are agreed upon by and between the parties aforenamed as follows vizt. . . . [Ralph Inman agrees for himself and his heirs that he will pay the £200 yearly to Elizabeth Smith's trustees or to any other person she designates, her coverture notwithstanding. He further agrees that he will keep detailed business records to submit to the trustees upon request. In return, he is granted the right to do whatever he wishes with all the annual income over £200.]

And the said Ralph Inman doth further Covenant that he will not assume any power over, or claim of property in any part of the personal Estate of the said Elizabeth Smith that she is now possessed of, as particularly mentioned and contained in an Inventory or Schedule thereof bearing even date with these

---

* Published with the permission of the Massachusetts Historical Society, Boston, from the James M. Robbins Papers, vol. 3.

presents and signed by all the parties herein named (saving the remainder aforesaid) but the same or the full value thereof shall upon his decease be by his Executors or Administrators delivered up and restored to her if living or to her aforesaid Trustees their Executors or Administrators or to such person as she or they shall appoint to receive the same, and if it shall so happen that said Ralph survives the said Elizabeth he shall as soon as may be after her decease surrender and deliver up unto her aforenamed Trustees their Executors or Administrators or to the Executors or Administrators of said Elizabeth in her will named or to such person or persons as she shall therein appoint to receive the same all and every part of the personal Estate Goods and Chattels in the Inventory or Schedule aforesaid or pay the full value thereof and shall retain and keep back no part thereof Fire, losses of debts, and other extraordinary casualties to be always exceptd.

And it is further agreed that the said Elizabeth Smith shall and may if she pleases at any time during the Coverture, make her last will & Testament or Instrument purporting her last will and Testament & thereby give bequeath and dispose of all and every part of her aforesaid personal and real Estate to any person or persons at her discretion to take effect upon her decease in case she should dye before him said Ralph Inman, And the said Ralph his Executors and Administrators in case he survive her shall permit the same to be proved and approved as her will and operate in the same manner as tho' she was not under Covert at the time of making such will or at the time of her decease. And it is further agreed that if the said Elizabeth Smith shall not make her last will & Testament, or any Instrument purporting the same that then the whole of her aforesaid personal and Real Estate shall descend and go to such person or persons as shall then be next of kin to said Elizabeth who shall be entitled to the same as tho' she had died sole and unmarried, and the said Ralph for himself his Executors and Administrators doth hereby Covenant to Restore to and pay the whole of said Estate to said next of kin accordingly.

And it is also agreed that all such debts as shall appear to be due from the said Elizabeth Smith to any person whatsoever before her Intermarriage with the said Ralph Inman shall be paid out of such of the Estate of said Elizabeth as shall upon said marriage come into his hands and the said Ralph shall not be subject or liable to pay the same or any part thereof out of his own proper Estate.

And it is also agreed that any Receipts or discharges that said Elizabeth may give to her aforesaid trustees or any other persons relative to the said Two hundred pounds sterling by her reserved as aforesaid shall be good and allowed by said Ralph her coverture notwithstanding.

And the said Ralph Inman for himself his heirs Executors and Administrators doth further Covenant grant and agree to and with the said Elizabeth Smith and the said Ezekiel Goldthwait & John Innes Clark Trustees as aforesaid their Executors and administrators that if it shall so happen that the said

Elizabeth survives the said Ralph she shall have full power & Right to possess
Enjoy and improve the whole farm and lands of the said Ralph Inman situate
in Cambridge aforesaid whereon the said Ralph Inman now dwells together
with the dwelling house stables outhouses and buildings as now occupied by him,
to hold the same with the incomes and profits thereof unto her the said Elizabeth for and during the term of her natural life or so long as she shall incline to
live there without paying any rent or consideration whatsoever for the same but
if she shall not choose or incline to live in said dwelling house herself but wholly
remove with her family therefrom then this Covenant so far as it respects her
living on said farm shall cease determine and be void at the time she shall with
her family wholly remove from the same and she afterwards shall not have or
pretend to any right or claim to said dwelling house farm and premises or any
part thereof.

And it is further agreed by the parties aforesaid that if said Elizabeth shall
incline to sell the whole or any part of her real Estate during the joint lives of
said Ralph and Elizabeth he the said Ralph shall with the said Elizabeth execute
any deed or deeds that shall be necessary for that purpose, and whatever sum
or sums of money he shall receive upon such sales shall by him be made and
added to the personal Estate of said Elizabeth and he or his Executors or Administrators shall be accountable to said Elizabeth Smith or to said Ezekiel
Goldthwait and John Innes Clark Trustees as aforesaid in the same manner as
for her other personal Estate as afore expressed unless the said Elizabeth shall
incline to apply it to any other use which she hereby reserves a right to do her
Coverture notwithstanding, but if she shall not otherwise apply it, the said Ralph
is to have and apply the interest thereof to and for his own use during their
joint lives. . . .

[Here follows a provision that the survivor of their marriage shall inherit
all of their combined possessions of furniture, linen, bedding, and plate—that
is, silver and other dishes and utensils.]

In consideration of the Covenants aforesaid the Elizabeth Smith for herself her heirs Executors and administrators doth Covenant and agree that in
case said marriage take effect and of her surviving the said Ralph Inman and
of his dying intestate that what is hereby secured to her and upon her receiving
the same she hereby excludes herself from all dower and thirds in his real Estate
saving her living on the farm and lands as aforesaid, and from all claim & demand upon any part of his personal Estate excepting the plate household goods
furniture and other chattels aforementioned and also such part as he may incline to give her by his last Will, if he should leave one. And the said Ezekiel
Goldthwait & John Innes Clark on their part grant and agree so far as concerns
them and is or shall be in their power that the covenants aforesaid shall operate
according to the true intent & meaning of the aforesaid contracting parties, and
that neither they nor their heirs Executors or Administrato[rs] shall do or
consent to anything whereby the Covenants or agreements aforesaid shall

be frustrated. In Witness whereof the parties aforesaid have hereunto Inter-changeably set their hands & seals the day and year first aforewritten.

Signed sealed & Delivered
in presence of us.—

Daniel Cooledge	*Ralph Inman*
Eliza. Cumming	*Eliz. Smith*
	Ezek. Goldthwait

Boston Feby 4th 1786 I Ralph Inman within named Do hereby acknowledge that the covenants herein contained have been performed by the trustees within named and I hereby release them from all demands and actions and causes of action on

account thereof	*Norman Brimmer*	*Ralph Inman*
witness	*M. Inman*	*John I. Clark*

Know all men by these Presents that I John Innes Clark, above named, do acknowledge to have received in my capacity of Executor to the within named Elizabeth Inman, with Edward Hutchingson Robbins and others of said Executors, all the securities, papers bonds & notes, referr'd to in said Covenant from said Ralph Inman, & that he hath in all respects fully kept & observed the same on his part, & in consideration thereof & of the sum of five shillings paid me by said Ralph, I do hereby release, & forever discharge him the said Ralph therefrom, hereby cancelling the same in every part—In witness whereof I the said John Innes Clark surviving trustee, the said Ezekiel & Elizabeth both deceased, have hereunto & seal this day of _____ In the year of our Lord 1786

Signed.   Sealed & Delivered
    In presence of us—

Last Will and Testament of Elizabeth Murray Inman, May 14, 1785

In the Name of God Amen I Elizabeth Inman,* Wife of Ralph Inman of Cambridge in the County of Middlesex Esq. being of Sound, disposing Mind & Memory do hereby make, and Ordain this my last Will & Testament (my coverture notwithstanding) An Authority to make which my Executors will shew —And Trust I commend my Soul into the hands of my Creator, relying on the Merits of my Saviour Jesus Christ for remission of all my Sins. My Body I commit to the Earth to be Buried as my Executors may think proper.

* Published with the permission of the Manuscript Division of the New-York Historical Society, from the Murray Family Papers, box 3.

As to my Worldly Estate, Both, Real Personal and Mixt I dispose & devise the same as here after Mentioned—Imprimis, I Direct that All my Just Debts & Funeral Charges be paid by my Executors as soon as possible after my Decease. . . . [She directs the payment of two specific outstanding debts.]

Item   I Give unto my much esteemed Friend the said Ralph Inman Esquire An Anuity of One hundred Pounds Sterling Money of Great Britain to be paid him yearly from the periods in the Manner and on the conditions hereafter provided and not otherwise.

Item   I Give to Mrs. Dorothy Forbes the Sum of five hundred Pounds Sterling provided She gives up or cancels my Bond conditioned for the Payment of that Sum.

Item   I Give to Miss Elizabeth Murray, my Neice the Daughter of James Murray Deceased the sum of One Thousand Pounds Sterling Money of Great Britain.

Item   I Give to my Neice Mary [Polly] Murray the Daughter of Doctor John Murray of Norwich in England the Sum of One Thousand Pounds Sterling Money of Great Britain.

Item   I Give unto Jacobina Butler [that is, Jackie Day; Wife of James Butler resident in Ireland & Daughter of Janette Barclay the Sum of One hundred Pounds Sterling. . . .
[Here follow bequests of £100 each to two young women evidently named after her and to the three children of Dorothy Murray Forbes.]

Item   I Give to my Cousins Jane & Anne Bennett Daughters of Andrew Bennett Esq. late of Chester in Scotland deceased the Annuity of forty Pounds Sterling . . . [here follow details of the annuity payments].

Item   I Give unto my Neices, Mrs. Dorothy Forbes & Elizabeth Murray as Daughters of my Brother James Murray Esq. Deceased the Portrait of the said James & Also the Portrait of My Self. I likewise devise unto them the said Dorothy & Elizabeth & their Heirs forever my Pew in the Chapel Church situate in the Town of Boston, Also my Tomb and whole Estate in the Chapel Burying Ground. . . .
[Gives a house and lot in Boston to Prudence Middleton Whipple, a niece of James Smith's through his first wife, and her husband.]

Item   My Will is that Mrs. Anne Powell the Wife of William Dummer Powell be paid & receive from my Estate hereafter described the lawful Interest of two Thousand Pounds Sterling which Interest is to be paid to her Annually for and During her Natural Life & for her own personal Use & Disposal, And that After her Decease the said Principal Sum of two Thousand Pounds Sterling be paid & distributed to and among her present & future Children in equal Portion that is to say Among those who survive her Decease Unless they leave Issue, which issue shall represent their [Decea]sed Parent. . . . [This bequest is to be paid by her two nephews

John Innes Clark and John Murray out of the income from two houses
and a distillery left to her by James Smith.]

Item my Wearing Apparell & cloaths of every kind I give to said Mrs. Forbes,
Mrs. Powell & sd. Elizabeth Murray in equal portions.

And as to the residue of my Estate whether Real Personal or Mixt, or
whatever, is not granted As aforesaid I hereby give Devise & Bequeath the Annual enco[me] thereof to my Brother the said Doctor John Murray and During
his Natural life the Principal or residue aforesaid. After his Decease I give
devise and bequeath to the remaining Children of my said Brother Doctr. John
Murray (excluding the said Mary Murray, Anne Powell & John Murray, already
Named as legatees), to hold to them their Heirs & Assignes the same residue
hereby Devis'd, being and to remain Changeable with the Support of my two
Black Servants Marlborough & Isabella, and with the Payment of the Annuities
herein before bequeath'd to the said Ralph Inman, Jane & Anne Bennett. . . .
[Here follow details of the payment of the annuities.]

Also my Will is that all legacies herein bequeath'd shall be by my Executors
paid as soon as may be After my Decease with lawful Interest till Paid.

And as to the said Ralphs Annuity, My Will is that the same commence
from the time and As soon As he shall surrender into the hands of any Executors all the Goods, Chattels & Estate of which at my Decease he shall be possessed
in my right or may appertaine to one, and all Writings, Papers & evidence of
property of any kind, which shall be Necessary to enable my Executors to execute
this Will & Testament and which they shall demand for that purpose, upon the
Accomplishment of which the said Ralph's Annuity is to commence & have effect
& not Otherwise. . . . [Here follow further details of the Bennetts' annuity.]

And I the said Elizabeth Inman do hereby revoke Disannull & make void
all former Wills by me at any time before made & established and establish this
to be my last Will & Testament Agreeable to the liberty reserved in my Marriage Contract. . . . [She names John Innes Clark, John Murray, Jr., and Edward
Hutchinson Robbins as executors, with authority to sell any of the estate if
necessary to carry out the terms of the will, and orders that each be given a
gold ring.]

In Witness Whereof I have hereunto set my hand & Seal this fourteenth
Day of May in the year of Our Lord One Thousand Seven[teen Hundred a]nd
Eighty Five

[torn]   *Eliz: Inman* & a seal

And at her request We
Subscribe As Witnesses

    James Lloyd
    John Amory
    Rufus G. Amory

Suffolk Ss:

The aforewritten Will being presented for Probate by John Innes Clark & Edward Hutchinson Robbins two of the Executors therein named James Lloyd, John Amory, & Rufus G. Amory, made Oath that they saw Eliza.[a] Inman the Subscriber to this Instrument sign & Seal & Also heard her publish & declare the same to be her last Will & Testament, and that when she so did she was of sound disposing Mind & Memory According to these Deponents best discerning & that they set to their Hands as Witnesses thereof in the said Testatrix presence.

Boston May 28th 1785

O. Wendell Jud. Probate

3 The Young Ladies Academy of Philadelphia

Ann D. Gordon

Girl in Blue by an unidentified artist. Courtesy of the Abby Aldrich Rockefeller Folk Art Center, Williamsburg, Va.

The Young Ladies Academy opened in Philadelphia in 1787, offering girls a chance for education in a school remarkably similar to academies for boys. Under the instruction of John Poor, girls could study such subjects as grammar, arithmetic, geography, and oratory, a combination recognized —for boys—as basic learning in a commercial society. More than its curriculum, however, marked this school as new. Influential men in the city took seriously the proposition that girls could and should benefit from schooling and contributed their time and talents to popularizing the idea. They called themselves the school's visitors until they incorporated the school in 1792 and became its trustees. Under their leadership the academy grew to be an independent institution, more stable than the schools or classes taught by private teachers, incorporated by the state, and free from religious affiliation. Located in the commercial and social hub of the new nation, the Young Ladies Academy rapidly achieved national fame, drawing students from as far away as the West Indies and Maine.

To its contemporaries the academy symbolized a change in men's thinking about women, and to historians it represents a departure in the history of women. Men founded it, taught in it, and created the records by which it can be studied, and yet the effects of their actions were felt by young women, each of whose lives changed because she attended the academy. The record of the Young Ladies Academy is entirely ideological, consisting of published addresses by trustees and students together with selections from the trustees' minutes published in 1794 to advertise the school.[1] As a consequence, its best foot is always forward. Historians are frustrated by the record in drawing conclusions about the significance of this or any academy to the radical transformation of women's public presence in America between 1750 and 1830. The questions are: Did the Young Ladies Academy and its contemporary girls' schools contribute to the changes, and if so, how?

The academy provided a miniature platform on which late eighteenth-century sexual politics came to life. It occasioned statements about

[1] Sources on the Young Ladies Academy include the following: *The Rise and Progress of the Young-Ladies' Academy of Philadelphia; Containing An Account of a Number of Public Examinations and Commencements; the Charter and Bye-Laws; Likewise, a Number of Orations delivered by the Young Ladies, and several by the Trustees of the Said Institution,* Stewart and Cochran, Philadelphia, 1794; Benjamin Rush, *Thoughts upon Female Education, Accomodated to the Present State of Society, Manners, and Government in the United States of America . . .,* Prichard and Hall, Philadelphia, 1787; John Swanwick, *Thoughts on Education, Addressed to the Visitors of the Young Ladies' Academy in Philadelphia, October 31, 1787 . . .,* Thomas Dobson, Philadelphia, 1787; Samuel Magaw, "An Address Delivered in the Young Ladies Academy, at Philadelphia, on February 8th, 1787, at the close of public examinations," *American Museum,* 2 (1788), 25–28. Unless otherwise noted, all subsequent quotations come from these sources.

the changes men anticipated in women and the hopes women held out for themselves. Everyone, it seemed, wanted change (except rare voices, not heard at the academy, speaking out against women's power to reason). They did not all agree about the reasons for change or the directions it should take but found common ground in the proposition that their school would bring about precisely the change they sought. Schools had the power to make or break a society because through them the rising generation acquired its values, and people's values determined the quality of life. This belief in school power was fundamental to social and political theory in the new republic, as well as to the ideas men held prior to the Revolution.

The decision to extend education to girls required that men and women apply complex traditions about the value of education, traditions that evolved for boys, to girls. Comparison between these traditions and the academy's intentions and policies shows how change came about and how volatile it was.

THE EDUCATORS

Trustees and visitors of the Young Ladies Academy looked to their own experience with schools to find models for training girls. Interest in women's education arose in Philadelphia among the men who knew the most about how schools were run and why they were important. The trustees were, almost to a man, college graduates. Some, such as the Reverend Robert Blackwell, earned honors from more than one of the colonial colleges. Graduated from Princeton in 1768, Blackwell received an honorary bachelor of arts degree from Columbia in 1770, his master of arts degree from Princeton in 1782, and doctor of divinity degrees from Pennsylvania and Princeton in 1788. William Rogers held degrees from Brown, Yale, Princeton, and Pennsylvania. Their common training and shared experience as students imposed responsibilities. Provost William Smith, of the College of Philadelphia, hammered home this theme to his students: "Consider yourselves . . . as distinguished above the Vulgar, and called upon to act a more important Part of Life." [2] The college graduates applied their training to the outstanding problems of their day, among which was numbered the level of education in society.

The arguments for schools employed in the 1780s and 1790s differed very little from those advanced in the middle of the eighteenth century. "The good Education of Youth has been esteemed by wise Men in

---

[2] William Smith, *A Charge, Delivered May 17, 1757, at the First Anniversary Commencement in the College and Academy of Philadelphia . . .*, B. Franklin and D. Hall, Philadelphia, 1757, p. 4.

all Ages," Benjamin Franklin had written, "as the surest Foundation of the Happiness both of private Families and of Commonwealths." [3] In 1749 the common sense of this observation persuaded Franklin's friends to open the Academy of Philadelphia for boys. Leaders throughout the colonies reached similar conclusions about the connection between training youth and ensuring the security of government, and the number of schools mushroomed from the 1740s until the outbreak of revolution. Most of them were secular, or at least interdenominational, and governed by laymen. Simultaneously, Presbyterians, Anglicans, Baptists, Lutherans, and other religious groups hatched plans for still more academies, competing among themselves for the spiritual loyalties of young men but, more significantly, spreading schools over the land.

The Young Ladies Academy's leaders took up the cause of education through teaching, founding new schools, and governing old ones. The ministers, in particular, taught school and served on the boards of colleges and academies. John Andrews, one of the original visitors of the academy, taught school to his young parishioners in Queen Anne's County, Maryland, after college, and during the war taught in rural Pennsylvania. In 1785 he returned to Philadelphia, where he had studied, to teach at the new Episcopal Academy for boys, in which trustee William White was a moving spirit, and from 1791 until 1813 he taught at the University of Pennsylvania. White, Thomas Mifflin, Jared Ingersoll, and James Sproat were among the college trustees represented at the academy, and Ashbel Green, Henry Helmuth, and Samuel Magaw were among the professors.

In one important respect this group of men broke with tradition. Few people, except Quakers and Moravians, stopped to ask why the "good Education of Youth" applied only to boys.[4] An academy designed according to Franklin's model would "supply the succeeding age with men qualified to serve the public," and yet, 40 years later, it was the graduates of such academies and colleges who led the way in supporting women's education. Their support, which not only led to the founding of the Young Ladies Academy but also furthered the formation of other schools for girls, was important because the visitors and trustees were leaders—principally as ministers, but also as prominent doctors and lawyers with national reputations.

[3] Quotation from Benjamin Franklin, *Proposals Relating to the Education of Youth in Pensilvania*, B. Franklin and D. Hall, Philadelphia, 1749, p. 5. Much of the material used in this essay is based on my dissertation: "The College of Philadelphia, 1749–1779: The Impact of an Institution," unpublished Ph.D. dissertation, University of Wisconsin–Madison, 1975.

[4] Priscilla Mason, in the documents following this essay, may refer to Quakers in her remarks about women and churches. Although the Quaker and Moravian schools, in and near Philadelphia, probably sped up the decision to educate girls in Philadelphia, the Young Ladies Academy came out of a different educational tradition. The connection between the two remains to be studied.

Bishop William White, first president of the visitors, had helped to reorganize the Anglican church into an independent, national Protestant Episcopal church. Benjamin Rush, doctor and inveterate essayist, served in the Continental Congress. Jared Ingersoll, one of Philadelphia's outstanding lawyers, also had served in Congress and, when the academy opened, sat in the Constitutional Convention. Thomas Mifflin, a merchant, a trustee of his alma mater, the College of Philadelphia, and a war hero, occupied himself with politics. The senior ministers of Philadelphia's Christian churches joined this influential group, bringing in addition their considerable influence within each denomination. They had the power to make women's education acceptable and fashionable as well as to define its form.

The Young Ladies Academy resembled earlier schools in everything but the sex of its students, because its founders selected from available models the features suitable to their experiment. In choosing the term *academy* they selected a type of school that had already proved its flexibility. Of Greek origin, the word implied higher forms of learning, but in the seventeenth and eighteenth centuries it differed in meaning from a college. The Academy of Philadelphia, for example, offered two programs —neither of them collegiate—distinguished by whether a boy needed to learn Latin and Greek. Those students intended for college, and hence for careers in law, medicine, and the church, prepared by studying the so-called learned languages. Students entering careers in trade or crafts could follow a program complete in itself and more appropriate to the demands of their future employment. It was this last application, neither preparatory for higher education nor equivalent to college, that became the most general meaning of academy after the Revolution and that suggested a model appropriate for girls.

Because the academy's purposes were basically secular, it could be interdenominational and tolerant of religious diversity. This too followed local practice. Among the ministers on the governing board were Presbyterians, Episcopalians, Lutherans, and Baptists, which enabled the school to attract students from as many churches. Presumably the Young Ladies Academy faced a situation similar to that of a new college: a small market needing every encouragement. A century of religious toleration had produced a unique condition of cooperation among churches in Philadelphia because none could claim a monopoly on power or wealthy parishioners. At the College and Academy of Philadelphia the trustees had committed themselves to sectarian balance and representation as the only way they could raise money and attract students. If anything, the Revolution had strengthened local resolve to be tolerant, even though such church schools as the Episcopal Academy could survive.

The curriculum for practical, self-contained academies received its classic statement in Benjamin's Franklin's proposal for an English School, written in 1751. Well versed in the educational proposals of John Locke and his English followers, Franklin distilled the requirements for good citizenship and the most useful topics from enlightenment philosophy into a rudimentary program concentrated on learning to write clearly and read critically. It would, in his words, fit boys "for learning any Business, Calling or Profession, except such wherein Languages are required" and "qualify them to . . . execute the several Offices of civil Life, with Advantage and Reputation to themselves and Country." The program proposed that boys first learn the rules of English grammar and spelling, advance to reading for oral effect and comprehension, acquire the rules of rhetoric and oratory, begin the study of history and the natural and mechanical sciences, practice composition—learning ethics and logic to aid them—and finally read widely of the best English authors.[5] Scientist and businessman that he was, Franklin also assumed that the boys would study *"Arithmetic, accounts,* and some of the first principles of *geometry* and *astronomy."* [6]

Girls at the Young Ladies Academy followed this course. At the earliest public examinations in 1787, girls demonstrated their proficiency in reading, writing, spelling, arithmetic, and geography. John Swanwick, a merchant and a visitor of the academy, expressed the hope that before long the list of achievements would include composition. By 1790, when the first diplomas were prepared for academy students, the list of subjects had grown to include spelling, reading, writing, English grammar, arithmetic, geography, rhetoric, and composition. During the school year in 1787, and perhaps later, special lectures were given at the academy on the principles of chemistry and natural philosophy. In 1789 mention was made of an introduction to astronomy at the academy. Sprinkled throughout the curriculum were lessons in what John Swanwick called "Christian knowledge."

THE FAIR SEX

The educators believed that woman's nature differed from man's except in its capacity to reason. They stood out from most eighteenth-century men because they built a school to celebrate the idea that women shared *so much* of man's nature. The most famous statement on girls' education in this period came from Benjamin Rush, who spoke to the students at

---

[5] Benjamin Franklin, "Idea of the English School, sketch'd out for the consideration of the Trustees of the Philadelphia Academy," in Richard Peters, *A Sermon on Education, Wherein Some Account is Given of the Academy, Established in the City of Philadelphia . . . Preach'd at the Opening thereof . . .,* B. Franklin and D. Hall, Philadelphia, 1751, p. 8.

[6] Franklin, *Proposals,* p. 12.

the Young Ladies Academy in July 1787 and published his address in Philadelphia and Boston shortly afterward. Rush concluded his remarks with a charge to the young ladies.

It will be in your power, LADIES, to correct the mistakes and practice of our sex upon these subjects by demonstrating that the female temper can only be governed by reason and that the cultivation of reason in women is alike friendly to the order of nature and to private as well as public happiness.

The trustees and the students believed themselves to be pioneers in what sometimes appeared as hostile terrain. The test of their joint venture would come in the students' ability to change men's minds about women.

But the changes that women might make were limited by a "natural" difference between the sexes and their distinctive duties. They called it woman's nature, but the trustees described her by social attributes. By nature she is "(what I look upon to be very little lower than the angels) sensible, virtuous, sweet tempered." She is "perfectly inoffensive, courteous and obliging to all," according to Samuel Magaw. On the basis of these qualities of womanhood, men defined woman's duties, insisting that they obeyed the laws of nature. Woman should cultivate "habits of obedience, and a placid, graceful attention to whatever duty she may be concerned in" and "not excessive refinement, or deep erudition." If she did not, then she violated her responsive and congenial qualities. All social duties, not just women's, derived from incontrovertible laws of nature. But the knowledge and training to analyze nature's evidence belonged exclusively to educated men who used their advantage to prescribe roles for women.

Rush interpreted the evidence: "The female breast is the natural soil of Christianity"; having a natural affinity for religion, he concluded, women should be responsible for its survival, because it "accords so admirably with all their accomplishments, and with all the excellencies of their nature." The act of assuming to set duties for women as well as the specific conclusions reached by these men underscored woman's subordinate role, but they did not rob her of all social influence. Women could be powerful indeed within their proper sector. John Swanwick, speaking to the girls a few months after Rush did, wanted them to assume the burdens of men's souls: "Like the guardian angels of our sex, they will gradually lead us to those celestial realms from which we have been exiled."

Harmony between sexual nature and social responsibility produced, in the minds of the educators, perfect partnerships between the sexes. Together, men and women filled the complement of socially useful activities. John Swanwick, for instance, recommended that women study the subjects that men were too busy to study so that between them they would share a full education. The ideal partnership assigned women specific value, albeit in relation to men's needs. "To give us happiness," Swanwick went on, "and to enable us to support the vicissitudes and misfortunes of the world, was the intention of a benevolent Deity, in adding women to the society of men."

Women bore the greater burden of things spiritual and moral because of their natural superiority in these realms. Swanwick described their religious influence in terms of conquest: "in proportion as they encourage [Christian knowledge] among the gentlemen, they will extend the limits of their empire, and lay the best foundation for . . . domestic life." Benjamin Rush argued that once women received education, they would have enough power over men "not only [to] make and administer [the country's] laws, but form its manners and character." This occurred not because they would enter the chambers of law but because they could threaten moral censure of men. Rush believed that "young men would . . . be restrained from vice by the terror of being banished from their company" and that "the patriot—the hero—and the legislator, would find the sweetest reward of their toils, in the approbation and applause of their wives." In effect, visitors offered women no more than the traditional powers of their sex: their wits and manners applied to a battle of the sexes. As a proud student put it, women had always enjoyed the power of their domestic quarrels, practicing "that species of female eloquence, of which husbands so much, and so justly, stand in awe."

Although the educators made the leap to count girls among useful, educable youth, they expected women to live entirely within their families; it was their nature to shine in the household, "to please, charm, and entertain, at home, among their families and friends." For Rush the drive toward family life came from within the girl: "To be the mistress of a family is one of the great ends of a woman's being." Education had only to draw out this impulse. A poetic gentleman who attended the Young Ladies Academy commencement in 1792 paraphrased a poem about gardening, one frequently used in references to schools, to suggest their natural step from girlhood to housewife. "Delightful task, t'expand the human mind, / To form the maiden for th' accomplished wife, / And fix the basis of a happy life!" When Rush and Swanwick spoke to the academy girls in 1787, they proposed that girls be taught some of the traditional arts and crafts of ladies: music, drawing, dancing, and foreign language (they omitted needlecraft). These, they argued, were not frills but useful skills, needed to fill that "portion of time that may fall heavy on their hands"—usually, for some reason, in the afternoons and evenings. Simply by learning to sing, a girl could expect to relieve "the distress and vexation of a husband—the noise of a nursery, and even, the sorrow that will sometimes intrude into her own bosom."

The actual emphasis in the academy was not on womanly arts but on subjects chosen to educate boys for their duties. Unless some portion of men's education was shared, the partnership between men and women could not survive. But the prescription that all women belonged in the home forced revisions in the explanations why children should study each subject. Most of the academy's courses developed skills in reading and writing. As James Sproat said, Philadelphia paid considerable attention to "the beauty of language and the elegance of every kind of writing." From John Locke to Franklin and beyond, the reasons for stressing these skills were twofold: Good writing indicated a person's social status and it equipped boys for public life and business. Only the first of these appeared as a reason for girls to master the new rules and uniformity governing English grammar and spelling. Benjamin Rush spoke of the "Pleasure and interest [that] conspire to make the writing of a fair and legible hand, a necessary branch of female education," and he warned the girls that carelessness in writing was "a mark of a vulgar education." Where men had need to write in order to set their ideas before the public, no such requirement arose in woman's sphere.

Arithmetic had become an important subject in the eighteenth century because, in Franklin's words, "no business, commerce, trade or employment whatever . . . can be managed and carried on without the assistance of numbers." [7] Did women then need arithmetic? Rush expected they might, to assist their husbands in business by keeping the books and to watch the family finances. Benjamin Say, another doctor, described women's use of numbers more actively: "to buy or sell advantageously—cast up accounts, and in general to transact such business as may be found occasionally necessary." Similarly, the reasons for studying science assumed a much smaller range of activity for women than for men. Even the most moderate introduction of boys to natural history or philosophy could be justified by their need to understand raw materials. Franklin, for example, wrote about the need "to understand many Commodities in Trade," to discover "new Instruments, Mixtures and Materials," and to acquire "Hints" of "new Manufactures, or new Methods of improving Land." [8] When Benjamin Rush lectured on chemistry and natural philosophy to students at the Young Ladies Academy in 1787, however, he discussed only those aspects of the subjects "adapted to the use and improvement of the fair," according to Swanwick. Rush himself described his purpose more precisely as to teach "such parts of them as are calculated to prevent superstition."

The extent of limits on women's lives that supporters of the academy took for granted can be best measured by the fate of oratory as a school subject. Oratory and rhetoric capped boys' education; it forced a student to apply everything he had learned at school in order to prepare

[7] Benjamin Franklin, "On the Usefulness of Mathematics," *Pennsylvania Gazette,* October 23, 1735.

[8] Franklin, "Idea of the English School," p. 5.

interesting and effective speeches, but more important, it set him up for
assuming leadership after school by the devices he had learned about
persuasion. In the phrases of Philadelphia's best-known professor of oratory, William Smith, it equipped boys with a tool akin to a sword for
guaranteeing justice and honor. The instrumentality of this purpose disappeared entirely at the academy, and oratory became a means to a peda-
gogical end, like learning the rules of grammar. Molly Wallace, a student
orator, protested that she had not learned her skill in order to make public
speeches and that she would not do so again after this exercise at her
commencement. She insisted that oratory taught her only "some valuable
habits, which, otherwise she can obtain from no examples" about speaking correctly; "we look not for a female Pitt, Cicero, or Demosthenes."

The Daughters

At the Young Ladies Academy, girls discovered a world different from
family life. Although it was not the intention of the school's founders to
pose such an alternative, it was a consequence of the educational system.
No one wanted to talk about it. It was cited as an advantage of the academy that students lived in families, not in dormitories. Family government and domestic life were the ends of a woman's education and should,
therefore, be its means. Local girls, the majority of students, stayed with
their parents, stepping out each day to school. Girls from other states, if
they followed the example of boys before the war, probably lived with
relatives or friends of their families and would be expected to honor their
hosts as their parents. "[E]minent danger" attended the practice of
boarding girls away from "an affectionate and pious mother" and "a
sensible and judicious father," Joseph Pilmore, a visitor, warned. Girls,
like boys, needed careful supervision; in the gardener's metaphors
abounding in educational addresses, parents helped the teachers to take
"special care . . . to prune the precious plants . . . and guard against
invading harm."

Attacks on boarding schools masked the contrast between any school
and family training. Since the 1750s, propaganda for founding schools
had compared the family unfavorably with professional educators. Founders of the College and Academy of Philadelphia charged that parents, and
especially mothers, muddled their children's education with emotions.
"Partiality and Indulgence render them unfit to be trusted with the sole
Care of the Children's Education," Richard Peters complained. Parents'
work had to become scientific: to read the "Visible Index to [a child's]
Disposition [and] Pointer to his Genius." These natural guides enabled
society to plan for the best use of each person's potential but needed
experts to follow their meaning. School also introduced children to a

broader view of life than any single family could do, so that educated young people acquired flexibility and dependability unknown to children kept within their family. The teacher, in John Locke's words, "set the *Mind* right, that on all occasions it may be disposed to consent to nothing, but what may be suitable to the Dignity and Excellence of a rational Creature." [9] Through school, the next generation learned to cope with freedom beyond the family.

Teachers, and in the case of the Young Ladies Academy, male teachers, intervened between the child and her parents. With John Poor at its head and, as far as is known, men assisting him, the academy gave precedence to men as the source of girls' domestic values. The girls respected and enjoyed John Poor. Using the literary skills he taught them, they composed a song for his wedding in 1790 and a poem about his marriage. His generosity earned him thanks from students at their commencement. But apart from his person, his role demanded honor.

I f modest merit is with honour crown'd,
O r happiness is by the worthy found,
H er grateful wish will not be in vain, who pays
N ot servile flattery, but deserved praise:
P raise to the man who thus employs his care,
O n wisdom's plan to form the youthful fair;
O h! may thy cares their just reward obtain,
R ich in each bliss, and only Poor in name.

Mothers and older women generally lost their central role in the education of daughters, at least in theory. Although most girls studied woman's work with their mothers before enrolling in school, mothers received no recognition in the academy, and the girls heard no mention of their future responsibility to train their daughters. When Benjamin Rush wanted to describe how important mothers were to the education of children, he spoke only of the need for "instructing their sons in the principles of liberty and government."

It was a habit of educators to paint grim alternatives to the discipline of schooling. For example, they portrayed boys drinking, gaming, and whoring instead of studying, and thereby heightened the value of school. But formal contrasts between school and family, in the instance of a girls' school, took on the appearance of a conflict between socially useful values and a stereotype of woman's culture. Because women lacked the benefits of school, they displayed minds "clouded with errors and superstitious notions in things appertaining to usefulness in this life, and the social duties which all ought to possess," according to Benjamin

[9] John Locke, "Some Thoughts on Education," in *The Educational Writings of John Locke,* ed. James L. Axtell, Cambridge University Press, London, 1968, p. 137.

Say. They filled their heads with fashion and indulged "a passion for reading novels" that ought to be "subdue[d]." The attack on novel reading, an attack much broader at the time than that mounted by the Philadelphia educators, was aimed equally at youth and adult. It encapsulated fear about women's lack of industry, their preoccupation with sex as social mannerisms, and their escape into fantasy. Novels symbolized the time that lay on women's hands and their escape from, in Rush's words, "that which is real."

The academy intended to change women's values through carefully regulated freedom, freedom that carried within it the possibility to break away from the stereotype. One of its methods was to emphasize the terms of friendship and esteem arising from the common experience of being students together in the academy. By 1788 more than one hundred students attended the school, "female pupils, exclusive of all male pupils, excepting such as are under seven years of age." Close ties grew among the girls, as graduating students often remarked. "[I]s it possible, my much respected schoolmates, that I shall be able now to take a final leave of you, with whom I have spent so many happy hours, our alliance seems too close, suddenly to be rent asunder." The break might be permanent for the students who traveled to the academy from: "Cape-Florida, Georgia, Carolina, Virginia, Maryland, Delaware, New-Jersey, New-York, Connecticut, Rhode-Island, Massachusetts-Bay, the Province of Main, Nova-Scotia, Canada, from several of the West-India Islands, and from various parts of the state of Pennsylvania." And yet, while they attended John Poor's classes, they were thrown together, "confine[d] . . . within the walls of an academy, a particular number of hours," as Ann Loxley described school to her classmates.

As students, the girls found bases for friendship different from those of their parents' lives: wealth, religion, social circle, or location. In school they were, more or less, individuals. Teachers and trustees took pains not to offend the religious preferences of families, for example, but at the same time they minimized the historical conflicts among rival Christian churches in favor of common education. When students took examinations in Christian knowledge, they competed for prizes identified by religious denomination. Anne McKean, daughter of Pennsylvania's Chief Justice, won the Presbyterian Prize in 1787, when Mary Meredith, daughter of a U.S. Treasurer, won the Protestant Episcopal Prize. But the school taught what was called "a rational, well-informed piety" that transcended doctrinal differences, and girls from the churches were mixed together. It would take more important principles than religion to distinguish one's friends.

The girls became, in their own word, "sisters." They were on their own to work and learn. Ann Loxley put it thus: "[W]ithout your particular attention and application, the sanguine expectations of your teacher and relations, will be forever baffled." The rules at the academy promised that "no bodily correction, nor harsh treatment of any kind be ever attempted." By all reports, the trustees observed "good order and respect for their superiors" among the students, but we lack the sources to know precisely how girls played together at school and whether they ever, like boys, prompted each other to mischief. Ann Loxley attested that they recognized constraints at school. She felt confined and knew her classmates shared the feeling, but she also recognized that her choice to win the esteem of her friends and the honors from adults was the central fact of her education. Among her "sisters," success or failure would be public events. The boys at the Academy of Philadelphia vandalized school buildings and harassed teachers, but rarely were they beaten for their infractions of the rules. Rather, teachers punished boys by humiliating them in front of their classmates and collected prize money for good boys by imposing fines on bad. That the boys should learn to evaluate their peers, recognizing and spurning the failures and honoring the successes, were lessons for manhood. "Any youth who might desire to break thro' the rules of this institution in his younger years," William Smith assumed, "can hardly be expected to submit to the rules of any institution when grown up."[10] The Young Ladies Academy paralleled boys' schools in confronting its students with a test of their characters.

Of all the qualities a girl might exhibit, it was her merit that the academy systematically rewarded. Competence in a subject—not age, not social standing, and not even length of attendance—determined a girl's progress through the school. Using the list of prize winners to trace recurring names, we find that some girls attended the academy for at least three years, but years did not necessarily correspond to the three classes. Ann Loxley stayed in the first class through the examinations of June and December 1789 and June 1790. The trustees allowed a girl to win the same prize at different examinations only if she had advanced to a new class in the meantime. Minimum enrollment, if a girl sought a diploma, was set at three months. Although her program might be unique and flexible, depending on how much she had learned, each student faced the challenge of public examinations to measure her achievement. All the girls were tested in a six-hour ceremony, quarterly in the first years of the school and then semiannually. The trustees read papers submitted anonymously by the girls and heard them spell, read, and otherwise demonstrate what they had learned. Prizes, paid for by the winners' parents, went to the best girl in each class for excellence in each subject, from "Good Behavior" to "Rhetoric." Diplomas were added in 1790. Finally, commencement became an elaborate and formal ceremony, at least by

[10] William Smith, "The College, Academy, and Charitable School of Philadelphia," *The American Magazine and Monthly Chronicle,* 1 (October 1758), 638.

1793. In that year a procession of the teachers, the students following two by two, and the trustees, led by their president and vice-president, marched in the streets to the Methodist church. There "they made a halt, when the Scholars separated on the right and left; then the Trustees passed between them into the House, followed by the Pupils,—Saluted by a band of music in the gallery." Before an audience of parents, townspeople, friends, and trustees, the best students—the valedictorian and the salutatorian—delivered orations.

THE YOUNG LADIES

The prizes and rituals implanted competitive spirit in young ladies. Known to contemporaries as *emulation,* the theory of motivating students by pitting them against one another came directly from boys' schools, where it was acknowledged to prepare them for a competitive world. Not only did emulation keep boys and girls at their tasks, but it taught them that industriousness and discipline produced the most important rewards. Emulation "alleviate[d] the fatigue, and enliven[ed] the hopes and expectations of the pupil" at the Young Ladies Academy. She struggled to earn "popular applause" and to win "this literary race." The visitors and trustees emphasized the combative character of public examinations in which girls "nobly contended . . . with very formidable and determined opponents, who disputed the ground . . . inch by inch." Even the losers were commended for their "praise-worthy perserverance and undaunted fortitude." The imagery contradicts the ideal of female delicacy. Each year the trustees' speaker at examinations expressed concern for the losers and stressed how close all the students had come to winning prizes, but they did not question the fitness of competition for their students. Girls were even urged to retain the habit, just as boys were. "The same desire to excel will always, I trust, accompany you through life," John Andrews told the girls after their examinations in 1789.

The academy reserved its highest honors for excellence in writing and speaking. It published examples of students' composition in 1794. *The Rise and Progress of the Young-Ladies' Academy* . . . contained a student's funeral oration, delivered in memory of Molly Say, an academy student, a number of poems, a song, an essay "On the Importance of an Early Application to Study," as well as the commencement addresses. Formulas governed the students' creations; only in brief flashes do their writings provide much insight on the authors. But the publication clearly set out to prove what girls could do and celebrated their achievements. One or two girls each year enjoyed the remarkable chance to deliver orations before a sizable audience. Most of these speeches followed a formula, derived from the rules of rhetoric, adapted to the ceremony of celebrating the academy's success as measured by the girls' achievements, and permeated with self-consciousness about the unique public character of their performance. After apologizing for appearing in public, the students thanked the trustees and their fathers for giving them the chance to attend school, and praised John Poor for leading them along "in the flowery paths of science." The orator turned then to her schoolmates. At the pinnacle of her own success, she urged the other girls to follow her example. Molly Say, daughter of a trustee, addressed her friends in September 1791.

I must, therefore, before I take my seat, intreat it of you to pay strict attention to the salutary advice of your Preceptor, and push on your studies through every branch of learning taught in this Academy, that you may be also entitled by our Trustees to a diploma, the highest honor you can receive.

She then took her fond farewell, remembering those "endearing ties, which have bound us together." For a moment she was a leader among women.

To the Reverend Samuel Magaw the girls' mastery of the English language was most remarkable, especially "at so early a time of life." Caught up in the spirit of competition at commencement, he went on to compare their achievements with men's. "It may be, you will be found to *take the lead* in these accomplishments, of *the most* of our *graduated* Sons." Imagine the proud smiles of the girls! But is this what the academy had aimed at—young men and young women competing against each other as writers of the English language? It had taught girls to compete against each other and shown them a system based on individual merit. Its students mastered literary arts that had no meaning if practiced in private and that depended on circulation, publication perhaps, and qualified criticism. Each student had the opportunity to discover her talents and make something of herself at the academy, measured against its particular standards, and she also learned that other girls had the same abilities: to reason, to work, and to succeed. She learned less about boys. "By the separation of the sexes in the unformed state of their manners, female delicacy is cherished and preserved," Benjamin Rush promised in 1787. But whatever special character she acquired through her sex, the academy student could hear in Samuel Magaw's address the plain fact of the matter: She had just completed an education identical to that received by many young men.

The academy students indicated an awareness of contradictions between their education and their future. The most striking and pathetic feature of their commencement addresses is the absence of a future. They offered no vision of life beyond school. Frequently they leapt from academic achievements to immortality, as if nothing lay between their youth and their death. Unlike male students, who looked forward to freedom and responsibility to a greater degree than school could offer, the young ladies reminisced about the singular times they had enjoyed at the academy. Molly Wallace, speaking to her classmates in 1792, put school soundly behind her in an oration explaining that she would never again speak in public. Eliza Laskey, valedictorian in 1793, made a poignant statement about the leavetaking that commencement forced on the girls. "Perhaps no other situation in life is like that of parting fellow students," she suggested. It was painful because "Our youthful age, our daily meetings, and our likeness of employment in the same literary pursuits have brought us acquainted with such ties of intimacy." Like her sister students, she sensed that one stage of her life was coming to an end, and she found no way to express hope for the next.

The rare student broke through the contradictions. She asked, in effect, why she could not pursue "any Business, Calling or Profession," having learned the prerequisites at school. Priscilla Mason, salutatorian of the class of 1793, posed the question. She conjured up a society with women in the "Church, Bar, and Senate." Her witty and well-argued speech attributed to education the power to make this change in women's circumstances and even suggested that it had been the intention of the academy's founders to do so. What but their lack of education had kept women down in the past, she asked. Certainly their natural talents matched men's. She showed by argument and personal example that women shared the necessary qualifications to be orators. Men had, however, denied the point, "seized the sceptre and the sword, . . . denied us the means of knowledge, and then reproached us for the want of it." Overlooking the contortions introduced to educational theory by such men as Rush, Priscilla Mason went straight to the heart of the traditions in noting that men's power alone prevented women from gaining the same benefits as men from the same education.

Priscilla's idea of how and why societies changed derived from republican political theory. It was a time for overthrowing arbitrary power and substituting new bargains based on the merits of argument and on qualifications. She had both. But "Our high and mighty Lords" had held despotic sway over women's lives. "They doom'd the sex to servile or frivolous employments, on purpose to degrade their minds, that they themselves might hold unrivall'd the power and preeminence they usurped." Her faith in argument sounds naive but very confident. The Young Ladies Academy testified to a change in men's attitudes. "Happily, a more liberal way of thinking begins to prevail. The sources of knowledge are gradually opening to our sex." The women were ready. The old barriers to their full participation in society would fall because men had shown their willingness to surrender prerogatives of arbitrary power. All that remained, she told her schoolmates, was to "qualify ourselves for those high departments—they will open to us."

THE FUTURE

The first students to appear on the early lists of prizewinners at the academy were daughters of Philadelphia's finest families, whose men had been successful merchants and public figures for two or more generations. A few of them were daughters of college graduates or of men whose names appeared as trustees in other schools and colleges. It was a stylish and relatively expensive proposition to educate a daughter; a son could earn back his tuition many times over after school, but a daughter would not. By 1794 the old names were less prominent, and among the newcomers were many more German and Scotch-Irish girls. Families of those two groups had been slower and more cautious than English merchants to send sons to college because they were uncertain of the influence it would have on their values and unconvinced of its purpose. Many Germans felt discouraged by the college's anti-German attitude. But after 1779 the numbers of students from both groups rose, when the University of Pennsylvania actively courted them and college education had more acceptance. Tapping these non-English communities for the highest form of girls' education may have similarly lagged; the English commercial leaders of Philadelphia took the advantages of education for their daughters more for granted and spent their money more casually.

Dolly Willing can typify the urban merchant's daughter, although her family's wealth was very great. Her father, Thomas, married into an extended family of merchants and merged two fortunes. He held high posts in the colonial government and served as a trustee of the College of Philadelphia. Anne Willing Bingham, Dolly's older sister, married one of the wealthiest young men to graduate from the College and, during the 1780s and 1790s, ruled Philadelphia as its most fashionable lady and finest hostess—counting Thomas Jefferson, for example, among her friends. Dolly, who was 15 when the academy opened, enrolled immediately and won a prize her first year there. That is the last mention of her name in the school's lists. Five years later she married her first cousin, Thomas Willing Francis, a college graduate and a merchant. Maybe she chose him herself, but the marriage of cousins among her family's social equals occurred frequently as a financial arrangement to consolidate portions of family wealth. She bore 10 children in 20 years—hardly conducive to the leisure her academy warned her about—and then outlived her husband by 32 years. Until changes occurred in the ability of families to set up their daughters so successfully, girls like Dolly had little reason to expect that an academy would alter the pattern of their adulthood.

It is possible that among the students there were girls for whom the training had more practical potential. Few of the German and Scotch-Irish girls could have come from families as wealthy as the urban merchants. At some point in the last two decades of the eighteenth century, more and more families judged it worthwhile to commit time and money to girls' education. The numbers of academies along the eastern seaboard and, later, inland through the mid-atlantic and northern states, showed that a demand existed. To an extent impossible to measure, this interest included a decision that education had practical application, not just to develop character and accomplishments, but also to prepare in case a girl needed to work. Although historians have demonstrated that women increasingly did have need to earn an income in the early nineteenth century, because they were single or because they were widowed without capital, we do not know how people made the transition to preparing daughters to support themselves and whether education became an equivalent to dowries, as among boys it sometimes substituted for a portion of their father's land. By the 1780s many women in American cities had no alternative but to work in the early spinning and weaving manufactories, just as there had been women with no choice but to enter domestic service. But somewhere on the social scale between them and the Dolly Willings, there were families without sufficient resources to supply daughters with land or income to attract husbands, for whom education provided an alternative. And there were families with enough consciousness about the precarious state of property and marriage to plan ahead for future security, to prepare girls for work as teachers, for example.

Awareness of the practical necessity for education showed up occasionally among the most advanced thinkers on woman's situation. Debates on womanhood flourished in newspapers and magazines over the last two decades of the century, and the goal of economic independence for women appeared as one consequence of applying current social and political theory to their sex. In her recent essay, "Daughters of Columbia," Linda Kerber singled out the theme of independence from scores of essays on womanhood that she studied.[11] Obviously, the women seized upon a word that resonated with experiences of the revolutionary era, but more than that, they grasped its ramifications should the principles of the Revolution be applied to every social relationship. Independence, most broadly and abstractly conceived, meant a chance to train their minds as men did and to understand life other than through domestic details. As good republicans, they knew that the success of government depended on the intelligence of its citizens, among which they numbered themselves. Some women asked for more than intellectual recognition. There were

[11] See Linda Kerber, "Daughters of Columbia: Educating Women for the Republic, 1787–1805," in *The Hofstadter Aegis: A Memorial*, eds. Stanley Elkins and Eric McKitrick, Alfred A. Knopf, New York, 1974.

signs of concrete problems that women faced and identified. They sought, for example, to control their own property, to have some way other than marriage to earn a living, and in extreme instances to have a voice in government. Education was only a first step, and its purposes covered the range of women's social relations. When women asked for schools, they asked men to rise to the standards they themselves had set for America and to provide women with its advantages, as Priscilla Mason had anticipated they would.

It is difficult to establish whether the men at the Young Ladies Academy simply did not hear the women or purposely ignored them. Rush, who said the most of any visitor or trustee about women's lives, used the revolutionary heritage in a different way and placed the interests of society in stable family life ahead of women's own interests. To women fell the burdens of a new society, such as a tightened economy that made it necessary for every man to work and for their wives to assist "as stewards and guardians of their husbands' property." American social mobility made it difficult to find good servants; domestic service had become "the usual retreat of unexpected indigence" and "servants possess[ed] less knowledge and subordination than are required of them." As a consequence, women took on more supervision over households than did women of their class in England. These were not the issues that women defined as major from their experience of marriage, work, and society.

There are strong indications that the educators at the Young Ladies Academy wanted to stem the tide of women's discontent. Samuel Magaw made a curious statement of historical interpretation. He doubted, he began, that the academy's founding should be regarded "as constituting an Era altogether new." He went on to explain himself.

Neither would I resolve the success herein that we have met with, to any thing like a sudden Revolution in the public ideas and impressions. The most interesting Reform, and most permanent in its effects, may perhaps, in the greatest number of cases, be brought about slowly and imperceptibly; while others again, are marked by a celerity almost astonishing. How this may be, as applied to the case before us,—I pretend not to decide.

But the moral he drew stressed contentment with "*this* extremely pleasing fact," that an "Improvement" in women's education "*exists.*" It is possible to read that passage as a caution to women to accept what they had received and not expect, as Mason did, a flood of changes to follow. It is also possible to read Magaw's remarks as a useful and practical estimate of what his society (and historians in ours) might expect from a change in education.

The changes would come slowly, principally because real social circumstances were left untouched by opening an academy. But the school's symbolic importance, its change in the culture and its contributions to students, pushed change ahead. Middle-class women took heart from the existence of academies, even when they didn't attend them. The schools of the late eighteenth century seemed to signal a new recognition of women's ideas, encouraging them to write more and to find places to have their work published. Women took a more prominent role in promoting their own education and organized themselves into societies for charitable works. In fact, they duplicated the academy experience among grown women: sociable groups, often working together on a project, and audiences for each other's essays. Had the trustees of academies taken their idea of women's future and worked backward to a design for education harmonious with the social experience they anticipated, the effects might have been slower. But, relying on a model harmonious with public life, they reinforced women's ambitions to take a larger part of life.

Documents

From the Valedictory Oration, Delivered by Miss Molly Wallace, June 20, 1792

The silent and solemn attention of a respectable audience, has often, at the beginning of discourses intimidated, even veterans, in the art of public elocution.* What then must my situation be, when my sex, my youth and inexperience all conspire to make me tremble at the talk which I have undertaken? But the friendly encouragement, which I behold in almost every countenance, enables me to overcome difficulties, that would otherwise be insurmountable. With some, however, it has been made a question, whether we ought *ever* to appear in so public a manner. Our natural timidity, the domestic situation to which by nature and custom we seem destined, are, urged as arguments against what I have now undertaken:—Many sarcastical observations have been handed out against female oratory: But to what do they amount? Do they not plainly inform us, that, because we are females, we ought therefore to be deprived of what is perhaps the most effectual means of acquiring a just, natural and graceful delivery? No one will pretend to deny, that we should be taught to read in the best manner. And if to read, why not to speak? For surely it cannot be a less necessary qualification for a young Lady to speak properly, than for her to read so, since she will, perhaps, rarely have occasion to read in public; tho' she may almost every day be obliged to speak, not only in the circle of her friends and acquaintance, but even before strangers, who will not often make the

* From *The Rise and Progress of the Young-Ladies' Academy of Philadelphia* . . ., Stewart and Cochran, Philadelphia, 1794, pp. 73–79.

allowances, which an awkward and uncouth mode of elocution would necessarily require. But yet it may be asked, what, has a female character to do with declamation? That she should harangue at the head of an Army, in the Senate, or before a popular Assembly, is not pretended, neither is it requested that she ought to be an adept in the stormy and contentious eloquence of the bar, or in the abstract and subtle reasoning of the Senate;—we look not for a female Pitt, Cicero, or Demosthenes.

There are more humble and milder scenes than those which I have mentioned, in which a woman may display her elocution. There are numerous topics, on which she may discourse without impropriety, in the discussion of which, she may instruct and please others, and in which she may exercise and improve her own understanding. After all, we do not expect women should become perfect orators. Why then should they be taught to speak in public? This question may possibly be answered by asking several others.

Why is a boy diligently and carefully taught the Latin, the Greek, or the Hebrew language, in which he will seldom have occasion, either to write or converse? Why is he taught to demonstrate the propositions of Euclid, when during his whole life, he will not perhaps make use of one of them? Are we taught to dance merely for the sake of becoming dancers? No, certainly. These things are commonly studied, more on account of the habits, which the learning of them establishes, than on account of any important advantages which the mere knowledge of them can afford. So a young lady, from the exercise of speaking before a properly selected audience, may acquire some valuable habits, which, otherwise she can obtain from no examples, and that no precept can give. But, this exercise can with propriety be performed only before a select audience: a promiscuous and indiscriminate one, for obvious reasons, would be absolutely unsuitable, and should always be carefully avoided. . . .

My dear School mates;

Before I bid you adieu, you will claim my particular attention; that I should endeavour to animate you in the prosecution of your studies; and that I should offer you my advice in a manner; which, at any other time, might be deemed arrogant, but which, the solemnity of the occasion may possibly justify. —We must be sensible, that we are favoured with opportunities of improvements, of which thousands of our sex are denied. This ought surely to inspire us with gratitude to the Author of the Universe, who hath distinguished us in a manner so singular, and with reverence and affection toward our parents and guardians, who, in many instances, have given us the advantage of instruction superior to that, which they themselves have enjoyed. We ought doubtless to emulate their virtues.—But, shall we equal them? If we do not, ignominy and reproach will inevitably be our portion. It is our duty then nobly to exert ourselves, and to shew, that the labour and care which have been bestowed upon us have not been bestowed in vain; and to prove that the female mind will reward the most assiduous culture. Our utmost efforts, however, will give us but a small portion of knowledge; and our improvements will be best shewn in the exercise of humility. Charity and modesty are the best evidences of a highly cultivated mind. Yet for these virtues we are not to mistake an affected and languid delicacy, which the misjudging have falsely called sensibility. There is a firmness, and there is an independence of sentiment, which, if tempered with an unaffected softness and gentleness, are peculiarly suited to the female character: —They give it a lustre which no borrowed charms can bestow; they are really necessary as the friends of virtue, and as a shield against the attacks and insinuations of artful flattery, of vice and of folly:—their charms are irresistable. There can be no occasion for me to urge the necessity, of reverence and obedience to your parents, your teacher and superiors. Time will teach you that these virtues are indispensibly necessary. The precepts of your teacher, you will particularly regard. He knows and will attend to your interest. However difficult some parts of your studies may be, in him you will always find attentive and willing assistance, ready to mitigate your labour, and smooth the path of science. In the most flowery and beautiful, we often meet with some small obstruction and difficulty, which in some measure, retard our glorious progress. But there are few difficulties we may not overcome by pursuing industry. That you *will* persevere, I persuade myself, that you may enjoy the fruits of your virtuous exertions, is my most sincere wish and the fondest hope of heart. And now I trust you will always bear me in mind that I shall ever be solicitous for your happiness. . . .

From the Salutatory Oration, Delivered by Miss Priscilla Mason, May 15, 1793

Venerable Trustees of this Seminary, Patrons of the improvement of the female mind; suffer us to present the first fruits of your labours as an offering to you, and cordially to salute you on this auspicious day. . . .*

A female, young and inexperienced, addressing a promiscuous assembly, is a novelty which requires an apology, as some may suppose. I therefore, with submission, beg leave to offer a few thoughts in vindication of female eloquence.

I mean not at this early day, to become an advocate for that species of female eloquence, of which husbands so much, and so justly, stand in awe,—a species of which the famous Grecian orator, Xantippe, was an illustrious example. Although the free exercise of this natural talent, is a part of the rights of woman, and must be allowed by the courtesy of Europe and America too; yet it is rather to be *tolerated* than *established;* and should rest like the sword in the scabbard, to be used only when occasion requires.—Leaving my sex in full

* From *The Rise and Progress of the Young-Ladies' Academy of Philadelphia . . .*, Stewart and Cochran, Philadelphia, 1794, pp. 90–95.

possession of this prerogative, I claim for them the further right of being heard on more proper occasions—of addressing the reason as well as the fears of the other sex.

Our right to instruct and persuade cannot be disputed, if it shall appear, that we possess the talents of the orator—and have opportunities for the exercise of those talents. Is a power of speech, and volubility of expression, one of the talents of the orator? Our sex possess it in an eminent degree.

Do personal attractions give charms to eloquence, and force to the orator's arguments? There is some truth mixed with the flattery we receive on this head. Do tender passions enable the orator to speak in a moving and forcible manner? This talent of the orator is confessedly ours. In all these respects the female orator stands on equal,—nay, on *superior* ground.

If therefore she should fail in the capacity for mathematical studies, or metaphysical profoundities, she has, on the whole, equal pretensions to the palm of eloquence. Granted it is, that a perfect knowledge of the subject is essential to the accomplish'd Orator. But seldom does it happen, that the abstruse sciences, become the subject of eloquence. And, as to that knowledge which is popular and practical,—that knowledge which alone is useful to the orator; who will say that the female mind is incapable?

Our high and mighty Lords (thanks to their arbitrary constitutions) have denied us the means of knowledge, and then reproached us for the want of it. Being the stronger party, they early seized the sceptre and the sword; with these they gave laws to society; they denied women the advantage of a liberal education; forbid them to exercise their talents on those great occasions, which would serve to improve them. They doom'd the sex to servile or frivolous employments, on purpose to degrade their minds, that they themselves might hold unrivall'd, the power and pre-eminence they had usurped. Happily, a more liberal way of thinking begins to prevail. The sources of knowledge are gradually opening to our sex. Some have already availed themselves of the privilege so far, as to wipe off our reproach in some measure. . . .

But supposing now that we posses'd all the talents of the orator, in the highest perfection; where shall we find a theatre for the display of them? The Church, the Bar, and the Senate are shut against us. Who shut them? *Man;* despotic man, first made us incapable of the duty, and then forbid us the exercise. Let us by suitable education, qualify ourselves for those high departments— they will open before us. They *will*, did I say? They have done it already. Besides several Churches of less importance, a most numerous and respectable Society, has display'd its impartiality.—I had almost said gallantry in this respect. With *others*, women forsooth, are complimented with the wall, the right hand, the head of the table,—with a kind of mock pre-eminence in small matters: but on great occasions the sycophant changes his tune, and says, "Sit down at my feet and learn." Not so the members of the enlightened and liberal Church. They regard not the anatomical formation of the body. They look to the soul, and allow all to teach who are capable of it, be they male or female.

But Paul forbids it! Contemptible little body! The girls laughed at the deformed creature. To be revenged, he declares war against the whole sex: advises men not to marry them; and has the insolence to order them to keep silence in the Church—: afraid, I suppose, that they would say something against celibacy, or ridicule the old bachelor.

With respect to the bar, citizens of either sex have an undoubted right to plead their own cause there. Instances could be given of females being admitted to plead the cause of a friend, a husband, a son; and they have done it with energy and effect. I am assured that there is nothing in our laws or constitution, to prohibit the licensure of female Attornies; and sure our judges have too much gallantry, to urge *prescription* in bar of their claim. In regard to the senate, prescription is clearly in our favour. We have one or two cases exactly in point.

Heliogabalus, the Roman Emperor, of blessed memory, made his grandmother a Senator of Rome. He also established a senate of women; appointed his mother President; and committed to them the important business of regulating dress and fashions. And truly methinks the dress of our country, at this day, would admit of some regulation, for it is subject to no rules at all—It would be worthy the wisdom of Congress, to consider whether a similar institution, established at the seat of our Federal Government, would not be a public benefit. We cannot be independent, while we receive our fashions from other countries, nor act properly, while we imitate the manners of governments not congenial to our own. Such a Senate, composed of women most noted for wisdom, learning and taste, delegated from every part of the Union, would give dignity, and independence to our manners; uniformity, and even authority to our fashions.

It would fire the female breast with the most generous ambition, prompting to illustrious actions. It would furnish the most noble Theatre for the display, the exercise and improvement of every faculty. It would call forth all that is human—all that is *divine* in the soul of woman; and having proved them equally capable with the other sex, would lead to their equal participation of honor and office.

4 Equality or Submersion?
Feme Covert Status in Early Pennsylvania

Marylynn Salmon

Elizabeth Canning being sentenced at the Old Bailey Court, London. Courtesy of The Historical Society of Pennsylvania.

Historians of the law have not yet reached a satisfactory definition of the relationship between husband and wife under the early American legal system.[1] Not one of the available definitions adequately explains the delicate balance that existed between wifely submission and independence of action. Some legal discussions emphasize the image of a dutiful wife, subject to her husband's will in all respects; others stress the image of an independent woman armed with her jointure and separate estate. Because sources supporting both these views can be found in eighteenth-century legal records, neither one should be considered in isolation. According to current historians, Sir William Blackstone's portrayal of complete male dominance over female stands at one end of this definitional spectrum, and Mary Beard's emphasis on female equality through the court of equity stands at the other. In the middle are Frederick Maitland's comparison to medieval guardianship and Richard Morris's claim of increased independence for colonial American women.[2] What is needed to replace these inadequate definitions is a discussion encompassing two distinct areas of the English legal system: the common law and equity.

THE COMMON LAW AND EQUITY COMPARED

The common law was the ancient law of England, founded upon custom and long usage, based on precedent. It frowned on change in almost any form and remained conservative in attitude toward the rights of women. The purpose of a court of equity was to facilitate justice in the face of hardened, frequently outmoded legal principles, and under its auspices judges were able to make decisions that opposed accepted common law precedents. For example, in both England and the colonies courts of equity supervised the administration of separate estates for married women, whereas common law courts refused to recognize such an innovation in the law of property. This conflict is typical of the relationship between the two branches of the law; it is a distinction that needs to be studied in order to demonstrate the role that each played in shaping the legal position of married women.

In 1765 Blackstone published his *Commentaries on the Laws of England*, a concise, readable discussion of English legal principles and statute law. It found instant popularity in both England and America,

[1] I would like to thank Mary Maples Dunn, Mary Beth Norton, and Lisa Joan Pollak for reading and criticizing this paper.
[2] Sir William Blackstone, *Commentaries on the Laws of England*, Clarendon Press, Oxford, 1765–1769, I; Mary R. Beard, *Woman as Force in History*, Macmillan, New York, 1946; Frederick Pollock and Frederick Maitland, *The History of English Law*, The University Press, Cambridge, 1952, II; Richard B. Morris, *Studies in the History of American Law*, Joseph M. Mitchell, Philadelphia, 1959.

and in the colonies it was regularly employed as a course of study for law students. Soon the primary reference work on the legal position of women was Blackstone's chapter on husband and wife. In cases concerning women, lawyers and judges frequently repeated his rhetoric, most often quoting this passage on the union of man and woman after marriage:

> *By marriage, the husband and wife are one person in law; that is, the very being or legal existence of the woman is suspended during the marriage, or at least is incorporated and consolidated into that of the husband; under whose wing, protection, and cover, she performs every thing. . . . Upon this principle, of an union of person in husband and wife depend almost all the legal rights, duties and disabilities that either one of them acquires by the marriage.*[3]

According to Blackstone, a woman was civilly dead after she married. Any separate legal identity that she possessed as a feme sole was destroyed by her marriage, subsumed under the identity of her husband, who thereafter performed all legal functions for the two of them. This observation, conveyed with a dramatic flair typical of the great English commentator, was indeed true for women under the common law. Prior to marriage, men and women held virtually equal positions before the law. As femes soles, women owned property, entered into contracts, bequeathed their possessions, or served as legal guardians or administrators of estates; in essence, they ordered their lives as they saw fit with little legal interference. The restrictions placed upon their activities were much more those of custom than of law.

Once women married, however, their legal standing changed. They acquired femes coverts status. A married woman did not own personal property. All personalty she brought into the marriage—clothing, furniture, or money, for example—automatically became her husband's. Any real property she owned became her husband's to manage, and as soon as they had a child that property became his for life as "tenant by the curtesy." Her wages were her husband's, and employers were sometimes directed to pay them directly to him. He also had a right to the person of his wife and could restrict her movements unless she sued for a legal separation. Although such separations were difficult to obtain, if she were successful, then his was the superior claim to the guardianship of their children.

These common law provisions reflect a subservient position for women within the colonial family structure. But it should not be assumed that the law restricted only women. After marriage men also found that

[3] Blackstone, *Commentaries*, I, 442.

their activities were hindered by family responsibilities. For example, the law required a man to cohabit with and support his wife and children. Although he held sole authority for the management of family property during his lifetime, he could not permanently alienate it without the consent of his wife. And at his death the law required him to devise at least two-thirds of his estate to his immediate family.

Although a man possessed powers of active control over his property, a married woman's safeguards under the common law were primarily defensive. The practical inability of a married woman to exercise any control over family finances placed her in a delicate, if not a dangerous, position. In a good marriage, a man provided for his wife, sought her advice and agreement on all transactions, and wisely anticipated unfortunate events, such as financial crisis or sudden death. With a sympathetic husband, a woman's life could be secure and her legal rights and liabilities reasonable; but with a poor businessman, an adulterer, or a deserter, she could be placed in an untenable position with no redress under the law. The common law view on the proper role of women was based on the ideal marriage; it was simply unrealistic.

It is not surprising, then, that arrangements developed outside the common law system whereby married women could own and control property separately from their husbands. Jointures, trusts, and marriage settlements served to protect them from the financial hardships brought about by the mismanagement of their estates. One example is a 1774 marriage settlement created by an engaged couple in Bucks County, Pennsylvania. They wrote:

That notwithstanding the intended marriage shall take effect and be solemnized, the said messuage, tenement, and tract of land shall be the proper and distinct estate of her the said Margaret, during their joint lives. . . . Matthew shall not do or suffer any act whatsoever, whereby Margaret shall or may be any ways frustrated or hindered in the giving, devising, or bequeathing, nor of holding, possessing and enjoying her own particular estate.

More common than marriage settlements were bequests made to married women with stipulations against the interference of husbands. In writing his will, Benjamin Franklin included this provision for a trust in his devise to his daughter:

With regard to the separate bequests made to my daughter Sarah in my will, my intention is, that the same shall be for her sole and separate use, notwithstanding her coverture, and I do give my executors so much right and power therein as may be necessary to render my intention effectual in that respect only. This provision for my daughter is not made out of any disrespect I have for her husband.

Similarly, Rebecca Lewis of Philadelphia wrote in her 1758 will:

I desire that £3 each year may be paid by my executors into the proper hands of my Aunt Esther Dunning, the wife of John Dunning, during her natural life, and not into the hands of her said husband, and her receipts alone without her husband, notwithstanding her coverture, shall be sufficient discharges.[4]

In these three cases, and in numerous others from the colonial period, women were given sums of money or land for their own use, removed from any control by their husbands. Such property settlements were a method of financial insurance for women under a legal system that gave men virtually absolute control over familial property management.

Specific legal forms designed to provide married women with financial independence had existed since the sixteenth century in England. As Mary Beard noted in *Woman as Force in History,* it was misleading of Blackstone to omit any discussion of these developments in equity from his influential chapter on the law of husband and wife. His common law definition was overly simplified, for with the protection of courts of equity femes coverts could own property, enter into contracts, and devise their estates, immune from their husbands' interference.

Beard was correct in utilizing the principles of equity for her definition, but it is unfortunate that she did not extend her study to include their practical application. We still do not know how many women actually employed marriage settlements or what the prevalent attitude was toward their use. It appears that they were not uncommon, especially among astute businesswomen such as Elizabeth Murray, but we should not assume that their existence demonstrates an equal legal position for women. The very fact that equity required a husband's consent to the creation of any separate estate detracts from the spirit of independence that Beard attributed to such an arrangement.

That this mere potential for independent action gave women a legal position of equality, as Beard claimed, is debatable. Accordingly, students of the law have tried to unravel the complicated question of feme covert status by comparing the husband-wife relationship to that between a guardian and his charge. As his wife's guardian, a husband possessed certain absolute rights over both her property and her person. For example, a married woman could not enter into a contract unless her

[4] *Barnes* v. *Hart,* 1 Yeates 222–223 (1793); Benjamin Franklin, Will (1790), in the Philadelphia City Archives; Rebecca Lewis, Will (1758), in the Philadelphia City Archives.

husband acted as a coparty. The courts reasoned that if a woman contracted alone, her potential default could result in her separation from
her husband through imprisonment. Tapping Reeve, Connecticut Supreme Court judge and founder of the first law school in the United
States, gave this rationale for the law on contracts:

> *The right of a husband to the person of his wife . . . is a right
> guarded by the law with the utmost solicitude; if she could bind herself
> by her contracts, she would be liable to be arrested, taken in execution,
> and confined in a prison; and then the husband would be deprived of the
> company of his wife, which the law will not suffer.*[5]

The definition of guardianship has not been used in discussions of
American law, but Reeve's comments demonstrate that it could well be
applied to certain aspects of the colonial American situation. We can cite
further evidence in support of this definition. Numerous legal opinions
equate the legal rights of women with those of two groups who were
under the guardianship of others: children and idiots. Although it was
sometimes (not always) noted that the judgment of a woman was not on
the same low level as that of a child or an idiot, her freedom of action
was as restricted as theirs due to her family ties. Her position, like theirs,
was a dependent one.

Although guardianship has several advantages as a framework for
understanding the relationship between husband and wife, its strong
implication of the feudal right, a relationship unfamiliar to the American
judicial system, results in a correlation that is ultimately unsatisfactory.
But the implication of dependency that existed in such a feudal relationship is a useful concept for understanding the position of women.

Although the rights of a married woman were not subsumed under
her husband's legal identity, they were circumscribed to a large degree. A
feme covert could indeed own property separately from her husband, but
only if he consented. If she created a separate estate in secret, against the
wishes of her husband, a court of equity would not enforce it. Friends or
relatives were permitted to create a trust for her without his permission,
but this too denotes her dependence on the generosity of others. Her
potential for control might be seen in her right to refuse permission for
the sale of the family real estate, but it is necessary to remember that she
possessed only a negative voice concerning such property transactions. She
had no comparable authority to initiate any financial agreement, and her
husband exercised absolute control over the rents and profits collected
from their property during his lifetime. Therefore, while femes coverts
could and did influence their own legal affairs, it was difficult for them to

[5] Tapping Reeve, *Domestic Relations*, Oliver Steele, New Haven, 1816, p. 98.

do so effectively. They had to work against a social system that offered them only the barest potential for independent action.

RULES AND PRECEDENTS IN PENNSYLVANIA: MARRIAGE SETTLEMENTS

The particulars of the female state of dependency can be examined most fruitfully by turning to the case law of one colony, Pennsylvania. Although each jurisdiction created its own body of laws by statute and by precedent, they overlapped in many areas, and lawyers often borrowed arguments or decisions from the courts of other colonies when a gap appeared in their own set of precedents. This discussion of the laws affecting women in one colony is therefore a reflection of general eighteenth-century attitudes. Pennsylvania was not representative in all its specific provisions for women, but the tone of the arguments in the judges' opinions was based on widely held assumptions about the proper social function of married women. To that extent, an analysis of the law of one colony is both useful and valid.

In this examination the law governing women's property rights will be discussed through Pennsylvania case law. The ability of married women to create antenuptial and postnuptial settlements and bequests, the problems of women's role in land conveyancing and their right to receive separate examinations, and the guarantee of dower rights will be used to define women's legal status, in order to reach an understanding of their accepted role in society.

By the end of the eighteenth century, marriage settlements existed in several different forms, but in the earliest years a court of equity would enforce separate estates only if they were made in the form of a trust. Such an arrangement vested the property in a third party who supervised the estate in the name of the woman. Depending on the nature of the settlement, the trustee either followed the instructions of the woman herself or acted as her business manager. If a woman had only limited control over her property, or no control at all, then she possessed a trust or a passive use. If she controlled the property through the trustee, then she possessed an active use—Elizabeth Murray's settlement was, for example, an active use. There was an obvious qualitative difference between active and passive uses, and the former became much more popular as time progressed. At the end of the century the logical conclusion to the active use was reached; women with separate estates were finally allowed to own and administer them in their own names, without the intervention of trustees. This was a significant legal development for women, indicative of a change in attitude toward their contractual abilities.

The case of *Barnes* v. *Hart*, tried in the Pennsylvania Supreme Court in 1791, serves well as a framework for understanding this change in attitude toward marriage settlements. It concerned the legality of an antenuptial agreement written in 1774 by Margaret and Matthew Henderson. Although Margaret took the precaution of arranging a separate estate, she did not create a trust with powers of administration. Instead she made a simple agreement with her fiancé. Under the provisions of the settlement Margaret agreed to share with her husband all the yearly profits of the property; they would use that income jointly for the duration of the marriage, but if Matthew died before Margaret then the whole estate remained hers. He possessed no authority to devise away any part of that property. In creating this settlement Margaret was primarily concerned that the estate remain within her own family. In the agreement it was stated:

> *That the said Margaret shall have full power and absolute authority by will and testament in writing, to give, devise and dispose of the said messuage and tract of land and expectancy to such persons, and for such uses, as she shall see fit, as fully as she could have done if the said marriage had never been solemnized . . . so that the same shall not be in the power or disposal of the said Matthew, or liable to any of his debts or incumbrances.*

Margaret died childless before her husband and executed a will in which she left the property to various nieces and nephews. Her husband's nephew contested the will on several grounds, two of which are important to this discussion. He claimed that the will of any married woman was void at common law, under statutes passed in the reign of Henry VIII and enforced in the colonies. And he noted that in Pennsylvania marriage agreements were valid only when the property was conveyed to trustees for the use of the wife. A simple agreement such as the one arranged by the Hendersons did not bind the legal heir.

Both arguments were undeniably true at the time that *Barnes* v. *Hart* was tried. A feme covert could not devise her possessions in any of the colonies unless she made formal arrangements for a separate estate. And up to this point, such arrangements in Pennsylvania were enforceable only when they existed in the form of a trust. The opinion of the court indicated, however, that it wanted to support the obvious intention of Margaret and Matthew Henderson in writing their settlement. Here a man had freely allowed his wife to convey her own property. Had she died intestate the nephew would have inherited the property, but instead he was given only a minor share. Margaret Henderson's desire to devise her estate to other relatives was clear, and so was her husband's willingness to let her do it. Sitting as a court of equity, the Pennsylvania judges felt compelled to follow the express intention of the two contracting parties, and not to rule for the heir-at-law simply on a technicality.

Chief Justice McKean wrote in his opinion, "The intention of the parties is plain, and admits of no doubt. Here was a fair agreement between them . . . and it has been frequently determined in the Supreme Court that a judge [in equity] will, to effectuate the intention of the parties, consider that as executed which ought to have been done." His associate, Justice Shippen, agreed. Shippen wrote, "I must confess that when this case first came to be argued before us, I was of opinion against the defendant. The old distinction between trusts and legal estates, as to a wife's power of appointment in pursuance of marriage articles, struck me forcibly. Upon more deliberate consideration I now think otherwise." [6]

In colonial America, the change from antenuptial agreements created only by trusts to simple agreements between engaged couples was in keeping with the legal climate of simplicity and practicality. Released from the fictitious forms of their legal predecessors, American lawyers tended to look with disdain on the complications of English land conveyances. Witness, for example, the tone of this discussion by Tapping Reeve. He was discussing the mode of conveying real property to a married woman rather than establishing a trust, but the principle was the same.

A, the husband of B, cannot convey real property to B. Yet if A conveys to C, a third person, who, by agreement, immediately conveys to B, A does in fact convey to B through C, who is only a conduit pipe, through which the title is conveyed to B. It is acknowledged, that such a conveyance by A to C, and then by C to B, would be valid. It is clear that such a mode of conveyance answers no purpose, except to preserve entire, without infringement, a maxim in preserving which there is no conceivable utility.[7]

Women could not create valid marriage settlements by this kind of simple contract once they married. Because husbands and wives could not legally contract with each other, a provision that was a logical extension of the woman's limited contractual abilities, the complicated procedure of a trust still had to be employed for postnuptial settlements. If a woman inherited property while she was a feme covert, she could maintain it separately only if her husband agreed to such an arrangement and if they jointly executed a trust for her benefit. The courts were consistently more conservative in handling settlements entered into after marriage, enforcing them according to the letter of the law, because they were philosophically opposed to independent legal actions by married women. Therefore, although the burden of creation always lay on the woman and her family, when postnuptial settlements were involved that burden became heavier.

Note the case of *Torbert* v. *Twining,* tried in the Pennsylvania

[6] *Barnes* v. *Hart,* 1 Yeates 222, 226–227 (1793).
[7] Reeve, *Domestic Relations,* pp. 90–91.

Supreme Court in 1795. It concerned a devise made by a father to his married daughter. In his original will he simply bequeathed the real estate to his daughter Beulah, but upon further consideration he wrote a codicil to the will in which he gave the property to trustees for the use of his daughter. The wording of the document was not perfectly clear, since there was no specific provision for Beulah Torbert's "sole and separate use" of the property. Therefore, Beulah's husband was able to contest the administration of the will successfully.

McKean wrote in his opinion that the court could not presume to guess the intention of persons in devising their possessions; rather, that intention had to be carefully explained in the wording of the will. In the absence of a clear wording, the court would be doing more than enforcing the provisions of a will—it would be actually writing the will itself. Although the testimony of witnesses in this case indicated that Beulah's father expressed his satisfaction with the codicil to his will by saying during his last illness that "he expected he had effected his purpose, and that her husband could not intermeddle with it," the court chose to reject such evidence of the old man's intent. Therefore, although he thought that he had been very careful in creating this trust for the benefit of his daughter, Beulah's father was finally unable to provide her with a guaranteed income.

The decision of the court in *Torbert* v. *Twining* appears puzzling at first glance. Sitting as a court of equity, the Pennsylvania Supreme Court was obliged to consider intent as well as the actual wording of the will. In fact, as the counsel for the defense pointed out, what other purpose could have been served by writing in the additional provision for a trust, if not to secure a separate estate for Beulah? A clue to the true reason behind this decision is found in a single sentence at the very end of the judges' decision. Prejudice against the case of Beulah Torbert is found in these words of Justice Yeates: "It appeared to us that Mrs. Torbert left her husband without cause, merely to found certain proceedings against him for divorce, in the state of Connecticut." Here was the crux of the matter. It was difficult enough for a totally respectable woman to receive justice under the intricacies of the American judicial system. No solicitude was demonstrated for a woman who willfully flouted the values of family life by deserting her husband and prosecuting him for divorce in another state.[8]

PROPERTY TRANSACTIONS

In the years before the Married Women's Property Acts—that is, before the middle of the nineteenth century—the only significant control a

[8] *Torbert* v. *Twining,* 1 Yeates 440 (1795).

woman exercised over family property was her veto power over any proposed land conveyance. Her consent to a sale was required for two reasons: to ensure her agreement to transactions involving the property that she had brought into the marriage, and to provide proof that she had formally relinquished all dower rights. Her consent was obtained in a formal manner, by a separate examination at the time that she entered into any manner of land exchange. Although justices of the peace tried to determine the true wishes of a woman at this time, such an examination was not a foolproof safeguard against her husband's coercion. Judges knew that a man could easily force his wife into executing a conveyance that she opposed, but they saw private examinations as a means of providing at least a minimum of justice. Justice Tilghman discussed the custom realistically in his opinion on *Jourdan* v. *Jourdan* (1823).

Examine the woman how you will, it is impossible to ascertain with certainty, whether she gives her free consent; her word must be taken for that; she may, in fact, be under terror, though she be examined in the absence of her husband. But there is a better chance for her speaking her real sentiments, in his absence, than in his presence; and it is difficult for the law to protect her further, than by giving her an opportunity of disclosing her mind to the magistrates, out of the presence of her husband.[9]

Even the minimal security offered by separate examinations was not always provided for femes coverts. The formal recording of these statements was not an absolute requirement of Pennsylvania law until 1770, although before that time careful persons may have requested such a procedure during a sale. The normal form of a land conveyance in the eighteenth century was a joint deed from the husband and wife to the purchaser, a comparatively simple arrangement that replaced the complicated fine and recovery of the common law. To complete a proper land transfer by fine and recovery, the woman had to be separately examined by writ. But for a joint deed conveyance this formal document was unnecessary. In Pennsylvania, at the time the conveyance was registered, the woman followed the local justice of the peace into an adjoining room, where he read the deed to her and assured himself that she understood its contents and the meaning of her consent to the sale. These safeguards completed, he recorded on the face of the deed her acceptance of the conveyance.

Until *Davey* v. *Turner,* tried in 1764, no one made objections to this simple conveyancing procedure. At that time an attempt was made to introduce the complicated English fine and recovery procedure into the body of Pennsylvania law, but the Supreme Court rejected the effort on the basis of Pennsylvania custom. Another challenge to the procedure

[9] *Jourdan* v. *Jourdan,* 9 Serjeant and Rawle 274 (1823).

arose in 1768 when, in *Lloyd* v. *Taylor,* counsel noted that there were many instances when women did not have even oral examinations at the time of land sales, much less examinations by writ. The attorney in this case thought that the Pennsylvania joint deed procedure should be strengthened by requiring the woman's separate examination at all times.

In *Lloyd* v. *Taylor* the feme covert signed the deed without undergoing formal questioning by a local justice of the peace. Her attorney argued that the conveyance was void, but the court accepted the informal arrangement, again on the basis of Pennsylvania custom. The judges believed that any possible coercion by the husband (there was evidence to that effect in this case) was secondary to the need for security in longstanding land titles in the colony. The opinion reports that "it had been the constant usage of the province, formerly, for *femes coverts* to convey their estates in this manner, without an acknowledgment or separate examination; and that there was a great number of valuable estates held under such titles, which it would be dangerous to impeach, at this time of day." [10]

The Supreme Court's decision on *Lloyd* v. *Taylor* obviously disturbed the colonial legislature, because two years later it passed an act requiring a private examination of the wife in every land conveyance. But by providing one model form for the separate examination, the lawmakers unwittingly opened the way for the execution of many technically flawed land deeds. In most areas local justices and recorders were unused to the required procedures, and omissions or errors appeared frequently. The courts soon realized that they could not enforce the legislative proposal without invalidating numerous land deeds. Therefore, they chose to support conveyances that had followed only the general form of the required procedure rather than its exact words. Yeates explained their reasoning in making the decision.

> *If a rigid pursuance of that form be absolutely necessary to bar the future claims of such women, I have no scruple in declaring that the acknowledgment of more than nineteen deeds out of twenty, which I have met with since the passing of that law, would be found miserably defective. Let any one examine his title papers to lands, and pronounce on the correctness of my remarks.*[11]

Although Pennsylvania judges were willing to overlook flaws in the administration of separate examinations, they were not willing to suspend the requirement altogether. The protection was there for any woman who knew enough to demand it. A feme covert's right to prevent the sale of family property was an acknowledgment of her independent legal

[10] *Lloyd* v. *Taylor,* 1 Dallas 17 (1768).
[11] *Shaller* v. *Brand,* 6 Binney 442 (1814).

stature, challenging the image of wifely submission presented by Blackstone. In Connecticut, where a man could alienate property without his wife's knowledge or consent, the principle of union was maintained. But in Pennsylvania a woman could effectively stop her husband from selling their land if she chose to do so.

Not all women wanted to fight against the land transactions that their husbands executed without their consent. Such a prosecution involved the use of formal legal machinery with its accompanying publicity. Some women did not even know about property sales until after they were completed. This was true in the case of the Chief Justice of the Pennsylvania Supreme Court, Thomas McKean, and his wife Sally. In 1779, when Mrs. McKean was away from Philadelphia visiting friends, the judge decided to sell all his real estate so that he could buy a country estate "whereon I may live cheap, and spend the remainder of my days in comfort." A few days later he wrote to his wife that he had sold her lot for £2,000, but had sold nothing yet of his own. Her response to that information must have been furious, judging by the next letter that McKean wrote to her:

I am to get the full value of the lott at the Bridge, and more than I believe any other person will ever offer for it—An unwillingness to sell it as it was your's, made me ask a price I did not expect to get, but it turned out otherways and I am contented, only you appear to be otherwise. . . . I thought you loved a Country life, but you seem now to prefer the Town—agreed; we will continue in one. The general character of the Lad[ies] is, that they are fickle, ever changing, & never satisfied, but I flattered myself you were an exception.[12]

After 1770 any conveyance, even the creation of a separate estate, was unenforceable without an oral examination of the woman. In the case of *West* v. *West* the marriage settlement of Mary and Joseph Willey was invalidated on that basis. In every other respect the couple had executed their deed correctly; as a postnuptial settlement it had to be made in the form of a trust. But the omission of Mary Willey's examination served to subvert her title and she was not allowed to devise the property that she had long considered to be her own. Her will did not stand against the legal claims of her husband's heirs because the settlement had been improperly constructed, and once that fact was proved there could be no other defense for her case. Without a separate estate a woman could never devise real property, even if there were evidence that her husband consented. The opinion of the court stated:

12 McKean Papers, Letterbook VI, f. 23–27, Historical Society of Pennsylvania, Philadelphia.

Now, if there is one principle of law more fixed than another, it is this: that a married woman cannot, by any mode of conveyance, except by fine and recovery (the separate examination of the woman with us being substituted for the fine), in any way, affect or change her real estate . . . for coverture is a civil disqualification at common law, arising from a want of free agency in the wife as much as from the want of judgment in the idiot.[13]

A feme covert's conveyance of personal property such as clothing or jewelry was equally restricted. It could be made only on an informal basis, with the permission of her husband. Such informal conveyances would not stand up in court if they were contested. Note the wording of this will by Mary Morgan:

Sensible as I am that a married woman hath no legal right to devise or will away what she possesseth of personal property without the consent of her husband, I think it unnecessary (whilst I set down to express in what manner I wish that my clothes and a few trinkets I have now by me may be disposed of amongst my relations as tokens of love and remembrance of me . . .) to attend to the usual form of making a will; I mean this therefore only as a memorandum for my dear Dr. Morgan not doubting but he will cheerfully acquiesce in what he knows to be my wishes.[14]

She then proceeded to give away favorite dresses, pieces of jewelry, and small cash bequests to her children, nieces and nephews, and friends.

We have noted that Pennsylvania waited until 1770 to formalize the married woman's right to a separate examination. Why did it take so long for the colonial legislature to enforce a standard common law procedure? Part of the reason for this deviation must be found in the nature of the colonial American legal profession. Most lawyers were self-trained and knew little of the complications of English land conveyancing; they were simply incapable of executing a fine and recovery. But a second reason appears to lie in the colonial attitude toward married women. It seems that female consent, or lack of it, did not overly concern either husbands, purchasers, or lawyers in their transactions of land conveyances before 1770. The courts consistently maintained that a woman's best interests were represented by her husband, an attitude that aptly demonstrates the position of dependency occupied by American women. Their legal identities were neither subsumed under those of their husbands nor

13 *West* v. *West,* 10 Serjeant and Rawle 446–447 (1823).
14 Mary Morgan, Will (1784), in the Francis T. Redwood Collection, Historical Society of Pennsylvania, Philadelphia.

disregarded, but their legal rights were minimal and easily ignored when they became troublesome.

DOWER RIGHTS

In another area of the law, Pennsylvania courts effectively destroyed an ancient English protection of the delicate position of femes coverts. Women had the right to receive support from their husbands' estates after they were widowed. In England and in almost all the colonies, Pennsylvania being a notable exception, widows were given at least one-third of the real property of their husbands for their livelihood. The dower right constituted a life interest only. It did not give a woman the privilege to sell or devise the property, but only to enjoy the rents and profits from the land during her lifetime. At the widow's death this land went automatically to the heirs of her husband. It must be stressed that the dower right of a widow represented only her minimal share of the family estate; her husband could leave her more or even the entire estate if he wanted to. In most cases, however, there were children to provide for, and the widow was normally granted only her legal dower right to one-third. In many instances this was probably a fair share, and in others children could be depended upon to help support their mother when the estate was not large enough to do so.

In his treatise on *Domestic Relations,* published in 1816, Tapping Reeve noted that a wife could not be barred from her dower by any action of her husband. This was undoubtedly the most valuable aspect of the English dower law. A husband could not sell any property during the marriage if the sale denied his wife dower. Unless the woman, by a separate examination, acknowledged her willingness to resign dower rights in the property, the sale would not hold against her claim. If a woman had been ill-treated in this manner, then at the death of her husband she could sue the present owner for her dower and be awarded her life interest by the court as though the sale had never taken place.

As Justice Shippen noted, the right of a woman to dower was "so sacred a right that no judgment, recognizance, mortgage, or any incumbrance whatever, made by the husband after the marriage, can at common law affect her right of dower: even the king's debt cannot affect her." [15] But then he went on to explain that in one area Pennsylvania did not uphold the common law tradition: Dower was not guaranteed to women whose husbands died in debt. Normally under the common law, personal property was used first to meet creditors' demands, and if that was insufficient, then the widow was granted her dower before the real property was

[15] *Graff* v. *Smith's Administrators,* 1 Dallas 484 (1789).

attached to pay the debts. The widow retained this property until her death. Then, and only then, could it be divided among the creditors. This ancient common law provision, stemming from a concern for the financially vulnerable position of married women, frequently served to keep widows off relief rolls.

In Pennsylvania, a concern for the rights of creditors weighed more heavily on the consciences of lawmakers than did their responsibility for the protection of married women's incomes. In the first legal code written for the colony, a provision unique to English law made lands liable to pay debts, one-third of the land if there were children and all of it if there were not. The Great Law of 1683 extended this provision, for under that code one-half of the land could be taken to meet the demands of creditors if there were children. By 1688 the colonial assembly determined that all of a man's lands could be applied for the payment of his just debts, leaving the widow and children, who might well have been ignorant of the family's financial situation, without any means of support. In 1700 the "Act for taking lands in execution for the payment of debts" revealed the attitude of the legislators. It explicitly stated that the purpose of the act was to protect the interests of creditors.

In a primitive society like colonial Pennsylvania, the only security that could be given for a loan was land, and it is important to remember that outside Philadelphia almost all the colony's wealth existed in the form of real property. Mortgaged property had to be forfeited at the death of its owner because the rents and profits from the land were never sufficient to pay off the money owed; forfeiture was the best way to repay creditors in a money-scarce economy. The maintenance of a strong credit base was viewed as essential to the stability of the young colony, and therefore the common law protection for widows was quietly pushed aside.

William Penn's sensitivity to the rights of creditors was responsible for this variation on the common law in his proprietary colony. Before they left England the first Pennsylvania colonists agreed to make their lands liable for the payment of debts. The enlightened policies of Penn regarding imprisonment for debt have always been used to demonstrate sympathy for the rights of debtors. But while Penn did maintain that it was impractical for such men to remain behind bars where they could not possibly work to repay their debts, he may well have been considering the rights of creditors more than those of debtors when he advocated their release. Certainly the laws that made lands liable to pay debts, and the provision that denied a widow her dower, point in that direction. The Proprietor's peculiar sense of responsibility toward creditors may explain why Pennsylvania alone of all the colonies changed the common law in this area, despite the fact that every colony faced the pressures of underdeveloped economies.

In 1793 Shippen looked back on the first legal code and wrote:

Our ancestors in Pennsylvania seem very early to have entered into the true spirit of commerce by rejecting every feudal principle that opposed the alienation and partibility of lands. While, in almost every province around us, the men of wealth or influence were possessing themselves of large manors, and tracts of land, and procuring laws to transmit them to their eldest sons, the people of Pennsylvania gave their conduct and laws a more republican cast, by dividing the lands, as well as personal estate, among all the children of intestates, and by subjecting them, in the fullest manner, to the payment of their debts.[16]

Pennsylvania, then, was one of the first colonies to loosen the old English dependence on land inheritances as the basis for status in society. Lands could not descend from father to son encumbered by unpaid debts or mortgages. While this practice was modern in principle, it was unfortunate that the laws dealing with married women's property rights did not keep pace with the new attitudes toward debt repayment. Legal records from the late eighteenth century reveal that women were denied support from their husbands' lands when creditors made claims on the estates.

In *Scott* v. *Croasdale* (1791), the counsel for the widow made a concerted effort to overthrow Pennsylvania's aberration of the common law. He reminded the court that dower was a favored area of the common law and tried to demonstrate the similarities between colonial law and the law of England. He argued that a woman could not lose her dower right unless she freely consented, but the opinion of the court was against his conclusions. The point was "too clear to bear an argument," for Pennsylvania had always maintained that the widow's right was secondary to that of the creditors.[17]

FEMALE DEPENDENCY UNDER THE LAW

The Pennsylvania dower policy gave to femes coverts a responsibility equal to their husbands for repaying family debts, but it did not give them any commensurate power to control the accumulation of those debts. In William Penn's colony, unity of person was applied as a legal principle to the detriment of married women, an application that weakens the arguments of historians who believe that American women occupied a stronger position in regard to the control of real property than did their English counterparts. Richard Morris has written:

As a result of the new economic conditions in the colonies, women, both married and single, were attaining a measure of individuality and

[16] *Morris' Lesse* v. *Smith*, 1 Yeates 243–244 (1792).
[17] *Scott* v. *Croasdale*, 1 Yeates 75 (1791).

independence in excess of that of their English sisters. . . . This independence brought about the obsolescence of the concept of the unity of husband and wife in marriage to form one legal personality which, for all practical purposes, was the husband.[18]

We have shown that in Pennsylvania the new economic conditions of colonial life did not create a liberal legal climate for femes coverts. Rather, the legal policies worked to deny women access to one of the unquestioned privileges of the English common law—dower. Women who executed land conveyances were also exposed to the inherent dangers of a primitive legal system that supported rather than damaged the concept of unity of person. Therefore, the legal position of women may well have been hindered as much as helped by the unsettled conditions of colonial American life.

The Pennsylvania legal climate was more liberal in certain other areas. Most important, its equity courts enforced marriage settlements on an increasingly flexible standard during the late eighteenth and early nineteenth centuries. The procedures necessary for a valid antenuptial settlement were simplified, and although judges might not personally approve of separate estates for married women, they enforced them according to accepted precedents. It does not appear, however, that this right to a separate estate significantly freed a feme covert from her position of legal dependency. Note the disapproving tone of this Pennsylvania Supreme Court opinion:

Separate examinations have been viewed with a jealous eye by Courts of Equity . . . the husband, by the law of this country, and of every well-regulated government, is the head of the family, and the best judge of their finances. A custom for a feme covert to surrender her copyhold lands held under a separate estate, without the consent of her husband, is bad; it is said to be contrary to the law and policy of the nation, and tends to make wives independent of their husbands.[19]

With such a conservative attitude dominant in American courts, it is not surprising that an established body of law regulating marriage settlements was very late in developing and that, once it had developed by the end of the eighteenth century, it was strictly enforced. Above all else, the law discouraged wives from becoming independent.

To summarize the image of dependency that existed for women under eighteenth century American law, it may be helpful to study the Pennsylvania feme sole trader statute, enacted in 1718. Pennsylvania

[18] Morris, *Studies*, pp. 128–129.
[19] *Torbert* v. *Twining*, 1 Yeates 438 (1795).

legislators followed the lead of London in allowing certain married women to conduct businesses in their own names. The wives of mariners or of men who were absent from the colony for long periods of time, of deserters, and insolvents could exercise all the legal rights necessary to engage in a business activity. They could enter into contracts, sue, and retain all profits for themselves. Similarly, they were liable for all of their own debts as though they were unmarried. The statute is liberal in tone. It gave to femes coverts commercial rights that they did not normally enjoy, providing them with the means to support themselves in the absence of their husbands.

But this statute did not indicate an acceptance of financial independence for married women. To the contrary, it served as a defensive mechanism, a last resort when normal family relationships failed. Only the wives of suspect individuals were allowed the benefits of feme sole trader status. Women who lived with their husbands did not qualify under the terms of the act. In large part, these provisions offered economic protection to young communities that did not have the means to provide public support for abandoned women and children. They also strengthened the position of creditors who wanted payment for the debts that the absent husbands had contracted, since feme sole traders often paid the sums their husbands owed.

Another provision of the feme sole trader act further delineated the dependent position of married women. The law stated that if a man remained away for an extended period of time, his estate could be taken by local officials and used to pay for the maintenance of his wife and children. The wife herself had no right to use any of her husband's funds in the meantime. Instead she had to wait for the court to authorize official action, which could take months or even years. And it is significant that when her husband's estate was finally attached for the payment of debts and family expenses, it was administered by local magistrates who might or might not consider the woman's wishes. Her potential for independent action in controlling family property was minimal in such a situation. The law protected her, but it did not give her financial independence.

This Pennsylvania statute exemplifies the confused logic behind the judicial attitude toward femes coverts. Ideally, the courts wanted a union of man and woman after marriage, but practically, they recognized that such a union ignored human nature. Thus, the law was a confused amalgam of principles, some liberating women from old common law restrictions and some placing them in the same subservient position they had known in medieval England. To provide some safeguards against the absolute authority of the husband, the courts accepted separate estates for married women but discouraged their use. Initially the courts allowed a husband to sell his wife's property without her permission and then retreated from that stand to require proof in writing of her consent. They allowed the wives of wandering men to maintain their own businesses but insisted on administering the man's estate for his wife rather than giving her control over its distribution. The most dangerous regression for Pennsylvania women was the loss of their dower right. The ability to create simple marriage settlements, unencumbered by third parties, was their most significant advance.

In conclusion, it must be said that women gained little, if anything, under the judicial system of early Pennsylvania. Their actions were still circumscribed by a social attitude of conservatism. Although some women benefited from the protections offered by courts of equity, others suffered in widowhood by the loss of their dower right. It has been assumed that the primitive practices of early American courts worked in favor of married women; now it can be seen that improvements did not always follow unconventional legal practices. The informality of the system could easily be as harmful as it was helpful.

Documents

Watson v. Mercer, 1820

The opinion of Justice Gibson in a Pennsylvania case concerning the use of separate examinations:*

"In no country, where the blessings of the common law are felt and acknowledged, are the interests and estates of married women so entirely at the mercy of their husbands as in *Pennsylvania.* The exposure of those, who, from the defenceless state in which even the common law has placed them, are least able to protect themselves, is extenuated by no motive of policy, and is by no means creditable to our jurisprudence. The subordinate and dependent condition of the wife, opens to the husband such an unbounded field to practise on her natural timidity, or to abuse a confidence, never sparingly reposed in return for even occasional and insidious kindness, that there is nothing, however unreasonable or unjust, to which he cannot procure her consent. The policy of the law should be, as far as possible, to narrow, rather than to widen, the field of this controlling influence. In *England,* the courts of equity will not assist the husband to obtain possession of his wife's personal property, although it becomes his absolutely on the marriage, before he makes an adequate settlement on her: here, he has the power to obtain her personal estate, not only without condition, but in some instances by means of the intestate acts, even to turn her real into personal estate, *against* her consent. In other countries, the wife's dower, that sacred provision which the law makes for her in return for the personal

* Reprinted from *Watson* v. *Mercer,* 6 Serjeant and Rawle 49 (1820).

property she brought her husband, and in recompense of a lifetime devoted to him and his children, is put beyond the reach of every effort which selfishness or profligacy can make, to deprive her of it: in this, it may be swept away by his debts, contracted in the gratification of his vices. In the country whence we derive our laws, the wife's land can be aliened only with her assent, deliberately expressed on a fair, full, and careful, separate examination, in a court of record: in this, the examination is considered a matter of such little importance, that it is entrusted to a justice of the peace, by whom it is sometimes entirely dispensed with in fact, but often slubbered over, even in the presence of the husband himself. These are considerations which induce the mind to pause, before it consents to adopt the rule, that the act of the magistrate is to be considered as having been rightly done till the contrary appear; and thereby to withdraw the only protection, inefficient as it is, which the law interposes in behalf of married women. Alienation of the wife's land, should not be of too easy access; but when a case occurs, as it undoubtedly sometimes does, where a sale is the best thing that can be done for the interests of all concerned, a strict adherence to the necessary forms requires but a moderate share of attention, and the exaction of it should, therefore, not be considered a hardship."

An Act Concerning Feme-Sole Traders, 1718

WHEREAS it often happens that mariners and others,* whose circumstances as well as vocations oblige them to go to sea, leave their wives in a way of shop-keeping: and such of them as are industrious, and take due care to pay the merchants they gain so much credit with, as to be well supplied with shop-goods from time to time, whereby they get a competent maintenance for themselves and children, and have been enabled to discharge considerable debts, left unpaid by their husbands at their going away; but some of those husbands, having so far lost sight of their duty to their wives and tender children, that their affections are turned to those, who, in all probability, will put them upon measures, not only to waste what they may get abroad, but misapply such effects as they leave in this province: For preventing whereof, and to the end that the estates belonging to such absent husbands may be secured for the maintenance of their wives and children, and that the goods and effects which such wives acquire, or are entrusted to sell in their husband's absence, may be preserved for satisfying of those who so entrust them, *Be it enacted,* That where any mariners or others are gone, or hereafter shall go, to sea, leaving their wives at shop-keeping, or to work for their livelihood at any other trade in this province, all such wives shall be deemed, adjudged and taken, and are hereby declared to

---

* From "An ACT concerning feme-sole traders" (1718), *Laws of the Commonwealth of Pennsylvania,* Philadelphia, 1810, I, 99–101.

be, as feme-sole traders, and shall have ability and are by this act enabled, to sue and be sued, plead and be impleaded at law, in any court or courts of this province, during their husbands' natural lives, without naming their husbands in such suits, pleas or actions: And when judgments are given against such wives for any debts contracted, or sums of money due from them, since their husbands left them, executions shall be awarded against the goods and chattels in the possession of such wives, or in the hands or possession of others in trust for them, and not against the goods and chattels of their husbands; unless it may appear to the court where those executions are returnable, that such wives have, out of their separate stock or profit of their trade, paid debts which were contracted by their husbands, or laid out money for the necessary support and maintenance of themselves and children; then, and in such case, executions shall be levied upon the estate, real and personal, of such husbands, to the value so paid or laid out, and no more.

II. *And be it further enacted,* That if any of the said absent husbands, being owners of lands, tenements, or other estate in this province, have aliened, or hereafter shall give, grant, mortgage or alienate, from his wife and children, any of his said lands, tenements or estate, without making an equivalent provision for their maintenance, in lieu thereof, every such gift, grant, mortgage or alienation, shall be deemed, adjudged and taken to be null and void.

III. *Provided nevertheless,* That if such absent husband shall happen to suffer shipwreck, or be by sickness or other casualty disabled to maintain himself, then, and in such case, and not otherwise, it shall be lawful for such distressed husband to sell or mortgage so much of his said estate, as shall be necessary to relieve him, and bring him home again to his family, any thing herein contained to the contrary notwithstanding.

IV. But if such absent husband, having his health and liberty, stays away so long from his wife and children, without making such provision for their maintenance before or after his going away, till they are like to become chargeable to the town or place where they inhabit; or in case such husband doth live or shall live in adultery, or cohabit unlawfully with another woman, and refuses or neglects, within seven years next after his going to sea, or departing this province, to return to his wife, and cohabit with her again; then, and in every such case, the lands, tenements and estate, belonging to such husbands, shall be and are hereby made liable and subject to be seized and taken in execution, to satisfy any sum or sums of money, which the wives of such husbands, or guardians of their children, shall necessarily expend or lay out for their support and maintenance; which execution shall be founded upon process of attachment against such estate, wherein the absent husband shall be made defendant; any law or usage to the contrary in any wise notwithstanding.

Mary Maples Dunn

Lucretia Mott. Reprinted with permission of Bryn Mawr College from the Photograph Albums of Carrie Chapman Catt.

Quaker women in colonial America are of special interest for a number of reasons. Their experience of life was in many ways so unique that broad generalizations about the history of colonial women do not altogether fit them. This is primarily because Quaker theology altered in significant ways the traditional view of women to which most Protestants adhered, and opened to its female adherents opportunities that most women did not have. Admittedly the Friends' influence on colonial women's lives in general was not great; very few Protestant sects followed the Quaker lead or adopted their doctrinal positions with respect to women. But the lives of Quakers do show us the way in which the Protestant revolution might have liberated women by allowing them some voice in doctrine, church government, and discipline, and therefore by giving them power and status more nearly equal to that of men.

The Protestant View of Women

Eve symbolizes those perceptions of women most deeply rooted in the Judeo-Christian tradition that the Quakers tried to overturn. Eve was a second thought, created out of Adam's needs. Eve was the first sinner because she was considered by Satan to be weaker of mind and more easily moved by evil argument than Adam, and also to have the power of the temptress over the man. After the Fall, or first sin, she therefore had to be put in a position in which she could not undermine man's relationship with God; her own relationship with God would be mediated by man.

This place in the universe came through the judgment of God Himself. His curse for her part in original sin was clearly stated in Genesis 3:16, "Unto the woman he said, I will greatly increase thy sorrows and thy conceptions. In sorrow shalt thou bring forth children, and thy desire shall be subject to thine husband, and he shall rule over thee." [1] Most Christians fully accepted this reading of the essential inferiority of women, which incorporated an intellectual component because of Eve's inability to resist Satan, a psychological component due to her role as temptress, and a biological component rising out of the curse of painful childbirth.

If Christians of most eras may be said to have discovered the nature of women in Eve, then Paul's writings set forth for most seventeenth-century Protestants the weaknesses typical of this nature and also some norms for female behavior and rules for the control of women. Paul's doctrine was of enormous importance in the seventeenth century

[1] All quotations from the Bible are taken from Lloyd E. Berry, ed., *The Geneva Bible: A Facsimile of the 1560 Edition*, University of Wisconsin Press, Madison, 1969. This was the Bible most commonly used by seventeenth-century nonconformists.

to the English Puritans, who wanted to purify the English church, and to dissenters like the Quakers, who created new sects. In both cases, godly people wanted to return to what they called the primitive church and tried to recapture the simplicity and fervor of the first Christians. Most of these people therefore accepted without question what they believed Paul was telling them about women. But it was possible to read Paul in several ways, and only a few radicals like the Quakers chose to interpret his writings in a way that would release women from traditional Christian restraints.

Women, as Paul understood them, were subject to particular weaknesses or sins (and so were men, of course, but theirs were different). Because they were seductive, women were apt to tempt men to acquire worldly possessions. Because they were intellectually weak, they were prone to gossip, scandal-mongering, frivolity. Paul apparently believed that disorder in the church at Corinth was due to female interference in the governance of the Christian community. The controls he suggested depended on male authority in the church, where women were to be silent and submissive. "Let your women keep silence in the churches," he wrote in his famous letter to Corinth, I: 14:34, "but they ought to be subject, as also the Law saith."

Male authority was also established in doctrine or teaching, as he made clear in the same letter, I:14:35, "And if they will learn any thing, let them ask their husbands at home: for it is a shame for a woman to speak in the church." It was not possible to construe these injunctions narrowly as to time and place—that is, only to Corinth—since the Apostle was equally specific in a later letter to Timothy, I:2:11–12, "Let the woman learn in silence with all subjection. I permit not a woman to teach, neither to usurp authority over the man, but to be in silence."

But Paul was also a little uncertain about his views of women. Surely the message of Christ must be available to all Christians equally. Paul apparently derived his rules for the submission of women from familiar customs. He may have asserted them at first only to correct an immediate situation in Corinth, and because he thought the second coming of Christ (and the end of human time) was imminent, making it unnecessary to worry about social order in detail. But he later reaffirmed those rules in the realization that the end of the world was not after all at hand. In other writings Paul had a more liberating message for women. This ambivalence in Paul, which was seized upon by George Fox, the founder of the Society of Friends, is seen in several places, in ways both small and great.

In Titus 2:3–4, older women were given a responsible teaching function—"teachers of honest things, they may instruct the young women, to be sober minded, that they love their husbands, that they love their children." Paul also insisted that women were to share equally in the benefits of the new spiritual order. He wrote to the Galatians 3:28, "There is neither Jew nor Grecian: there is neither bond nor free: there is neither male nor female: for you are all one in Christ Jesus."

Furthermore, even in the first letter to the Corinthians there is some confusion, since Paul said in I:11:3–5, "But I will that you know, that Christ is the head of every man: & the man is the womans head: and God is Christs head. Every man praying or prophecying having any thing on his head, dishonoreth his head. But every woman that prayeth or prophecieth bareheaded, dishonoreth her head: for it is even one very thing, as though she were shaven." The implication of women's inferiority to men is clear, but the possibility of their speaking in church is also clear and this in the same letter in which he commanded silence. The ancient tradition of women prophets, who were a part of God's revelation, also receives recognition, a position of potential authority over doctrine that in other ways Paul denied to women.

THE QUAKER VIEW OF WOMEN

Quaker women were not bound by these scriptural prescriptions and definitions, as other Protestant women were. By the time Quakers established themselves in any number in America, the sect had already come through the experimental stage of the founding years and had resolved most major questions of doctrine and of church governance as they applied to women. Women had the support of the leaders of the Quaker movement. Both George Fox and Margaret Fell championed female ministries and inclusion of women in the governance of the Society. Moreover, Quakers very early began to accept their identity as a "peculiar" people who marked themselves as social deviants by manner of speech, refusal to take oaths, plain clothing, and aggressiveness in their women.

Quakers, in common with other radical seventeenth-century English sects like the Anabaptists (but unlike more moderate groups like the New England Puritans), believed in spiritual rebirth, direct inspiration by the Divine Light, and lay ministries. These doctrinal positions were important to women. Friends insisted, first and foremost, on the possibility of being reborn in the spirit, or experiencing a conversion, a personal sense of Christ within oneself. Having Christ within meant the presence of an informing, indwelling Divine Light. Sex bias had no place in this conversion experience; there was nothing inherent in the female to prevent her spiritual rebirth, to hinder the work of the Divine Light. As George Fox put it, in an interesting variation of

Paul's message to the Galatians, "Ye are all one man in Christ Jesus."

Through emphasis on the Divine Light, which was viewed as a continuing revelation, or new prophecy, Friends could ignore ancient limitations on women by claiming that the new Light could, at a minimum, show the way to new understandings of earlier revelations. This was crucial to the definition of the female role. For example, the curse laid on women in Genesis, seen by many as the fundament of female inferiority and submission, was reinterpreted by George Fox, who considered the spiritual regeneration of the converted as a triumph over this curse.

Fox maintained that prior to the original sin of Adam and Eve, men and women were equal; after their rebirth, or conversion, this equality returns: "For man and woman were helpsmeet, in the image of God and in Righteousness and holiness, in the dominion before they fell; but, after the Fall, in the transgression, the man was to rule over his wife. But in the restoration by Christ into the image of God and His righteousness and holiness again, in that they are helpsmeet, man and woman, as they were before the Fall." We also have statements by women, emphasizing God's curse of the serpent, Genesis 3:15: "I will put enmity between thee and the woman, and between thy seed and her seed; he shall break thy head, and thou shalt bruise his heel." Thus, woman was given a role in redemption, and Quaker women could address each other as "you that are of the true Seed of the promise of God in the beginning, that was to bruise the Serpent's head." [2]

Fox and the female Friends of the formative generation would not accept the restrictions imposed by Paul on the women of Corinth, by Puritans on the women of New England, by Presbyterians on their female followers, or by Anglicans on the women of Virginia. The Quakers dismissed these rules as not pertaining to the regenerate—those in whom Christ dwells. As Fox put it, "and may not the spirit of Christ speak in the Female as well as in the Male? is he then to be limited?" [3] Margaret Fell was certain that Paul spoke to Corinth alone, or to certain women only. On the issue of learning from husbands, she pointed out that not all women marry; and in fact it was acceptable to Quakers that some women stay single.

This tolerance of unmarried women was also unusual. Protestants generally rejected the idea of nunneries and emphasized marriage as the

[2] Milton D. Speizman and Jane C. Kronick, eds., "A Seventeenth-Century Quaker Women's Declaration," *Signs: Journal of Women in Culture and Society*, 1 (Autumn 1975), 235.

[3] The first two quotations from George Fox are from *A Collection of Many Select and Christian Epistles, Letters and Testimonies*, T. Sowle, London, 1698, II, 323–324. The third is from *Concerning Sons and Daughters, and Prophetesses Speaking and Prophecying, in the Law and in the Gospel*, MW, London, n.d., p. 9.

only appropriate career for women. But we know that an appreciable number of Quaker women never married, at least in the eighteenth century, and we even know something about their lives. For example, Elizabeth Kendall, an English Quaker and public minister, never married but lived with her friend, Mary Bundock, also unmarried. They lived together for nearly 30 years and, as they put it, "entered into Partnership in which we dwelt together in great Love and Nearness." [4] We can see from this that the Quaker attitude toward regenerates allowed them to live in ways that did not conform to the usual social patterns, and allowed some women to live totally outside the lines of male authority established in Genesis and Paul.

George Keith, a young Quaker who later came to America and developed more conservative religious views, defended the proposition that women, when they had Christ within, could be both prophets and ministers. He used as a text the woman from Samaria (John 4:28–30) who proclaimed Christ although she did not, he pointed out, have a university education. Quakers produced additional Biblical evidence to prove that women often played active and prophetic roles: Miriam, Hannah, Mary Magdalen, Susannah, Mary, and Martha were only a few of their crowd of witnesses.

This doctrinal position was important not only for women, but also for all Quakers. It was the logical conclusion to their protest against an ordained ministry as authorities on revelation. Just as any man could be a minister, so could any woman; their qualifications were not external, but internal. Having exposed and solved for themselves contradictions in Christian messages to women, Friends proceeded to go their own way. Fox's first disciple was probably a woman, and if Fox was the father of Quakerism, then Margaret Fell was its mother.

Women in the Friends' Ministry

The first and most notable way Quaker women acted upon the Society's policy of tolerance was to engage in the lay ministry, even when some opposition existed. Through this ministry they could influence questions of doctrine. The process by which a woman committed herself to a public ministry was initially internal. She had to be convinced not only of the presence of Christ within, but also that He spoke through her. She might be very uncertain of herself and need support and encouragement from other Friends. When her work as a public exponent of the truth was established, she might well believe herself called to carry that truth abroad.

[4] "The Testimony of Mary Bundock Concerning Elizabeth Kendall," Am. 0885, f. 5, Historical Society of Pennsylvania, Philadelphia.

One woman, Jane Hoskins, said of herself: "Lord I am weak and altogether incapable of such a Task. I hope thou will spare me from such a Task. I hope thou will spare me from such Mortification, besides I have spoken much against women appearing in that Manner." [5] When she first tried to speak she could not utter a word, but other Friends sensed her worth and urged her to go on trying. Eventually she became a widely traveled minister, speaking in meetings in all the North American colonies, the West Indies, and Great Britain.

In the early years of the Society, these missions were designed to proselytize; later, as the Friends became more withdrawn, they were intended to help keep the faith strong. Of the first 59 publishers of the truth who came to America from 1656 to 1663, nearly half (26) were women; of these 26, only 4 were traveling in ministry with their husbands. Many of these women exhibited enormous courage and bravery in the face of the frequently hostile environment and establishments.

Mary Dyer is the most famous of these early American Quakers. She had emigrated to Massachusetts in 1634 or 1635, where she became a follower of the well-known Antinomian, Anne Hutchinson. When Hutchinson was excommunicated, Mary Dyer also left the church and followed her into banishment in Rhode Island. On a trip to England in the 1650s, Mary Dyer met George Fox and became a Quaker. When she returned to the colonies in 1657, she began her public ministry in the New England Puritan communities that had previously banished her. She was expelled from both Boston and New Haven but had the temerity to return to Boston four times after Massachusetts passed a law banishing Quakers under pain of death. Once she was condemned to death but set free at the last moment, as she stood under the gallows. On her fourth trip she was again sentenced, and she was hanged in 1660. She may have forced the Puritans to come to grips with their intolerant hostility to nonconformists; she may have been unusual in courting death in Massachusetts; but she was not unusual in her determination to spread the Quakers' message.

The later ministry, in which women were equally active, could also take them far afield. More typically, however, women and men in the eighteenth-century ministry traveled to established meetings to help maintain a high level of religious experience. These women apparently did not travel very far during childbearing years, unless they were unmarried, and the ministry was often a wonderful opportunity for a new career after the menopause. They generally traveled with another woman minister and lived on the hospitality of the meetings they

[5] "A Short Narrative of the Life of Jane Hoskins," Quaker Collection, Haverford College Library, Haverford, Pa.

visited. Fortunately, many of these ministers left journals describing their experiences.

Susannah Morris did not start her ministry until after her children were born, but then visited Friends in Carolina, Virginia, and Maryland; twice she went to Europe, once for nearly three years, and the second time at age 63. At 70 she was still on the go. Jane Hoskins followed a similar itinerary, although she started much younger and did not marry until she was 45. Margaret Ellis, who was Welsh and shy about her English, also traveled widely and seems to have assumed a special ministry to blacks and to laborers in iron works. All these women had the active support of their own meetings, which sometimes financed ocean voyages, and they were heard with respect at other meetings. Susannah Morris's proudest accomplishment was the reconciliation of two neighboring groups of Friends in Holland who, ten years before her visit, had formed one meeting but then quarreled so ferociously that they had separated into two meetings.

THE WORK OF WOMEN'S MEETINGS

The other area in which Quaker women engaged most actively was the women's meetings; we find them playing a strong part in church governance, discipline of women, and control of church membership. Some historians have assumed that women's meetings were established to give women enough authority to keep them happy but not enough to make them powerful. The records of women's meetings, which exist in considerable number, do convey a sense of lesser bodies with relatively little money and without the quasi-judicial function of men's meetings in dealing with conflict and controversy. But from the beginning Fox was concerned about the role of women, and his message to them was unconventional; and the Fell women, Margaret and her daughter Sarah, had a great deal to do with the formation of early women's meetings and saw them as an instrument for the expansion of the woman's role.

We know that some American women were active in establishing meetings, and not only meetings for women. As late as 1751, when Abigail Pike and her husband, John, moved to Cane Creek on the North Carolina frontier, she and a Friend, Rachel Wright, rode 20 miles through the wilderness to the nearest quarterly meeting to ask that a monthly meeting be established at Cane Creek. The request was granted, and the minutes show both women active in the local meeting as well as a traveling frontier ministry.

Not all Friends agreed that women should have separate meetings. A minority of males actively attacked the establishment of women's meetings and believed to some degree in male superiority. The Wilkinson-Story schism in England in the 1660s was in large part the result of some men's objections to the founding of women's meetings, and particularly to the fact that they would have to submit to the women in questions of marriage. There was also some opposition throughout the colonial period to the principle of sexual equality in the meeting. But men's meetings sometimes helped to assert the authority of the women's meetings. The Narragansett, Rhode Island, Men's Meeting was asked to sign certificates of dismissal for women who were moving from one meeting to another; these dismissals (proving that the women in question were members in good standing) had already been signed by the women's meeting. The men replied that this would "degrade" the women's meeting, and stated their belief that "both male & female are all one in Christ Jesus."

The Quaker meeting structure was complicated. As it developed in Pennsylvania, for example, there was a local weekly meeting for worship and local preparative meetings—business meetings that got ready for the monthly meeting. The monthly meetings were also business meetings, made up of the representatives (sometimes called overseers) from several weekly meetings that formed a small geographic cluster within a county. Quarterly meetings were county-based. There was also a yearly meeting that took up larger questions of policy; it was colony-wide, including West New Jersey, and met in Philadelphia and Burlington in alternate years until 1760, when separate yearly meetings were established. The Philadelphia Yearly Meeting was the largest and most influential of the yearly meetings.

All the business meetings had separate meetings for men and women, except the Select Meeting (the meeting for ministers and elders), which also had yearly, quarterly, and monthly components. Although the Select Meeting was set up by the yearly meeting in 1714, it was not until 1740 that women were required to be included as elders. They had, however, been included as ministers from the beginning; Rachel Cowgill of Bucks, Pennsylvania, was the first, and there were very few years between 1714 and 1776 when women were not appointed by Bucks to attend the Select Meeting. Thus, women were included in every part of the Friends' meeting structure and hierarchy.

This meeting structure had an added advantage for women. We believe that many colonial women, particularly the country women, led rather isolated lives. But Quaker women had a circle of Friends whom they saw with some regularity, and who were scattered throughout the colony. Quaker communities in different yearly meeting structures also tended to keep in touch with their fellow believers by means of traveling ministries and circular letters. The West Indies and Great Britain were a part of this larger circle, and women in small towns in

New Jersey or North Carolina had an active sense of sisterhood stretching from Philadelphia to London or from Boston to Barbados.

The first American women's monthly meetings were formed in 1681, on the advice of a yearly meeting held in Burlington, which decided that, since Friends were becoming more numerous, it was necessary to establish a women's monthly meeting "for the better management of the discipline and other affairs of the church more proper to be inspected by their sex." [6] It is possible to watch through the records of monthly meetings the slow growth of organization and organizational skills at these "grass roots" levels. At first the women were apt simply to record the fact that they met, but soon they began to see what business they should undertake. They disciplined women whose behavior was questionable, sent committees to visit women who were not attending meetings, began to collect small sums of money to distribute to the poor. They appointed representatives to the quarterly and yearly meetings and decided who might go out on public ministries.

Not all of these women's meetings were assertive; some seemed at first to defer in some matters to the men. For example, the Bucks, Pennsylvania, Quarterly Women's Meeting was uneasy about contributing to the yearly meeting without seeking consent from the men. Other meetings seemed to take pleasure in vigorous decision making; in meetings with stable memberships, such as Chester, Pennsylvania, we find older women like Grace Lloyd year after year accepting responsibility for female behavior and for female participation in quarterly and yearly meetings. These women must have been of tremendous importance in socializing young women to an active role.

An important symbolic act occurred in each meeting as women became accustomed to managing their affairs. They invariably decided to buy a record book (an important investment) and to appoint a clerk. Thereafter, the book was tangible evidence of their activity. Equally important, as Friends began to build permanent meeting houses in the eighteenth century, women acquired their own space. In England, apparently, a separate room, loft, or gallery was provided for women's meetings, while men used the principal room that was also used for worship. The meeting in Tuckerton, New Jersey, built in 1709, had a little wing for women's meetings. But the more common and very ingenious American device was a set of sliding partitions that could divide the meetinghouse down the center. Women sat on one side, men on the other. During the meeting for worship the partitions were open and all worshiped together, but during meetings for business the partitions would come down, thus providing women and men with separate spaces for the conduct of their separate business.

6 Preface, Burlington Monthly Meeting, Women's Minutes, 1681–1747, Friends Historical Library, Swarthmore College, Swarthmore, Pa.

Women's most important function in the American meetings, ultimately, was their share in protecting the institution of marriage and maintaining the unity of membership. Certainty that partners were free to marry was important in a mobile group, and particularly in America, which was an immigrant society. Hence, people who wanted to marry, if they were not native to the meeting in which they expected to wed, had to produce certificates from their prior meetings, showing them to be free and single. It was equally important to know that they were Friends, to guarantee the marriage would be "in unity": Friends had to marry Friends, both parties had to demonstrate membership in good standing, and they had to marry in meeting. Marriage out of the meeting, if not truly repented, led to exclusion from membership for the couple, and sometimes for their parents if they could be shown to have been negligent. This exclusiveness tried to guarantee that both partners to a marriage would remain active in the meeting.

Women's meetings generally appointed several members to oversee a marriage. This involved interviews with the couple, not only to verify their intentions, but also to make certain both were convinced Quakers who would be active in raising their family in the Society. The overseers looked into the couple's reputation and material considerations. Marriages were first proposed in the women's meeting, but the men's meeting cooperated, and the marriage could not take place until the meetings agreed. The women sent representatives to the wedding to make sure all was done with dignity and decency according to the Friends' mode.

The wedding was like a meeting for worship. Everyone entered and sat in silence, until someone was moved to speak. A minister might exhort. The couple, following the Spirit, would in due course rise and pledge themselves each to the other. At the conclusion everyone present signed a certificate as witnesses. After the meeting there was usually a meal. The Friends' mode for postnuptial entertainment was moderate rather than severe, and weddings were festive occasions. For example, the Chester, Pennsylvania, Women's Monthly Meeting disapproved of having strong liquor passed around at weddings; but they thought it was acceptable to put the drink on tables, where those who wanted it could serve themselves.

This rigorous protection of marriage in unity was combined with regular disciplining of men and women who were lax in their attendance at meeting. Absences, if prolonged, were noticed, and a committee (Quakers loved committees) was sent to inquire why the absentee was staying away. Those who did come were watched for evidence of slackness or lack of devotion; the Chester women felt called upon to protest the indecent custom of taking snuff during meeting. Through these disciplines, women's meetings played a great role in maintaining a family-based membership in the Society of Friends, one in which neither sex dominated in number, and women retained some share of power.

Women could also look to the meeting for help in times of difficulty. All women's meetings collected funds for the poor or for people in crisis. Widows in particular found themselves both comforted and controlled by the meeting. It gave them help if they were poor or if they were in need of assistance to provide for their children. If they wanted to remarry, the meetings, both women's and men's, were slow to give permission. They were particularly anxious that remarriage should not take place before the first husband's estate was settled and his property secured to his children. This was certainly to the advantage of orphaned children (especially girls), who could count on the fact that the meeting would take care of them; but it was not always welcomed by the widows.

Agnes Strickland of Wrightstown, New Jersey, a public minister, wanted to remarry before her first husband's estate was settled and her children's property secured. The meeting tried to help but was worried about the children in this case because neither Strickland nor her prospective husband was being cooperative. Time dragged on and Agnes and her intended set up housekeeping without benefit of matrimony. The meeting was scandalized and outraged; Strickland was forbidden to preach. It was five years before she was readmitted to her ministry and all was forgiven.

THE CUSTOMS OF A PECULIAR PEOPLE

The family base of membership helped maintain communal ties within the Society, which slowly became a more and more closed group that did not so much seek new conversions as socialize its young and discipline its members to its distinctive customs and social patterns. Quakers were in many ways a peculiar people; their exceptional view of women was only one of a number of characteristics differentiating them from their neighbors. This distinctiveness was decidedly an advantage for the women, whose unusual role in the ministry and the meeting might otherwise have been identified as uniquely deviant. It is possible that the Quakers became a closed, withdrawn society in part so that the women could live more comfortably with a social role that was not universally acceptable.

The thrust and origin of some of the Quakers' unusual social attitudes is to be found in the same doctrines that liberated women. All those in whom Christ was believed to dwell were thought to be essentially equal, even when they did not equally share in material wealth or social position. Thus, Quakers adopted, for example, what they called plain language, or *thee* and *thou* instead of *you*. In the seventeenth century the word *you* was used between equals, *thou* to an inferior. The use of *thou* with everyone underlined the message of equality of people in every station or of either sex.

We can find active practice of this doctrine affecting the lives of women. For example, Jane Hoskins came to America at age 19 in 1712, worked as an indentured servant and then as a wage servant, and was eventually taken into the household of Grace and David Lloyd of Chester, Pennsylvania, as a housekeeper or upper servant. She always joined the family to eat, to meet guests, and to attend meetings. Because she was a public minister, the Lloyds supported her ministry.

Clothing also distinguished the Quakers. Women were urged to dress plainly, without the extravagant hoops, petticoats, and high head-dresses that were fashionable at one time or another in the eighteenth century and that differentiated the idle rich from the hard-working poor. They did not spurn color or fine fabrics but deplored excess. Their styles did not keep pace with the mode, but neither were they static and ridiculously old-fashioned. When Rachel Budd and Isaac Collins were married in Philadelphia in 1771, she wore pale blue brocade with matching high-heeled shoes; but after the meeting she immediately put on the apron that was the badge of Quaker women. Rachel Budd's apron was white, but most eighteenth-century Quaker women always wore the green apron, the badge that marked them out, the common element of dress that bonded together all Quaker women of every condition.

Country female Friends, and women in the ministry in particular, had to be good horsewomen, too, and for horseback they wore a "safeguard," a sort of outside petticoat that protected their going-to-meeting clothes from mud. Horse and safeguard together suggest their freedom of movement as well as the distinctive style that set Quakers apart. A non-Quaker woman who visited Pennsylvania in 1784 wrote: "They are very shiftable. They ride by themselves with a safeguard, which, when done with, is tied to the saddle, and the horse hooked to a rail, standing all meeting time as their riders sit." [7]

MARRIAGE AND FAMILY

The lives of these Quaker women, who set themselves apart from the rest of the community, revolved around the meeting and the family, and the two were intimately connected. Because of the disciplined nuclear-family base for membership, Quaker families engaged in a de-

[7] As quoted in Amelia Mott Gummere, *The Quaker: A Study in Costume,* Ferris & Leach, Philadelphia, 1901, p. 155.

liberate process of socializing children to the meeting. Women ministers frequently spoke of parental duties during meeting. Elizabeth Wilkinson, a visitor to New York in 1761, commended parents for their practice of bringing children to the meeting and for the good behavior of the children, but she also called on women to "bring up their children in the reading of scriptures." [8]

If a family did not control its children, and particularly if they allowed them easy friendship with young non-Quakers (especially of the opposite sex), then the meeting would intrude with advice, admonition, or even disownment. Some meetings adopted a practice of sending "weighty" (that is, proved and loyal) Friends, both men and women, to visit families to see that family socialization was being carried on, and they held both parents responsible. A mother's duty was therefore intricately bound up with her religious life. In this respect, her experience was not unlike that of others of her Protestant sisters; but in other sects in the eighteenth century men (fathers) no longer saw parental duties in those terms.

Quakers used the conventional rhetoric of their times to describe marital relationships, and although they reinterpreted Paul on the women's role in the church, Quaker men were apt to describe the wife's position in relation to her husband in Pauline terms of submission. However, both wife and husband had to submit to the disciplines of the meeting and of Quaker life. If difficulty within a marriage was reported to the meeting, a women's meeting might send a committee to inquire into the problem and try to resolve it. Because there was a women's meeting that could assert its authority over husbands as well as wives, and because the Society was so family centered, a marriage between Quakers offered a partnership within meeting and family life that was unusual in American female experience.

The age at which a young Quaker woman first married was generally rising during the eighteenth century, from about 22 to a little over 23, a pattern similar to that of other colonial groups. She would be a few years younger than her husband. At least half of Quaker brides could expect to live with their husbands for 30 years or more, and very few would separate or divorce. If a woman outlived her husband, she was less likely to marry again than were other colonial women. Childbirth was a central drama in the marriage, and a Quaker couple, like other American couples, could expect to have six or seven children.

The attitude of truly convinced Quaker women toward their children and childbirth was not as conditioned by the anxiety and guilt that marked the equally devout of other sects. The concept of original

[8] "A Journal of a Religious Visit to Friends in America by Elizabeth Wilkinson," 975 B, f. 39–40, Quaker Collection, Haverford College Library, Haverford, Pa.

sin did not enter Quaker mothers' evaluations of themselves or of their children. Margaret Morris, a pious New Jersey Quaker whose first child died in infancy, had moments of self-blame during the child's illness but assured herself that God "will not visit the sins of the fathers upon the children," and when the baby did die she prayed God to "accept of him a saint, spotless & innocent as I receiv'd him from thee." [9] The idea that an infant was innocent was unusual, and it must have altered, in subtle ways we do not yet understand, the relationship between a mother and her children. The triumph over the curse of Genesis may have had far-reaching results on human personality.

But the celebration of infant innocence did not necessarily guarantee that a woman would depart from traditional child-rearing techniques. Some Quaker women apparently had to put children out to nurse, and the wealthy frequently hired wet nurses. But female ministers spoke out against these practices, on grounds of infant health and infant development. Sophia Hume, one of the most prominent of American ministers, called the practice cruel and asked, "how can we reasonably expect that a Stranger should take the due and tender Care, and faithfully discharge so troublesome an Office, which a Parent suppos'd to have a natural Engagement for her Infant, declines." [10]

The education of a girl took place at home, where she learned her domestic arts; in the meeting, where she was introduced to community religious life at about the age of 5; and sometimes at school. Quaker girls who lived within the boundaries of Philadelphia Yearly Meeting were most apt to have some formal schooling, and there was a minimum requirement that girls who would become members of a women's meeting should be able to read and write and do some arithmetic. These were skills required for the work of the Lord as well as the domestic circle. Girls of wealthy or urban families might learn foreign languages, fancy needlework, or even mathematics, but there was no real pressure on girls or women for intellectual achievement. Even for men the values of the meeting were always more important than anything else.

QUAKER PRINCIPLES AND THE POLITICIZATION OF WOMEN

Despite the best efforts of Friends to control the lives of their young, in the mid-to-late eighteenth century, marriage out of unity greatly increased. This did not bring a relaxation of the insistence on unity and family support for the meeting; instead, offenders were disowned,

[9] Margaret Morris, "Copybook," 975 A, 1760, Quaker Collection, Haverford College Library, Haverford, Pa.
[10] As quoted in J. William Frost, *The Quaker Family in Colonial America*, St. Martin's Press, New York, 1973, p. 72.

and the size of the Society as a whole dwindled dangerously. The reasons for these defections are uncertain, although historians have offered a number of explanations, the most familiar of which concerns Quaker disciplines.

It has been suggested that it was particularly the affluent who were prepared to leave the meeting by "marrying out," and perhaps more narrowly the wealthy urban Quaker merchants who felt confined by their Quakerism, unable to enjoy the pleasures and perquisites of wealth. But until careful statistical analysis of marriages out of unity is completed, it is not possible to verify this conclusion. Even the most cursory reading of minutes shows young people marrying out of both rural and city meetings, in areas where there was a concentration of Quaker population as well as areas where Quakers were few in number and widely dispersed.

It has also been suggested that marriages out may have resulted from tensions placed on the traditional patriarchal family by the greater role allowed women, which in turn created role conflicts for the men. However, it has also been shown that in mid-century there was a movement to tighten discipline even further and place even greater emphasis on the family as the center of Quaker life.

A more satisfactory explanation for Quaker conflict, and one that helps us understand the role Quaker women would play in postrevolutionary America, might be found in the larger social and political context of the American colonies. The most influential American center of Quakerism was in Pennsylvania. The colony had originally been founded by William Penn as a haven for Quakers and other persecuted people of God, but Penn had envisaged it also as a "Holy Experiment" in which Friends' communal values, and the persuasion and consensus that governed the meeting, would provide a model for governance of the colony. From the very beginning, Quakers had enthusiastically assumed political power and public responsibility. This was clearly a man's world, but the men brought with them the moral tenets of the meeting, in which women had some voice.

In the early years there was no agonizing conflict between politics and conscience. Quakers were fairly frequently divided over local issues, and this was a matter of concern to some Friends. There were colonial wars, but Friends in power were able to find ways to offer support to neighbors or raise money for "the king's use" without doing serious violence to their pacifist testimony; after all, war never really came to Pennsylvania itself. In fact, Pennsylvania had undergone a period of unparalleled growth and prosperity from its founding until 1755. Pennsylvania's farmers were growing in number and producing great surpluses; Philadelphia was the major American port city, through which came a steady stream of immigrants and cargo. Both rural and urban Quakers were creating comfortable, even affluent, lives.

The toleration on which the colony was based was an important ingredient in its rapid population growth, but as a result the Quakers fairly quickly became a minority group. They maintained a majority in the legislature because the German settlers, particularly the pietists, were content with the Friends' leadership and their economical management of government. The Quakers' opposition was the Proprietors' party. William Penn's sons had become Anglicans, and they wished to increase their Pennsylvania profits and power. The Quakers rallied their non-Quaker followers (the Quaker party) behind antiproprietary tax and money issues. Until 1755 they did so with considerable success.

In 1754 the situation changed rapidly and, for Quaker leadership, disastrously. The French had seized control of the upper Ohio Valley and were arming hostile Indians on the Pennsylvania frontier. Sporadic Indian raids in the west were disturbing many of the Quakers' allies who, when they sought protection, found themselves confronting both the Quaker tradition of fair dealing with the Indians and Quaker pacifism. The proprietors, anxious for support in the west and eager to demonstrate their loyalty to the crown, insisted that the Assembly pass a bill to raise taxes for defense of the frontier.

The Quakers were resourceful; they proposed a bill including tax and money powers that they knew the governor would refuse to admit. The Quaker party was for the moment willing to follow this lead, particularly since Benjamin Franklin was dexterously providing some defense for the frontier by creating a volunteer force that exempted the Quakers. Nevertheless, the French and Indian War, a full-scale imperial conflict, was already under way, and Pennsylvania's desperate balance of interests could not survive. Thoughtful Friends probably understood that an increasingly sophisticated and complicated empire would constantly create for them crises of conscience that their political allies would not share.

As the crisis deepened, the scene shifted to London. The proprietors represented the Quaker party as irresponsibly pacifist and totally unwilling to support the mother country in the war, and asked the crown, whose first interest was war, to help obtain an act of Parliament barring Quakers from seats in the Pennsylvania Assembly. The Quaker party, in its turn, looked to the crown to dispossess the proprietors and set up a royal government; to prove their loyalty, they were prepared to support the war. In neither case would Quakers be able to retain their political power.

The London Yearly Meeting mustered all of its lobbying power to prevent an act of Parliament directed against Quakers and strongly urged their colonial colleagues to step down from office as a part of the solution to the crisis. Thus was their dilemma driven home: Pennsylvania Quakers must either compromise on matters of principle, or they must give up the leadership role they had enjoyed. Some Quakers chose compromise, with the result that they lost status in the Society. Strict Quakers retreated immediately to the meeting. Ten pacifists resigned from the Assembly, others refused to run for office, and many refused to vote.

Events after the French and Indian War moved too rapidly for strict Quakers ever to recoup their losses. If they could not countenance war, neither could they support rebellion. The psychological loss to Quaker men of Pennsylvania must have been tremendous, because they lost more than power. The foundation stones of their sense of themselves as Americans had been destroyed. The origins of Pennsylvania were in them and in their religion; now they were outcast. And what had happened so dramatically to them would now be repeated for other Quakers who could not set aside their peace testimony, or their membership in a trans-Atlantic society, in order to support the Revolution. They followed the lead of Pennsylvania. What could fill this void, allow them to retain their distinctiveness, and still provide a public role and public service that would link them with their past?

In this crisis situation the Quakers exerted their most stringent disciplines on their membership. Pressure was put on the compromisers; they must move out of politics or out of the meeting. Many went, including the halfhearted. The Society was drastically reduced in number, and those who remained had to discover ways to rechannel their old political energies, to maintain some of their old influence, and to convince the non-Quaker world that their kind of political morality had social value.

The solution they arrived at gave the Quakers a new and lasting role in American political life. They became a public moral force, associated with humanitarian causes frequently designed to focus attention on the failure of government and society to provide social justice. They began in the 1750s by trying to protect and befriend Indians who were now without Friends in government. They even tried to negotiate Indian peace. They moved on to found or support a wide variety of public charities and ultimately to the greatest crusade, abolition of slavery. They were to become a powerful political force, but one operating entirely outside formal political organization.

This change in political role and direction had great significance for Quaker women. Women had long since been outspoken on many issues now occupying the men, and when public matters were also moral ones, Quaker women held opinions and had no difficulty in expressing them in meeting or even in other public places. In mideighteenth century Margaret Ellis undertook a special mission to Negroes, for example. Elizabeth Wilkinson, an English Quaker who visited America, warned American Friends in 1762 not to settle on lands to which Indians had claims, and at least one woman said she was "thankful in her heart" for the warning. But women could not vote, hold office, or exert general public leadership.

The public world was customarily a man's world, and even the Quakers' new involvement was not generally organized through the meeting, where women were accustomed to play an active role, but rather through public associations and committees. However, the Quaker men validated the public role of reformer for the entire Society, and this new politics was not carried on in an arena that was by law exclusively for men. Quaker women were bound to follow this lead. They were accustomed to creating structures parallel to those of the men for the business of religion. They had organizational skills that few other women had as yet learned. They were used to public speaking, dispensing charity, exerting moral discipline. Most important of all, they took themselves seriously.

Obviously, public roles were limited during the Revolution when Friends were, by virtue of their pacifism, the objects of hostility and suspicion. But there was a remarkable spate of activity in the postwar period. Female benevolent societies, organized by Quaker women to help poor women of all sorts, sprang up soon after the war in major centers like Philadelphia and Wilmington. Schools for poor girls and Negro women were organized and conducted by Quaker women.

Friend Prudence Crandall was arrested in Connecticut for admitting a Negro girl to her school, otherwise attended by white girls, in 1837. Lucretia Coffin Mott, a Philadelphia Quaker who hailed originally from Nantucket, helped found the Philadelphia Female Anti-Slavery Society in 1833; William Lloyd Garrison would not at first admit women to the American Anti-Slavery Society, but a Quaker woman like Mott knew how to organize a parallel group of women. Sarah Pugh, another Quaker, was for many years the head of the organization. Mott also organized the Anti-Slavery Convention of American Women in 1837. When the World's Anti-Slavery Convention, which met in London in 1840, excluded female delegates, it was Sarah Pugh who wrote the protest and Lucretia Mott who led the public attack on the policy. Eight years later, four Quakers—Jane Hunt, Mary McClintock, Margaret Coffin Wright, and Lucretia Mott—joined Elizabeth Cady Stanton to convene the first women's rights conference in Seneca Falls, New York.

According to *Notable American Women, 1607–1950: A Biographical Dictionary,* 40 percent of female abolitionists were Quakers; of feminists born before 1830, 19 percent were Quakers; of suffragists born before 1830, 15 percent were Quakers. Since 2 percent is a generous estimate of Quakers in the total American population in 1800, it is clear that Friends were represented in the leadership of these causes in numbers completely out of proportion to their numbers in the nation. Perhaps we may conclude that although other Protestant sects did not adopt the doctrinal positions that liberated Quaker women in the seventeenth century, Quaker women eventually helped lead the way to the political positions through which women might liberate themselves.

Documents

A Seventeenth-Century Quaker Women's Declaration

From our Country Women's meeting in Lancashire to be Dispersed abroad among the Women's meetings every where.

Dear Sisters.*

In the blessed unity in the Spirit of grace our Souls Salute you who are sanctified in Christ Jesus, and called to be Saints, who are of the true and Royal offspring of Christ Jesus. . . . To you that are of the true seed of the promise of God in the beginning, that was to bruise the Serpent's head, and which is fullfilled in Christ Jesus of which we are made partakers, which is the seed the promise is to . . . for we are all the children of God by faith in Christ Jesus, where there is neither male nor female &c. but we are all one in Christ Jesus. . . .

And Christ Jesus in the dayes of his flesh, had a dear and a tender care and regard unto women, who received many gracious blessings and favours from him: he despised not the woman of Canaan. . . . And also the woman of Samaria, John 4. . . . See what love and plainess he manifested unto this woman, not despising her, nor undervalluing her, in the least: but he spoak the plaine everlasting truth unto her, and set up that worship of his own spirit unto her there, which remaines, and will remain forever, glorious praises to his holy name, forevermore. . . .

And let us meet together, and keep our womens meetings. . . .

And also, to make inquiry. . . . If there be any that walks disorderly. . . . Then send to them . . . to Admonish, and exhort them. . . .

And if any transgression . . . amongst women or maids, that hath been more publick . . . then let them bring in a paper of condemnation, to be published as far as the offence hath gone, and then to be recorded in a booke.

And if there be any that goes out to Marry, with priests, or joineth in Marriage with the world, and does not obey the order of the Gospell as it is

* From Milton D. Speizman and Jane C. Kronick, eds., "A Seventeenth-Century Quaker Women's Declaration," *Signs: Journal of Women in Culture and Society,* I, No. 1 (Autumn 1975), 235-245.

established amongst friends, then for the womens monthly meeting to send to them, to reprove them, and to bear their testimony against their acting Contrary to the truth. . . .

And dear sisters it is duely Incumbent upon us to look into our families, and to prevent our Children of running into the world for husbands, or for wives, and so to the priests: for you know before the womens meetings were set up, Many have done so, which brought dishonour, both to God, and upon his truth and people. . . .

And likewise, that the women . . . take care, against tithes. . . . Since the priests claimes,, and challenges a tithe, which belongs to women to pay, as well as the men, not only for widdows, but them that have husbands, as piggs, and geese, henns and eggs, hemp and flax, wooll and lamb: all which women may have a hand in. . . .

And also all friends, in the womens monthly . . . that they take special care for the poore, and for those that stands in need. . . .

Also let Care be taken that every particular womens monthly meeting, have a booke to set down, and record their bussinesses and passages in, that is done or agreed upon . . . let the book be read, the next monthly meeting, and see that the business be performed, according to what was ordered. . . .

And also that the collections be set downe, in the booke; and that the Receipts, and disbursments of every particular meeting, be set down in their booke, and read at their womens monthly meeting, that every particular meeting may see and know, how their collection is disbursed. . . .

This is given forth for Information, Instruction, and Direction. . . .

Monthly Meeting of Women Friends, Westbury, Long Island, 1708

To friends of yᵉ monthly meeting att Jericoe

Dear friends * these few lines may Certifie that I did through weaknes & for want of keeping to yᵗ spirituall measure of gods grace in my own heart give way to yᵉ weak & naturall parte so as to sufer my daughter Sarah to marry contrary to the good order of truth & with one that was nott in unity with friends to the greif of the faithfull & truly sencible amongst us and my own sorrow & condemnation: but it was my weakness as before expressed I being but very weak in some things but truly hope itt may be as a warning to mee for time to come to be more carefull how I act in any such thing without taking the advise of faithfull friends

Martha Pearsall

Hempstead Harbour
23 of 4th mon: 1708 [June 23, 1708]

* Published with the permission of Friends Historical Library, Swarthmore College, from Westbury [Long Island] Monthly Meeting (Women), 23. 4th mo. 1708.

Monthly Meeting of Women Friends, Chester, Pennsylvania, April 26, 1714

The ffriends * that carried the cloath to Mary Edwards for her Mother gave an acount that she Recd it kindly & is Loath to be troublesome to ffriends but if the Meeting is free to send her a litell money she shall take it in Love soe the Meetting hath ordered to be sent in Money further for her mothers use 20 shilling.

Hannah Hill's Recommendations for Quaker Dress and Conduct, 1726

From Women ffriends at the Yearly Meeting held at Burlington [New Jersey], The 21st. of the 7th. Month, 1726 [September 21].

Dear and Well-beloved Sisters: †

A Weighty Concern coming upon many ffaithful ffriends at this Meeting, in Relation to divers undue Liberties that are too frequently taken by some. . . . Tenderly to Caution & Advise ffriends against those things which we think Inconsistent with our Ancient Christian Testimony of Plainness. . . .

As first, That Immodest ffashion of hooped Pettycoats. . . .

And also That None of Sd ffriends Accustom themselves to wear their Gowns with Superfluous ffolds behind, but plain and Decent. Nor to go without Aprons. . . . Nor to wear their heads drest high. . . .

And that ffriends are careful to avoid Wearing of Stript Shoos, or Red or White heel'd Shoos. . . .

Likewise, That all ffriends be Careful to Avoid Superfluity of Furniture in thier Houses. . . .

And also that no ffriends Use ye Irreverent practice of taking Snuff, or handing Snuff boxes one to Another in Meetings.

Also that ffriends Avoid ye Unnecessary use of ffans in Meetings. . . .

And also That ffriends do not Accustom themselves to go in bare Breasts or bare Necks.

There is Likewise a Tender Concern upon our minds to recommend unto all ffriends, the Constant use of ye plain Language. . . .

Dear Sisters, These Things we Solidly recommend. . . . That we might be unto ye Lord, A Chosen Generation, A Royal Priesthood, An Holy Nation, A Peculair People. . . .

Signed on behalf & by ordr of ye sd meeting By

Hannah Hill

---

* Published with the permission of Friends Historical Library, Swarthmore College, from Chester [Pennsylvania] Monthly Meeting of Women Friends, 26. 2nd mo. 1714.
† From Amelia Mott Gummere, *The Quaker: A Study in Costume*, Ferris & Leach, Philadelphia, 1901, pp. 152–154.

On the Sickness and Death of Her Infant Son, by Margaret Hill Morris, 1760

Oh Lord! * thou who gave him best knows when to take him—from his birth
have I endeavour'd to live loose from him, & not to let my natural affection
make me desirous of his life, when I'm certain that if thy wisdom sees fit to re-
call him it will be best for him . . . & it has been a close trial to me, this his
tedious sickness, often fearing that for some omission of mine the dear babe
was afflicted . . . but thou who are merciful will not visit the sins of the fathers
upon their children—for thou has said the soul that sins it shall die. . . . I dare
not wish his life or death—thy will be done. . . . I thank thee that thou art
pleas'd to accept of him a saint, spotless & innocent as I reciev'd him from thee.
Oh! that he may be as acceptable an offering as Abraham's only son was in thy
sight. . . .

On Entering Public Ministry, by Rebecca Jones, 1758

Very frequently I was seized with an apprehension that, if I was faithful to the
manifestations of Divine grace, † the baptizing influences thereof would be witnessed for the cleansing, purifying, and preparing my spirit, rightly to engage in
the Lord's work: at which my heart trembled within me, and I very much
feared. . . . And, though in meetings both for worship and discipline, my duty
was often pointed out to me, yet, the fear of marring the Lord's work, a sense
of my own weakness, the situation in which I was placed in the world, the
prospect of much suffering awaiting me, but, above all, a sense of the purity
and stability necessary for those who fight the Lord's battles . . . I say all these
things mightily humbled me, and reduced me to the brink of the grave I went
alone—I kept silence—I refrained from my natural food, and my sleep departed
from me. . . . I carried my burden from one month to another, and from meeting to meeting, until the 7th month 9th, 1758, in an evening meeting, finding
no excuse would longer do, and that faithfulness was required . . . I stood up in
great fear and trembling, and expressed a few sentences very brokenly. I returned home with the promised reward of peace, which I had long sought in
vain, but, now that I had given up to the Lord's will, was favored to obtain it.
This was my first public appearance.

* Published from the Quaker Collection with the permission of Haverford College
Library from Margaret (Hill) Morris, 1737–1816, Copybook.
† From William J. Allinson, ed., *Memorials of Rebecca Jones*, Henry Longstreth,
Philadelphia, 1849, pp. 12–13.

Part Three
Nineteenth-Century America

The Paradox of "Women's Sphere"

Mary Beth Norton

Visions of a preindustrial golden age may have clouded
historians' eyes and prevented them from perceiving the realities
of women's experience in colonial America, but equally strong,
simplistic, and erroneous notions of domestic oppression have
characterized their view of American women's lives in the
nineteenth century. After approximately 1820 many aspects of
the female experience changed dramatically, some as a direct
result of technological development, others as a consequence
of new social and political attitudes that affected both women
and men.

A wide variety of new options opened to women. Instead
of resigning themselves to isolated married life on a farm,
girls in the nineteenth century could contemplate living in
cities and working in factories; attending high school and
college; pursuing careers in teaching or librarianship or perhaps
even medicine; joining female benevolent societies; becoming
foreign missionaries; working for the abolition of slavery, or
the attainment of women's rights, or the reform of social institutions like orphanages and insane asylums; founding settlement
houses in immigrant ghettos; or writing novels and short stories
aimed at their female contemporaries.

Of course, not all these options were open to every
nineteenth-century girl. Few blacks, even after emancipation,
could take advantage of them, and sometimes for whites they
were not options but necessities. Working-class daughters did
not choose to go to work, they had to. Genteel middle-class
single women (either never married or widowed) often turned
to teaching or writing to support themselves. But even though
individuals may not have had many choices, American women
as a group engaged in a far greater range of activities, and had
a far greater range of experiences, than their grandmothers had.

Ways of life that had existed in America and Europe for
many centuries were breaking down. Agricultural society was
giving way to industrialization; the quiet rural life was succeeded
by existence in noisy, crowded cities. From lives governed by

the duration of sunlight and seasonal rhythms of planting, cultivation, and harvest, Americans had to adapt to an existence increasingly ruled by clocks, to workdays measured in hours of toil rather than by tasks accomplished. It was not until the 1920 census that a majority of the American population was revealed to be living in urban areas, but long before that the changes had made a telling impact on the lives of women in the United States.

THE PRESCRIPTIVE PITFALL

The extreme complexity of the social, economic, and political patterns in the nineteenth century makes it hard to discern common denominators in women's experience, and perhaps this is the reason that historians studying the period have often taken the easy way out, examining the published literature that told women how to behave rather than investigating the realities of their lives. Nineteenth-century prescriptions for proper female behavior make wonderful targets for sarcasm and anger: They are so alien to twentieth-century minds that it is hard to treat them with respect.

After reading the hundredth, or even the tenth, earnest injunction to "young ladies" to be pious, submissive, and chaste, one either finds it difficult to take the message seriously or, on the other hand, becomes so incensed that a calm, detailed analysis of the material proves to be impossible. Yet the accessibility of this literature and the relative ease with which it can be surveyed have led to numerous studies based on role prescriptions. Even when the authors of such works disavow any intention to imply that nineteenth-century women lived entirely in accord with the principles set forth for them, they sometimes forget their own disclaimers and slip into assuming that the ideal equalled reality.

Many difficulties are raised by such analyses. Historians do not know how many people read the books in question or how women reacted to their contents. One scholar has in fact suggested that many of the most popular of such works were probably bought by doting parents or grandparents as "proper" presents for their daughters, who may never have read them at all. Thus, the relationship between the books and the women they were intended to advise has not been adequately explored.

The stress on directions for proper behavior, even when combined with an investigation of how women actually lived, appears to indicate a causal relationship. Taking this emphasis seriously can lead to an assumption that women took little initiative in shaping their own lives, that they merely followed the path laid out for them by men and by a few prominent members of their own sex. That this view of female passivity is dangerously erroneous can be demonstrated by referring to numerous biographies of suffragists and to some studies of ordinary women. What these works show is that women, individually and collectively, may not have been the sole mistresses of their fates, but neither did they instantly acquiesce in everything they were told to do.

Also, one must ask whether the roles laid out in the prescriptive literature were intended to apply to all nineteenth-century American women. And of course the answer is an emphatic no: The advice books were intended for an audience of middle- and upper-class white northern urban women, at a time when a majority of Americans still lived on farms and the urban middle class was relatively small. Blacks and immigrant whites as well as all working-class Americans were entirely excluded from the purview of the prescriptive literature. There is also an abundance of evidence to indicate that many nineteenth-century women within the intended readership of the advice books explicitly rejected these role models.

A study of the prescriptive literature can, however, be useful. But the advice books must be seen in their proper context, and for what they were: expressions of social norms formulated largely by men, outlining ideal types of female behavior. It is possible to understand the impact of the roles laid out for white women in nineteenth-century America only through detailed studies of how individuals and groups of women were affected by the role expectations. This is one of the major contributions of Carol Berkin's essay on Charlotte Perkins Gilman, for in Gilman's life one can see how a unique woman struggled to escape from the ideological constraints on her actions.

A historian confronting the issue of nineteenth-century femininity is faced with a paradox. On the one hand, woman's ideal role was so sharply defined as to be oppressive. On the other hand, the century also saw the founding of the women's rights movement, the burgeoning of higher education for women, and the entry of women into professional occupations like teaching and librarianship. Furthermore, the experience of females from racial and ethnic minorities bore little or no relationship to the established norms. What is one to make of it all?

DIVERSE EXPERIENCES

When seen in contrast to the colonial period, the diversity of experiences of nineteenth-century American women is truly extraordinary. What follows is an all-too-brief survey of some of those experiences.

Many white women still lived on farms, like their eighteenth-century mothers and grandmothers. But because the period after 1815 witnessed the great westward migration of the American people, at least some nineteenth-century women lived in circumstances closer to the seventeenth century than to the eighteenth. Like their earliest American ancestors, they too were pioneers, carving out homes, farms, and eventually towns from land not previously settled by Europeans. Like their female forebears, they lived in an environment with an unbalanced sex ratio, for the movement west, like the earlier Atlantic migration, brought a preponderant majority of young males into the new settlements. Because of the isolation of the frontier, women had to learn the skills their great-grandmothers had known, and they too had to cherish the rare social occasions that broke the rural monotony. Studies of the diaries of pioneer women show how the sex roles learned in eastern areas broke down under the stresses of frontier life. But the diaries also demonstrate the tenacity with which women clung to the familiar elements of their existence.

Black women participated in the same population movements, as slave owners transferred their work forces into the rich, newly opened lands of the Gulf Coast states. Many black families were probably irreparably divided by the migration, for, even if a planter took all his slaves with him, large numbers of blacks had spouses and children on other plantations. Nevertheless, research has shown that slaves quickly re-established family patterns similar to those in eastern states, with comparable marriage and childbearing practices. Many cotton and sugar plantations of the Southwest were larger than the biggest eastern establishments, and so the slave population was even more concentrated in a few areas than it had been previously. One consequence was the flowering of an Afro-American cultural tradition, centering to a large extent on Christianity and its promises of spiritual freedom to a people in bondage. Women as well as men helped create that culture and pass it on to succeeding generations.

For the first time in American history, the number of blacks who were enslaved was decreasing. As the years passed, the free black community that had begun to take shape after the

American Revolution grew ever larger. Free black men and women lived and worked in northern and southern cities, and two free black women—Sojourner Truth and Harriet Tubman—emerged in the forefront of the abolitionist movement. Even though only the northern states formally abolished slavery within their borders, individual emancipations in the slave states enlarged the numbers of freed-men and -women long before the mass emancipation following the northern victory in the Civil War.

In the context of sex roles, it is instructive to note that freed black husbands and wives tried, if they could, to organize their families in such a way that the woman would not have to work outside the home. The meaning of this deliberate reversal of slave patterns has not yet been fully explored, but it does not necessarily indicate that the prescriptive literature aimed at whites was now affecting blacks as well. Rather, the laboring wife was probably seen as a badge of slavery—as indeed she was—and therefore to reject bondage also meant to reject slave female work roles. It goes without saying, though, that ex-slave families were often unable to achieve this goal, because of wage discrimination against blacks.

In any discussion of the westward migration of whites and blacks, one must not forget the Native American families that were being forced from their traditional homelands as the line of settlement pushed inexorably onward. Some tribes resisted violently, others did not, but in the end many had to leave areas where their people had lived for generations, if not centuries, and move onto reservations, some of them located in environments not easily adaptable to their former ways of life. Although little scholarship has focused specifically on the roles of Indian women during this time of trouble, they must have borne the brunt of many of the changes in their society because of their traditional role as cultivators of the land. When that land changed from the forest soil of northern Georgia and Alabama to the dusty vastness of Indian Territory (Oklahoma), as it did for the Cherokees, the adjustment must have been difficult indeed.

And what of the white women who did not move west? Their lives were also changing under the impact of the increasing industrialization and urbanization of the eastern and midwestern states. The rise of textile manufacturing in New England meant that eastern women could put away the spinning wheel and the hand loom forever. Daughters of northeastern farm families could now find employment in the textile mills of

Lowell and surrounding communities in Massachusetts and Rhode Island. Ironically, these rural girls composed America's first true industrial labor force in the 1820s and 1830s, until they were replaced by the Irish immigrants who flooded the New England states in the 1840s. As other industries began to develop, they too turned for the bulk of their labor force to the immigrant men, women, and children arriving in the United States from Europe and Asia. The womenfolk in such families worked along with the men to create a better life than that which they had left, but the vivid description of life in urban tenements drawn from memoirs and contemporary observers makes one wonder about their success.

As for the northern middle-class women who were the targets of the prescriptive writers, their lives also diverged from earlier patterns. One of the signs of the changes that occurred in cities and smaller communities was the amazing growth of female organizations in size and number. Whereas women's organizations were a rarity in colonial America, consisting perhaps of a few isolated prayer groups and an occasional combination of female merchants, every nineteenth-century American town had its female benevolent and reform societies. Initially many of these groups were church related, sponsoring foreign missionaries or the publication of Bibles for distribution to "benighted heathen" abroad, or concentrating on reform efforts closer to home. Such groups ran schools for orphan girls, attempted to reform prostitutes, and promoted temperance. Eventually organizations with secular concerns were also founded, the most notable of which were the various organizations interested in women's rights.

For obvious reasons, historians have long been attracted to the study of these organizations, whose very emergence seems to belie the historical interpretation stressing the passivity and submissiveness of nineteenth-century women. Yet until quite recently the treatment of the National American Women's Suffrage Association was filiopietistic in its orientation, and the biographies of its leaders lacked much critical bite. But in the past few years specific studies of leadership and tactics in the suffrage groups have been published, and this portends well for the future of analytical inquiry into their activities. Although they have admired the suffragists' determination and their commitment to idealistic goals, historians have usefully pointed out some of the failings of the movement as it developed, especially its eventual concentration on suffrage to the exclusion of other concerns, its compliance with the antiblack prejudices of its southern white members, and its reliance on the argument that voting by educated middle- and upper-class white females could help to negate the supposedly uninformed votes of blacks and the "immigrant hordes."

Women from other social ranks also joined organizations. Female workers first formed local unions and then organized the Women's Trade Union League to coordinate their activities nationally. Black women, who were not admitted to the white female organizations, formed separate clubs, but they were more likely to concentrate on the betterment of their race than on foreign missions. Throughout American society, women excluded from the male worlds of politics and economic leadership banded together to achieve mutually acceptable ends. In the all-female organizations they learned organizational skills they could never have exercised had they participated only in male-dominated clubs. Accordingly, the sexual segregation we deplore in the twentieth century did have its positive side for our female ancestors.

Indeed, some historians argue that the rigid domestic role outlined in the prescriptive literature might have had its positive aspects as well. They reason that although women were confined to the home, it was nonetheless *theirs*. Women's presumed expertise in homemaking and child rearing made the domestic sphere wholly feminine, a realm upon which men were not supposed to intrude. Whereas in the colonial era fathers had had the primary say in child rearing, in the nineteenth century mothers were assigned that task. As a result, women gained more control over their own lives and those of their children than had previously been the case. The birthrate dropped steadily in the United States after 1800, despite the fact that dependable birth-control devices were introduced only in fairly recent years, and now a historian has suggested that women's newly acquired domestic power might be a cause of that decline in fertility. The theory remains to be proved, but it does open new avenues of inquiry as historians seek to explain the drop in the birthrate.

This new emphasis on "domestic feminism" has led to a reevaluation of women who had previously been ranked as anti-feminists because of their opposition to women's suffrage. Most notable is the case of Catharine Beecher, educator and author of the popular *The American Woman's Home,* the single most comprehensive book of household advice published in the nineteenth century. In her speeches and writings Beecher outlined a special role for women in American society, based on their domestic identity. Instead of arguing that women should seek such male prerogatives as voting, she stressed that they should develop their inherent capacities for nurturance and conciliation in order to effect changes in American society.

In the twentieth century the women's movement took a direction other than the one Catharine Beecher favored, and so she was, in effect, cast into outer darkness, until it came to be recognized that she was just as committed to improving women's condition as were the advocates of female rights. She simply chose another method of advancing her position; because the suffragists regarded her as an enemy does not mean that historians have to accept their failure to distinguish the underlying unity of the seemingly variant approaches to women's status.

A RESOLUTION OF THE PARADOX

Is there a way in which all the widely varying lives of nineteenth-century American women can be fitted together into a whole? At the moment the answer must be no, but perhaps a start might be made by raising a crucial question. Why were nineteenth-century Americans so obsessed with the idea of women's sphere? Although seventeenth- and eighteenth-century American writers occasionally addressed themselves to the issue of the proper role of women, the torrent of works on that theme printed during the decades between 1820 and 1900 was unprecedented.

One way of viewing this prescriptive literature is to recognize that it came in response to the changes that have been briefly outlined here. If no one questions a role, if there are no pressures placed on its maintenance, then there is little reason to define it carefully and exactly, nor is there a need to write about it repeatedly. It was precisely because the traditional housewifely role was being challenged—not only formally by women, but indirectly through industrial hiring practices and other means—that it had to be defended as staunchly as possible. And the same challenges also led to the position adopted by Catharine Beecher and the other domestic feminists. No longer could the female role be taken for granted: It had to be rationalized, justified, sustained for reasons other than mere custom and tradition.

The same debate, of course, continues to the present day, and in many ways the paradox is still with us. Can it ever really be resolved?

John Harper's article on the campaign against any form of planned parenthood in nineteenth-century America directly addresses the public issues posed by the private decisions made in many families to control fertility. Although it is impossible to measure statistically the relative prevalence of different methods of birth control, Harper shows that abortion and various sorts of mechanical aids were widely employed to reach the desired end. The fact that so many women went to such lengths to avoid or terminate pregnancies demonstrates the depth of their commitment to decreasing the size of their families. And the reaction of male doctors and public officials alike indicates the challenge such private determinations could present to public policy.

When large numbers of American families decided to limit their fertility, the birthrate declined, and white men concerned about maintaining Anglo-Saxons as the dominant group in the United States began to be concerned about the fact that the birthrate of the immigrant and black populations of the country remained high. They envisioned a society in which their kind of folk were outnumbered by groups they believed to be genetically inferior. And so they launched a counterattack on abortionists and distributors of birth-control devices, in order to try to stop the dangerous trend.

In a sense, they succeeded; but in another sense, they failed. They did not arrest the fertility decline, which continues to this day, but on the other hand they were the forerunners of modern "right to life" groups who still argue that women should not be able to obtain abortions freely. The potential contradictions between private decisions and public policy thus extend into our own time.

What Harper demonstrates on a social level, Carol Berkin shows in her examination of the personal life of Charlotte Perkins Gilman. Even though Gilman has a vaunted reputation as an independent reformer, Berkin clearly outlines the difficulties she met in her attempts to break free of the confines of the prescribed role for nineteenth-century American women. Gilman may not have read prescriptive literature, but she had absorbed its message. Torn between accepting and rejecting domesticity, she finally reached a resolution of her dilemma in her late second marriage. The public-private conflict lay within herself, as she presented a confident image to the world yet inwardly wrestled with the implications of following her own desires instead of acceding to the wishes of others. It is in studies such as this that we can assess the impact of behavioral expectations on nineteenth-century women far more successfully than if the role prescriptions are examined in isolation.

In times of trouble, Charlotte Perkins Gilman found solace in female companions, and two of the other three essays in this section demonstrate the importance of female networks and support groups for women of the middle and working classes. When Mary Lyon wanted to raise money to establish Mount Holyoke Female Seminary, she turned to women's religious societies; when the Irish Collar Laundry laborers of Troy, New York, struck their employers, they did so with a sense of solidarity as both workers and women. In each case success was largely predicated on a recognition of female identity on the part of participants in the movement, and on their willingness to act upon that shared identity. Their femininity tied women together in a way that nothing else could; it may not have broken down class barriers, but it did forge strong alliances among women of the same class, allowing them to unite to achieve common goals. For the genteel middle-class whites of western Massachusetts, that goal was founding a school that could educate themselves, their daughters, and their sisters to be teachers; for the Irish working women of Troy, the goal was increased wages that would more adequately compensate them for their labor.

In newly settled California, women were so scarce that no opportunities existed for female Chinese immigrants to join together in similar fashion. Few in number, controlled by pimps, husbands, and employers, the seamstresses, prostitutes, and others largely had to make their own way against all the odds. That some succeeded is a testimony to enormous courage and resourcefulness; that many died is evidence of the harsh conditions under which they lived and worked. Their experience demonstrates vividly that being female in an overwhelmingly male society did not necessarily convey benefits. Quite the contrary: In this instance at least, it led instead to vicious exploitation.

The theme that runs through all the articles is the nineteenth-century woman's search for autonomy, both collectively and individually. Charlotte Perkins Gilman thought most systematically about the quest, but Mary Lyon also explicitly sought to prepare her students for lives independent of their families. Similarly, women who adopted various means of limiting their fertility tried to attain control over their own lives, and the Collar Laundry workers wanted to establish a union that could protect them from exploitation and that could give them some measure of independence from the whims of their employers. The California Chinese too wanted and fought for such independence, but they had to do so as individuals and thus they had less chance for success. It seems as though, in the end, nineteenth-century American women were not so submissive and domestic after all.

6 *Private Woman, Public Woman:*
The Contradictions of Charlotte Perkins Gilman

Carol Ruth Berkin

Charlotte Perkins Gilman. Reprinted with permission of Bryn Mawr College from the Photograph Albums of Carrie Chapman Catt.

Once upon a time, 10-year-old Charlotte Perkins wrote in 1870, the good King Ezephon and his besieged kingdom were saved by the heroic battle-field performance of Princess Araphenia, only daughter of the king. Araphenia had not vanquished the wicked enemy alone, however; she had magical help from the fabulous Elmondine, beautiful visitor from a distant planet. Bejeweled and bewitching, Elmondine had come to a lonely Araphenia in the palace garden and had offered advice and assistance. To save the king and his kingdom, Elmondine created, out of thin air, an army of a thousand men. And to the young earthly princess, this fairy princess gave a magic sword with which to fight and an invincible horse on which to ride while disguised as a warrior-prince. When victory came, the brave girl threw off her disguise, and her astonished father embraced her.

Tales like this one appear in different versions throughout Charlotte Perkins's diaries.[1] The central characters remain the same in each story: a young woman who can, through some magic, overstep the prescribed boundaries of her life and enter into active participation in the great struggles between good and evil in her society; an older woman, resplendently female yet wise and independent and powerful, who guides the novice's path; and always a grateful father whose respect had been won.

Charlotte Perkins was a young girl with an active fantasy life and a lonely reality when she spun these tales. But as a mature woman of 50, she continued to write stories of wise, older women, strong and independent doctors or philanthropists, who appeared out of nowhere to guide some struggling girl to maturity. The setting was no longer fabulous, but the characters were unchanged.[2]

No Elmondine ever appeared in the life of Charlotte Perkins Stetson Gilman. But for many younger women—in her lifetime and today—she has seemed to play that fabled role herself. Writer, philosopher, socialist, and feminist, Gilman has come to stand for the potentialities of American womanhood. She appears very much the self-made woman, overcoming sexual stereotype and social pressures to emerge as a woman of depth and dimension.

Valuable as this Elmondine may seem to those searching for a model, Gilman did not come from a distant planet, free of the conflicts that a woman might have faced at the turn of the century or faces today. Nor was she magically transformed by any fabulous figure into a secure, stable, integrated personality without the marks of a difficult childhood. Her life bears witness to the difficulties of feminism, not as an ideology or a

1 In this essay, all materials from Gilman's diaries and personal correspondence with family and friends are drawn from the Charlotte Perkins Gilman Papers, Schlesinger Library, Radcliffe College, Cambridge, Massachusetts.
2 See, for example, the novelettes serialized in *The Forerunner* (1911–1916), reprinted by Greenwood Press, New York, 1968.

political commitment, but as a personal experience. Charlotte Perkins Gilman struggled for intellectual and emotional liberation, hampered through much of her life by an internalization of the very split vision of masculine and feminine spheres and destinies that, in her work, she would expose as artificial. She struggled later in her life to achieve a balance between independence and an interdependence with others. This essay seeks to chart her personal confrontation with feminism, because it is in that experience that she may serve as a model for American women.

SELF-IMAGES: CHILDHOOD AND ADOLESCENCE

Charlotte Perkins was born on July 3, 1860.[3] Her parents' family trees, rooted in New England soil, were already intertwined, with cousins marrying cousins in discrete confirmation of their pride in association. Her father was a Beecher, grandson of Lyman Beecher, and nephew, as Charlotte put it, of twelve "world servers," a young man nearly smothered in the mantle of reform. Frederick Beecher Perkins's mother had been a rebel of sorts, the odd sister who had never taken any interest in public affairs.

Frederick Beecher Perkins struck a compromise between family tradition and maternal heresy: He dedicated himself to the pursuit of knowledge, thus satisfying his own personal desires in the interest of society. It was his world service to know everything, in case anyone might ask. He was quick tempered, sensitive, with a well-mannered hostility to authority. He was never much of a financial success and never seemed to care. In 1858 Perkins married his 31-year-old cousin, Mary Fitch Wescott of Providence, Rhode Island. As a girl, Wescott had been "the darling of an elderly father and a juvenile mother," a naive, lovely, flirtatious girl who broke hearts and prompted numerous proposals at first sight. Her own branch of the family was known for its strong attachment to one another and its indifference to the outside world.

If Mary Fitch Wescott had been naive and frivolous as a maiden, her marriage cured her of both failings with cruel abruptness. Within less than three years she bore three children. The eldest died. Thomas Perkins and his younger sister, Charlotte Perkins, survived. When the exhausted mother was told that another pregnancy would kill her, her husband abandoned her.

The dissolution of the Perkins family worked upon the consciousness and character of each member differently. Despite the poverty, the humiliating dependence on family charity that kept her moving from home to

---

[3] Gilman's own account of her family history and her life, from which much of the information in this essay is drawn, can be found in her autobiography, *The Living of Charlotte Perkins Gilman*, D. Appleton-Century, New York and London, 1935.

home and city to city, Mary Perkins never voiced a word of criticism at her abandonment. Thus, her children were left to struggle with its mystery. Their father's motives could only be imagined and their mother's continuing attachment to him only accepted as a reality.

Mary Wescott Perkins kept her silence, but she drew from this marital experience a lesson that surely helped shape her daughter's life. She learned, she said, that affection was a fatal vulnerability. What was true physiologically became for her psychologically true as well: Love could kill. She strove, therefore, with devotion and steely determination to arm her own children against emotional disappointment. She resolved to nurture stoics, immune to rejection because no appetite for love had been developed. This denial of affection to her children was, of necessity, also self-denial; out of love for her children she kept her distance from them. "I used to put away your little hand from my cheek when you were a nursing baby," she once remarked with pride and regret to her adult daughter. But her stoicism was acquired rather than natural, and there were lapses; in secret moments, when she thought her daughter Charlotte safely asleep, she held and caressed and kissed her.

It was Charlotte Perkins—precocious, intensely lonely, isolated from other children by her family's nomadic life, and alienated from her brother by his teasing style and his "bad" behavior—who bore most heavily the burden of her mother's contradictions. From Mary Wescott Perkins she learned the unintended but crucial lesson that there was a public, rational, independent self and a secret, emotional, vulnerable self. The young girl took the public self to be estimable and held the private self suspect. By the age of 10 she had constructed this dichotomy.

Her childhood diaries reveal a self-consciously stoical Charlotte, a character ruthlessly creating itself, always disciplining and reprimanding, always self-critical, trusting in rigorous programs for self-improvement to overcome unacceptable character traits. This was, for her, the real Charlotte Perkins. Yet she indulged a secret self. At night she immersed herself in a rich fantasy life, allowing her imagination to transport her to beautiful and exotic paradises where (as she later remembered) "the stern restrictions, drab routines, unbending discipline that hemmed me in became of no consequence." But allowing free rein to her imagination provided more than an escape from drab situational realities. Her fantasy worlds were never so randomly constructed as she might have believed. Repeatedly she peopled them with open and affectionate maternal figures who provided her with the secrets to winning a father's affection and esteem.

As sustaining as she knew her fantasy worlds to be, Charlotte Perkins felt the need to prove that she kept her imagination under control. Unwilling to relinquish it, she struck a bargain with herself that would preserve it: "Every night," she wrote, she would think of pleasant things that could really occur; once a week, of "lovelier, stranger things"; once a month, "of wonders"; and once a year, of "anything."

This bargain held until her adolescence. When she was 13, as Gilman recalled in her autobiography, her mother discovered the evening fantasies and ordered her daughter to end them. To this, Gilman wrote, an obedient child instantly acceded. Perhaps, however, Charlotte Perkins demanded of herself that the fantasies be abandoned, or transformed into something less disturbing to her conscious self. Such a transformation did occur, for even as she dissolved the kingdom of Ezephon she began to nurture an absorbing enthusiasm for the "things that could really occur" in the world of science and sociology. Social "wonders," existing and potential, began to preoccupy her; physics, with the power of its absolute laws, made magic pale; and the plausible utopias the social reformer could design were "lovelier stranger things," than the fairy kingdoms had ever been.

The bridge between the old fantasy world and the new scientific one was her own role in them. In either setting, Charlotte Perkins's part was heroic. In the new and less-disturbing secret life that took shape, she dreamed of becoming a renowned world server, a major figure in the reorganization of her society. The shift in focus to the real world offered her a better chance to release her productive and constructive energies. But lost in this transformation was the expression of a desire for intimacy and the frank recognition that loneliness was a negative condition.

Her imaginary worlds had helped her confront her feelings. They were populated by individuals who came to cherish her and to love her and, thus, to end her emotional isolation. But in the new world of social realities, Charlotte Perkins saw herself befriended by no one in particular and a friend to no one but impersonal humanity. In such a self-image, loneliness was elevated to a necessity; it was transformed into the price one paid for the heroic self. Through the prism of her new ambitions, the years of stoical training at last revealed their clear purpose. Her mother had intended to prepare her for survival only; now Charlotte Perkins saw that self-denial and discipline prepared one not simply to endure life, but to perform great deeds in it.

As this perception of her life hardened into an ideology, Charlotte Perkins lost the power to discern genuine interests from defensive commitments. The attraction of social reform became a shield against the appeals and the dangers of personal intimacy. The two modes of living were forced into contradiction. Armed with a rationale for dismissing her feelings, she often refused to probe their meaning. Some emotions she could incorporate into or redefine within her heroic image. Responses and impulses she could not thus account for, she simply denied. Her conscious certainty masked her deep ambivalence.

Her new self-image and its ambitions drew Charlotte Perkins to a closer identification with her father. He loomed in her mind—as figures often do who are not familiar realities—as the embodiment of his ideals rather than his performance. His reputation as a humanitarian was as well known to her as he was unknown. His apparent dedication to public service contrasted, in her mind, with her mother's slavish commitment to her children and the narrow circle of domestic life. Certain that her mother led a "thwarted life," she became equally certain that her father did not.

Thus, attraction to Frederick Perkins increased, even as the key to gaining his attention seemed to be found. Charlotte Perkins had sought that attention before, appealing to him to write to her because she was lonely. Appeals for support and approval now gave way to requests for reading lists in history, anthropology, and science. To these came speedy and lengthy replies. In this manner she reached out to him, speaking of her intellectual isolation, not a personal loneliness but an absence of tutelage and collegiality. No one at home, she wrote, could understand as he could her ambitions to relate to social issues. It was in this shared breadth of vision that she pressed their kinship. But for all her efforts to rise above "personal pain or pleasure," her disappointment at his frequent coolness and distance slipped into the letters. "Should I continue to write," she asked after a long period without response from Frederick Perkins, "for I am anything but desirous to intrude."

Her mother conveyed a sense of danger in the admission of personal needs, and her father seemed simply to dismiss them as trivial. Thus, both parents denied the validity of feelings to their daughter. But without knowing it, mother and father conspired in a second way. The young Charlotte Perkins came to believe that the compensations for self-control and self-negation were real in the public sphere and were only a mean mockery in the circle of the home; that the avenue to satisfaction and the path to despair were as inevitably separated as this man and woman. She must choose between them. And she must be allowed to choose between them. The choice was a demand upon her own resources; the possibility of choice was a demand upon the society in which she lived. The Victorian society she encountered seemed more hostile than receptive to her pursuit of a public life, and this would direct her reformist energies to the place of women in American society.

The new self-image that took shape in the early 1870s may have cushioned Charlotte Perkins while family relationships and economic circumstances disintegrated further. In 1871, after a decade of separation, Mary Wescott Perkins began a suit for divorce. Her motives are unknown, but the decision brought a dramatic alteration in her public image. When the divorce came in 1873, Mary Perkins was no longer a loyal and suffering wife; she had become a scandalous divorcée. Once-sympathetic Beechers and Perkinses closed their doors to her, and she and her children were left entirely on their own.

In 1873 the three moved to Providence, Rhode Island. They spent a brief time experimenting in cooperative living. When this failed, the Perkinses settled into independent poverty. While her mother struggled to support the family, Charlotte struggled for autonomy. At 15 she openly challenged her mother's rule of complete obedience, with ironic success. Free of parental control at last, she promptly disciplined herself: She swore to give total obedience to her mother until she reached age 21.

Superficially the results of rebellion and of defeat were one and the same; in more ways than she yet understood, Charlotte Perkins remained a dutiful daughter. Her real rebellion was not in character but in the uses to which she intended to put the stern self-discipline and the dire vision of a woman's lot in the world that were her inheritance. Mary Wescott Perkins intended to protect her daughter from disappointment, and to prepare her for life. But that protection was situational: It was in marriage, as wife and mother, that Charlotte Perkins was expected to face her tests. Charlotte Perkins intended, however, to escape marriage, to avoid the despair and defeat it guaranteed, and to meet her test in a world her mother could not know or imagine.

The reality of her adolescent years offered few opportunities to test the meaning of her commitment to spinsterhood. Her mother's excessive restrictions on Charlotte Perkins's social life limited her access to men and even to women. Without any real attachments and always desperately lonely, she fell back upon her imagination for relief. She formed a wild and absorbing crush on an actor she had seen perform but had never met. She nursed an adoration of an older woman who had been only casually kind. In her diaries she regularly denounced love and marriage, yet she filled its pages with speculation: "Who will you marry?" "What will be his age?" "What will you wear on your wedding day?"

QUESTIONS OF FRIENDSHIP OR MARRIAGE

At the age of 18 Charlotte Perkins described herself in her diary: "18 years old. 5'6½" high. Weigh some 120 lbs or thereabout. Looks, not bad. At times handsome. At others, decidedly homely. Health, perfect. Strength —amazing. Character—ah! . . . I am not in love with anybody; I don't think I ever shall be." This was written in January 1879. In February a short diary entry reasserted her lack of attachments. "No Valentines! No Regrets!" Perhaps there were no regrets. But in March of that year, her mother allowed Charlotte to accompany her on a visit to relatives in Cambridge and Boston. Here, suddenly, the 18-year-old found herself the belle her mother had so often been in her own youth. She was surrounded by young college men, courted by Arthurs, Edwards, and Charles Walter Stetson, a "Nice boy . . . but young." She frankly enjoyed the flirtation, and when she returned home in July, her mood grew gloomy.

That fall she returned to Cambridge and then went to Connecticut, and again was faced with a happy embarrassment of beaux. Back home in November, she kept herself busy writing letters to her new male friends, among them a younger cousin from Connecticut, George Houghton Gilman. For several months letters passed between "Dear Ho!" and "Dear Chopkins," and it was to Houghton Gilman that she most openly wrote of the boredom and the tension of living under the heavy hand of her mother. On March 6, 1878, she had chastised herself in her diary: "I must really abolish all desire for comfort or any sort of happiness if I expect to have any peace." But back in Cambridge for New Year's Day 1880, she recorded with pleasure a day of excitement and expectation, the "best day of my life."

Charlotte Perkins was nearly 20 when this brief flurry of social life broke the monotony of her Providence existence. When the excitement ended, she settled once more into biding her time until, at 21, she could embark upon her own life. Even in her impatience, however, she knew that things at home had greatly improved. She had studied art, and recently had enjoyed some independent income through the sale of miniatures and other decorative pieces. She found release for her physical energies—and an opportunity for sorority—at a local woman's gymnasium.

And despite her mother's continuing interference with her life—reading her mail, intercepting and rejecting social invitations—Charlotte Perkins had established her first genuine friendships with other women. One of these women was Grace Channing, daughter of a noted New England clerical family, a girl with a background similar to Charlotte's. Together, Grace Channing and Charlotte Perkins wrote plays and poems to entertain themselves and their families. But most intimate and most important was the friendship formed with Martha Luther, a young girl who for almost four years held Charlotte Perkins's unguarded confidence.

These friendships were hard-earned. Charlotte Perkins was as deeply wary of them as she was eager for them, thinking affection to be a trap and a drain on one's energies, but feeling it as a voluntary vulnerability. To protect herself, she compelled Martha Luther to make a pact, pledging that their affection would be "permanent and safe." Even with such a guarantee, Charlotte worried that she would jeopardize the relationship either by excessive demands for affection or, conversely, by sudden withdrawals of affection. "I was always in a fervor," she later recalled, "that for a time I should want to see her continually, and that there would be spaces when affection seemed to wane."

Sometime before the end of 1881 Martha Luther married and moved from Providence. Perkins felt the separation keenly, experiencing the old isolation and loneliness more intensely after the years of sharing with Luther. She was, by her own account, in a vulnerable state when, in January 1882, Charles Walter Stetson re-entered her life. Like Perkins, Stetson had trained as an artist. Art was an immediate bond between them, though perhaps it involved more competitive tension than either thought to admit. Even deeper was the bond of circumstance. "He was," Gilman later recalled, "a great man—but lonely, isolated, poor, misunderstood." Stetson's state of mind and worldly condition seemed to mirror her own perfectly. The two quickly fell in love and, within a short time, Walter Stetson proposed.

The effect of Stetson's proposal upon Charlotte Perkins was deep and disturbing. It came in her twenty-first year, and thus it set her cruelly at odds with herself. She was, by the terms of her bargain with herself, free at last of parental control. She felt an urgency to give her past meaning by pursuing its heroic dreams. Her self-esteem depended upon an energetic dedication to her social goals. To abandon the pursuit of a life of world service before it had begun, and to embrace instead love and marriage, would be to shatter a self-image that had, despite its problems, been sustaining.

Just when she needed most to understand what she truly desired and what she might realistically work to have, Charlotte Perkins was most completely at a loss. She could not separate her genuine commitment to social reform from the power she had invested in it to justify her emotional isolation; and because she had invested her commitment with that power in order to defend against emotional rejection and disappointment, she could not risk disarming it in the face of a proposal of marriage, with its confusing threats and promises of intimacy. She loved Walter Stetson and wanted to be with him. But she could neither overcome the powerful image of her mother's thwarted life nor separate that image from the institution of marriage itself; the two concepts were merged.

In order to avoid confronting her confusion, Charlotte recast her dilemma. She posed the choice as one between two mutually exclusive duties rather than two strongly felt desires. She faced, she told herself and Charles Walter Stetson, a decision to be made between a duty to life and a duty to love. Thus she distorted her feelings and the issues entirely; she sacrificed any awareness of her positive yearnings for both choices in order to avoid the reasons for rejecting either. In her diaries and her letters to Stetson, she hid behind a rhetoric of obligation and self-sacrifice that not even she could resist in the end. She made no effort to accommodate both duties. She was protected from this approach not simply by her psychic patterns, but also by her sociological perceptions. For women, life and love were not overlapping spheres. Men could have marriage and careers; women, responsible for home and children, could not. A sense of injustice that she could not entirely hide sprang from the fact that it was exactly this social division of labor and duties that she intended to reform.

For months, Charlotte Perkins pleaded with Walter Stetson for delay. This she won in large part simply by her indecision. Although he suffered, she felt she suffered more, because she was torn this way and that, and had, she told him, no peace. "How often one duty contradicts another," she exclaimed when, in the midst of reading in order to acquire a "general notion of how the world worked," she stopped to write him a letter. "And what a world of careful practice it needs to distinguish the highest!" It was the skill required to distinguish the highest duty that she felt sorely lacking. And this, she argued, accounted for her delay.

"I am not a tenderhearted child," she assured him, and herself, "neither am I an impulsive girl: But a clearheaded woman who is weighing a life time in her hands." How could she know what she would lose or gain if she had no experience of either life? On marriage and motherhood there were, she knew, all-too-many voices of authority to guide her. "This is noble, natural and right," said "all the ages." Her own body, she admitted, urged her to yield. Against her independence ran "all the ages" as well, for "no woman yet has ever attempted to stand alone as I intended." The grandiosity of this statement was entirely innocent, although it did not reflect social reality.

In the 1880s American women of her race and region were experimenting with independence. The existing social currents for change had, in fact, suggested to her the role of public woman and reformer; her ambitions confirmed that the struggle had already begun. Of course, the general contours of her society reinforced both her notion of women's segregated sphere and the heretical quality of her career aspirations. But when Charlotte Perkins spoke of standing alone, it was the expectation of emotional isolation rather than the concrete problems of economic support or practical opportunities that gave force to her personal drama.

What did she want to do? She had taken care to bury the answers and could not now plumb her own depths. She tried to clarify her thoughts in letters to Walter Stetson, in soliloquy rather than conversation. But she could not explain—or understand—herself. Why, she wrote, do I hesitate? Life with him promised paradise, she said, but love seemed to ask "more than I can give." Repeatedly, and with an unwitting callousness for his feelings, she pressed for a relationship that was limited, a friendship, like the one agreed upon with Martha Luther, that would free her from the necessity of choice. Companionship and friendship would satisfy her; why must there be love and marriage? "I ought not to complain of being offered the crown of womanhood," she confessed, voicing her own and her mother's tenacious romanticism about all that they feared; but she did not fully wish to accept it.

Slowly the choice crystallized into one of duty to submit and endure, or duty to rebel. Posed in these terms, love lost all its positive potential, and independence had its romance restored. But at the last moment, with frustrating perversity, she denied even her own freedom and responsibility to choose. Instead she bowed to the moral imperative of finding one's "right duty." The "right duty" was surely the more difficult one.

As she weighed each choice, her pride—and the hint of pleasure—in her insistence "that my life is mine in spite of a myriad lost sisters before me" made her crucially uneasy with the choice of independence: thus, she chose marriage. On December 31, 1882, she wrote in her diary: "With no pride, with little hope, with uncertain occasional happiness, with no glad energy and living power; with no faith or nearly none, but still, thank God! with firm belief in what is right and wrong; I begin the new year."

A deep nostalgia and a sense of loss showed in her diary for 1883 as she made plans for marriage. Self-pity, wholly shrouded from her own consciousness, marked every page. Dread—equally of unhappiness and of happiness—pervaded this secret record of events.

Marriage, Motherhood, and Collapse

On May 2, 1884, Charlotte Perkins and Walter Stetson were married. Despite all her mother's care and preparation, despite her own, Charlotte Stetson entered marriage as an innocent and a romantic: "My Wedding Day . . . HOME. . . ."

I install Walter in the parlor and dining room while I retire to the bed chamber and finish its decoration. The bed looks like a fairy bower with lace, white silk, and flowers. Make my self a crown of white roses. Wash again, and put on a thin shift of white mull fastened with a rose bud and velvet and pearl civeture. My little white velvet slippers and a white snood. Go in to my husband. He meets me joyfully; we promise to be true to each other; and he puts on the ring and the crown. Then he lifts the crown, loosens the snood, unfastens the girdle, and then— and then. O my God! I thank thee for this heavenly happiness! O make me one with thy great life that I may best fulfill my duties to my love! to my Husband!

May was filled with diary reports of great personal happiness and a total commitment of energy and ego to cooking, baking breads, visiting, and house care. She aimed for perfection and was furious at any domestic failures. Culinary errors made her "disgusted with myself." By mid-June efforts to prove herself a perfect wife were interrupted by an illness that left her weak and bedridden. By June 25 she was miserable, not because of domestic failures, but now because her "old woe"—"conviction of being too outwardly expressive of affection"—had begun to fill her with fears of driving Walter Stetson away. Assurances by her husband could only temporarily ease her mind. In early August she learned she was pregnant.

Through most of her pregnancy, Charlotte Stetson was both sick and depressed. The physical incapacity and loss of the body tone she had acquired through hours in the woman's gymnasium disturbed her, and they no doubt contributed to her sense of unnatural lethargy and of a passivity she held in contempt. Holding herself in ever lower esteem as the months went by, she feared Walter Stetson must share her disgust with herself. But her husband—almost stubbornly—proved sympathetic and supportive. "He has worked for me and for us both, waited on me in every tenderest way. . . . God be thanked for my husband!"

The pregnancy brought her little pleasure. Still, as the months passed, Charlotte Stetson began to adjust to her child-to-be in the terms she best understood: in the language of duty. Her hopes, she wrote, were that the child she carried would be a "world helper" and that she herself could serve the world by a devotion to the child. "Brief ecstasy, long pain. Then years of joy again," she wrote on the morning of March 23, 1885, when Katherine (Kate) Beecher Stetson was born.

But pain and joy seemed to wage a confusing struggle that left her helpless. Despite desperate efforts to be a perfect mother, Charlotte Stetson had given over the care of her daughter to her own mother by August 1885. Depressed, ill, bedridden, she had few days without "every morning the same hopeless waking." She could not explain her deepening depression. Her child was lovely, her husband was loving; she berated herself for not regaining control over her emotions and carefully shied away from locating in her illness any hostility or anger. She was suffering, she was certain, from a new disease called "nervous prostration," and she came to fear that she had contracted an infection of the brain.

Walter Stetson, however, surmised that marriage and motherhood were his wife's problems. Although he did not understand why this was the case, he accepted it. That fall he offered her a separation. But with desperate insistence Charlotte Stetson refused this relief. "He cannot see how irrevocably bound I am, for life, for life. No, unless he dies and the baby die, or he change or I change there is no way out." The dilemma was once again, if not of her own making, at least one she would not allow to be too easily resolved. She could not permit herself to be relieved or consoled; she was invested in this painful punishment. And, with the unintentional blindness of the determined sufferer, she forced husband, daughter, and mother to participate in her nightmare.

Then, in the summer of 1886, Charlotte Stetson bowed to family urgings and left, alone, for California. She looked forward to a host of reunions, visiting her brother Thomas in Utah, her father in San Francisco, and her good friend Grace Channing in Pasadena. The trip restored her health and spirits almost magically. The lush, rich floral splendor of Pasadena satisfied her childhood dreams of beauty; to her, the city was Edenic.

But her return home brought immediate relapse into illness and despair. That winter her husband took her to the famous woman's doctor, S. Weir Mitchell, for treatment at his clinic. Here, her worst fears that either love or "her driving force" must be relinquished were given confirmation by a representative of that impartial science she had always trusted. Mitchell, famous for his belief that anatomy was a woman's destiny, argued that the passivity of the womb must be echoed in the woman's daily life in order for true health to be hers. He prescribed for Charlotte Stetson a totally domestic life, the constant companionship of her child, and an absolute end to any writing or serious reading. Determined to obey this dictum of absolute domesticity, Charlotte Stetson reached the dangerous edge of insanity.

This total collapse, with its admission of failure and its punishment, seemed to release Charlotte Stetson from her commitment to her marriage. Every effort had been made. Thus, in early 1887 she agreed to a separation from her husband. She had, in significant if shrouded ways, recapitulated her parents' marital history. Her mother's physical danger from childbearing found its counterpart in her own near-insanity. But the Stetsons' separation, unlike that of Frederick and Mary Wescott Perkins, had no taint of a husband's abandonment.

Walter Stetson remained nearby, visiting whenever his wife allowed, some weeks coming to see her every day. He brought her gifts, cared for Kate when his wife or child was sick, and, as Charlotte Stetson frequently recorded in her diary with gratitude, did not press any demands upon her. Yet when she looked at the examples of marriage and motherhood around her, she identified with the despair of vulnerable and abused women. "Talked with Mrs. Smythe," she wrote on February 20, 1887. "She is another victim! Young, girlish, unexperienced, sickly, with a sickly child, and no servant . . . ignorant both, and he using his 'marital rights' at her vital expense."

By the end of the year, Charlotte Stetson had begun to think again of California and its healing effect on both body and mind. In 1888, with her daughter and her mother, she set out once again for Pasadena. She had done her duty to love; now she meant to fulfill her desire "to have my utmost capabilities called out in some necessary work."

THE CALIFORNIA YEARS

In this manner, the Charlotte Perkins Gilman known to us through her books, lectures, novels, magazine articles, and poetry began her career. If this were a fairy tale, the woman who left New England "ashamed, degraded and despairing" to become an independent woman and a leading intellectual and social critic of her day would have soon experienced the personal satisfaction and self-esteem her achievements should have brought her. But this woman was who and what she was, and like us all she carried her past into her present.

With her mother (soon to develop cancer) and Kate, Charlotte Perkins Stetson lived a precarious existence, economically and emotionally, in California. She was formally uneducated, and unskilled except in commercial art. This occupation she did not pursue. Her goal was a public life and her career the preaching of a gospel of reform. She tried to support her family by giving public lectures on reform topics, but the proceeds from a passed hat were small. Extra income came from taking in boarders. Debts piled up; soon the triad was moving from house to house in a nomadic pattern reminiscent of her own childhood. If her experience as the head of a husbandless household echoed her mother's years of struggle, Stetson's love life became an odd parody of her marriage.

In 1890 she formed a relationship with another woman writer. The affair was not necessarily sexual; the intensity of emotion did not demand, though it may have included, physical expression. Perhaps Stetson was only seeking a friendship similar to the sustaining one with Martha Luther, but with "Dora" she accepted the subservient and self-negating role she had always associated with "wife." The aspects that had driven her from marriage she now experienced with, even seemed to invite from, Dora. Dora was generous with money, and Charlotte, who would take no financial aid from her estranged husband, accepted assistance from Dora—with every string attached. In return for the money and the companionship, Charlotte provided Dora with her domestic services, "making a home for her," and with intellectual support, cheating her own career by "furnishing material for [Dora's] work."

But the companionship was not so gentle and constant as that she had received from "her dear boy," Walter. Dora was an openly abusive partner. She was "malevolent. She lied . . . she drank . . . she swore freely, at me as well as others. She lifted her hand to strike me in one of her tempers." This affair, begun with the decade, ended when Dora left Charlotte in 1893. From this demeaning experience, Charlotte Stetson refused to learn anything except disappointment. She did not examine her choice of loves or raise any questions about what the affair reflected of her needs and her insecurities. She would only chastise herself in her diary: "Out of it all I ought surely to learn final detachment from all personal concerns."

These private turmoils did not prevent, but coincided with, Charlotte Stetson's growing recognition as a public figure. Her skills at extemporaneous speaking had earned her little money in her early years in California, but they had brought her a reputation, just as her first essays and published articles had brought national notice. Her radical views on the rights of labor and of women, on child care, and other social reforms earned her influential friends in California, as well as the expected enemies. In an essentially conservative state, there were nevertheless several active women's organizations and a few lively communities of intellectuals and writers. These groups welcomed Charlotte Stetson without hesitation, helped her find speaking engagements, and encouraged her to develop and expand her ideas.

Through her work with women's organizations like the Pacific Coast Women's Press Association, she made contact with the national leaders of the women's rights movement—Stanton, Stone, and the settlement house organizer, Jane Addams. To these friends and associates Charlotte Stetson appeared as an energetic, creative, remarkably productive, and admirable woman. But this image contrasted sharply with her own critical sense of herself. In her public life, as in her private life, she seemed determined to demean herself. She was not to be applauded for her raw energy or its constructive channeling, she felt. In reality, she was no better than a cripple; illness, fatigue, and the accompanying mental lethargy that she insisted were the legacy of her married life had permanently damaged her intellectual abilities. She was certain never to realize her potential, and thus she was a disappointment to herself, as she should be to others.

In her first year in California, amid the confusion of establishing a new life, with financial worries and a young child to care for, she had written 33 articles and 23 poems. But this was not enough to bring a sense of satisfaction. In every possible way she seemed to flee the self-esteem her work could and, by her own declared philosophy, should provide. She was hampered by an inability to take her work (rather than herself) seriously. Her speaking and her writing she dismissed as "natural" for her and therefore not to be confused with true work. Work she defined as everything she could not do easily, well, or at all, and she could not hope to do such work because her nervous condition prevented it. Thus, she felt her marriage remained with her; she had not escaped.

It was not the marriage itself that Charlotte Stetson remained wedded to, but rather her concept of her feminine identity. This identity was rooted in disappointment and the thwarted life. As she moved into what she viewed as a masculine sphere, the world of the mind and of action, she would not abandon its opposite. Ironically, though perhaps not surprisingly, the very things she defined as legitimate, enviable intellectual work—"reading, going into a library, learning languages"—were her father's skills, joys, and professional duties as a librarian. And these were, she insisted (and thus it was so), the achievements her past made impossible.

INTELLECTUAL CONTRIBUTIONS

But Gilman's abilities were extraordinary. Quick, creative, able to grasp immediately the essentials of an argument and to generalize from seemingly disparate particulars, she had trained and tutored herself well during her lonely youth. Her true genius lay in her ability to transform her personal contradictions into valuable and legitimate insights on social problems and on the institutions and ideologies that created and sustained the problems.

In her ability to bridge the gap from personal experience to social understanding, she liberated her intellect from the immobility she protested she suffered. What fueled the process was her conviction that social solutions could be found that would some day obviate psychological dilemmas like her own. In this there was potential irony, for she had committed her energies to the elimination of a source of her creativity.

The intellectual framework of her insight was that of the evolutionary and progressive social analysts of her era. Like Lester Ward, Edward Bellamy, and other social critics of the late nineteenth century, she believed that the always shifting patterns of social organization could be understood, predicted, and to some extent manipulated if the evolutionary laws Charles Darwin had discovered were properly applied to human society. By understanding the laws of sociology, human participation in the shaping of human destiny was possible—and, for the concerned citizen, imperative.

Charlotte Perkins Stetson Gilman, like her peers, wrote and lectured to suggest the appropriate actions. For committed evolutionist reformers like herself, change was synonymous with progress. No matter how dark or regressive they might seem, the past and the present always served as a useful and ultimately justifiable base for a better future. Thus, there was equanimity in her perspective, despite the tone of urgency or impatience in pressing reform or the polemical style of her argument. She was dedicated to prodding for changes she was convinced would eventually come. It was only a matter of when and how smoothly the changes would arrive.

Gilman's own work was devoted to the analysis of the relationship of women to their society.[4] Her ideas were not formally or systematically

---

4 Gilman's books, published between 1898 and 1935, are: *Women and Economics*, Small, Maynard, Boston, 1898; *In This Our World*, Small, Maynard, Boston, 1898; *Concerning Children*, Small, Maynard, Boston, 1900; *The Home: Its Work and Influence*, McClure, Phillips, New York, 1903; *Human Work*, McClure, Phillips, New York, 1904; *What Diantha Did*, Charlton, New York, 1910; *The Man-Made World*, Charlton, New York, 1911; *His Religion and Hers: The Faith of Our Fathers and the Work of Our Mothers*, D. Appleton-Century, New York, 1923; *The Living of Charlotte Perkins Gilman*.

presented until *Women and Economics* was published in 1898, but they had been formulated many years before and were already introduced in the work of her California days. As a historical social anthropologist, she traced the rise and institutionalization of patriarchy as a necessary step in human growth and progress. Until the development of modern industrial society, this patriarchal structure with its rigid segregation of women into sex-related functions had been essential for race preservation. But modern society no longer required such a segregation, nor its aggrandizement to the male of privilege and power through the monopoly of the social sphere. The laws and customs sustaining male monopoly on socially productive activity were now clearly without legitimacy. This kind of social division of labor was neither permanent nor fixed by nature; permanent sexual differences did not, as social conservatives argued, mean permanent differences in capacity for social productivity.

Women's potential for contribution in the social—or, as Gilman called it, the human—sphere must now be released and realized. This would mean a radical restructuring of the society, which would be resisted by men jealous of their privileges and by women ignorant of their deprivation. But, she wrote in 1912: "Social evolution has never waited for the complete enlightenment of mankind."

Gilman's vision of the future did not eliminate the genuine sex-related functions. Reproduction remained woman's specific natural specialization, essential to the preservation of the race. But she wholly renounced the traditional social institutions and duties that surrounded this sexual function. In books like *The Home* or in her *Forerunner* essays, she entirely dismantled the imprisoning female sphere of home-making and child care.

Astute and direct, Gilman located the institutionalization of women's oppression in the home and the family, and in the conditioned mentality that channeled all love and all sense of responsibility and potential for self-esteem into limited personal relationships rather than social activities and humanitarianism. Women were not merely trapped in the home, but also psychologically crippled so that they must only hope to remain there. Not only was their world too narrow, but they could not hope to master it. The sphere itself, with its multiple and dissimilar duties, its undifferentiated requirements, its mystique that forbade systematic training for what was "natural"—this chaotic agglomeration called home and child care could not be successfully managed by the average woman.

The fault lay with the role, not with the woman, Gilman insisted. Only a total disassembling and rationalization of "women's sphere" would be acceptable, with each component of women's traditional roles transformed into a modern, scientific, and professional activity. Once this process had begun, women could abandon their old tasks with confidence that none suffered as a result. They could release their energies in the larger world. Professional "baby gardens" or nurseries, professional food services, and house-cleaning services—on these Gilman's hopes rested. Woman's role would thus disappear, and she would not be accused of deserting it.

Femininity itself would be redefined and attainable: "As women grow, losing nothing that is essential to womanhood, but adding steadily the later qualities of humanness, they will win and hold a far larger, deeper reverence than that hitherto vouchsafed them. As they so rise and broaden, filling their full place in the world as members of society, as well as their partial places as mothers of it, they will gradually rear a new race of men, men with minds large enough to see in human beings something besides males and females." [5] Gilman's woman of the evolutionary future would be Elmondine, female and independent, at ease with her sex and her work.

Yet, ironically, Gilman's new woman carried with her the crucial social and psychic trappings of the old. Gilman, like many of her contemporary feminists, could not ultimately envision woman liberated from the task of nurturance itself, could not imagine woman pursuing work for her own personal satisfaction or solely for its challenge to her mind and ambitions. Although she was genuinely radical in the surgery she wanted to see performed on society and all its sacred institutions in order to free women from a sex-defined sphere of domesticity, her goal was to expand the area in which women might serve, not be served. Admittedly she placed the same standard of morality upon men; a desire to cooperate with and to contribute to the welfare of the greater society was, if anything could be said to be, the defining impulse of true humanity.

Here was the reform vision of her century, perhaps, but those who struggled to meet its demands with an obliteration of self were too often women like Charlotte Perkins Gilman. Too many of her own psychic struggles were over defining *self,* its boundaries never stable, the distinction between self-fulfillment and selfishness never clear. She had married, driven to a great extent by a repulsion at her *pride* in defining herself as a woman different from others and independent. Her self-esteem was stifled once she achieved that independence because, to take pride in her own creativity and talents, to cherish them for their own sake, could only be understood as selfish. Surprisingly, she would have more success in her private life resolving this dilemma of self and selfishness than her intellectual work incorporated or revealed.

Gilman's feminist ideas were shared by other women of her generation. Although her radical programs, such as dismantling the home, were resisted by feminists and nonfeminists, her central analysis of women and

---

[5] Charlotte Perkins Gilman, "Are Women Human Beings? A Consideration of the Major Error in the Discussion of Woman Suffrage," *Harper's Weekly* (May 25, 1912).

society was embraced. In her thinking and writing, in the realm of ideas, she was not isolated from others, but had found companionship.

THE RETURN EAST

In 1895 Stetson left California. Within those eight years she had established herself as a writer, admired in literary as well as intellectual circles and praised by social reformers across the country. She had lectured for socialist and women's organizations. She had edited a financially unsuccessful but intellectually exciting radical newspaper. She had helped organize and had participated in women's conferences that earned her a place among the leading ranks of international feminists. She had organized a unique employment office, through which "day work" domestics could find temporary jobs. She had written about evolutionary socialism, anthropology, history, and feminism. But at the age of 35, when she left for the East, she judged herself a failure.

Charlotte Stetson returned East alone. Her mother had died in 1894. That same year Walter Stetson had remarried, choosing his ex-wife's friend Grace Channing as his bride. To many people's surprise—and disgust—Charlotte Stetson appeared delighted with this match. Soon after their marriage, she sent Katherine to live with them.

The decision to relinquish Katherine had been characteristically a blend of rational considerations and deep emotional ambivalence. Her relationship with Katherine was so complicated by fears of failure to be a good mother, by self-conscious and rigid pursuit of a program of "good mothering," and by doubts about its success, that her daughter made her both anxious and guilty. Like her own mother before her, she found it difficult to express directly the love and sympathy she felt for Katherine, often because she feared it would burden the child in some way.

She chose, again as her own mother had, to be useful to her daughter, to protect her by building in her a "right character." She substituted the doctrines of "understanding and self-control" for Mary Wescott Perkins's "obedience and discipline," and she produced a perfectly behaved, sober, responsible, emotionally distant young girl. When in 1894 Charlotte Stetson decided to send her daughter to the more stable home of the Stetsons and thus to the care of Grace Channing, she refused to let Katherine see that the separation would hurt her. In this way, she said, she protected Katherine from any uneasiness at deserting her mother. The cost of this denial Charlotte Stetson thought only she had to absorb.

Nothing she ever did raised such hostility or brought her such notoriety as this act of voluntary separation from her child. She was labeled an unnatural mother, accused not of failing as a mother but of renouncing her duty to be one. Duty and self-indulgence seemed to reverse themselves in the public eye, like a reflection in the mirror: She thought she was helping Katherine by giving her up; the newspapers said she was freeing herself. Her critics' insight was only semantic: The freedom they spoke of, a self-conscious self-interest, was not yet within her reach.

The year 1895 was spent in Chicago, with Stetson working for Jane Addams in the Chicago settlement-house projects. In January 1896 she attended a suffrage convention in Washington, D.C., where she met and befriended the famous pioneer in American sociology, Lester Ward. Between January and July of that year she took to the road, lecturing and giving guest sermons at 57 different churches or meeting halls in the Corn Belt.

In the midst of a hectic schedule she found time in April to visit New York City where her father, now remarried, had settled. Stetson liked her new stepmother and her grown daughters. Her father seemed content, their meeting was warm, and she allowed herself the sweet contemplation of a home at last—with her father. But by November 1896, when she returned to New York, Frederick Perkins had been moved to a sanatorium. He was helpless, growing rapidly senile as the arteries in his brain hardened. Her own intellectual powers were on the rise; his had ebbed. He would not be there to welcome or commend her to the larger world he had so long symbolized.

The next two years were important ones in Stetson's life. Free entirely of personal ties, she devoted herself to her work. She kept up an extraordinary pace, traveling for months at a time, lecturing, attending feminist meetings and conventions, and in her uncommitted hours, reading and writing. Everywhere she went she was confronted by the tangible evidence of her success. Men and women greeted her in each town, receptive to her ideas and eager to be near the energy she radiated. Younger women confessed that she was their model of independent womanhood. Her litany of self-doubt and self-criticism was weakened by this daily routine confirmation that she was indeed what she had wished and worked to be.

Reality thus seemed to catch up with Stetson during these years, and the passage of time seemed to make her more comfortable in her chosen role as spokeswoman for reform. Yet surely this maturation process pointed to a new receptivity to self-esteem. Perhaps the loss of both her parents freed her from the need to view her life in the old pattern of dichotomous loyalties and aversions, a duality that allowed her no victory without its companion, defeat.

One thing is clear: The acceptance of her success changed her understanding of her personal loneliness. Loneliness lost its heroic quality and she came to feel it not as a necessity or a punishment or the price of success, but simply as an emptiness. This changed perception influenced the course of her renewed friendship with Houghton Gilman.

MARRIAGE AND WORK: RESOLUTION

On March 8, 1897, Charlotte Perkins Stetson visited Houghton Gilman's New York office for advice on a legal matter. It had been almost 20 years since "Ho" and "Chopkins" had exchanged letters, yet Houghton recognized her at once. "This," she later wrote, "was the beginning of a delightful renewal of an earlier friendship."

George Houghton Gilman was seven years his cousin's junior, a handsome, courtly, intelligent man. He was gentle, steady, generally likable. He had for most of his life been burdened with responsibility that had tied him down, emotionally and financially, for his mother was an invalid, his brother Francis a dwarf. These family obligations, heavy enough to oppress others, seemed not to embitter Houghton Gilman or to produce in him any debilitating sense of lost opportunities. He may have lived a circumscribed life, but he nevertheless found enjoyable moments and interesting pastimes. He was modestly ambitious and honorable; he liked his work as an attorney. He was not politically active or much attuned to the issues that so engrossed Charlotte Stetson. But he very much enjoyed her company.

Charlotte Stetson was obviously pleased with the new friendship and could not stay off the subject of Houghton Gilman, even in a letter to her daughter. "Last week I made a delightful discovery! Found a cousin! . . . This cousin is Houghton Gilman . . . he is now a grown man nearly thirty, but when I remember him he was just your age." Then, only a few sentences later, she found herself writing: "To return to my newly discovered cousin; he is in the 7th regiment, and is going to take me to see them perform next Tuesday."

By March 18 the cousins were corresponding again, as they had decades ago. Charlotte, full of things to say and feelings to show, chose to write them to "Ho" even though they were both in New York City. "In some ways," she explained, "paper is freer than speech." The paper served her well, for the letters are frank and intense. "What a good time I did have the other night!" she wrote on March 18. "You now float and hover in my brain in a changing cloud of delectable surroundings."

Enjoying Houghton Gilman's company and his confidence seemed to reinforce Charlotte Stetson's awareness of how carefully she had repressed her feelings over the last several years and had escaped dealing with them by a frenzy of activity. "These years, when I stop doing things and my mind settles and things come up into view, most of these are of so painful a nature that I have to rush around and cram them back into their various (right here I have to stop and write a poem on 'Closet Doors' . . .)." But Gilman had created a mental space for her. "Now when I am quiet," she wrote, "there's a pleasantest sort of feeling—warm and cosy and safe."

Although her friendship with Gilman had allowed her room to test her capacity for affection once more, and helped her come to terms with its long absence, she was still wary and insecure. She often insisted that the relationship was platonic, familial, with herself the idiosyncratic but interesting older cousin and him the elegant and courtly young boy who found her educational and amusing in a maiden-aunt fashion. "I am looking ahead and wishing most earnestly and tenderly that you may have such a house as you deserve and one of the very charmingest of wives," Charlotte Stetson typically included in a long and effusive letter, using her pose as "Aunt Charlotte" like a talisman against disappointment.

As the odd courtship continued, these letters became—as those to Walter Stetson had once appeared to be—an open battleground for her conflicting emotions. But Charlotte Perkins Stetson had grown. There may have been defensive cul-de-sacs and charades, but there was nevertheless a true effort to discover her feelings, to know her desires, and to act as she wanted to act rather than as she ought. She knew that Houghton Gilman made her feel good about herself, good enough for her to admit how very low her self-esteem had always been. "Truly Houghton, for all the invulnerable self-belief and self reliance which I have to have to live at all, you have no idea how small potatoes I think of myself at heart, how slow I am to believe that anyone's kindness to me is other than benevolence."

Houghton Gilman could not help but know. She had revealed her insecurity in every letter, in a transparent flippancy that was too earnest to be coy. "It won't surprise me in the least when you get over liking me as they all do," she had written, and in a hundred different forms she repeated the same fears over the next years. It was an appeal for reassurance woven into the letters with others. "Do [my letters] annoy you? I couldn't write for a week cause this fear depressed me," she wrote while in Kansas; "*Say* you like me if you do—often!" she added to a letter that summer.

For four years Charlotte Stetson confided her present and her past to Houghton Gilman, in a dialogue largely with herself. And, although much of the content was self-denigrating and self-pitying, there were moments of a new comfortable feeling about herself. She began to treat herself well, to buy clothing, and to indulge in gratuitous touches of luxury. She had begun to celebrate herself. Although this delight in self would previously have repelled her, now she began to accept personal pleasures that harmed no one by their fulfillment. Most important, she re-examined the very basis of affection.

Duty, she discovered, could not always promote or sustain love. "I have loved many people, in various ways, mostly because they needed it," she wrote Houghton, "but . . . the way you make me feel is different. It is not merely in the nature of wanting you—in the sense of a demanding personal affection, or even of—well, any kind of hungriness. And it is not at all in the sense of wishing to serve . . . the uppermost feeling is of pure personal gratification because you are so!"

What surprised Charlotte Stetson most was that the frank commitment to love did not destroy the sense of commitment to her life's work. Self-denial and self-satisfaction were not after all mutually exclusive rulers of character and destiny; there was room in her to accommodate both states. Her work improved, she told Houghton, her energies increased, her desire to write was not diminished but intensified. She had moments of genuine optimism. "The new charmed being now accepted by Madam Conscience, who has been struggling violently to choke it up for some time past, works admirably and I begin to see my way to let out more love towards Kate, too."

In truth, Charlotte Stetson was at the peak of her career when she wrote these letters to Houghton Gilman. *Women and Economics* was published in 1898 and won instant international acclaim. Even before it was published she was at work on a second book. In the summer of 1899 she returned to England, a star among equals at the international women's conference. Her lecture tours at last showed a profit, with Houghton Gilman acting as her agent and adviser. Her personal philosophy, equating living with growing, had once located growth in the soil of pain, denial, and disappointment. Now she conceded a growing that was expansive and inclusive. What could be a clearer sign of the changes in Charlotte Perkins Stetson than that she had at last developed a sense of humor. The heroic figure could now laugh a little at herself.

In June 1900 Houghton Gilman traveled to the Midwest to meet Charlotte Stetson. She was in the midst of a speaking tour; he had taken the summer away from his law practice. They had not seen each other for almost a year. On June 11 they were married. Of this wedding day, Charlotte Perkins Gilman, now 40, wrote:

Monday . . . Our Day . . . the end of waiting, not to let the happiness blind and mislead me—dull my sensitiveness, check my sympathy, stop my work. It will not, I know; it has not so far and it will not. On the contrary I shall do more work and better. . . . I suppose I shall get used to love and peace and comfort and forget to be grateful everyday! But I doubt it. The other life has been too long. . . . I have liked as well as loved you from the first. . . . So strong and quiet and kind . . . to your pure and noble Manhood I come humbly, gladly full, bringing all that I have and am—willing to be taken as I am. . . . I am coming to be your happy Wife.

Gilman's new confidence in the harmony possible between her public and private lives proved well founded. For 34 years her personal happiness neither hampered her work nor eroded her feminist perspective. When, on August 17, 1935, she ended her own life to avoid debilitation by cancer, she was no longer an influential figure in the world of ideas or politics. The war and the decade that followed had destroyed the world she knew. The era of optimistic reform had passed; and the search in the 1920s by young women for self-gratification and satisfaction without any commitment to public service had made her militant but nurturant feminism obsolete. Despite her eclipse, Charlotte Perkins Gilman continued to write and to advocate the restructuring of society. Her last book, however, was not social anthropology but autobiography, charting an inner odyssey to both independence and interdependence. It was a conscious effort to mark the path for other, younger women.

In the end, Charlotte Gilman's philosophy and her psychic needs seemed, after all, to be one. She sought a social and a psychological androgyny: a full humanity, to be experienced by each individual, that would create harmony among them through shared experience rather than the isolation and dualism of the sexually segregated world into which she had been born. She sought the pride in contribution and participation that ensured self-esteem, and the condition of independence that ensured equality. She sought the integrated self, and even at those moments when she felt it impossible for herself in her own lifetime, she was determined to secure it for future generations of women and men.

Documents

Two Callings, by Charlotte Perkins Gilman, 1903

I

I heard a deep voice through uneasy dreaming,*
A deep, soft, tender, soul-beguiling voice;
A lulling voice that bids the dream remain,
That calms my restlessness and dulls my pain,
That thrills and fills and holds me till in seeming
There is no other sound on earth—no choice.

"Home!" says the deep voice, "Home!" and softly singing
Brings me a sense of safety unsurpassed;

---

* Published with permission from the Charlotte Perkins Gilman Collection, Schlesinger Library, Radcliffe College, from *The Home: Its Work and Influence*, New York, 1903.

So old! So old! The piles above the wave—
The shelter of the stone-blocked, shadowy cave—
Security of sun-kissed treetops swinging—
Safety and Home at last! . . .

I shrink—half rise—and then it murmurs "Duty!"
Again the past rolls out—a scroll unfurled;
Allegiance and long labor due my lord—
Allegiance in an idleness abhorred—
I am the squaw—the slave—the harem beauty—
I serve and serve, the handmaid of the world.

My soul rebels—but hark! a new note thrilling,
Deep, deep, past finding—I protest no more;
The voice says "Love" and all those ages dim
Stand glorified and justified in him;
I bow—I kneel—the woman soul is willing—
"Love is the law. Be still! Obey! Adore!"

And then—ah, then! The deep voice murmurs "Mother!"
And all life answers from the primal sea;
A mingling of all lullabies, a peace
That asks no understanding; the release
Of nature's holiest power—who seeks another?
Home? Home is Mother—Mother, Home—to me. . . .

II

A bugle call! A clear, keen, ringing cry,
Relentless—eloquent—that found the ear
Through fold on fold of slumber, sweet, profound—
A widening wave of universal sound,
Piercing the heart—filling the utmost sky—
I wake I must wake!—Hear—for I must hear!

"The World! The World is crying! Hear its needs!
Home is a part of life—I am the whole!
Home is the cradle—shall a whole life stay
Cradled in comfort through the working day?
I, too, am Home—the Home of all high deeds—
The only Home to hold the human soul!

"Courage!—the front of conscious life!" it cried;
"Courage that dares to die and dares to live!
Why should you prate of safety? Is life meant
In ignominious safety to be spent?
Is Home best valued as a place to hide?
Come out, and give what you are here to give!

"Strength and Endurance! of high action born!"
And all that dream of Comfort shrank away,
Turning its fond, beguiling face aside;
So Selfishness and Luxury and Pride
Stood forth revealed, till I grew fierce with scorn,
And burned to meet the dangers of the day. . . .

"Duty! Unlimited—eternal—new!"
And I? My idol on a petty shrine
Fell as I turned, and Cowardice and Sloth
Fell too, unmasked, false Duty covering both—
While the true Duty, all-embracing, high,
Showed the clear line of noble deed to do.

And then the great voice rang out to the sun,
And all my terror left me, all my shame,
While every dream of joy from earliest youth
Came back and lived!—that joy unhoped was truth,
All joy, all hope, all truth, all peace grew one,
Life opened clear, and Love? Love was its name!

So when the great word "Mother!" rang once more,
I saw at last its meaning and its place;
Not the blind passion of the brooding past,
But Mother—the World's Mother—come at last,
To love as she had never loved before—
To feed and guard and teach the human race.

The world was full of music clear and high!
The world was full of light! The world was free!
And I? Awake at last, in joy untold,
Saw Love and Duty broad as life unrolled—
Wide as the earth—unbounded as the sky—
Home was the World—the World was Home to me!

The Forerunner *Editorial, 1911*

. . . The need The Forerunner seeks to meet is not of a general and popular sort, but is no less real for all that; being the demand of a rather special group of people for clear expression of their rather special views.*

The main ground of appeal of this magazine, is the Near Sure Perfectly Possible Improvement of Life; offering to that end its quota of thought and feeling, its presentation in fact, fiction, fable, fancy, verse, and prose.

* From *The Forerunner*, 2 (1911), 28–29.

Its view upon the Woman Question is that which sees women as human beings, not merely struggling for freedom, privilege and power, but as heavily behind hand in their duty to the world; holding in their gift a mighty fund of Love and Service which we can no longer do without.

It sees in Socialism the natural evolution of our economic system; long since begun, now already introduced in many lines in varying degree, sure of ultimate adoption, and calling for the intelligent study and recognition of every conscientious citizen. . . .

Excerpt from The Crux, *1911*

[Vivian] sat with her shapely hands quiet in her lap while her grandmother's shining needles twinkled in the dark wool, and her mother's slim crochet hook ran along the widening spaces of some thin, white fuzzy thing.* The rich powers of her young womanhood longed for occupation, but she could never hypnotize herself with "fancy-work." Her work must be worth while. She felt the crushing cramp and lonliness [sic] of a young mind, really stronger than those about her, yet held in dumb subjection. She could not solace herself by loving them; her father would have none of it, and her mother had no use for what she called "sentiment." All her life Vivian had longed for more loving, both to give and take; but no one ever imagined it of her, she was so quiet and repressed in manner. The local opinion was that if a woman had a head, she could not have a heart; and as to having a body—it was indelicate to consider such a thing.

"I mean to have six children," Vivian had planned when she was younger. "And they shall never be hungry for more loving." She meant to make up, to her vaguely imagined future family, for all that her own youth missed. . . .

* From *The Forerunner,* 2 (1911), 45. *The Crux* is a serial story.

7 *The Founding of Mount Holyoke College*

Kathryn Kish Sklar

Portrait of Mary Lyon. Original in Mount Holyoke College Library.

The 1830s marked a turning point in many dimensions of American female experience. Especially important were the changes the decade witnessed in women's education, epitomized by the founding of Mount Holyoke Female Seminary in South Hadley, Massachusetts, in 1837. Even before the seminary opened its doors, its founder, Mary Lyon, predicted that it would inaugurate "an era in female education." "The work will not stop with this institution," she told a friend shortly after the ceremonial placement of the building's cornerstone, and subsequent years proved the accuracy of her statement.[1] Mount Holyoke, innovative among female educational institutions because of its solid financial base, its commitment to instructing girls drawn from all economic levels, and its advanced curriculum, served as a model for many women's colleges founded later in the century. Accordingly, an examination of the circumstances surrounding its inception can reveal the impulses behind the significant advances made in female education during the antebellum period.

To some degree Mary Lyon's successful attempt to establish an institution of higher learning for women in 1837 was unique in the annals of female education in the nineteenth century. Her institution was designed for and funded by families of average wealth, unlike the seminaries that preceded it in the 1820s—such as Emma Willard's in Troy, New York, or Catharine Beecher's in Hartford, Connecticut— and unlike the colleges such as Vassar, Smith, and Wellesley, that followed it in the last third of the nineteenth century, which were designed for and funded by a wealthier constituency. Mount Holyoke was nevertheless a logical product of its time and place and of a founder whose own personal experience was replicated to some extent in the lives of many of her less-distinguished female contemporaries.

Mary Lyon: The Early Years

Born in 1797 in Buckland, Massachusetts, Mary Lyon was raised by her mother after her father died when she was only 5. Jemima Shepherd

[1] Unless otherwise indicated biographical information on Mary Lyon and quotations are from *The Power of Christian Benevolence Illustrated in the Life and Labors of Mary Lyon,* compiled by Edward Hitchcock, D.D., LL.D., President of Amherst College; with the assistance of others, 9th ed., Hopkins, Bridgman, Northampton, 1851. For descriptions of institutions modeled on Mount Holyoke, see Sarah D. (Locke) Stow, *History of Mount Holyoke Seminary, South Hadley, Mass. During its First Half Century,* 1837–1887, Mount Holyoke Seminary, Springfield, 1887, pp. 327–347. The only scholarly biography of Mary Lyon is Elizabeth Alden Green's as yet unpublished "Life of Mary Lyon."

Portions of the research for this essay were supported by a Summer Stipend from the National Endowment for the Humanities, for which the author is grateful.

Lyon provided her daughter with a model of a woman who was a "presiding angel of good works" for the neighborhood, and in later years Mary called her "that dearest friend of my young heart." Certainly her father's death drew the girl closer to her mother, and her relationship with this "dearest friend" could well have been the source of her lifelong respect for and loyalty to her sex.

But the death of her father had another important effect on the shape of Mary Lyon's life: As a widow, Jemima Lyon had few financial resources, so her daughter was forced to contribute to her own support at an early age. In 1814, when she was 17 years old, Mary Lyon started her career as an educator by contracting to teach in a town school in nearby Shelburne during the summer months. Her pay was 75 cents a week, plus the board and room she received by "boarding round" with Shelburne families, who were in turn reimbursed for their expenses by the town selectmen.

FEMALE EDUCATION IN NEW ENGLAND, 1760–1840

In choosing to make her living by teaching, Mary Lyon was following in the footsteps of many other young New England women of her generation. But employment in the town schools had only recently become an occupation open to females. Before 1780 most publicly supported schools in Massachusetts towns had been attended exclusively by boys and were taught solely by men. Even though state education laws required all towns to maintain district schools to teach "children" reading, writing, and arithmetic, girls were usually denied access to these institutions, just as they were automatically excluded from the grammar schools (also town supported), which trained college-bound boys in Latin and Greek.

Thus, colonial parents who wanted their daughters to learn to read, write, and cipher had to pay for that privilege, sending them first to the dame schools that were also attended by younger boys, and then perhaps to a local female academy that offered instruction in music, fancy needlework, and dancing. The women who ran these schools, generally in their own homes, lacked any sort of special training for the task; they combined occasional instruction with other domestic duties in order to support themselves and their families.

Given the erratic nature of this education, it is not surprising that Kenneth Lockridge, who has investigated literacy patterns in prerevolutionary New England, has estimated the literacy rate of women there to be only half that of men (about 45 percent of women as opposed to 90 percent of men). But by the time Mary Lyon began to teach, this discriminatory pattern had been seriously eroded, if not completely eliminated. The federal census of 1850, which first measured literacy by sex, registered equal and universal literacy skills among white native-born New England men and women. Because such skills were acquired early in life, and because the population of 1850 included a sizable number of women who grew up between 1780 and 1820, it is obvious that a substantial improvement in female education occurred during those decades.

Although by approximately 1810 girls were accepted in town schools throughout Massachusetts (Mary Lyon attended a Buckland school in 1803), the process by which they were included varied considerably. One of the leaders in opening district schools to girls was Sutton, a relatively poor agricultural community in Worcester County, which as early as 1767 paid women teachers to run summer sessions for local girls.

Interestingly, Sutton violated state law by not supporting a grammar school until the 1790s, even though it had established a system of 14 district schools by the 1770s. This suggests that one factor in Sutton's commitment to the basic education of its daughters was its concomitant lack of interest in producing a well-educated male elite. By 1773 the selectmen of Sutton were already devoting half of their education appropriations to the instruction of girls—a proportion that continued throughout the rest of the century—and it is clear that the town fathers preferred to have all their children learn the rudiments rather than to concentrate their resources on the training of a few boys in Latin and Greek.

This trade-off between the basic instruction of all children and the advanced education of a small number of male youths is apparent when Sutton's actions are contrasted to those of Northampton, a commercial town in the Connecticut Valley located near South Hadley and the eventual site of Mount Holyoke Seminary. In 1800 the selectmen of Northampton spent as much to support one grammar schoolmaster as the leaders of Sutton spent year round on seven district schools, and as late as 1788 these selectmen voted explicitly "not to be at any expense for schooling girls."

In 1792 an outlying district of Northampton finally obtained the selectmen's permission to include girls in a coeducational summer session taught by a man, but not until several of the town's citizens won a ruling from the Massachusetts attorney general that "girls had rights and could not be excluded from school" did the selectmen begin to consider altering their policy. They implemented the change slowly and reluctantly, being prodded by a town committee's recommendation in 1801 that women be employed to teach girls. Only in 1810, however, were the committee's suggestions for the systematic employment of female teachers fully effectuated.

Mary Lyon and other women hired by town selectmen to teach in public schools between 1780 and 1820 differed markedly from their predecessors, the proprietors of dame schools, in two important ways. Whereas teaching in dame schools was a female occupation governed by custom, teaching in town schoolhouses meant entering a male occupation governed by state regulations that applied equally to both sexes. The first systematic revision of state school laws after the Revolution, in 1789, was also the first to mention schoolmistresses along with schoolmasters. That law required that teachers of either sex be certified as competent before being employed, and specified the ways public funds were to be raised for their salaries. Their positions of public authority gave young schoolmistresses a new kind of prestige in their communities. As one woman who taught in a district school in this period put it, "she who could preside with dignity in the school room commanded respect elsewhere." [2]

Also, whereas women of all ages taught in home dame schools, the vast majority of those who taught in town schoolhouses were young and unmarried. Most were between the ages of 16 and 23, the average age at marriage, and turnover was high among them. Because women could be paid significantly less than men—perhaps one-half or even one-third the salary of a male schoolmaster—town selectmen increasingly hired females. By 1837 Massachusetts district schools employed three women for every two men, and by 1850 there were two women for every man employed. As a result of high turnover rates and the widespread employment of women, it has recently been estimated that by 1837 one of every five native-born white Massachusetts women had taught school at some point during her life, whereas the equivalent male proportion was one in seven.[3]

Most of Mary Lyon's female contemporaries went no further than sporadic district school teaching. But in 1817, after three summers of teaching at that level and as many winters of instructing children in private families, she entered the coeducational Sanderson Academy in Ashfield "resolved," according to her biographer Edward Hitchcock, "to prepare herself particularly for teaching." She paid the tuition of two shillings a week with savings from her previous jobs and by doing spinning and weaving for local families.

The academy, located less than five miles from Mary Lyon's birthplace, had been founded in 1816 by Alvan Sanderson, the town's Congregational minister. It was one of a number of private academies that

[2] Massachusetts school laws for 1789 are in *Massachusetts Perpetual Laws*, Thomas & Andrews, Boston, 1801, pp. 39–45; Anon., *Bessie or Reminiscences . . . by a Grandmother*, J. H. Benham, New Haven, 1861, p. 185.

[3] Thomas Woody, *A History of Women's Education in the United States*, Octagon, New York, 1974, I, 497; Richard M. Bernard and Maris A. Vinvoskis, "The Female School Teacher in Ante Bellum Massachusetts," *Journal of Social History*, 10 (March 1977), 333.

offered an equal education to men and women, emphasizing a practical curriculum and the study of natural philosophy (physics). Sanderson, like others of its type, neither provided training in such traditional female skills as sewing or music nor developed a specific vocational rationale for the education of women. Mary Lyon later described Sanderson as "the school where I was principally educated, and to which I feel in no small degree indebted." Certainly her later stress on an academic curriculum for women and her emphasis on the spiritual training of her charges can be traced in part to her experience at the academy.

Alvan Sanderson exemplified the vital links forged between church and school in this rocky and hilly hinterland west of the Connecticut River. Ashfield contained one of the largest Baptist communities in New England, and "awakened" or evangelical religion was especially strong there, imbuing all aspects of life with spiritual urgency. Mary Lyon's great-grandfather, Chileab Smith, had been a lay patriarch among Ashfield Baptists, "whose right to worship without taxation he had won in 1773 after a long struggle culminating in an appeal to London." [4] Jemima Lyon had raised her children in the Baptist faith, which meant that they were not baptized until after they had experienced personal religious conviction, or "conversion from their sins." The spiritual state of young children was therefore more than a nominal concern around Ashfield, and this concern prompted closer ties than usual between church and school.

These ties contained an unexploited potential for the advancement of female education. Ministers encouraged female teachers like Mary Lyon to exercise spiritual authority and leadership in their schools, transforming their task of instilling "virtue" in their pupils from a nominal to a vital responsibility, and viewing the training of female teachers as a sacred as well as a secular undertaking. When Mary Lyon was herself teaching at Sanderson a few years later, visiting ministers emphasized her spiritual responsibilities to the teachers she was training. As she described one visit:

After expressing a great interest in the school on account of its influence on society, and on account of its containing so many teachers for district schools the ensuing summer, he said that he had been anxious for its spiritual prosperity. He only said it, but it found a resting place in my heart, and there it has rested.

This religious aspect of teacher training accounted for the uniqueness in Mary Lyon's later fund raising, which succeeded in raising a new scale of funding for female higher education for a new middle-class constituency.

[4] Sidney R. MacLean, "Mary Lyon," in *Notable American Women, 1607–1950,* ed. Edward T. James et al., Harvard University Press, Cambridge, 1971, II, 443.

MARY LYON'S FUND-RAISING TECHNIQUES

We can see this uniqueness in fund-raising circulars Mary Lyon wrote between 1834 and 1836 for Mount Holyoke. These circulars made four basic points: like male colleges, the seminary was to be permanently endowed by the whole Christian community; like male colleges, it was designed to cultivate Christian activism in its students; like male colleges, it was designed to draw students from moderate circumstances as well as from wealthy families; and unlike male colleges, but parallel to their chief goal of training ministers, Mount Holyoke's primary function was to train female teachers.

Thus, Mary Lyon imitated the funding principles on which new male colleges, especially Amherst, were founded—widespread support "from liberal Christians in common life" who contributed because "the prospect was held out that it would be a college of high standing where the expenses would be low, and that it would be accessible to all." When "the Christian public" responded with 15,000 dollars in two years' time, Mary Lyon concluded: "I doubt whether any benevolent object, not excepting even the missionary cause has ever, within two years from its commencement, made a great advance in gaining access to the understanding and hearts of the people."

This initial endowment was nearly four times greater than the financial resources with which Willard and Beecher began their seminaries in the 1820s. Perhaps because they relied more heavily on tuition fees to meet their annual expenditures, many female seminaries were costlier than male colleges. As Reverend Mark Hopkins, President of Williams College, said in 1840: "In some cases the expense of sustaining a young lady in school for a year was more than double what was required to give a young man the advantages of a college course." [5]

Mary Lyon succeeded in obtaining a new scale of funding, which freed her from placing the burden of profit or of institutional development on tuition fees. Costs at Mount Holyoke were one-third those paid by students at Willard's Troy Female Seminary. Lyon's new scale of funding therefore significantly benefited "the adult female youth in the common walks of life."

How did she do it? In this essay we view three factors that contributed to her success: the ideological and religious example of Reverend Joseph Emerson; the partnership she formed with Emerson's assistant, Zilpah Grant; and the loyalty she retained to her social and economic origins. Emerson's example provided her with theoretical and behavioral

---

[5] Stow, *History of Mount Holyoke*, p. 9. See Alma Lutz, *Emma Willard, Daughter of Democracy*, Houghton Mifflin, Boston, 1929, p. 89 for Willard's estimate that a year's study at Troy cost 200 dollars in the 1820s. All italics in this essay appear in the original quotation.

connections between evangelical religion and female teachers; Grant's assistance provided her with fund-raising experience; and her adherence to her origins made it possible for her to exploit an untapped source of support for higher female education—the same popular roots that had nourished change in female primary education before 1820.

Before enrolling at Emerson's Ladies Seminary in 1821 Lyon contributed to her support by "weaving heavy blue and white coverlets, a kind of work requiring strength equal to that of a man and therefore commanding more pay than common labor." After a harrowing three-day journey with a close friend from Ashfield and her father in their family carriage, the two young women joined others from nearby Boston and from towns throughout New England.

The Influence of Awakened Religion

Reverend Joseph Emerson had been dismissed from his pastoral labors by his Beverly congregation in 1816 due to ill health, but his insistence on religious conversion as a criterion for church membership, which was opposed by his more decorous parish, probably also contributed to his dismissal. The seminary he established in nearby Byfield infused vocational training for female teachers with the experiential and ideological power of awakened religion. His efforts were reinforced by the able assistance of his wife, Rebecca Hasseltine, sister of New England's first missionary heroine and martyr, Nancy Hasseltine Judson, and with the help of Abigail Hasseltine, "preceptress" for many years at Bradford Academy.

In the 1820s Joseph Emerson was one of the strongest supporters of and advocates for female teachers. As his biographer and brother, Ralph Emerson, wrote:

He was born for the very work of teaching and especially of teaching females. His specific object now was, to render their education more solid and much more extensive. . . . His object was not merely to have a good seminary of his own, but also to benefit other teachers, and to raise up a multitude more, of the right stamp, and ultimately to fill the land with such seminaries and schools.

At Emerson's school all learned "an increased sense of the responsibility of the maternal relation," and in keeping with this emphasis, turned their attention "from the fancy work of the fingers to the great subjects of thought in science and religion." But the seminary's main purpose was to benefit female teachers.[6]

[6] Rev. Ralph Emerson, *Life of Rev. Joseph Emerson, Pastor of the Third Congregational Church in Beverly, Mass. and Subsequently Principal of a Female Seminary,* Crocker and Brewster, Boston, 1834, pp. 248 and 431.

Like Willard and Beecher, Emerson advocated a reorientation of female higher education away from the development of leisured skills (such as instrumental music or fancy sewing) designed to polish the rudiments of home learning. These skills, in Willard's words, merely fit women "for displaying to advantage the charms of youth and beauty," and prepared "them to please the other [sex]." [7] Whereas higher education had formerly prepared young women for the marriage market and had focused on skills useful in establishing a husband-wife relationship, these innovators in the 1820s found a new rationale for female education in the mother-child relationship and its vocational equivalent—the female schoolteacher.

In her *Plan for Improving Female Education,* presented to the New York legislature in 1819, Emma Willard argued that female seminaries deserved the support of public funds because:

properly fitted by instruction, women would be likely to teach children better than the other sex; they could afford to do it cheaper; and those men who would otherwise be engaged in this employment, might be at liberty to add to the wealth of the nation, by any of those thousand occupations, from which women are necessarily debarred.[8]

Willard's argument did not succeed in gaining the financial support of the New York State Legislature for female seminaries, but it did represent the strongest grounds on which to base such an appeal.

In his 1822 *Discourse on Female Education* Joseph Emerson echoed Willard's view that more women should join men in "the business of teaching," because "their instructions are at once more excellent and less expensive." To this economic argument, however, Emerson added the buttresses of evangelical religion. Endowing the vocation of teaching with sacred agency, he said that teachers could "do more to enlighten and reform the world and introduce the millennium than persons of any other profession except the ministers of Christ," and he believed that females were as good as if not better than males in this redemptive work. Calling for improvements in female education commensurate with female responsibilities, Emerson urged that "something must be *done* in order that females may attain that dignified and elevated rank in society for which the God of nature, as well as the Bible, has manifestly designed them." In conclusion Emerson pointed to two hopeful portents of positive change in the immediate future: benevolent activism among mature women, and the desire among average women for improved education.

---

7 Woody, *Women's Education,* I, 345.

8 Emma Willard, *An Address to the Public Particularly to the Members of the Legislature of New York, Proposing a Plan for Improving Female Education,* J. W. Copeland, Middlebury, Vt., 1819.

Emerson praised female benevolent activity in general and declared:

As woman was the first in the transgression, so she appears to have been most active to deliver the world from the dreadful effects of her horrid apostasy. . . . The numerous and noble institutions that so distinguish and bless the present day have been greatly promoted by female exertions. They have been urged forward by female hands, by female tongues, by female prayers.

Praising female support of education and the American Education Society in particular, he quoted from a recent report of that society, which was founded in 1815 to meet the rising demand for charitable support among the growing numbers of indigent young men preparing for the ministry at college.

The Female Auxiliary Education Society of Salem and Vicinity, has been perseveringly engaged five years, and has contributed $695.03. The Contributions of the last year exceed those of any preceding year. The Female Auxiliary Society of Boston and Vicinity has in three years contributed to the funds $1,119.32. The Graham Society of Boston from Jan. 1817 to Jan. 1821, have aided 42 beneficiaries of the American Education Society, in articles of clothing to the amount of $626.27. . . . Of fifty-eight societies which are auxiliary to this, thirty-one are composed of females.

Educational auxiliaries, one of the most common forms of female benevolent activity, were described by Lucy Stone, later an important abolitionist and suffragist, and a member of such an auxiliary in West Brookfield when Mary Lyon spoke to it in 1837:

Little sewing circles were formed where rich and poor women met to sew, either for a fair to raise money or for garments to be given directly to the young men whom the education societies aided. "Help educate young men! Help educate young men for ministers and for missionaries!" was the constant appeal made to women. Was it a wonder that as young women drew the needle they also drew the conclusion that if education was so necessary for men it must be valuable for women who were to stay at home? [9]

In 1822 Joseph Emerson did not call on women to channel their fund raising into the support of female education. During the next 15 years, however, female benevolent associations grew in numbers and in experience, making them ripe for Mary Lyon's appeal.

[9] Elinor Rice Hays, *Morning Star, A Biography of Lucy Stone, 1818–1893*, Harcourt, Brace & World, New York, 1961, p. 26.

Between 1776 and 1811, religious institutions ceased to be supported by taxes levied on all households regardless of their church attendance, and came instead to rely on voluntary contributions. Partly in response to this "disestablishment," an increasing number of churches and ministers revived the seventeenth-century emphasis on the church as a voluntary community whose membership was defined not only on the basis of geography, but also on the ability of each prospective communicant to experience a spiritual rebirth, the authenticity of which might be examined by the minister, deacons, or entire congregation. During the "Great Revival" of 1800 to 1840, the social and economic power of an awakened laity compensated for the withdrawal of state support and transformed female church members, who had since 1660 constituted a numerical majority within most churches, into an active agency for the redemption of the world.

Between 1810 and 1840 the numbers and size of New England female religious, charitable, or reform associations grew dramatically. At the peak of the Great Revival in the 1830s a significant proportion—at least one-third and probably a majority—of adult women were members of one or more such associations. The records of the Grafton Female Moral Reform Society, near Sutton, listed approximately one-third of the town's adult women as members between 1838 and 1840. This coalescing of the female religious laity into a variety of voluntary associations usually began under the nominal leadership of the minister, but frequently (as in the case of Female Moral Reform Societies) they developed into legally autonomous female corporations.

In such organizations single women often acted as treasurers, because married women could not hold and transfer money or engage in legal contracts. Although legally disabled upon marriage, around 1810 mature women, in combination with a few single or widowed women and in alliance with the church, began to exercise a new kind of collective power within their communities. During this period the American Education Society and its female auxiliaries also grew at a rapid pace. In a recent study David F. Allmendinger has estimated that by 1838 the society supported one out of seven young men enrolled in New England colleges.

As Nancy F. Cott recently pointed out in *The Bonds of Womanhood: Woman's Sphere in New England, 1780–1835*, male associations formed during this period for a variety of political, civic, and professional goals as well as for religious or charitable purposes, but female associations were almost exclusively religious or charitable. One obvious reason for this distinction was the general exclusion of women from public life. Another reason can be found in the benefits women derived from such associations. Cott concluded that women supported religion faithfully because, "No other avenue of self-expression besides religion at once offered women social approbation, the encouragement of male leaders (ministers), and, most important, the community of their peers." At Emerson's Seminary Mary Lyon learned how this approbation, encouragement, and community could sustain the lives of young female teachers. She may also have realized that a connection could be made between the collective strength of organized female benevolence and the advancement of female education.

In addition to their "more excellent and less expensive" teaching as young women and their active enlistment in the cause of redemption as mature women, Emerson pointed to another hopeful sign for change in female education—the eagerness with which older women of average economic circumstances promoted their daughters' as well as their own schooling:

So many thousands of American mothers, impressed with the importance of knowledge which they do not possess, are willing to rise up early, to sit up late, to eat the bread of the most rigid economy, to exert themselves to the utmost, that their daughters may be favored with the means of improvement, very greatly superior to what they themselves had possessed; and that so many females are making such vigorous efforts, to enjoy and improve the means of their education, and are not ashamed to become fellow pupils with those who have not seen half so many summers themselves.

Encouragement of Female Education

Emerson put his prescriptions into practice by raising funds for students who received little or no economic support from their families. His public announcement for a "Course of Lectures on Astronomy" in Boston in 1819 stated that the proceeds:

are to be appropriated to the charitable purpose of aiding pious and indigent young ladies in obtaining an education, with a view to qualify themselves for the important business of teaching. There are few objects for which charity is solicited, which, in proportion to the expense, promises greater benefit to society.

His announcement noted that class inequities in education affected females in ways they did not affect males:

It is the happiness of the present age, that female education is much more attended to than it was in ages past. Indigent females, however, many of whom with the advantages of education, might embellish and improve society, are left without resource. They are destitute of various means of acquiring an education, which are possessed by the other sex; and the Education Society, it may be remarked, do nothing for females. This benevolent object, therefore . . . must commend itself, with peculiar claims to every friend to female improvement as well as to literature and religion.

At the end of his lecture series Emerson had "at least $350 to carry home to my poor scholars." [10]

As well as generating economic support for less wealthy students, Emerson promoted what might be called ego strength or psychological autonomy in his students through the conversion processes of evangelical religion. At the beginning of each term he invited those who "were professors of religion, or hoped they had been renewed by divine grace," to remain in the seminary hall during a recess period. Then he urged them to use their influence on their fellow pupils and announced a weekly prayer meeting to which the whole school was invited.

Mary Lyon described the results of Emerson's policy in a letter to her mother, saying, "an increasing anxiety for a revival in the seminary began to prevail," with those who already considered themselves saved laboring for the conversion of the others. This conversion process had two stages: a recognition of the obstacles within one's own heart to the Savior's "special presence and works," and the transcendence of those obstacles through complete "trust in God." Students learned to monitor their own spiritual progress and to receive assistance from their peers while they were "passing this critical period, this all important moment of their lives." Lyon and others were especially grateful for "the solemnity, affection, and tender solicitude" of Zilpah Grant, Emerson's assistant, who spoke at religious meetings "in the most interesting and affecting manner."

Peer solidarity developed in a context removed from normal family influences. "Imagine to yourself," Lyon wrote her mother, "a little circle of about forty females, almost excluded from the rest of the human family, all appearing as solemn as eternity." This solidarity was reinforced the night before their departure for home at the end of the school term, when, Lyon wrote, several "met at our chamber after school for prayer. We had an impressive season." Religion was the basis of a "community of feeling" among Emerson's students in which, one observer noted:

They were all led to drink into one and the same spirit; and to feel that they had a great work before them in life, and that they were to aid

[10] *Life of Joseph Emerson,* pp. 250–251.

*each other in this work. . . . This laid the foundation for a new and
kindred feeling of an exalted and permanent character.*

"We learned to consider each other as sisters," Zilpah Grant said,
"and this feeling did not cease with our connection with the school." [11]
The benefits of awakened religion were therefore threefold. Conversion,
or spiritual rebirth, promoted self-esteem in young women by giving
them the feeling "that they had a great work before them in life." It
promoted psychological autonomy by emphasizing God rather than
family as the organizing principle of personal identity. It promoted
solidarity among young women by encouraging them to express their
"affection and tender solicitude" for one another.

THE CREATION OF A NEW INSTITUTION

In his address on *Female Education* Emerson concluded "that the period
is not remote, when female institutions very greatly superior to the
present, will not only exist, but be considered as important as are now
our colleges for the education of our sons." But, he added, "Where such
an institution shall be erected, by whom it shall be founded, and by
whom instructed, is yet for the hands of Providence to develop."

In a manner that combined "the hands of Providence" with changing social and economic circumstances, Mary Lyon established during the
winters between 1824 and 1831 the prototype of an institution "as important as" male colleges. At Buckland, near Ashfield, this school combined
evangelical religion, prospective female teachers, and class consciousness
in ways that earned extensive popular support and established the basis
for her funding appeals of 1835 to 1837.

It was there Lyon first conceived of "a seminary which should be
so moderate in its expenses as to be open to the daughters of farmers
and artisans, and to teachers who might be mainly dependent for their
support on their own exertions." Between 1824 and her decision in 1834
to devote herself to full-time fund raising for an endowed institution of
her own design, however, Lyon's loyalties and energies were divided
between her work at Buckland and the professional alliance she formed
at Byfield with Zilpah ("Polly") Grant.

Polly Grant grew up in northwestern Connecticut in circumstances
very similar to those Mary Lyon had known around Ashfield. Grant's
father died in 1796 when she was 2 years old, and her widowed mother
(also named Zilpah) raised five children on their small and isolated farm.
But there was one salient difference between Lyon and Grant; Grant's

[11] *Life of Joseph Emerson*, p. 425.

mother committed suicide soon after her remarriage in 1820. From 1821 until her retirement and subsequent marriage around 1840, Zilpah Grant suffered long periods of emotional and physical collapse. Her partnership with Lyon dissolved in 1833, after they tried and failed to secure financial support from wealthy benefactors for an "Emersonian" approach to female education.[12]

Their first joint venture between 1824 and 1827 at Adams Academy in Londonderry, New Hampshire, was a telling prediction for the future. Adams began as a coeducational academy with an endowment from a wealthy benefactor of 5,000 dollars. But after a bequest of 4,000 dollars by a "single gentleman" for the female department only, it reincorporated on a new basis in 1823 and became one of the first institutions endowed exclusively for girls. Grant agreed to manage the school on the condition that "one seventh of the study time should be devoted to the Bible," and "there was to be special instruction for those who wished to become teachers." She and Lyon eliminated "ornamental branches" of study, emphasized "solid training," and promoted "guidance and control of the heart" through religious awakening and commitment. "The plan may be called *Emersonian,* though considerably altered to meet our particular purpose," Lyon wrote.

In 1824 theirs was the first female academy to issue diplomas or a "testimonial of approbation" to those who had completed a full course of study. Their spiritual leadership was much in evidence. Lyon, who had recently joined the Congregational church, wrote her sister, Freelove: "We believe the Holy Spirit is now with us by his special operations. It is now a very critical period." They also recruited the older generation in this effort, asking "several mothers who have daughters here to supplicate the influence of the Spirit on this institution every Wednesday morning between eight and nine oclock."

Using religion to gain the loyalty and support of mothers as well as daughters, Adams Academy might have marked "an era in female education" if its (male) trustees had not put a stop to these Emersonian methods by unilaterally announcing that "music and dancing" would be offered at the school in the future, and teachers would be selected "who will not attempt to instill into the minds of their pupils the peculiar tenets of any denomination of Christians, but will give that general instruction wherein all Christians agree." [13]

The evangelical movement was growing rapidly in New England churches in the 1820s, but all Christians did not agree that spiritual rebirth was a necessary part of a godly or moral life. Unitarians were first

[12] Sydney R. MacLean, "Zilpah Polly Grant," in *Notable American Women,* II, 73–75.
[13] Marion Lansing, ed., *Mary Lyon Through Her Letters,* Books, Inc., Boston, 1937, pp. 50, 65, 70–71.

among these, and most of Adams's trustees were adherents of this theo-
logically "liberal" and nonevangelical outgrowth of Congregationalism.
By reinstating music and dancing, the trustees endorsed genteel female
skills appropriate to the parlor or the sitting room. By substituting more
general ethical training for the psychological processes of conversion,
they lessened the degree to which pupils could "drink into one and the
same spirit; and feel that they had a great work before them in life."
Refusing to teach dancing on grounds that it would disrupt their schedule, Grant left for the newly incorporated Ipswich Female Seminary near
Boston, and Lyon returned to Buckland, where she cultivated more
intensely the winter school she had been developing since 1824.

The Buckland and Ipswich Schools

Buckland school began with 25 female pupils, doubled its size the next
year, grew to 74 when Lyon returned to it in 1828, and had an enrollment of 99 the next year. Its low tuition of 3 dollars a term was less than
half that charged at Ipswich Female Seminary, making it accessible to
"the daughters of farmers and artisans" and self-supporting teachers. Her
Buckland school

*became the resort of many who had been or expected to be teachers. The
celebrity of the school in that region was such, that to have attended it
one or more terms became a letter of recommendation to a candidate
for teaching. . . . Though the word had not yet found its way thither,
it was, to all interests and purposes, a* normal *school.*

Neighboring towns began to appoint school committeemen in the
fall instead of the spring in order to make their selections from pupils in
Mary Lyon's school. Local religious leaders were equally strong in their
endorsement, since "ministers in the sanctuary, when they prayed for
colleges, did not forget the school at Buckland." To the churches in the
vicinity the school became a "consecrated spot," and "in many a working
man's house, at many a family altar, that school was remembered with
earnest prayer and with pious gratitude," because "daughters who went
thither thoughtless and bent on pleasure, returned home serious, and
bent on doing good."

Some of them, however, would not return home. By 1820 parents
in this declining farming region were experiencing a massive loss of their
young, especially of their sons, through migration west. But unmarried
daughters were less free to seek their fortunes elsewhere. As Hitchcock
dramatized the conflict such departures entailed:

*Fathers, with trembling lips, would ask, "Why do you want to go away?
Is not your father's house a pleasant home to you? Is there anything you
do not have? Why do you wish to leave us?" The daughter pleaded that
a younger sister would be company, eyes and feet for her parents; that
she could be spared, and not much missed; that, in some other spot, she
might minister to the wants of young minds; and by such considerations
would win the father's consent to her departure.*

Thus, religious commitment allowed young women to resist the "family
claim" on their services and greatly facilitated their entrance into the
larger world of social service.

Mary Lyon's advice to students in 1832 showed how religious commitment also provided psychological assistance in such moments of risk-
taking and personal choice, allowing a young woman to take a first step,
even though she might not know where it would lead her.

*Take all the circumstances, and weight them candidly, taking the Bible
for your guide, and asking God to enlighten your mind. . . . You may
see but one step where you can place your foot; but take that, and another will then be discovered, and if you can see one step at a time, it
is all you ought to ask.*

This was good advice for a generation that faced new occupational
options. Religion supplied the means for young women to develop autonomous personal goals commensurate with their new economic ability to
support themselves away from home. "I would have all contented, wherever Providence may place them," Mary Lyon said in 1829, "whether
or not they may be favored with the society of father or mother, brother
or sister."

Such migration-assisting religious advice became even more important in Mary Lyon's teaching after 1830, when she left Buckland to
work with Zilpah Grant at Ipswich Female Seminary. About 20 of her
Buckland students went with her. Ipswich attracted students from greater
distances and propelled them further, as missionaries and teachers. There
she and Grant engaged in extensive fund raising, building Ipswich into
one of the leading female seminaries in the country. They employed
Emersonian principles, concentrating on training female teachers and
supplying them with religious commitment.

Like Emerson's school, theirs lacked a rent-free structure, and students were scattered in neighboring homes rather than boarding together
as a collective unit. But Grant and Lyon saw collective living as essential

to their character-building and academic goals. In the words of their first fund-raising circular: "The whole should resemble a well-regulated voluntary association." They first sought funds for "a seminary building" and "a boardinghouse . . . for one-hundred and fifty boarders," but due partly to apathy among the prospective trustees and partly to illness affecting Grant, this effort collapsed in 1831. Subsequently they designed an ambitious new institution, the New England Female Seminary for Teachers, which closely resembled Willard's proposal of 1818 except that it appealed to private sources of funding among "friends of education and of evangelical religion" rather than the state legislature.

When this proposal also failed, one prospective trustee concluded: "I must confess that the best men in the community do not favor our plan of a female seminary as much as I anticipated." Mary Lyon's analysis of their failure was perceptive. She concluded that "the attention of the community" could not be gained on the purely educational grounds they had used to argue for "the superior literary and scientific advantages of a permanent school." Rather, "some peculiar and tangible feature, addressing itself to the feelings and perceptions of the middling classes of society, must be used as a lever for moving public opinion and obtaining the needed funds."

Realizing that her own creative energy was best expressed in class as well as religious terms, Mary Lyon wrote to Hannah White, her assistant at Buckland:

During the past year, my heart has so yearned over the adult female youth in the common walks of life, that it has sometimes seemed as though a fire were shut up in my bones. I should esteem it a greater favor to labor in this field than in any other on which I have ever fastened my attention.

Recognizing that Zilpah Grant's preference for a life-style that transcended her own social origins prevented her from joining Lyon in such a field, Lyon wrote Grant in 1833: "If I should separate from you, I have no definite plan. But my thoughts, feelings, and judgment are turned toward the middle classes of society. For this class I want to labor, and for this class I consider myself rather peculiarly fitted to labor."

Believing that the cultural institutions of religion were the best means of reaching this class, she wrote Grant: "If the institution is ever founded, it will be safe only in the hand of God, and under God, in the arms of the whole benevolent community, including not only the rich, but the poor." Lyon adopted the "peculiar and tangible feature" of religious sponsorship in her independent fund raising after 1833. This allowed her to combine two powerful support systems reaching deep into the "middling classes" of New England life—the ministry and the female evangelical associations. Although the former provided her with endorsements and protection, she relied on women to generate most of her funds.

FUND RAISING FOR MOUNT HOLYOKE

"Skilled in the art of dealing with the 'gentlemen,'" in September 1834 Lyon selected trustees who endorsed the religious and class principles of her fund-raising efforts, and protected her from "fear of the effect on society of so much female influence, and what some will call female greatness." One trustee, Reverend Theophilus Packard of Shelburne, had four months earlier gained the official endorsement of the Association of Ministers in both Franklin and Hampshire counties for the establishment of an endowed female seminary under Mary Lyon's direction. Packard's daughter, Louisa, had been a student and assistant teacher at Lyon's Buckland school.

Powerful male supporters like Amherst's Edward Hitchcock defended her fund-raising efforts against religious conservatives, who attacked her educational qualifications, her right to identify her cause with the church, and her masculine style.[14] In her defense Hitchcock spoke for the religious constituency to which Mary Lyon appealed, saying:

Let the Ipswich and Mount Holyoke Seminaries be blest, as Amherst has been, with revivals of religion every year, nay almost every term, and they may be sure, however they may be sneered at and ridiculed by [some] individuals, that they stand fast in the affections, and may rely upon the pecuniary support, of the greater part of the religious community.

And he spoke for the economic constituency for which she labored, asking:

Is it no honor for females to make efforts and sacrifices of a masculine character, that they may elevate the literary and religious condition of their sex, especially of those who for want of pecuniary means have been unable to enjoy the best opportunities?

Half of Lyon's trustees were enthusiastic supporters from her home region, and half were prestigious and nominal eastern supporters who

14"Paterfamilias" to the Editor of *Boston Religious Magazine*. Ms. Mount Holyoke College Library: College History and Archives Collection. A covering letter by Edward Hitchcock shows this to have been written by him in June 1837. Mary Lyon chose not to submit the letter for publication, but Hitchcock must have made the same arguments orally.

had been associated with fund raising for Ipswich. Therefore, Lyon could recruit funds from both regions. She began, however, not with wealthier or influential gentlemen, but with "the ladies of Ipswich."

Because students at Ipswich Female Seminary "had been accustomed, once or twice a year," to contribute to local benevolent societies, Lyon's appeal "exclusively to ladies" for 1,000 dollars in seed money fell on fertile ground. Calling for "a separate and independent institution, similar in character to the Ipswich Seminary," but "founded and sustained by the Christian public" and expenses "reduced one third or one half," she "held before them the object dear to her heart—the bringing of a liberal education within the means of the daughters of the common people, till it loomed up to them, for the time, as it did before her eyes."

Walking from door to door in Ipswich, Lyon "told the husbands, in a very good-natured but earnest way, that she had come to get them to cut off one little corner of their estates, and give it to their wives to invest in the form of a seminary for the daughters of the common people." The result was that "Ladies who in ordinary subscriptions, to benevolent objects, did well to put down their fifty-cents, gave her five or ten dollars of hard-earned money, collected by the slow gains of patient industry." Lyon subsequently distributed a large number of circulars through her male support-system, such as the packet she sent Thomas White in Ashfield saying, "I do wish our farmers would look at this and see what can be done." But women remained the central focus of her fund-raising campaign of 1835–1837.

Finding her bodily presence more powerful than her letters, "she went to many towns and met the ladies, to inspire them with zeal for the work," and "with her impassioned eloquence, she stirred up the spirit of emulation by holding up the example of the Ipswich ladies."

As Lucy Stone described the effect of Lyon's appeal on her sewing circle:

Those who had sewed and spent time, strength and money to help educate young men, dropped the needle and toil and said "Let these men with broader shoulders and stronger arms earn their own education, while we use our scantier opportunities to educate ourselves." [15]

Relying on organizations like sewing circles or on individual local women, such as Mrs. Abby Allen in South Hadley, a former teacher and "the acknowledged leader in all benevolent enterprises," to organize local donations, Lyon described her seminary as "another stone in the foundation of our great system of benevolent operations." By transcend-

[15] Hays, *Lucy Stone*, p. 26.

ing local boundaries, this system made possible a new scale of funding for female education. As Lyon declared in a printed letter addressed to "Dear Madame" soon after the cornerstone was dedicated, "hundreds of individuals in more than sixty different towns" had proved untrue "the principle so long acted upon that Christians are not required to contribute for the building up of any female seminary, unless it be established in their own town!"

Grass-roots financial support within the "Christian community" meant, she said, that "it will no longer be doubted whether the work of supplying our country with well qualified female teachers shall be allowed a standing among the benevolent operations of the day." Less than three months later, in January 1837, her contributors had increased to more than 1,800 individuals in 90 towns, who pledged 27,000 dollars in addition to South Hadley's 8,000 dollars and Ipswich's 1,000 dollars.

To critics who thought her aggressive fund raising was unseemly in a woman, Lyon said:

What do I do that is wrong? . . . I ride in the stage coach or cars without an escort. Other ladies do the same. I visit a family where I have been previously invited, and the minister's wife, or some leading woman, calls the ladies together to see me, and I lay our object before them. Is that wrong? . . . If there is no harm in doing these things once, what harm is there in doing them twice, thrice, or a dozen times? My heart is sick, my soul is pained with this empty gentility, this genteel nothingness. I am doing a great work. I cannot come down.

When questioned as to the motives of women who donated "under her persevering eloquence and prolonged urgency," she would reply: " 'Get the money,' closing her hand to suit the action to the word, 'Get the money; the money will do good.' "

By December 1841, a new wing had been added to the original building and more than 50,000 dollars had been raised and expended for the seminary. By the time Lyon died in 1849, Mount Holyoke annually trained more female teachers than any other institution, including the three state normal schools established by the Massachusetts Board of Education in 1839 to 1840 through an allocation of 20,000 dollars, half of which came from a private donor. As of 1851 the seminary had received donations worth 70,300 dollars. Until 1853 tuition and boarding fees at Mount Holyoke were 60 dollars a year.

The significant change and innovation that Mount Holyoke promised at its founding seems to have been amply fulfilled in practice after 1837. At least three-quarters of its students during the seminary's first 50 years became teachers. By the 1840s the missionary movement was as strong there as it was among their brothers at Amherst or Yale. Because they were systematically recruited for such partnerships by spiritually ambitious young men in about a dozen New England colleges, and because missionary organizations denied sponsorship to single women, many found higher callings in foreign fields as wives of missionaries.

Mount Holyoke's curriculum matched this seriousness of purpose. Latin, the language of the church, was ambitiously emphasized in the curriculum and was required for admission by 1847. Science classes were frequently taught by Professor Hitchcock, who gave lectures on human anatomy in the 1840s illustrated by the most advanced equipment, including a manikin with detachable organs. David F. Allmendinger is currently studying the social origins of early Mount Holyoke students and has estimated that they closely resembled the class composition of contemporary male colleges, in which approximately one-third were to some degree self-supporting, or came from families who could not afford to pay all or part of their expenses.[17]

Historians have generally assumed that the ideological context in which female institutions first achieved collegiate parity with male colleges was the secular or scientific milieu of the last third of the nineteenth century, when Vassar, Smith, and Wellesley were founded. By the time these institutions were founded college students of both sexes, probably including those at Mount Holyoke, were drawn almost exclusively from wealthy or professional families, and historians have generally assumed that funding for the first significant advance in female education came primarily from wealthy sources. But Mount Holyoke's early history requires us to re-examine these assumptions, since it was established at the height of the greatest religious revival in American history, and initiated a "new era in female education" for "the adult female youth in the common walks of life."

Documents

To the Friends of Christian Education, 1835

After much deliberation, prayer, and correspondence, the friends of the Redeemer have determined to erect a school for the daughters of the church, the object of which shall be to fit them for the highest degree of usefulness.* The

---

17 Woody, *Women's Education*, I, 361; *Louise Porter Thomas, Seminary Militant: An Account of the Missionary Movement at Mount Holyoke Seminary and College*, Mt. Holyoke College, South Hadley, 1937; MacLean, "Mary Lyon," in *Notable American Women*, II, 443–447; David F. Allmendinger, Jr., "The Social Origins of Early Mount Holyoke Students," paper delivered at Mount Holyoke College, January 1976. I am grateful to Professor Allmendinger for permission to refer to this research in progress.
* Reprinted from Edward Hitchcock, *The Power of Christian Benevolence Illustrated*

justly celebrated school at Ipswich embraces the principal features which we wish this to possess. We will state the outlines of our plan.

1. The seminary is designed to be permanent; to be under the guardianship of those who are awake to all the interests of the church. It will not, under God, depend upon the health or the life of a particular teacher, but, like our colleges, be a permanent blessing to our children, and to our children's children.

2. It is to be based entirely on Christian principles; and while it is to be furnished with teachers of the highest character and experience, and to have every advantage which the state of female education in this country will allow, its brightest feature will be, that it is a school for Christ.

3. It is located at South Hadley, Massachusetts, on the banks of the Connecticut, at the foot of Mount Holyoke, in the centre of New England, easy of access from all quarters, and amid the most lovely scenery. In selecting the location, the committee had in view centrality, retirement, and economy, morality, and natural scenery.

4. The buildings are to be adequate to receive and board two hundred young ladies.

5. It is designed to cultivate the missionary spirit among its pupils; the feeling that they should live for God, and do something as teachers, or in such other ways as Providence may direct.

6. The seminary is to have a library and apparatus equal to its wants; to have its internal arrangements such that its pupils may continue to practise such habits of domestic economy as are appropriate to the sex, and without which all other parts of education are purchased at too dear a rate.

7. The seminary is to be placed on such a foundation by the Christian public, if they sustain our views, that all the advantages of the institution may be afforded so low, as to be within the reach of those who are in the middle walks of life. Indeed, it is for this class principally, who are the bone and sinew and the glory of our nation, that we have engaged in this undertaking. The wealthy can provide for themselves; and though we expect to offer advantages which even they cannot now command, yet it is not for their sakes that we erect this Christian seminary, and thus ask the funds of the church. In regard to this, we hope and expect that it will be like our colleges, so valuable that the rich will be glad to avail themselves of its benefits, and so economical that people in very moderate circumstances may be equally and as fully accommodated. We expect that distinctions founded on such incidental circumstances as wealth will not find a place within its walls, any more than they do at the table of Jesus Christ.

8. In order to establish such a seminary, the committee believe that the Christian public must be invited to contribute a sum not less than thirty thou-

in the Life and Labors of Mary Lyon, Hopkins, Bridgman, 9th ed., Northampton, Mass., 1851, pp. 212–213. This circular was written by three trustees, the Reverends John Todd, Joseph Penney, and Roswell Hawks, from material supplied by Mary Lyon about her prospective seminary.

sand dollars. While every thing is to be done on a scale as economical as possible, yet the committee feel that the materials and work should all be the first of their kind. Of this sum, the village of South Hadley has contributed eight thousand dollars, which, with the subscriptions of the few who, in addition, have been invited to contribute, makes the sum already raised about one third of the amount specified.

Letter from Mary Lyon, 1836

Dear Madame,

. . . The time has now come when we must make our arrangements for furniture.* For this we must depend principally on ladies. We have no doubt but the call will be promptly met. In all our progress, ladies have been prompt to do all that we have asked. . . .

. . . [W]ould not the ladies in your place consider it a privilege to furnish one of these chambers? Would you not consider it a privilege to bring the subject before them so fairly, that they will do it with promptness?

Among the means essential to the safety of the nation, many are convinced of the necessity of urging into the field a multitude of benevolent, self-denying female teachers. Many of the most candid and discriminating, who have the advantage of observation on the subject, are convinced that all other means without this will be insufficient. Fill the country with ministers, and they could no more conquer the whole land and secure their victories, without the aid of many times their number of self-denying female teachers, than the latter could complete the work without the former. But what can be done? . . .

This work of supplying teachers is a great work, and it must be done, or our country is lost, and the world will remain unconverted. If we begin, we must go on; the more we do, the more we must do. The more we attempt to supply, in this particular, the wants of our country, the more its wants will be made manifest. What instrumentality shall ever meet this demand? Why is it, that so much should have been seen, and acknowledged, and felt on this subject, without an attempt to apply the sovereign remedy, which has been so successfully applied to every other want? It has seemed that the church had been fully convinced, that there was but one grand means of meeting any great public demand of the Redeemer's kingdom—a union of disinterested labors and contributions is the grand means. When the church early felt her need of the services of young men, she began to found colleges; and as the demand for their services increased, and became more manifest, she went on founding colleges,

* Reprinted from Edward Hitchcock, *The Power of Christian Benevolence Illustrated in the Life and Labors of Mary Lyon,* Hopkins, Bridgman, 9th ed., Northampton, Mass., 1851, pp. 232–235. Excerpt of October 1836 letter.

till more than eighty have been reared in our country, and more than thirty theological seminaries. But this was found to be not sufficient, and the American Education Society came into existence, and has been going forward with an increasing magnificence and glory, scarcely equalled, except by the importance of its object. All these are so many public voices from the church, calling upon young men, and entreating them to enlist in her service. But what has been the voice of the church to female teachers? Has it not been, *"We need not your services: go on to serve yourselves—to serve the children of this world—to serve the mammon of unrighteousness. We can save our country, and convert the world without your aid."*

Selected Massachusetts Township Boundaries, c. 1818

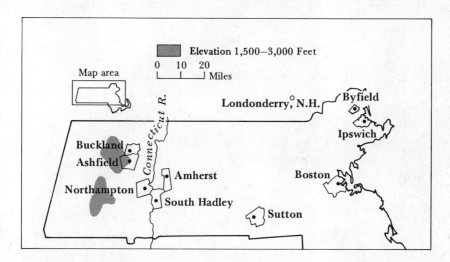

8 *And We Are Nothing but Women: Irish Working Women in Troy*

Carole Turbin

Woman Ironing by Edgar Degas. Courtesy of the National Gallery of Art, Washington, D.C., Collection of Mr. and Mrs. Paul Mellon.

*You know what a union is . . . you know full well the value
of cooperation; we have been out of money six weeks and but two
of our number have given in. I fancy but there are few men's
organizations that can show such a record, and we are nothing
but women.*

> Esther Keegan, Vice President of the Collar Laundry
> Union of Troy, New York, to the Workingmen's Union
> of New York City, July 2, 1869. (New York World,
> July 3, 1869).

A REMARKABLY SUCCESSFUL WOMEN'S TRADE UNION

It has often been observed that women's labor activity in the United States
in the mid-nineteenth century was sporadic, short-lived, and unsuccessful.
As dependents whose proper sphere was fireside and nursery, working
women's role in the labor force was incompatible with the conditions
necessary for permanent trade union organization. Women did not devote
time and money to union activity because they did not regard themselves
as permanent members of the work force. Moreover, they were occupied
with household duties after their hours of wage labor and were too shy
and retiring to participate in organizations that required speaking in
public and assuming leadership. Also, since women were the most unskilled, low-paid workers of the day, they lacked the leverage to bargain
with employers and the resources to weather hard times and strikes.
Finally, some women workers faced hostility from working men because
men believed that women competed for their jobs and reduced their
wages to the low level of women's earnings. As helpless, degraded workers
on the lowest levels of the working class, most women wage earners did not
engage in labor activity to protect their interests as workers.[1]

The Collar Laundry Union of Troy, New York, does not fit this
characterization. Other working women periodically went on strike and
some organized small unions that lasted as long as a year. But the laundresses' union was larger and more permanent than many men's locals
during these decades. This women's union consisted of at least 400 members at its peak and existed for almost 6 years (from February 1864 to
September 1869). Other women workers improved wages and working
conditions from time to time. But the laundresses raised their wages to
a level almost equal to the average earnings of working men. Also, they

[1] John B. Andrews and W. P. D. Bliss, *History of Women in Trade Unions,* Arno Press,
New York, 1974 (reprint of 1911 edition), pp. 17–18, 45–49, 140–145; Theresa Wolfson,
The Woman Worker and the Trade Unions, International Publishers, New York,
1926, pp. 90–97, 157–158; Eleanor Flexner, *Century of Struggle,* Atheneum, New York,
1970, Chap. 9, especially p. 137.

accumulated a fund large enough to provide security during strikes, illness, or death in the family. Further, the laundresses did not face hostility from male workers, but formed a close alliance with the male-led labor movement. Male unionists considered the Collar Laundry Union the only " 'bona fide' female union in the country." [2] In light of the obstacles to labor organization that women faced, why was the Collar Laundry Union so successful?

THE INGREDIENTS OF SUCCESSFUL TRADE UNION ACTIVITY

The women who organized the Collar Laundry Union were not transient workers who had little reason to attempt to improve their condition as workers. Like other working women in the nation, the Troy laundresses as a group were permanent members of the industrial work force. Although individual women may not have remained in the labor force all their working days, women were essential to industrial production, and by the mid-nineteenth century they were a substantial percentage of the industrial labor force. Labor historian David Montgomery points out that by 1870 one-quarter of the wage earners in nonagricultural occupations were female. Of these, 70 percent were domestic servants. But of the remaining 30 percent, most were industrial workers. Over four-fifths of women industrial workers were employed in some branch of apparel making, including hoopskirt making and parasol and umbrella sewing. The remaining one-fifth were schoolteachers, clerks in stores, or worked in numerous other industrial occupations employing women, such as paper box making, cigar making, and printing.[3]

Troy's laundresses were an important part of that city's permanent industrial work force. They were not domestic servants or washerwomen who did personal laundry, as the term laundress suggests, but industrial workers who ironed newly manufactured detachable collars in commercial laundries. Employing about 600 women, Troy's approximately 14 laundries performed one step in the production of detachable collars for the city's prosperous shirt, collar, and cuff industry. In keeping with the increasing division of labor of the day, the laundering process was divided into separate steps—washing, starching, and ironing—and individual

---

[2] For basic facts about these unions, see: Flexner, *Century of Struggle*, pp. 131–141; and Andrews and Bliss, *Women in Trade Unions*, pp. 105–110. The following essay is based primarily on fuller information found in newspapers published in Troy and New York City, the labor press, Susan B. Anthony's *The Revolution* (New York, 1868–1872), and proceedings of meetings of the National Labor Union and the New York State Workingmen's Assembly. This quote is from the *Workingman's Advocate*, June 26, 1869.

[3] David Montgomery, *Beyond Equality: Labor and the Radical Republicans, 1862–1872*, Vintage Books, New York, 1967, p. 33.

workers specialized in only one operation. And in keeping with craft unionism, each group of workers formed separate organizations, although sometimes they engaged in labor activity together. Also in keeping with craft unionism, the women who formed the union were the most skilled workers in the shops—the ironers. In Troy the union was often referred to as the Collar Ironers' Union.

Troy's shirt, collar, and cuff industry was not a minor local industry in a backwater town. Troy was an important industrial center with two major industries—shirt, collar, and cuff manufacturing and the iron industry. These industries' products, as well as textiles and other goods produced in surrounding Albany and Cohoes, were shipped all over the United States via the Hudson River and the Erie Canal, which connected the East to the Midwest through the Great Lakes. The relatively small-scale collar laundries were interdependent with Troy's shirt, collar, and cuff factories, which produced most of the detachable collars and cuffs sold in the nation. The 15 factories employed a total of 3,128 women. Although it was a local industry, it was seventh in capital investment of all the 23 apparel industries in the state, including New York City's already vast clothing industry. Today Troy is still nicknamed "Collar City." [4]

Many members of the Collar Laundry Union were not permanent workers. Working men and women agreed with other Americans that ideally women should remain at home in their proper sphere and husbands should earn enough to support their families. Thus, in Troy as in other communities, less than 1 percent of the women in the labor force were wives living with their husbands.[5] Another much larger group (about 17 percent of the Troy laundresses in 1865) were widows with small children. But by far the largest group of working women in the nation were young single women who lived with their families. Some of these women may not have been willing to devote time and money to trade union activity because they did not regard themselves as permanent

[4] Daniel Walkowitz, "Statistics and the Writing of Working Class Culture; A Statistical Portrait of the Iron Workers in Troy, New York, 1860–1880," *Labor History,* 15 (Summer 1974), 416–460; *New York State Census,* 1865, p. 478.

[5] All percentages for age, birthplace, occupation of male relatives, and marital status are based on the manuscript censuses for Troy in 1865 and 1870. The census is an extremely imprecise tool for studying working women in this period. Many employed women do not appear in the census and enumerators often omitted households or invented families. But a comparison of data indicates that we can make some rough estimates. For example, in 1865 the proportion of widows to single women is about the same for laundresses as it is for most employed women (13 percent for collar stitchers, 20 percent for other sewing women, and 20 percent for other female industrial workers). Similarly, in 1870 there is a dramatic rise in the number of widows among the laundresses (44 percent) as well as among other employed women (34 percent for collar stitchers). The consistency of this rise suggests that it roughly reflects the marital status of the female work force.

workers. Young single women who anticipated marrying and raising children probably regarded their employment as temporary. Even widows dependent entirely on their own earnings probably hoped to remarry and leave the work force. Yet the collar laundresses did seek to improve their condition through trade union activity. To understand this, we must look more closely at the significance of women's temporary role in the work force.

The fact that Troy's laundresses worked only temporarily did not mean that their occupation was a fleeting moment in their lives, not worth improving through trade unionism. These working women were not laboring to buy themselves luxuries; many were the sole supporter of their family. Augusta Lewis, President of the Woman's Typographical Union No. 1 of New York City, observed that many of the laundresses "had aged parents, younger brothers and sisters, and some had their own children besides themselves depending on their wages." In 1865 Kate Mullaney, the laundresses' president, was supporting herself as well as her mother, Bridget, age 55, and two younger sisters.[6] Many others had to work even when the male head of household was employed. A study by the Massachusetts Bureau of Labor Statistics in 1872 shows that the yearly expenses of a family of four amounted to about $776.86. But during these years the average yearly income of wage earners was only $611.00. The report concluded that even when the head of the family worked steadily, had only two children, and did not indulge in luxuries such as Christmas presents, toothbrushes, and toys for the children, the average working man's family could not keep out of debt without the income of other family members. Clearly, working-class women's proper role included the role of provider.

For women like Troy's laundresses, some form of employment was a familiar experience in every stage of life. In many working-class families, daughters joined the work force as soon as they reached a suitable age, often entering the same occupation as their older sisters or other female relatives. Those who married in their early twenties probably did not work for more than five to seven years. But women who did not marry remained in the work force much longer. Because most working-class women were employed at one time or another, and because at any given time some female family members were working for wages, working-class women were constantly reminded of the necessity of earning a decent living. Although they may not have been permanent workers as individuals, they had good reason to protect their rights as workers.

The collar laundresses' position in the work force and the community was worth defending. Like many industrial workers during this period, the collar laundry women were largely of Irish background. In

---

[6] The description of Mullaney and her family and the following discussion of work patterns are drawn from the manuscript census for Troy in 1865 and 1870.

fact, over three-quarters of the laundresses were of Irish descent. In contrast, only one-half of other female industrial workers, and about 30 percent of sewing women were Irish-born or the children of Irish immigrants. Only domestic servants were more overwhelmingly of Irish background than collar laundresses.

Mid-nineteenth-century immigration patterns in the United States partially explain the overwhelming proportion of Irish women employed in the laundries. Many Irish immigrants found their way to Troy because the Hudson River provided convenient transportation from New York City, and Troy's industries promised employment. By 1865 Irish immigrants constituted almost one-quarter of Troy's population; the American-born children of these residents makes the proportion even higher. Since most of these people were working class, probably more than one-half of Troy's working class was of Irish descent.[7]

This is not to say that Troy's laundresses came from the city's poorest families. Irish workers did labor in the most menial occupations, such as day labor and domestic service, but many Irish families achieved a much higher status through employment in Troy's iron industry. This industry included several large iron and steel works and many smaller foundries that produced stoves, ranges, bells, wheels, and other iron products. Some skilled occupations like pattern-makers in the foundries and nailers and spikers in Burden's nail factory, employed largely workers of American background. But men of Irish descent constituted the largest number of workers in each of the three largest skilled branches of the iron foundries—molders, puddlers, and heaters and rollers. Since most of these men arrived in America with few industrial skills, they experienced considerable upward mobility through the iron industry.[8]

Troy's laundresses were part of a well-organized labor movement led by these highly skilled, largely Irish iron molders. In the 1860s and 1870s the most well-organized workers were highly skilled, well-paid men of American background. But in Troy the most well-organized workers were skilled iron workers, chiefly stove and range molders. From about 1860 to the 1880s the Troy Iron Molders' Union No. 2 was one of the most influential locals in the International Iron Molders' Union, and this national union was in turn one of the three or four most powerful national trade unions. In Troy the molders helped organize strikes, meetings, and trade union picnics that contributed to other workers' labor activity or celebrated working-class solidarity.[9] The Troy *Press* viewed one picnic as a symbol of this unity: "Capital, with her high head, proud mein and plethoric purse, is at Saratoga or Newport. Labor, with her

[7] Montgomery, *Beyond Equality*, pp. 35–40; Walkowitz, "Statistics," p. 422; *New York State Census*, pp. 11–12, 151–152.
[8] Walkowitz, "Statistics," pp. 435–444.
[9] Walkowitz, "Statistics," pp. 426–428.

brawny arms, independent spirit and moderate share of greenbacks is at Winnie's Grove. Hurrah for Winnie's!"

What was the collar laundresses' status in this working-class community? Although many laundresses came from the families of unskilled workers, an even larger group came from families on the highest levels of the working class. For example, in 1865 about 30 percent of the laundresses' male relatives were unskilled workers like laborers or porters, but only about 11 percent of sewing women's male relatives were unskilled. Also, about half (52 percent) of laundresses' male relatives were skilled workers like carpenters, blacksmiths, or molders. This figure is about the same for other Troy working women—for example, 59 percent for sewing women's male relatives. The laundresses' status was consistent with both the low status of Irish workers in general and the relatively high status of many Irish families in Troy.

The characteristics of the laundresses' occupation itself fit in with their mixed status in Troy's working class. In general, work in commercial laundries carried less status than other industrial occupations like needlework. Although laundering was probably not any more fatiguing and health-impairing than sewing and factory work, working conditions involved strenuous physical labor. Esther Keegan reported that laundresses stood on their feet almost all of their 11 to 14 hours of labor in shops as small as 16 feet square. Temperatures reached the "nineties" in the winter, and in the summer it was so hot that laundresses often had to "forgo their work for two or three weeks at a time from sheer inability to perform it." Ironers were required to continually lift hot heavy irons, and starchers' fingers became sore from constant immersion in starchy water. Keegan asserted that because of these conditions, laundresses frequently contracted consumption: "None but the strongest could stand it."

Laundering was also less ladylike than other women's occupations. While women from prosperous families may have done their own fine needlework, they rarely did their own laundry. People invariably compared laundry work to taking in washing, which was one of the most menial, poorly paid women's occupations. Thus, although laundry work was an industrial occupation, it was less genteel and respectable than dress-making, millinery, or even routine hand-stitching. Women of American background who had more options for employment probably preferred the more ladylike occupations of sewing or light industrial work.

Collar laundering was, however, more prestigious than domestic service. Working-class women considered the work of cooks, chambermaids, and housekeepers degrading because it involved serving or cleaning up after others and did not provide the independence of a wage. Women who needed servants bemoaned the fact that most Americans "would rather want bread than *serve* to gain it." [10] Therefore, while laundry

[10] Oscar Handlin, *Boston's Immigrants, 1790–1880*, Atheneum, New York, 1972, p. 61.

work was not a prestigious occupation for women of American background who could get other work, it was a good occupation for Irish women who wished to rise above employment in service occupations.

Unlike taking in washing and domestic service, laundering offered the independence of a wage and regular employment. Also, thanks to the union, laundresses' earnings were comparatively high. In 1872 the average earnings of working women amounted to $299.00 per year, or $1.16 per day, $6.96 per week, a figure close to the average earnings of working men ($13.44 per week). Collar laundering combined the disadvantages of unladylike labor with the advantages of industrial work. It attracted women from lower levels of the working class who were able to get better employment than domestic service, and those from higher levels who were willing to endure hard physical labor for high wages.

Of the several laundering steps, collar ironing was the most prestigious. It was not a skilled trade, since it involved a task familiar to many women and did not require knowledge of many complicated processes. Nevertheless, handling the heavy hot irons required physical strength, endurance, and a skill that could only be acquired through two to four weeks of intensive training. According to employers, good ironers were not easy to come by, and the ironing skill was worth more than that of starchers and washers. In the small world of commercial laundries, ironers were the aristocracy of labor.[11]

The collar laundresses' organizational structure and level of skill helped them to defend their right to earn a living in the occupation in which they were trained. The ironers organized by the work they did in their shop as well as by sex. This organizational structure was typical of craft unionism; workers who did different kinds of labor in one industry almost always organized separately. But it was also useful for women to organize separately because women who organized into men's locals were at a disadvantage. They faced male workers' antagonisms more directly and were more reluctant to speak up at meetings and take leadership roles. The few women who did belong to men's locals, like women cigar makers, were less effective unionists because their interests were submerged and isolated.[12] Working women like the laundresses who formed separate organizations could develop their own leaders and adopt strategies and tactics tailored to their particular work situation.

Kate Mullaney was aware that it was important for working women to organize independently from men. A reporter who interviewed Mullaney in September 1868 argued that the organization of New York City's working women lagged because women were not confident of their own abilities to be "presidents and secretaries" of trade unions. In defense of

11 Norman Ware, *The Industrial Worker, 1840–1860*, Quadrangle Books, Chicago, 1964, pp. xviii–xxi; Montgomery, *Beyond Equality*, pp. 140–148.
12 Flexner, *Century of Struggle*, p. 137.

her sisters, Mullaney responded that "there are numbers of ladies connected with the laundry union who were just as competent as any gentlemen." Probably because she realized that some women were at first reluctant to speak up at meetings or take leadership roles, she offered to send laundry union members to New York City to help women organize. If "ladies from New York" were not "competent," she would "send some from Troy and pay their expenses until such time as they were able to educate some of their own." According to Mullaney, New York's working women could overcome these difficulties with the help of other women workers rather than male trade unionists. Clearly, the laundresses' strategies were shaped partly by their status as women.

The ironers also used their position as semiskilled workers in strategies that contributed to their union's success. In this period, skilled workers were the most well organized partly because their skill was a valuable commodity that they could withhold from employers.[13] An incident that occurred early in September 1868 indicates that employers could not maintain a profitable level of production with inexperienced hands. Having given in to wage increases since 1864, the laundry proprietors tried to undermine the union by persuading nonunion ironers in the city's largest laundry to train new hands to replace workers in union shops. It would not have been necessary for the owners to use this tactic to weaken the union if they could have simply fired the union ironers and replaced them with new hands. Mullaney reported that the employers' tactics failed because the nonunion ironers, "seeing what the result would finally be, for their own protection, joined the union in a body." The owners' need for experienced labor enabled the ironers to strengthen their union even further. The laundry proprietors could not maintain full production levels during a strike even while scab workers were being trained. As employers themselves admitted, it took "some time to teach the newcomers the business." Even with a few weeks of training, the inexperienced workers' skill was not equal to the dexterity and speed of the striking ironers.

This tactic of withholding labor was successful partly because laundry proprietors were relatively vulnerable to employees' concerted action. As operators of a small-scale service industry, the laundry owners had fewer resources than the collar manufacturers with which to weather reduced production during strikes. Even more important, the laundry owners' position in the business community enabled them to pass on any increased labor costs to the collar manufacturers. The manufacturers had to absorb these costs. Despite the manufacturers' extensive resources and markets, they were dependent on the laundries' services to prepare their products for sale. The ironers' three-month strike in 1869 demonstrates

[13] Montgomery, *Beyond Equality*, pp. 140–148.

the importance of these factors in the union's success. In previous strikes the laundresses had conflicted only with the laundry proprietors, but in 1869 they faced a more formidable foe. That year the laundry proprietors combined with the much more powerful collar manufacturers. More than any other factor, the manufacturers' resources and strategies determined the strikes' outcome—the demise of the Collar Laundry Union.

The strike officially began on May 29, and on June 1 the manufacturers met publicly to plan their resistance. Their strategies were carried out on two fronts. They pressured the proprietors into holding out indefinitely by refusing to send new collars and cuffs to any laundry employing union ironers, and they helped the laundry owners obtain a new work force by helping them recruit and train new hands. Also, the manufacturers attempted to undermine directly the union's efforts to weather the strike. They tried to create a negative image of the union through the local press, which they virtually controlled. They prevented the few collar manufacturers in other cities from patronizing the union's cooperative laundry even though it claimed it could provide the same services for 25 percent less. Under these circumstances, the collar ironers' tactics were much less useful.

The collar manufacturers and laundry owners combined to prevent future wage increases. They aimed to do this not simply by opposing the present increase, but by finally eliminating the union. One indication that this was their motivation is the substantial evidence that the conflict was actually initiated by the laundry owners.[14] The ironers had demanded and received a wage increase in July 1868, and the starchers received an increase in March 1869. The third conflict began when the laundry owners demanded that the ironers equalize wages paid for work on different-size collars within each shop. When the ironers complied by decreasing rates for some work and increasing rates for other work, there was a general increase of about $1\frac{1}{2}$ cents per dozen collars. Although the proprietors had demanded the equalization, they refused to pay the increase.

The manufacturers claimed through the local press that this increase was the issue of the strike. They maintained that the ironers already received extraordinarily high wages for only ten hours of light labor per day, and that women foolish enough to be influenced by "outside busybodies" deserved to lose their jobs. Troy's collar factories, they argued, were already being undersold by the few collar manufacturers in other cities. If the ironers continued their unreasonable demands, Troy's collar industry would be destroyed and thousands of residents would suffer. The Troy *Daily Whig* asked, will "this new collar-a" prevail?

Although Troy's press was not as biased as the strikers claimed, it

---

[14] There is some evidence that the collar manufacturers were behind the initiation of the strike, but there is not enough data to confirm the role they played at this stage.

did suppress an essential fact that was revealed in New York City's newspapers: Once the ironers went on strike for the increase, some employers offered to rehire them at slightly higher wages on the condition that they give up their union. Kate Mullaney told the Workingmen's Union of New York City on July 2, 1869, that the laundry union's employers "do not care for the money." They were willing to pay the increased wages, but they insisted that the ironers "must give up" their union. Esther Keegan maintained that the ironers would make "every concession," but "it would never do to give up" their union. "We are determined not to yield." From a trade unionist's point of view, the strike was a lockout in which employers would not rehire union members unless they gave up their union. Like the iron molders' Great Lockout of 1866, the issue of the ironers' strike was "union or no union."

Partly because the combination of employers was so formidable, the ironers also chose another strategy for obtaining their rights: They formed a producers' cooperative, essentially a joint stock company financed through selling shares. In the late 1860s many prominent trade unionists believed that strikes could eliminate only the worst effects of wage slavery. They argued that producers' cooperatives enabled workers to escape wage slavery permanently by transforming themselves into small businessmen.[15] Iron molders were among the most enthusiastic advocates of cooperation, and their iron foundries in Troy were among the most successful cooperative enterprises in the nation. Following the example of molders and others, the collar ironers laid plans for a cooperative laundry in early June. In July, when it was apparent that local manufacturers prevented out-of-town manufacturers from supplying the cooperative with newly made collars, the union expanded the project to include a cooperative collar-and-cuff manufactory. As Mullaney wrote in a letter to Susan B. Anthony which appeared in *The Revolution* in April 1870, the "girls" hoped "to proceed on a purely business basis, by doing the work . . . themselves." They hoped eventually to "buy up all the stock and hold it for their own benefit." If the project had succeeded, the laundresses would have transformed themselves into small businesswomen who were not dependent on wages for survival.

Despite the ironers' determination and the trade union movement's generous support, the union was dissolved in early September 1869, and the cooperative was disbanded in 1870. The cooperative was doomed largely because of problems inherent in this form of producers' cooperative, and partly because it could not compete with Troy's powerful collar manufacturers. But the project's failure was probably also due to the fact that the ironers were women. No matter how efficient the ironers' enterprise was, and no matter how much expertise and financial aid male

[15] Montgomery, *Beyond Equality*, pp. 154–155, 227–229.

trade unionists contributed, prospective buyers were not likely to take women seriously as manufacturers.

The demise of the union and the cooperative does not mean that the laundresses were helpless women or degraded workers who had no bargaining power. They successfully resisted employers' appropriation of an unfair share of the profits their labor produced for a much longer period than most male workers did in these decades. They could do this for the same reasons that working men were able to improve wages and working conditions—by making the most of their employers' need for trained labor, and by taking advantage of the owners' vulnerability and their position in the business community. The ironers lost this leverage only when the proprietors increased their strength by combining with the manufacturers. The ironers' leverage was decreased even further a few years later when collar manufacturers found a more effective way to avoid absorbing laundry owners' increased labor costs: By the late 1870s the manufacturers incorporated the laundries into the collar manufactories. The collar ironers were "nothing but women" who faced more disadvantages than male workers. But like other relatively successful women and men unionists, they faced their employers primarily as workers.

The laundresses withstood employers' efforts to break their union for several months because their alliance with other workers—male trade unionists—made their strategies and tactics more effective. Male unionists cooperated with the ironers despite the fact that the antagonism between men and women workers were as deep as other hostilities dividing American wage earners. Just as working men were threatened by unskilled "green hands," especially if they were black or Chinese, they were also threatened by women workers. Working men not only believed that women took men's jobs and reduced their earnings, but they also thought that women wage earners were out of their natural sphere.[16] Because of these beliefs, sometimes male workers were not willing to provide women wage earners with the aid that unskilled or semiskilled workers urgently needed to organize effectively. Yet they did aid the laundresses.

How firm was this alliance between collar laundresses and male trade unionists? The ironers' relationship with the male-led trade union movement began with their friendship with Troy's iron molders. This relationship in turn began with the laundresses' first efforts to organize, lasted until at least 1870, and continued into the 1880s, if not longer. Esther Keegan reported that the molders' union introduced the laundresses to the principles of trade unionism in February 1864. During the period of economic difficulties just after the beginning of the Civil War, their "weeks' wages could only buy a pair of shoes." They "asked higher wages," but "were not listened to." But when they organized into a union

16 Montgomery, *Beyond Equality*, p. 147.

on the advice of the molders, they "got the advance they asked for." By 1869 almost all shops were organized and the union included about 430 members.

In the ensuing years the laundresses showed their appreciation and the molders reciprocated. At the first molders' picnic on July 18, 1864, about 4,000 people watched the presentation of a blue silk banner to Henry Rockefeller, the Troy molders' president. The banner pictured on one side a furnace in full blast with men "pouring off" the molten metal and on the other side a figure of justice below an eagle. Ribbons on one side of the banner bore the inscription: "Presented by the Collar Laundry Union of Troy to the Iron Molders' Association." Two years later, in April 1866, the laundresses donated the enormous sum of 1,000 dollars to the molders during their Great Lockout. In return, in September 1868, William Sylvis, President of the National Labor Union and the IMIU, appointed Kate Mullaney Assistant Secretary of the NLU. Remembering the laundresses' loyalty, the molders were the ironers' staunchest supporters during their 1869 strike. Dugald Campbell wrote, "The laundry girls have stood by the moulders in their hour of adversity and they to a man will do the same to them." In gratitude, the laundresses dedicated a poem to Campbell which began:

> *See Labor's Champion, so nobly contending,*
> *Who fights for the down-trodden toilers the while;*
> *Whose life's wholly spent their condition amending,*
> *Despite every slanderer that would him revile.*

Trade unionists in New York City and elsewhere also stood by the ironers in 1869. In early July Kate Mullaney and Esther Keegan visited New York City in order to solicit contributions for their cooperative and strike fund from the city's prosperous unions. Almost every union in the city responded with generous amounts of cash. By September, contributions totaled 4,510 dollars.

Ironically, the least generous organization was the Workingwomen's Association of New York, which was organized by Susan B. Anthony in September 1868. Although working women were active in the association in the first weeks, by July 1869 the members were all prosperous middle-class women. Most of these middle-class women were more concerned with working women's difficulties than other suffragists. According to a report in the New York *World* on July 3, Mullaney observed that she came before them to request contributions because she "understood that they were an association of working-women." But "as she looked around them" she could tell that "they were not the working-women whom she had been accustomed to see. She had to work all day in the shop, and this she did not think, judging from their appearance, that they did." Augusta

Lewis, who accompanied Mullaney, later wrote: "Although the society comprises many wealthy ladies, they raised $30 for the laundresses of Troy. As a society, either the want of knowledge, or the want of sense, renders them, as a workingwomen's association very in efficient." Elsewhere, Lewis wrote that compared to the Workingwomen's Association, the laundresses' union was a "real workingwomen's association." Suffragists made immeasurable contributions to improving women's condition, but women trade unionists considered male trade unionists to be firmer allies than suffragists were.

The state's trade unions generously aided the ironers in part because the strike was one of the few that was officially endorsed by the New York State Workingmen's Assembly. Trade unionists resented "begging expeditions" that visited New York, because contributing to strikes depleted their treasuries and weakened their ability to resist their own employers. In response to this problem William Jessup, President of the New York State Workingmen's Assembly, instituted a policy of investigating conflicts when strikers requested aid in order to determine whether they were worthy of contributions. If he deemed them worthy, Jessup issued an official circular explaining the strike's cause. The ironers' 1869 strike was one of only two conflicts that year endorsed in this manner. Significantly, the other worthy strike was the New York City Bricklayers' strike for the eight-hour day. Troy's iron molders, Troy's labor movement, and New York State's trade unions were the ironers' loyal allies.

Since most working men were threatened by women workers, why did male unionists rally behind the laundresses' union? A New York State Bureau of Labor Statistics Report of 1886 suggests that the iron molders and laundresses were allied because the laundry women were an important source of income for molders' families. The census manuscript adds some support to this argument. While 14 percent of the laundresses' male relatives were molders in 1865, molders constituted only 8 percent of collar sewers' male relatives, and 5 percent of sewing women's male relatives. Although 14 percent does not represent very many individuals, slightly more laundry women than other working women were related to molders. These family ties may have reduced antagonisms between male and female workers in collar laundries and iron foundries. Shared ethnic identity may have augmented these ties. Living in the same neighborhoods and participating in Irish political and nationalist organizations, Troy's Irish working-class community was particularly close-knit.[17] Troy's laundresses and molders probably had more ethnic and family ties than other female and male workers.

But family ties and shared ethnic identity cannot provide a full explanation for this alliance. If the alliance was based entirely on these

---

17 Walkowitz, "Statistics," pp. 433–435.

ties, then the ironers' union would have to be viewed as an isolated example that depended on the external aid of relatives or membership in an ethnic community. The union's strength, commitment to trade unionism, and firm alliance with male trade unionists could not have been based on external aid alone, but must have also depended on the ironers' own efforts as wage earners. Also, family ties and ethnic identity cannot explain why workers organize, because these ties do not necessarily lead to a commitment to trade unionism. In order to organize successfully the laundresses also had to develop a commitment to trade unionism through their own experiences in bargaining with employers. In order to form firm alliances with other workers the laundresses had to have common interests as wage earners who were attempting to counter the power of capital. These common interests also explain the laundresses' alliance with the national trade union movement.

It was possible for some male workers to ally with women on the basis of shared interests as wage earners and for others to be hostile to working women because working men's situation as men and as trade unionists was inconsistent. As American workers, male unionists were threatened by women working for wages. However, working men also recognized that women worked because they had to, that women workers had a right to protect themselves from employers, and that working women, like men, could obtain this protection only through trade unionism.

But working men's fear of women's competition was so strong that working men could cooperate with women wage earners only under circumstances that mitigated this threat to their livelihood. Three kinds of circumstances seemed necessary for this cooperation: With few exceptions, male and female wage earners cooperated only when male workers believed that women were not directly competing with men; this kind of cooperation occurred when working women were not helpless but proved the unionists' adage that "those who would be free must themselves strike the first blow"; most important, working men cooperated with women workers when they derived some direct benefit from working women's labor activity.

Most male-female cooperation in the 1860s and 1870s occurred between men and women who labored in different branches of the same industry. For example, members of the Daughters of St. Crispin stitched shoes in the same shops as male Crispins. In these situations male and female wage earners were not competitors, because they did work strictly reserved for either sex. Their cooperation strengthened the bargaining position of both sexes, since their efforts were aimed at the same employers.

In Troy and other communities cooperation also occurred between women and men who were employed in entirely different industries with different employers. In this case, women's unions were beneficial to men in another equally important way: They made substantial contributions to the solidarity of the working-class community. Troy's trade union movement was a major center of labor activity partly because iron molders and other skilled workers not only protected their own interests, but also helped draw other less-skilled workers into the local trade union movement. The molders helped establish Troy's Trades' Assembly in 1864 and organized huge picnics and demonstrations that mobilized thousands of workers in Troy and neighboring communities. Not only did they help the collar ironers organize, but they also aided others who were less likely to organize on their own, such as day laborers, tailoresses, and dressmakers. Unlike needlewomen in other communities, these Troy sewing women were continuously organized for at least a year.[18] Workers of different backgrounds, levels of skill, and stages of organization could depend on each other for support.

The ironers' independence and commitment to trade unionism made them particularly deserving of support. William Sylvis noted that "the Troy girls" worked hard, "doing what they could in a practical way to work out their own salvation. They have acted upon the old saying, 'Who would be free themselves must strike the blow.' " Having experienced labor activity on their own, the ironers developed a deep commitment to trade union principles. As Esther Keegan put it, the ironers militantly resisted employers' efforts to break up the union because they were "not willing to go back to that state of slavery in which" they "were six years ago." The union was the "mother of their success," and their success in turn was the mother of their firm commitment to trade unionism.

The ironers and other female trade unionists in Troy not only received aid but also made their own contributions to the unity of labor against capital. The dressmakers' and milliners' unions contributed to the bookkeepers' strike for a wage increase in 1864. The ironers not only supported the molders in 1866, but donated the large sum of 500 dollars to the New York City Bricklayers' strike in 1868. As a Troy molder put it, "The ironers . . . have always been noted for their liberality in assisting other trade unions on strike."

The laundresses also contributed to the solidarity of the national trade union movement. Their contribution to the molders' lockout was a donation not to a local conflict, but to Sylvis's strategy to counter a national association of manufacturers formed to weaken the IMIU. Similarly, the bricklayers' strike was part of the strategy of the state's eight-hour movement to enforce an eight-hour law recently passed by the state legislature. Like their allies, the laundresses protected not only themselves and their neighbors, but also the working-class movement as a whole.

The ironers' 1869 strike and their cooperative were major contributions to this movement. William Jessup described the strike as an attempt by "the employers and manufacturers to destroy the union by starving its members into subjection to accept the employers' terms." Like the molders' and bricklayers' conflicts, the ironers' strike was not a maneuver for temporary advantages, but a struggle for the American workers' right to organize. The Troy printers' resolution summed up the trade unionists' view:

It is the duty of all trades' organizations to resist such attempts upon trade union principles. . . . We must sustain and uphold the right of those who labor to consult together and determine upon the rate at which their labor shall be sold for the enrichment of capital.

Moreover, the laundresses were also taking the "higher step" of cooperation. Jessup's circular asking the state's trade unions to contribute to the ironers argued that:

The Collar Laundry Union does not ask you to contribute to support them in idleness while they are on strike. They desire to enter into co-operation by organizing manufactories of their own on the cooperative principle. The object is feasible. . . . Let us all contribute with a willing heart and an open hand.

Despite the fact that the strike failed and the cooperative foundered, the ironers' leaders continued to be committed to trade unionism, and male trade unionists continued to stand by them. As valuable members of the trade union movement, the ironers continued to be deserving of support. Sharing the interests of wage earners who sought to protect themselves through trade unionism, the collar ironers were "bona fide" trade unionists.

WOMEN TRADE UNIONISTS' SELF-PERCEPTION

The women who formed the Collar Laundry Union overcame formidable obstacles to trade union organization. Women who overcame these barriers must have been forceful individuals who developed the abilities to articulate clearly their conclusions and to plan strategies and tactics to achieve their goals. But the laundresses' success was not due to the fact that some were exceptional individuals. They were successful because they shared more characteristics that enabled workers in general to form permanent unions than did other female industrial workers. The laundresses were successful for the same reasons that male trade unionists were.

The factors contributing to the laundresses' success reveal that they organized primarily as workers rather than women. Coming from the same level of the working class as many male unionists, their organization reflected the characteristics of their occupation and their employers, divisions between workers based on level of skill, nationality, religion, and sex, and characteristics of the labor movement in their community. They came to the same conclusions about the relationship between labor and capital, adopted the same strategies and tactics, and formed the same alliances as male unionists.

Other characteristics of women's unions in the 1860s and 1870s in the United States support the conclusion that the laundresses organized primarily as workers rather than women. The collar laundry women were part of a female trade union movement within the national labor movement. New York City's newspapers reported on March 11, 1870, that representatives of the seven women's unions in the state, including the laundry union, met in the city's Cooper Institute to organize the Working-women's State Labor Union (WSLU) of New York. The formation of the WSLU is significant because it tells us that the laundresses' union was not unique, but was one of many women's unions in the region during these years. The laundresses were not isolated but were in close touch with other women unionists. These women developed the same forms of organization, ideologies, strategies, and tactics as male unionists.

An important conclusion about women trade unionists' consciousness of themselves as workers and as women emerges from this examination of male and female trade unions. Esther Keegan's address to the Workingmen's Union indicates that Keegan, like other women unionists, viewed herself primarily as a wage earner who was also a working-class woman—that is, Keegan recognized that the laundresses were "nothing but women" whose dependent status shaped their ability to organize as successfully as men. But this status was in turn fundamentally shaped by the disadvantages they shared with working-class men who were also dependent on wages for their livelihood. Thus, to the extent that women trade unionists organized as women, they identified with other working-class women, not with women of other social classes. Conscious of their identity as wage earners, they did not identify with women's rights advocates who would probably never have to work for wages. Women trade unionists like Troy's laundresses organized as women within their own social class.

This conclusion is not meant to argue that working women in the mid-nineteenth century did not identify with issues relevant to women of all levels of society. Women unionists did not agree with suffragists that "the ballot, in the World of work is [woman's] only shield and protection." But they did firmly believe that in principle women should have the ballot. Further, this conclusion is not meant to argue that all working women in all times and places will always identify primarily with working-class men rather than with women of other social groups.[19] These con-

19 *The Revolution,* January 15, 1868 (quote); New York *World,* September 18, 1868;

clusions indicate that for these women at this time and place, class interests were more important than interests shared with women of other social groups.

Documents

Linen and Collar and Cuff Manufacture and the Working-women's Union, 1873

When all these sewing processes are at last complete, the collars—and so of other articles, for we are following the fortunes of the collar as a representative of the rest—are transferred to the laundry, where a second series of eleven processes is gone through with, besides the mere transfer.* These are as follows: (1) Washing in suds, to remove the manufacturer's "dressing" from the goods; (2) bleaching, by means of hyperchloride of soda; (3) application of dilute sulphuric acid, to complete the bleaching process; (4) washing in suds, to remove the acid; (5) boiling; (6) rubbing and rinsing; (7) bluing and rolling; (8) starching with thin starch; (9) starching with thick starch; (10) drying; (11) ironing.

These operations are greatly facilitated by the arrangement of fitting up of the different rooms, and by various devices for economizing labor and power. Thus a peculiar formation of the stove for heating irons keeps forty of them hot all the time, with a small average consumption of coal; the order of the tubs used is such as to make the progress of the goods easy through the successive processes, etc. The starch used is not of wheat, but of corn, which is found to be equally efficient, cheaper, and much less disagreeable to the fingers of the operatives. This is a pretty important consideration, for it is found to make the difference between sore fingers and healthy ones,—that is, work or idleness,— besides pain, which is sometimes no small item, as the very agonizing inflammation called felon has occasionally been somewhat frequent among those who work in the starching rooms.

. . .

This firm, on the contrary, is well satisfied with that sort of success which is the only really desirable one in business—honest gains from enterprise, industry, and fair dealing. Steady kindness, and at the same time as much strictness as is necessary, keep them popular with their hands, of whom they employ

---

New York *Sun*, February 9, 1870; *The Revolution*, February 24, 1870; New York *World*, March 11, 1870; Nancy Schrom Dye, "Creating a Feminist Alliance: Sisterhood and Class Conflict in the New York Women's Trade Union League, 1902–1914," *Feminist Studies*, 2, No. 2 and 3 (1975), 24–38.

* Reprinted from Horace Greeley et al., *Great Industries of the United States*, J. B. Burr and Hyde, Hartford, Conn., 1873, pp. 614 and 616.

from five hundred to eight hundred. This treatment, and the pleasant quarters afforded to their operatives, secure the important advantage of steady help. Some of those in the establishment have been with the firm for twelve years or more; and it has repeatedly happened that those who left, for one or another reason, have returned and asked to be employed again, having found neither their new employers nor their new quarters as comfortable. This amicable state of things does not however, prevent a strenuous adherence to their rights. A few years ago, a so-called "Workingwomen's Union" was set up among the hands, and at once went to work to raise wages. Apparently there was a measure of justification for the step, since the required advance was granted, as was another within a few months. A third, however, met with a prompt refusal; the manufacturers, though not organizing into any formal body, agreed to put a stop to the performances, the Messrs. Cluett being among the very first in taking this ground. The demand of the "Union" was peremptorily refused, work stopped, the ill-advised strikers were let alone until they returned to work at previous rates, and the Union was exterminated, as no member of it would be employed. [*Note:* The firm of George B. Cluett, Brother & Co., later became a national producer of men's shirts, The Arrow Company, a division of Cluett, Peabody, and Co., Inc.]

A "Spicy" Letter from a Workingwoman, 1869

It was my pleasure a few weeks since to visit a real workingwomen's association, the Collar Laundry Union of Troy, New York.* I use the word real to designate it from imaginary workingwomen's associations who theorize, while this organization has proved "that those who would be free themselves must strike the blow!"

For many years past the collar laundries of Troy have employed several hundred women to wash, starch, and iron collars brought fresh from the manufacturer, preparatory to their sales in stores. Summer and winter from dawn to dark sometimes "till midnight, their work was to stand over the washtub, over the ironing table, with furnaces on either side, the thermometer averaging 100° for wages averaging from $2 to $3 a week each. Many of those thus employed had aged parents, younger brothers and sisters, and some had their own children, besides themselves, depending on this pittance for an existence. A representation of their necessities and individual appeal for an increase of salary received the usual answer to such demands—"That if dissatisfied there were plenty of women who would be glad to get work at any price." At last that bugbear of capitalists was resorted to, and they formed a trade union, whereby through their own

---

* Reprinted from the New York *Sun*, July 5, 1869. Although the letter is not signed, biographical details provide strong evidence that the writer was Augusta Lewis, president of the Women's Typographical Union No. 1 of New York City (organized from October 1868 to 1874).

exertions and their faithfulness to their organization they have increased their wages to $8 to $14 per week by working on an average from twelve to fourteen hours per day. Meantime their employers' profits are $85 per day. The laundresses' organization is at present in difficulty not of their own seeking. (The cause of the trouble was stated in Tuesday's *Sun*.) The employers are very willing to pay less for small collars, but refuse to pay the increase for large collars. Some [employers] say they will pay the scale provided the Union, which has increased their wages, is dissolved. It will then be in their power to decrease the wages, and the women, justly regarding the union as the mother of their success, refuse the terms. Having been educated as to the knowledge of their true interests by organization, they now desire to take a step higher and form a cooperative laundry, thus becoming their own employers, a form of organized labor to which even the most fastidious cannot object. I am not a resident of Troy, nor a worker or member of the Laundry Union, but I am a workingwoman who has had to work very hard for a very small sum, and my sympathies are ever with those who struggle in poverty to earn an honorable living. It is the duty and interest of every workingman and woman to extend a helping hand to those women of the Collar Laundry Union of Troy. . . . Fathers and mothers whose daughters are sheltered and protected by home and wealth, remember the workingwomen. It is uncertain how long you or your protecting care and wealth will be spared. Neither your daughters nor you know but they might yet have to earn their own living. At eight years of age the writer of this lived in Brooklyn Heights, and attended one of the most aristocratic schools in the City of Churches; a servant carried her books to schools, but at the age of seventeen she carried her lunch to work, and stood behind the counter of a Broadway store from eight in the morning 'til eight in the evening for $2 a week, and was asked by the forewoman: "Why not dress more stylishly; well-dressed saleswomen commanded better custom, and gave an air of dignity to the store." With such remuneration and such remarks, who dare deny that prostitution is at a premium. Yes, and will be until women are paid a living price for their labor. Let those who contribute to Magdalen Societies to reclaim the fallen do that which will prevent the necessity for such institutions, and wherever they see women striving to better their condition give them substantial aid.

Others will be encouraged by their success, and be stimulated by their example to seek to elevate their own condition, as the female cap makers of this city are now doing.

Whatever the evils of society are, let us not contribute to them by refusing to do the good that lies in our power at the present moment. In thus elevating one class of workingwomen, the good results will be felt by every other, and in future let us hope that when, from choice or necessity, women are compelled to earn their own living, it will not be a reproach but an honor to be, as I am.

A Working Woman

9 Chinese Immigrant Women in Nineteenth-Century California

Lucie Cheng Hirata

Chinese woman. Courtesy of United Press International.

The decades between 1850 and the turn of the century were the period of rapid development of the American West. Leading that development and to a large extent functioning as the core of the West was California, where the Gold Rush began in 1848. Once the discovery of gold became widely known, the population increased sharply and had to be fed, clothed, housed, and entertained. What characterized California in the mid-nineteenth century was its heterogeneous labor force, consisting of peoples from Europe, the Americas, and Asia, and individuals from diverse occupational backgrounds. Most of this population consisted of young men between the ages of 15 and 24. Although women were also part of the migration, their number was small. For example, in 1850 there were more than 12 men to every woman in California. The sexual imbalance and the youthfulness of the population had a number of consequences for the role of women in the development of California.

Despite the increase in population, the supply of labor lagged behind demand. The small number of women were therefore given more opportunities to participate in the labor force, and fewer restrictions were placed on them. Women were found in such occupations as mining and logging as well as teaching and nursing. Although some occupations were clearly dominated by men and other occupations were chiefly women's jobs, the range of options was wider than women could find on the economically more developed East Coast.

Services normally performed by women in the family were performed by women outside the family for the bachelor population. Most of these services were wage labor in the most backward sector of the economy. Domestic servants, laundresses, and prostitutes fell within this category and were the largest occupational groups among the female population.

Although natural resources and demographic factors defined the general pattern of women's work roles in nineteenth-century California, these factors alone do not shed light on the specific patterns exhibited by women from different national groups and different class backgrounds. For example, some of these groups, such as immigrant women from non–English-speaking countries, were precluded from certain occupations that required more fluent knowledge of the English language. In other words, though the general pattern of women's roles in developing California is more or less known, to date very little has been written about the particular functions of the women of any specific racial or national group.

We will discuss the major roles that Chinese immigrant women played during this period, describing their lives and experiences and relating them to the development of this frontier society.

THE STORY OF AH-CHOI

The discovery of gold in 1848 along the Sacramento River brought thousands of immigrants to California. In San Francisco, where miners from nearby sites congregated during the winter and immigrants gathered before entering the mining areas, prostitution became a lucrative business. The demand for prostitution was met by women of varying racial and national origins, including Chinese women from Hong Kong, Canton, and its surrounding areas.[1]

During the first few years of the Gold Rush, Chinese prostitution in California was characterized by individual initiative and enterprise. Like their white counterparts, many Chinese prostitutes during this period were able to accumulate sufficient capital to leave the profession. Some of them returned to China as relatively affluent members of the business community; others remained in America and either continued in prostitution as madams or invested in other businesses. A second distinctive feature of this early period was that the Chinese prostitutes received white clients almost exclusively.

The first Chinese female resident in America was believed to be a domestic servant who arrived in San Francisco as a member of the Gillespie household in February 1848. The second arrival was said to be a 20-year-old prostitute, named Ah-choi, who landed in late 1848 or early 1849. She differed from her sisters of the later period of Chinese prostitution in one important respect: She was her own free agent and succeeded in accumulating enough money to own a brothel within two years.

Ah-choi's social background is not known.[2] Judging from the evidence that she could speak some English, had enough money to make the trip from Hong Kong to San Francisco, possessed jewelry and fancy clothes on arrival, and had the know-how to set up a business immediately afterward, it seems likely that she was already a fairly successful prostitute or even a madam in Hong Kong who catered to the foreign trade. Like her male countrymen, she took advantage of the opportunities provided by news of the discovery of gold.

During the first two years after gold was discovered in California, it was not unusual for a miner to wash or dig up 100 ounces of gold a day. Ah-choi was able to charge one ounce of gold or 16 dollars per visit

[1] The following discussion on Chinese prostitution is a brief summary of the author's forthcoming paper, "Free, Enslaved, and Indentured Workers in 19th-Century America: The Case of Chinese Prostitution," *Signs* (1979).

[2] However, there is a great deal written about her. See, for example, Herbert Asbury, *The Barbary Coast*, Alfred A. Knopf, New York, 1933; Charles Dobie, *San Francisco's Chinatown*, Doubleday, New York, 1964; C. Y. Lee, *Days of the Tong Wars*, Ballantine, New York, 1974; and Wu Shang-ying, *Mei-guo Hua-qiao bai-nian ji-shi*, Hong Kong, 1954. Many of the details in these works are contradictory.

and still attract a line of waiting customers a block long. This fee was not exorbitant; successful European prostitutes were known to have charged much more.[3] Almost all of Ah-choi's customers were non-Chinese. Ah-choi's income must have offset her expenses by a large margin because by 1850, just about two years after her arrival, she had made enough money to make trips to Hong Kong and Canton and to import more Chinese women for her business. In 1852 she moved from her first place of business off Clay Street and opened up a larger house on Pike Street.[4]

Ah-choi was able to pay her passage to America; other free-agent prostitutes during this initial period emigrated under different circumstances. A popular social novel in the late Ch'ing dynasty contained a supposedly true story of a Cantonese prostitute who was brought to San Francisco by her American paramour when she was 18. After seven years she returned to Hong Kong with approximately 16,000 dollars, married a Chinese laborer and, because of her special knowledge of American trade, opened a store that sold only foreign goods.[5] While the details of this story may be suspect, it seems plausible that some women came to the Golden Hills as prostitutes and made enough money to open up businesses in America or China. The scarcity of women and the affluent condition of the men made it possible for prostitutes of different nationalities, mostly European, to amass a small fortune in a short period of time.

THE ORGANIZATION OF PROSTITUTION

This period of free competition among owner-prostitutes did not last very long, and there were not many free agents, mostly because of the prohibitive cost of passage. In 1852, of the 11,794 Chinese in California, only 7 were women, 2 of these were independent prostitutes and 2 others were known to have been working for Ah-choi. Despite their small numbers, it was clear that a considerable sum of money could be made in the business. That prospect attracted Chinese entrepreneurs, who organized various aspects of the business.

By 1854 Chinese prostitution in San Francisco had become a highly organized institution under the control of Chinese men, and its network extended across the Pacific to Canton and Hong Kong. The persons chiefly responsible for this trade included the procurers who kidnapped, enticed, or bought the women; the importers who brought them into

---

[3] For example, one European prostitute in the West was reported to have charged 1,000 dollars per night in the 1850s. See Dee Brown, *Women of the Wild West*, Pan, London, 1975, p. 70.

[4] Curt Gentry, *Madames of San Francisco*, Doubleday, New York, 1964, pp. 50–60.

[5] Wu Yan-ren, *Er-shi-nian mu-du guai xian-zhuang*, n.p., 1903.

America; the brothel owners who lived by their exploitation; the Chinese thugs who collected fees for protecting them from other thugs; the white police and officials who collected money for keeping them from being arrested; and the white Chinatown property owners who leased their land and buildings for exorbitant rents.

As California gained its reputation as a fast-growing area, industries developed and labor was in demand. American businessmen had long been aware of the coolie trade that supplied indentured Chinese laborers to Australia, Peru, British West Indies, Cuba, and other countries, and some began to import Chinese laborers for mining, construction, and other physical work. But the majority of Chinese immigrants to California during the nineteenth century came not as coolie labor but by means of the credit-ticket system.[6] With the cooperation of the Chinese Six Companies, large numbers of Chinese laborers arrived, and when the first transcontinental railway was being built in the 1860s, more than 11,000 Chinese workers were recruited for the project. The Central Pacific Railroad as well as the many other feeder lines Chinese laborers helped to construct were vehicles for the dispersion of the Chinese population. Although San Francisco remained the county with the largest concentration of Chinese, by 1870 Chinese were found in every county of the state, and by 1880 their numbers in all but eight counties increased. While the total Chinese population in California increased from 34,933 in 1860 to 75,132 in 1880, the number of Chinese women only increased from 2,006 to 3,686. The tremendous increase of the Chinese male population without a corresponding increase in females provided a rare opportunity for the Chinese to accumulate money. While some Chinese businessmen set up small factories, shops, and restaurants, others organized as secret societies (tongs), established gambling joints and opium dens and developed the female trade.

There is no accurate count of Chinese prostitutes in California during the nineteenth century. But the manuscript population census from 1870 identified prostitution as an occupational category. If we juxtapose the census figures with those reported by Chinese and American observers, it is possible to derive some fairly credible estimates.[7] In 1870, among the 3,536 adult Chinese women in California, there were approximately 2,157 whose occupations were listed as prostitutes, and a majority of them (67 percent) were concentrated in San Francisco. By 1880, although the total number of Chinese women in California changed

6 Thomas Chinn, *A History of the Chinese in California*, Chinese Historical Society, San Francisco, 1969.

7 Unless otherwise noted, all numbers and demographic characteristics concerning Chinese women in California during the nineteenth century are computed from the U.S. Manuscript Population Census for California for 1860, 1870, and 1880. The 1890 census was destroyed in a fire.

little, the number of prostitutes declined greatly. Among the 3,171 adult women, only 759 were listed as prostitutes. The decline is reflected even more sharply when we focus on San Francisco. Although 79 percent of the Chinese women in San Francisco were prostitutes in 1870, only 28 percent were so listed in 1880. Who were these women? How did they come? And what were their living conditions?

NINETEENTH-CENTURY CHINA AND METHODS OF PROCUREMENT

Like male Chinese laborers, who were first welcomed with open arms to California and then persecuted and excluded, the Chinese prostitutes faced similar treatment by the white population. This change in attitude is reflected in the accounts of nineteenth-century writers. Their works tended either to dwell on the exotic or to exaggerate the evil. Nevertheless, if selected cautiously and juxtaposed with other sources including those published in Chinese, these works can provide useful information in the construction of the history of Chinese prostitution.[8]

An examination of the available sources indicates that the most prevalent means of procurement were, in descending order, luring and kidnapping, contractual agreements, and sale.

Because of population pressure, class exploitation, and foreign imperialism, some areas in nineteenth-century China were so impoverished that many peasant families could not make ends meet even after a year's hard toil. To survive, a family, particularly in times of natural disaster and war, was frequently compelled to resort to mortgaging, infanticide, and the abandonment or selling of children. Female children were particularly vulnerable for both economic and social reasons. Since most productive labor was dependent on physical strength, female workers were less valuable than male ones. In any case, female labor would only contribute to the husbands' families. Furthermore, in patriarchal and patrilineal Chinese society, only males could carry on the ancestral line, and thus, it was always the girls in the family who were the first victims of extreme poverty.

One preferred solution for relieving the family of its female members was prostitution because it was remunerative: The family did not have to provide for the girl's upkeep and her sale or part of her earnings could help support the family. Parents sold their daughters and husbands sold their wives for various reasons, but the most fundamental one was survival—survival of the more "important" members of the family for

---

[8] In addition to the titles cited in footnote 2, see also California Senate Report on Chinese Immigration, 1878; San Francisco Board of Supervisors Special Committee Report on Chinatown, 1885; U.S. Congress Joint Special Committee to Investigate Chinese Immigration Report, 1877. For a complete listing of sources used in this paper, see Hirata's forthcoming article.

the preservation and continuation of the lineage. Sometimes the parents sold their daughters in order to pay the bride price for a wife for their son. At other times daughters and wives were sold to pay a debt, and often they were given as mortgage security and became slaves through foreclosure. The Wells Fargo History Room in San Francisco contained a brief report of a Chinese man in California who sold his daughter in order to have the passage money to return to China. A number of prostitutes in San Francisco were originally orphans who were sold into brothels by their relatives. Young girls sold to masters or mistresses as *mooi-tzai* (domestic slaves) were often resold into brothels when they reached 12 years of age. Brothel owners in San Francisco often informed their agents in Canton and Hong Kong of an appropriate purchase price to ensure a large profit.

Sometimes the agents were not successful in getting enough females on the market to fulfill their orders. They would then send subagents into the rural districts to lure or kidnap girls and young women and forward the victims to the shipping ports. Quite frequently those individuals who did the luring were emigrants from the same communities who had returned temporarily for a visit. The baits used included promises of marriages, jobs, or education. Two cases illustrate how this was perpetrated. The first case, which also reveals his attitude toward Chinese women, was related by a missionary:

> In the village of Paak Mok Tong, close to the great city of Canton lived a dainty little maid, Ah Yee. She was a refined, sensitive little creature, and really quite beautiful. Her father was dead. There was a family to support and her mother was poor. Then along came Jeah Sing Fong, a dashing young adventurer, who had lived some years in the United States and had returned to China with many grand airs. He was attired in the height of fashion and came, he said, to seek a wife, and take her back to "The Flowery Country" (America), there to share with him the prosperity which abounds in the "Golden Hills" (California).
>
> Ah Yee's mother listened to his story. Her bosom swelled with pride as she heard this young cavalier declare his love for her daughter. She sighed with relief when the agreement was concluded, for she felt that now the family would not suffer from want. So Ah Yee became a happy bride and set sail for America with Jeah Sing Fong.
>
> Upon their arrival at San Francisco they engaged a room in the Golden Gate Hotel on Grant Avenue where an older woman, King Fah, came to call upon the young newlyweds. Nine days later, Jeah Sing Fong departed, leaving his bride in the keeping of King Fah who took her to what she called her home and led her into a small room in a house on Spofford Alley.[9]

[9] Charles Shepherd, "Chinese Girl Slavery in America," *Missionary Review*, 46 (1923), 893–895.

The second case comes from an autobiographic account of Wong Ah-so:

> I was born in Canton Province [sic], my father was sometimes a sailor and sometimes he worked on the docks, for we were very poor.
>
> I was 19 when this man came to my mother and said that in America there was a great deal of gold. Even if I just peeled potatoes, there, he told my mother I would earn seven or eight dollars a day, and if I was willing to do any work at all I would earn lots of money. He was a laundryman, but said he earned plenty of money. He was very nice to me, and my mother liked him, so my mother was glad to have me go with him as his wife.[10]

It turned out that the man was given money by a brothel owner to buy a woman for prostitution. After two weeks in San Francisco's China-town, Ah-so was turned over to her owner. Similar experiences were told by Gion Sing and Chun Ho and reported in the United States Industrial Commission Report of 1901.

Kidnapping and stealing young girls and women for purposes of prostitution was not uncommon in traditional China. Sometimes the victims were invited to see the big American steamer anchored at the docks, and while they were enjoying the tour, the boat would start on its way to San Francisco. More often, kidnapping was carried out by force, and the victims were frequently daughters of relatively well-to-do families. On an official visit to the United States in 1888, Chinese envoy Fu Yun-lung composed a memorial that was inscribed on the gravestone of a Cantonese woman who had committed suicide after being kidnapped and sold into prostitution in San Francisco.

TREATMENT IN AMERICA

Not infrequently, kidnapping of Chinese females also took place in California. The *Alta California* and the San Francisco *Bulletin* carried many such news stories.

Many brothels in San Francisco during this period seemed to have had an arrangement with their workers similar to that described as the Chinese contract coolie system that dominated early emigration to Cuba and Peru. They were brought in under a contract of body service for a specified time, usually four to five years, during which they received no wages, and if they succeeded in working out their terms of service, they could, theoretically, get out of the business.

The traffic in women became more difficult after the passage of the

---

[10] Fisk University, Social Science Institute, *Orientals and Their Cultural Adjustment*, Nashville, Tenn., 1946, p. 31.

political code and other laws allowing the commissioner of immigration to prevent certain classes of people, including "lewd or debauched" women, from immigrating to California. These laws did result in an immediate but short-term drop in the number of female arrivals. However, as with many such laws, these did not stop the importation of women but instead had the effect of subjecting women to the indignities of close scrutiny both in Hong Kong and San Francisco, and making it more expensive to import women. Chinese women were landed under false pretenses concocted by the secret societies that were importing prostitutes. Tongs were also believed to have smuggled in women attired as boys, or hidden in buckets of coal, or concealed in padded crates labeled as dishware. The Chinese who were engaged in this business found that they had to share their profits with the United States Consulate in Hong Kong, the white lawyers and immigration inspectors in San Francisco, and consequently they raised the prices. Girls who were originally sold for 50 dollars at Canton now brought 1,000 dollars in the San Francisco market.

After the women were landed in San Francisco, they were transported to Chinatown and housed in temporary quarters known as the *barracoons,* where they were displayed for bids. Except for a few women who were bought by the well-to-do Chinese as concubines, the rest ended in brothels of various grades. While a small number were recruited to high-class dens where they would serve an exclusively Chinese clientele, the majority found themselves in brothels where, due to their comparatively low fees of 25 to 50 cents, they tended to attract white and Chinese customers. The latter type of prostitutes were often mistreated by their owners as well as by their customers. A few brothel owners, for example, occasionally beat some of them to death, and white men often forced them to engage in aberrant sexual acts, or, worse yet, occasionally shot them.[11]

Prostitutes of the highest grade lived in upstairs apartments in Chinatown and had a more or less long-term regular customer or customers. Very often the client was also the owner. It is not always accurate to characterize these women as prostitutes. Some may have been concubines and others may have lived in polyandry. They were often attractive and expensively adorned. While they may have appeared to be well treated, they were nevertheless chattels who could be sold by their masters at will. Essays and short stories written during the period tended to portray them as extremely vain. One story related the tale of a young man who labored day and night for three years in order to save 400 dollars to redeem his sister from a "humiliating and secret bondage." But the sister liked the life that she led with good dinners and pretty

11 *The Golden Hills News,* July 29, 1854 (in Chinese).

things and did not want to leave. She stole the money from her brother and bought a sealskin coat. The brother promised her owner that he would work hard for three more years to get the money again. As he left brokenhearted, she murmured: "Fool!" [12]

Most of the lower-grade prostitutes lived in the street-level compartments usually not larger than 4×6 feet and facing some dim alley. There were a few articles of furniture—a bamboo chair or two, a washbowl, and hard bunks or shelves covered with matting. The door usually held the only window in the room, and it was always covered with bars or a heavy screen, behind which the women, dressed in cotton tunics and trousers, could stand and call to passersby. The women were served two or three meals a day, the evening one usually consisting of a huge mound of rice and a stew of pork, mixed with hard-boiled eggs, liver, and kidneys.[13] The more fortunate ones were sometimes asked to entertain at parties given by tong leaders and Chinese merchants. They did not have regular wages, but instead were allowed to keep the jewelry, silk, and cash gifts given by their customers. This is perhaps why some prostitutes were able to send money to their parents in China. Although the amount is not known, it seems clear that some of the remittances that emigrant communities in Kwangtung received during the nineteenth and early twentieth centuries were from prostitutes in California.

The managers of the brothels, called "mothers" by the prostitutes, were not always the owners. Tong members who actually owned prostitutes often asked their wives or mistresses or an older prostitute to manage them. Normally half of the earnings of the prostitutes would go to the mothers and half to the owners.

Owners of brothels often also owned opium dens and gambling joints. Some prostitutes were addicted to opium and/or gambled excessively. The owners often loaned them money to feed their habits so that they would not only be dependent on the owners for these services, but they would also become more deeply indebted to them. From the point of view of many prostitutes, opium smoking was probably the only way they could find relief, and gambling the only avenue to an alternative life. Women who were desperate committed suicide by swallowing raw opium or drowning themselves in the bay.

The more fortunate ones were redeemed and married, mostly to Chinese workers. There did not seem to be the same stigma attached to prostitution among the Chinese masses as there was among whites. Part of the reason might be that prostitutes in China were generally not seen as "fallen women" or "degenerate women who craved for lust," but very often as filial daughters who obeyed the wishes of family. Although

[12] Sui Seen Far, "Lin John," *Land of Sunshine,* 10 (1899), 76–77.
[13] Dobie, *San Francisco's Chinatown,* p. 243.

prostitution was definitely not considered an honored profession, particularly among the gentry, women who were able to get out of it were usually accepted in the working-class society.

Apparently quite a few women in San Francisco were able to leave the brothels, although not without struggle, and often at tremendous risk. Throughout the mid-nineteenth and the early twentieth centuries, reports of such instances abound. Typically, a woman would run away to the missions, the police stations, or to her lover, with the hired tong soldiers on her trail. They might succeed in kidnapping her directly or, failing that, resort to other methods. The tongs often utilized the American courts to get her back. They would file a charge of theft, claiming the woman had absconded with some clothes or jewelry. After the police had located the woman, the tong would hire white lawyers to pay her bail and then return her to the brothel.

When this maneuver was not effective, tongs would put up public announcements on Chinatown walls warning others who might assist her escape and offering rewards for her capture. If a specific man was known to have run away with her, the tongs would offer a reward for him, dead or alive. Such rewards sometimes could run into the thousands, depending on the value of the woman involved. Stories were told of cases where the man and woman would leave the area in disguise or hidden in wooden boxes and flee to another place. Some telegrams between Chinese men in Marysville, Downieville, San Francisco, and other places revealed that a network of search and return was in operation at least during the 1870s.[14] Once caught and returned to the owner, the prostitute was likely to be whipped or beaten, resold, or sent away to the mines. Prostitutes in the mining areas, serving both white and Chinese clients, were often much more ill-treated than their counterparts in San Francisco brothels.

In order to prevent the woman from escaping, tongs were known to give the local police a retainer. Until 1877, a Special Police Force was engaged in a quasi-official capacity as peace officers in Chinatown. They received no set wages, but derived their incomes from the Chinese residents. At one point they were reported to be earning 1,000 dollars per month. They normally collected 50 cents a week from each prostitute and admitted that whenever there was a crackdown on prostitution, their income would be reduced.

If the prostitute did not succeed in escaping from the clutches of her exploiters, her life in the brothels probably would not last beyond four or five years. The length of a Chinese prostitute's working life in San Francisco did not seem to differ from that of other prostitutes in other large cities during this period. With a complete lack of medical care, many prostitutes became ill after a short time. The abundance of

[14] *California Chinese Chatter*, Dressler, San Francisco, 1927.

Chinese advertisements for a "secret formula" for curing syphilis and gonorrhea during this period testified to the prevalence of such illnesses. Although some doctors blamed the Chinese prostitutes for spreading the diseases to the white population, it was pointed out by other physicians that these illnesses were equally, if not more prevalent among white prostitutes in San Francisco. Though they rarely led to death, these illnesses were often causes of sterility.

Money Earned by Prostitutes

How much money did the average Chinese prostitute make for her owner during the length of her servitude? We have no direct information on this question. However, we can venture some estimates. The lowest grade of prostitute received 25 cents to 50 cents per customer. According to the literature on prostitution in general, an average full-time worker would receive at least four to ten customers per day. The contracts mentioned earlier bound the prostitute to at least four years of servitude and indicated that she would work 320 days per year. An absence of more than 15 days would subject her to a penalty of working one extra month. This means that at an average of 38 cents per customer and seven customers per day, a lower-grade prostitute would earn about 850 dollars per year and 3,404 dollars after four years of servitude. Since women in the inferior dens were kept at the subsistence level, the cost of maintaining them must not have exceeded 8 dollars per month or 96 dollars per year per person. Furthermore, the average capital outlay—that is, cancelled debt or the purchase price of a woman—usually amounted to an average of 530 dollars. These calculations indicate that the owner would begin to make a profit from the prostitute's labor in the first year of her service! Considering the average size of the brothel, which was about nine in 1870, this would give the owner a gross of 7,650 dollars per year. Subtracting rent and maintenance of the women, the owner would end up with an average of no less than 5,000 dollars. Even if we added other expenses, such as paying protection fees to the police and tax to the tongs, the profit the brothel owner received would still compare very favorably to the average income of other occupational pursuits that he or she might engage in, which was less than 500 dollars per year. These figures applied only to the lower grade of prostitutes; the higher grades would charge more for their services.

The most profitable situation from the procurers' point of view would be to get the girls to go with them voluntarily to San Francisco. In one case, the procurer succeeded in painting a glowing picture of California, and with 98 dollars obtained the consent of the mother to have her daughter go with the mistress. Upon arrival she sold her for 1,950 dollars and thus pocketed a profit of at least 1,702 dollars including transportation. The girl worked two years for her owner, earning no less than 290 dollars per month. At the end of the two years she was sold for 2,100 dollars.[15] The gross income that the brothel owner received from her labor as a prostitute was 5,580 dollars. Even if she was kept at a higher standard of living, the net profit must have been no less than 3,000 dollars in two years. All of these calculations do not even take into account the sewing and other forms of work that the women were assigned to do in the brothels during the day. The exploitative relations between the prostitute worker, the procurer, and the brothel owner are clearly indisputable. The huge profits made from their exploitation were invested into other businesses, both in California and in China, in the form of mercantile or industrial capital.

OCCUPATIONAL TRENDS

Although the majority of Chinese immigrant women in California in the 1860s and 1870s worked as prostitutes, others were scattered among different occupational groups including "keeping house," a designation used by census takers primarily as the occupation of unemployed house-wives. For instance, in 1870, of the approximately 3,536 Chinese adult women, 21 percent were recorded to be "keeping house." As mentioned before, the largest employed group was prostitutes, accounting for 61 percent of all women. The remaining 18 percent were distributed among a variety of occupations, none of which can be labeled white collar.

By 1880, a number of trends seem evident. As indicated in the table below, there were some changes in the first ten largest occupations from 1860 to 1880. But the changes did not signify a tendency toward upward mobility among Chinese women. The occupations remained largely the same except in different rank order. To a considerable extent, these changes in rank order can be related to the changes in economic development and the resulting population movement of Chinese women.

When the method of mining changed from placer mining to mechanized mining, and the organization of production changed from small independent miners to capitalist mining companies, the number of independent Chinese miners dwindled, and the Chinese along with other laborers were recruited to work for mining companies. Among them were a small number of women, whose numbers declined with the development of mining technology. Specifically, the number of Chinese women engaged in mining dropped from 63 in 1860 to 29 in 1870 and to 11 in 1880, or from third place to fifth and then to ninth place. This pattern of decline reflected not only the changing mode of production but also the persecution and subsequent departure of Chinese workers from the mines into railroad building and other pursuits. This relationship is corroborated by the fact that among the small number of female laborers

15 *U.S. Industrial Commission Report*, 1901, p. 783.

Occupations of immigrant Chinese women

1860	1870	1880
Prostitute	Prostitute	Keeping house
Wife or possible wife	Keeping house	Prostitute
Laundress	Servant	Seamstress
Miner	Laundress	Servant
Servant	Seamstress	Laundress
Laborer	Miner	Cook
Seamstress	Housekeeper	Needlework
Housekeeper	Fisherman	Entertainer (actor, theatrical performer)
Cook	Shoe binder	Laborer
Gardener	Cook	Miner
Lodging house operator	Laborer	Lodging house operator

SOURCE: Compiled from the manuscript population censuses of California, 1860, 1870, and 1880.

in 1880, a majority were identified as railroad laborers, the first time that this designation appeared in the manuscript population census. These female railroad workers, between the ages of 24 and 40, were found rooming together near Truckee. Additional evidence of the relationship is provided by the increase in the proportion of Chinese women in San Francisco. While in 1880, more than half of the Chinese women were found living in San Francisco, only one-third resided there in 1860.

If we compare the occupational distribution of Chinese women with that of all California women during the same period, we find that the former were not represented in the white-collar occupations like nursing and teaching, occupations that ranked among the top ten for California women as a whole. Their concentration in the least-esteemed occupations reflected the lack of employment opportunities for Chinese women, not only in relation to Chinese men but also in relation to white women.

INCREASING NUMBER OF CHINESE HOUSEWIVES

The second trend in occupational change during this period was the increase in the number of housewives. While the total number of Chinese adult women decreased somewhat, those designated as keeping house doubled from 753 (21 percent) in 1870 to 1,445 (46 percent) in 1880. Most of this increase occurred outside of San Francisco County.

It is necessary to point out that keeping house was only one of the roles performed by Chinese married women, many of whom were also wage workers or worked in small family-operated businesses. A few married women even worked as prostitutes. The designation keeping house was given only to women who were not performing household functions for pay, and who reported no other occupations. Among all married women in 1880 about 72 percent were classified as such.

The increase of married women during this period cannot be explained by new immigration alone, since the total number of women in California actually declined and it is unlikely that a large number of prostitutes went back to China while wives came. The partriarchal family system in China, the successive restrictions placed on immigration by United States authorities, the racial hostility against the Chinese all combined to retard the immigration of Chinese women. Therefore, it is very likely that a proportion of the married women in 1880 were former prostitutes.

It has often been stated that only merchants and the well-to-do could afford to send for their wives from China. Although the more affluent Chinese men were more likely to have their wives and concubines live with them in California, particularly after the 1882 Exclusion Act, at least until 1880 a considerable number of workers also lived with their wives. The 1880 census is especially useful for studying the family structure of the Chinese because it identifies the relationship of each member of the household with the household head. An examination of these manuscripts enables us to make some observations about the married Chinese women in California, and about their family structure.

The traditional Chinese family of three generations in one household was apparently not transplanted into California. We found no complete three-generational families in the 1880 records. Occasionally a grandfather was found living with his son's family, but such phenomena were extremely rare. More typically, the family structure included a married couple, the husband about 14 years older than the wife, and no child. The average age of wives was as high as 30.2, and the lowest recorded was 16. It seems that the account of the 14-year-old Chinese mother reported by Foote in 1878 was an exception rather than the rule. One expression of racial hostility in the late nineteenth century was the fear that there would soon be a permanent yellow population in California. Given the facts that the average number of children per Chinese family was only 0.70 and the average age of Chinese wives was over 30, many were nearing the end of their reproductive cycle, and given the declining number of female immigrants in 1880, such fear seemed more like hysteria.

Family size was obviously related to the class status of the male head of household. Although the average family size among workers was

2.4, that among the merchants and business owners was 4.1. Some families of the petit bourgeoisie had as many as 9 persons.

The life of a Chinese businessman's wife was quite different from that of a laborer's. Although both were likely to have come from Canton, the merchant's wife was usually of middle-class background and the laborer's wife was more often the offspring of a peasant family. The former lived in seclusion, generally upstairs from her husband's place of business. Her quarters were usually furnished with Chinese tables and chairs and decorated with Chinese ornaments. Until she gave birth to a child, she was unlikely to be seen in public places. Sui Seen Far, a Eurasian woman writing in the nineteenth century, described the social life of these Chinese women in the following passage:

> *Now and then the women visit one another; and when they are met together, there is such a clattering of tongues one would almost think they were American women. They laugh at the most commonplace remark and scream at the smallest trifle; they examine one another's dresses and hair, talk about their husbands, their babies, their food; squabble over little matters and make up again; they dine on bowls of rice, minced chicken, bamboo shoots and a dessert of candied fruits.*[16]

Since well-to-do families had house servants, their women did not have to perform daily maintenance chores such as cooking, laundering, and cleaning. They usually filled their leisure time with needlework to be used as presents for distant relatives or as ornaments on caps for husband and children.

These descriptions applied only to less than 1 percent of Chinese married women. The rest led a much less comfortable life. Although many of the women married to the less prosperous Chinese had two sets of responsibilities, one related to a job outside the home, the other related to being a wife, most were not employed and were identified as keeping house. But it would be grossly incorrect to conclude that most wives did not work. It was with good reason that wives were often given the occupational designation keeping house if they were not wage earners. For those households where a woman was so designated, a study of the number of residents per household revealed that at least 20 percent of the households had boarders or lodgers. In some households, the number of boarders reached 38, although 2 or 3 seemed to be the most common. Under these circumstances, the work of the housewife must have been

[16] Sui Seen Far, "The Chinese Woman in America," *Land of Sunshine,* 6 (January 1897), 62.

considerable and no less trying than a job outside the home. Further-more, housewives of small businessmen who could not afford to hire servants often helped out in the business without being recorded. It was also highly probable that many women did piecework at home for sub-contractors but did not report these activities to the census taker.

Even if she were "just a housewife," her life could not have been an easy one. Food had to be cooked, clothes mended and laundered, rooms cleaned, and children tended. Many married women made cloth-ing and cloth shoes for their families.

OTHER OCCUPATIONS OF WOMEN WAGE LABORERS

The third observation that can be made from the table is the rise in the number of Chinese women engaged in wage labor. Despite the significant decrease of women recorded as prostitutes, they remained the largest occupational group aside from keeping house, comprising 24 percent of the total of Chinese women in 1880. The sewing trade, including occupa-tions such as seamstress, tailoress, and dressmaker, jumped to the second largest place in the rank order of employment, rising from 36 (1 per-cent) in 1870 to 192 (5 percent) in 1880. Actually, the number of Chinese women engaged in sewing for pay must have been more. The San Francisco *Alta* reported that one Chinese official estimated about 764 women depended on sewing for their livelihood. As would be expected, sewing was predominantly an urban pursuit. Unlike the increase of women who kept house, which took place mainly away from San Fran-cisco, the growth in the sewing occupation was exclusively a San Francisco phenomenon. Even then, Chinese women engaged in the sewing trade were outnumbered by Chinese men at a 10 to 1 ratio. It was not until the twentieth century that Chinese women took this occupation over from the men.

Except for their occupational distribution there is very little infor-mation concerning the Chinese female wage earner in nineteenth-century California. The seamstress might be either married or unmarried. If unmarried she tended to live together with other seamstresses. Most of the married seamstresses were widows or women whose husbands were in similar lines of business, such as tailoring. Regardless of their marital status, they tended to work at home, receiving their work from Chinese subcontractors. Contemporary writers told of their working from dawn till late at night in exchange for very low wages. It was reported that few sewing factories paid women the standard wage of 2 dollars per day; most paid much less. The California State Bureau of Labor Statistics claimed that women normally received only 50 cents per day for sewing and repairing clothing. This was the chief reason that the report gave for the prevalence of white prostitution.

The female Chinese servant was mostly found in white families. If she were married, her husband would most likely be found working for the same family. The husband was often the cook and his wife the domestic who cared for the household. Her duties included cleaning, washing, and caring for children. Often she was asked to sew or mend for the family also. A nineteenth-century writer reported such a woman being made a spectacle by the white children, who charged visitors 5 cents for a look at her.

Sometimes Chinese servants were also found in well-to-do Chinese families. Some were older women in their late 40s or 50s who, as the census indicates, might be widowed or former prostitutes.[17] But many of these female servants were young and single, often in their early teens. Some might have been brought by the families from China and were held for an indefinite period of time. Others, like prostitutes, were bought from poor families in China. What follows is a typical story, dated 1876, of a Chinese female child who was sold as a domestic slave.

> *I was born in Sin Lam, China, seventeen years ago. My father was a weaver and my mother had small feet. I had a sister and brother younger than myself. My father was an industrious man, but we were poor. My feet were never bound; I am thankful they were not. My father sold me when I was about seven years old; my mother cried. I was afraid, and ran under the bed to hide. My father came to see me once and brought me some fruit; but my mistress told me to say that he was not my father. I did so, but afterward I felt very sorry. He seemed very sad, and when he went away he gave me a few cash, and wished me prosperity. That was the last time I saw him. I was sold four times. I came to California about five years ago. My last mistress was very cruel to me; she used to whip me, pull my hair, and pinch the inside of my cheeks.[18]*

Although we find such female child domestics in California, there is no evidence that a similar situation existed for male children. This difference again is attributable to both economic and social factors. Female children more than male ones were sacrificed for the survival of the family. And because owners of female child domestics could always look forward to selling the girl when she came of age, they could benefit not only from her service as a servant but also from her sale as a commodity.

California in the mid-nineteenth century was a fast-developing frontier society. The sexual imbalance and the youthfulness of the male

[17] Dorothy Gray, *Women of the West*, Les Femmes, Millbrae, Calif., 1976, p. 69.
[18] Otis Gibson, *Chinese in America*, Hitchcock, Cincinnati, 1877, pp. 220–221.

population had particular consequences for women. Although demographic factors delimited the general forms of women's participation in this development, racial hostility, cultural traditions, and internal class structure fostered the particular roles that Chinese immigrant women fulfilled. The racial, sexual, and class biases of most nineteenth-century writers have left an image of Chinese women as either degenerates by nature or helpless robots. White observers tended to emphasize the exotic or the evil, and Chinese writers tried to counter with exaltations of a few upper-class or highly educated women. Hidden from history are the experiences of the majority of early Chinese immigrant women, who tried to survive within a complex structure characterized by racial antagonism, sexual oppression, and class exploitation. This essay is only the beginning in uncovering the history.

Documents

The Ratio of Chinese Women to Men Compared to the Ratio of Women to Men in the Total Population of California, 1850–1970

	Chinese Males per 100 Females	Total Males per 100 Females
1850	39,450.0[a]	1,228.6
1860	1,858.1	255.1
1870	1,172.3	165.4
1880	1,832.4	149.3
1890	2,245.4	137.6
1900	1,223.9	123.5
1910	1,017.0	125.4
1920	528.8	112.5
1930	298.6	107.6
1940	223.6	103.7
1950	161.9	100.1
1960	127.8	99.5
1970	107.0	96.9

a There were only 2 Chinese women in 1850.
Source: Ratio for Chinese from 1850 to 1960 based on *Californians of Japanese, Chinese, and Filipino Ancestry: Population, Education, Employment, Income,* Department of Industrial Relations, San Francisco, 1965; 1970 ratio based on U.S. Bureau of the Census, *Historical Census of the United States,* Bicentennial Ed., U.S. Government Printing Office, Washington, D.C., 1975.

☙

Chinese in California: Distribution by County, Number of Women, and Percentage of Population, 1880

County	Number of Chinese Females	Percentage of Females in Chinese Population	Percentage of Chinese in Total Population
Alameda	35	0.8%	7.0%
Alpine	2	11.8	3.2
Amador	64	5.7	9.8
Butte	100	2.6	20.3
Calaveras	64	6.1	11.4
Colusa	23	2.4	7.4
Contra Costa	2	0.3	5.8
Del Norte	9	2.1	16.8
El Dorado	80	5.4	13.9
Fresno	45	5.6	7.9
Humboldt	15	6.2	1.6
Inyo	11	12.2	3.1
Kern	53	7.5	12.5
Lake	1	0.2	7.1
Lassen	2	4.0	1.5
Los Angeles	53	4.5	3.5
Marin	38	2.9	11.7
Mariposa	55	7.9	16.1
Mendocino	10	2.9	2.7
Merced	31	5.4	10.2
Mono	49	13.5	4.8
Monterey	22	5.9	3.3
Napa	12	1.3	6.8
Nevada	93	3.1	14.4
Placer	76	3.5	15.4
Plumas	21	2.4	14.1
Sacramento	162	3.3	14.2
San Benito	1	0.4	4.3
San Bernardino	2	1.6	1.6
San Diego	22	9.6	2.7
San Francisco	1,980	9.1	9.3
San Joaquin	12	0.6	8.2
San Luis Obispo	10	5.5	2.0
San Mateo	6	1.0	6.9

Chinese in California (cont.)

County	Number of Chinese Females	Percentage of Females in Chinese Population	Percentage of Chinese in Total Population
Santa Barbara	10	4.4	2.4
Santa Clara	66	2.4	7.7
Santa Cruz	14	2.7	4.1
Shasta	19	1.4	14.1
Sierra	42	3.4	19.0
Siskiyou	55	3.5	18.2
Solano	14	1.4	5.4
Sonoma	15	1.7	3.5
Stanislaus	53	10.2	5.9
Tehama	27	3.5	8.3
Trinity	27	1.4	39.0
Tulare	23	7.1	2.9
Tuolumne	50	6.2	10.3
Ventura	4	3.1	2.5
Yolo	9	1.5	5.2
Yuba	101	4.7	19.0

SOURCE: Figures for the Chinese are computed from the manuscript population census of 1880. Table prepared by Paul Nakatsuka and used with permission.

A Chinese Prostitute's Contract, 1886

The contractee Xin Jin became indebted to her master/mistress for food and passage from China to San Francisco.* Since she is without funds, she will voluntarily work as a prostitute at Tan Fu's place for four and one-half years for an advance of 1,205 yuan (U.S. $524) to pay this debt. There shall be no interest on the money and Xin Jin shall receive no wages. At the expiration of the contract, Xin Jin shall be free to do as she pleases. Until then, she shall first secure the master/mistress's permission if a customer asks to take her out. If she has the four loathsome diseases she shall be returned within 100 days; beyond that time the procurer has no responsibility. Menstruation disorder is limited to one month's rest only. If Xin Jin becomes sick at any time for more than 15 days, she shall work one month extra; if she becomes pregnant, she

* Translated by Lucie Cheng Hirata with permission from *Pigtails and Gold Dust* by Alexander McLeod, The Caxton Printers, Ltd., Caldwell, Idaho, by permission.

shall work one year extra. Should Xin Jin run away before her term is out, she shall pay whatever expense is incurred in finding and returning her to the brothel. This is a contract to be retained by the master/mistress as evidence of the agreement. Receipt of 1205 yuan ($524) by Ah Yo. Thumb print of Xin Jin in the contractee. Eighth month 11th day of the 12th year of Guang-zu (1886).

Map of California Counties, 1880

SOURCE: California County Fact Book, County Supervisors Association of California, Sacramento, 1963.

10 *Be Fruitful and Multiply:*
Origins of Legal Restrictions on Planned Parenthood
in Nineteenth-Century America

John Paull Harper

Madame Restell. Courtesy of General Research and Humanities Division, The
New York Public Library, Astor, Lenox and Tilden Foundations.

> *She had stated that during her pregnancies she had suffered*
> *so much discomfort that she had determined to bear no more*
> *children. She procured a piece of steel wire as long and as large*
> *as an ordinary knitting needle. . . . She had laid herself upon the*
> *bed and passing this wire up the vagina, pushed it, as she*
> *thought, very gently, into the uterine canal. Suddenly it slipped*
> *up and disappeared.*
>
> T. Gaillard Thomas, "Death From an Attempt at Criminal
> Abortion," American Journal of Medical Science, 65
> (1873), 406–407.

During the nineteenth century, American public leaders developed a legal policy to, in their term, "suppress" trade in goods and services for planned parenthood.[1] Although this restrictive legislation failed to abolish all such illicit practices, government officials prevented medical experts from openly dispensing relatively safe methods of controlling fertility. Therefore, many women needlessly perished by their own hand or in the hands of incompetent medical practitioners.

What had motivated the men who increased the dangers of planned parenthood? Historians like Carroll Smith-Rosenberg and G. J. Barker-Benfield have depicted the restrictive legislation as an irrational social policy. They contended that sexually insecure men, including, in Barker-Benfield's view, at least one alleged latent homosexual, compulsively adopted this policy to reaffirm their psychic domination over women. Because these authors found a lot of irrational sexist rhetoric in the propaganda against planned parenthood, they mistakenly assumed that the men who inspired this policy sought the oppression of women as an end in itself. Smith-Rosenberg and Barker-Benfield overlooked perhaps more chilling evidence that rational policy makers thoughtfully proposed the restrictive legislation in order to combat what they judged to be a population problem.[2]

ORIGINS OF A CONTROVERSY

In 1837 Reverend Horace Bushnell, an influential Congregational spokesman, assailed planned parenthood in his speech to the Phi Beta Kappa Society at Yale College. "We hear of one whole people," he stated in

[1] The term *planned parenthood* in this essay denotes a conscious decision to control fertility by abortion or contraception.

[2] Carroll Smith-Rosenberg and Charles Rosenberg, "The Female Animal: Medical and Biological Views of Woman and Her Role in Nineteenth-Century America," *Journal of American History*, 60 (1973), 332–356; G. J. Barker-Benfield, *Horrors of the Half-Known Life: Male Attitudes Toward Women in Nineteenth-Century America*, Harper & Row, New York, 1976.

reference to the French, "who are in danger of dwindling to absolute extinction, by force of this simple cause." The clergyman expressed concern about such "vices and degraded manners" as abortion and contraception in his own country. Bushnell proposed that government officials ban planned parenthood to head off the decline of "the Saxon stock" in the United States. "Do I speak of enforcing morals by law?" he cried. "Certainly I do. Only a decent respect for the blood of the nation requires it."

While Bushnell presented the first known public warning about declining fertility, other professional men had earlier anticipated this incipient social problem. In fact, physicians like John B. Beck of New York had been promoting legal restrictions on abortion for two decades. Beck, a prominent young physician in New York City, originally raised the issue of abortion in 1817 in a scholarly monograph on infanticide. He explained that medical scientists had discovered many methods of inducing premature delivery, including "emmenagogues" like "ergot," "savine," and "pennyroyal," and "the introduction of an instrument into the womb, which, by rupturing the membrane, destroys the child." Beck proposed legislation banning this medical treatment for planned parenthood. In 1823 he reiterated his opposition to voluntary abortion, apparently persuading New York lawmakers to address this issue in a general revision of the state criminal law.

New York legislators included legal restrictions on abortion in the revised statutes of 1829. By this law:

> *Every person who shall wilfully administer to any pregnant woman, any medicine, drug or substance whatever, or shall use or employ any instrument or other means, with intent thereby to destroy such child, unless the same shall have been necessary to preserve the life of such woman . . . shall, upon conviction, be punished by imprisonment in a county jail not more than one year, or by a fine not exceeding five hundred dollars, or by both such fine and imprisonment.*

Lawmakers in other states followed suit, gradually adopting the New York state code over the following two decades.

Meanwhile, in 1839 Hugh L. Hodge, Professor of Obstetrics at the University of Pennsylvania, condemned abortion in *An Introductory Lecture to the Course on Obstetrics.* "Human existence commences at conception," Hodge insisted. "[T]he embryo is endowed, at once, with the principles of vitality; and, although retained within the system of its mother, it has, in a strict sense, an independent existence. It is capable of thought, of reflection; it has a perception of that which is beautiful, of that which is right—of that which is wrong, of virtue and vice. . . . Abortion," he concluded, "is murder."

Hodge confined his remarks to speculative hypotheses about the maturity of embryos, completely ignoring the question of health in this lecture purportedly for medical students. The omission was not simply oversight, for Hodge personally prescribed abortions for health care. He opposed such medical treatment only as a means of planned parenthood.[3]

A RADICAL IDEA

If public leaders deemed family limitation a menace to society, radical intellectuals espoused planned parenthood to improve the lot of individuals in society. Robert Dale Owen, the British emigré, was the first to raise this issue in the United States. He summarized his ideas about family limitation in *Moral Physiology; Or, A Brief and Plain Treatise on the Population Question* in 1830. In this treatise, Owen emphasized economic incentives for controlling fertility.

In how many instances does the hard working father, or more especially the mother, of a poor family, remain slaves throughout their lives, tugging at the oar of incessant labor, toiling to live, and living only to die; when, if their offspring had been limited to two or three only, they might have enjoyed comfort and comparative affluence!

The radical publicist also advocated planned parenthood for health care.

How often is the health of a woman giving birth every year to an infant —happy, if it be not twins!—and compelled to toil on, even at those times when nature imperiously calls for some relief from daily drudgery— how often is the mother's comfort, health, nay, her life, thus sacrificed!

Owen proceeded to discuss several common methods of preventing conception. He rejected "the sponge"—"inserted into the vagina"—for being "of doubtful efficacy," and "the *baudruche*"—"a skin covering the penis"—for being "in every way inconvenient." He prescribed, instead, *coitus interruptus*, or as he put it, "complete withdrawal, on the part of the man, immediately previous to emission. *This is*," he promised, *"in all cases, effectual."* Owen found immense interest in his treatise and distributed 2,500 copies in less than a year.

<hr />

[3] Horace Bushnell, "The True Wealth or Weal of Nations," in *Representative Phi Beta Kappa Orations*, ed. Clark S. Northup, Elisha Parmele Press, New York, 1930, p. 14; John B. Beck, *Infanticide*, J. Seymour, New York, 1817, pp. 40–85; N.Y. Rev. Stat. (1829); Hugh L. Hodge, *Introductory Lecture to the Course on Obstetrics*, Lydia R. Bailey, Philadelphia, 1839, pp. 9–15.

Charles Knowlton, a country doctor in Massachusetts, also advocated "checks to conception" in *Fruits of Philosophy; Or, The Private Companion of Adult People* in 1832. He, like Owen, wanted to mitigate economic distress among the poor, as well as improve the health of women generally. "[M]uch misery may be prevented," he wrote, "by preserving the character of the lecherous, by preventing artificial abortions, and by diminishing infanticide."

Knowlton prescribed a method of contraception that he claimed as his own invention.

It consists, in syringing the vagina, soon after the male emission into it, with some liquid which will not merely dislodge all the semen, as simple water would do—the female being in the most proper position for the operation—but which will destroy the fecundating property of any portion of the semen that may remain. . . . [He suggested] *solutions of almost any astringent vegetables, as white oak bark, hemlock bark, red rose leaves, green tea, raspberry leaves and roots, etc.*

Knowlton personally peddled his book throughout Massachusetts. But, in February 1832, officials in Taunton arrested and fined him. He was again arrested in Lowell the next month. The district attorney charged that the physician had unlawfully distributed "a certain lewd, wicked, scandalous, infamous and obscene printed book, entitled 'Fruits of Philosophy,' purporting to give directions and disseminate a knowledge of means whereby men and women may indulge in carnal intercourse without becoming parents and evade the course of nature by means of chemical agents."

Knowlton stood trial before the Court of Common Pleas in Lowell in December 1832. A jury found him guilty of a misdemeanor at common law, and the judge sentenced him to "three months confinement at hard labour in the house of correction." The experience did not seem to deter Knowlton, for officials arrested him again at his home in Ashfield the next year. The district attorney ultimately dropped the charges when Knowlton agreed to stop peddling his book. But if Knowlton had at last given up dispensing his *Fruits of Philosophy*, other radicals continued distributing it for many years. In 1852 a physician noted that he had discovered Knowlton's book "in nearly every part of our wide-spread country." [4]

---

4 Robert Dale Owen, *Moral Physiology*, Wright and Owen, New York, 1831, pp. 33–61; Charles Knowlton, *Fruits of Philosophy*, F. P. Rogers, Philadelphia, 1839, pp. 7–86; *Commonwealth v. Knowlton*, Knowlton MSS, Middlesex County Courthouse, Massachusetts; [William A. Alcott], *Physiology of Marriage*, John P. Jewett & Co., Boston, 1852, p. 180.

POPULAR PLANNED PARENTHOOD

Doctors and reformers were not alone in their interest in family limitation. Medical entrepreneurs, acting in defiance of traditional social mores, had begun promoting goods and services for controlling fertility.

Madame Restell, "Female Physician," began publishing advertisements "To Married Women" in the New York *Herald* in November 1839. Restell promoted "Female Monthly Regulating Pills" for "all cases of suppression, irregularity, or stoppage of the mensus," costing "$1 a box," and "Preventive Powders" for "married ladies whose health forbids a too rapid increase of family" costing "$5 a package." She also offered her personal "treatment" for "all cases of irregularity" at her office and residence on Greenwich Street.

Other medical entrepreneurs were quick to adopt Madame Restell's advertising techniques. Madame Costello began publicizing "Female Monthly Pills" in the *Herald* in 1841, and Madame Demain began promoting "Female Monthly Regulating Pills" in the Philadelphia *Public Ledger* the next year. Dr. Melveau began proffering "Portuguese Female Monthly Pills" in the New York *Herald* in 1842. By 1843, Dr. Peters advertised "French Renovating Pills" in the Boston *Daily Mail,* and the next year Dr. Kurtz promoted "German Female Monthly Pills" in the *Daily Mail.* Mrs. Mitchell proffered "English Female Regulating Pills" in the Philadelphia *Public Ledger,* and Dr. Carswell and Dr. Hanley began publicizing a "medical and Surgical Institute" for "ladies troubled with irregularity" in the Boston *Daily Mail* in 1847. In the same year, Dr. Walter Scott Tarbox could be found handing out circulars advertising a "Family Regulator, or Wife's Protector" on the streets of Boston. "It is easily introduced by the female," Tarbox explained, "and does not diminish in the least the enjoyment." He sold this rubber diaphragm for five dollars. Thus, with enthusiasm, these medical entrepreneurs introduced popular planned parenthood in the United States.[5]

THE TIGHTENING GRIP OF THE LAW

Public leaders responded immediately to the medical entrepreneurs by launching a legal offensive against the Mrs. Mitchells and Madame Costellos who hawked their wares and skills publicly. On March 22, 1841, a New York City grand jury condemned Madame Restell's advertisements as "an abomination in this noble city," and early the next morning she was arrested. The district attorney charged that the defendant "wilfully,

---

[5] "Dr. Cameron's Patent Family Regulator," Walter Scott Tarbox MSS, Suffolk County Courthouse, Massachusetts.

wickedly, etc. did use and employ certain instruments, to wit, one piece of wire and one pair of pliers, with intent thereby then and there to procure the miscarriage of Mrs. Anna Maria Purdy" in July 1839. Madame Restell stood trial before the Court of General Sessions in July 1841. But Mrs. Purdy was not in the courtroom. The prosecution's chief witness had died of an undisclosed ailment that April. The district attorney, however, submitted a deposition, allegedly obtained from Anna Maria Purdy a month before her death, as the primary evidence against the defendant. The jury found Madame Restell guilty of a misdemeanor.

The New York Supreme Court, however, reviewed a writ of error in July 1842. "The general rule in criminal cases is, that the witness must appear in court and be confronted by the accused party," the judges observed. "The only exception to this rule at common law, is that of *dying declarations,* in prosecutions for homicide." Thus, they reversed the decision against Madame Restell.

Undaunted by her days in court, Madame Restell promptly resumed promoting planned parenthood. Just as promptly, medical men renewed the campaign to imprison her. Gunning S. Bedford, Professor of Midwifery at New York University, assailed Madame Restell's "prodigal destruction of human life" in a speech to the New York Academy of Medicine in 1846. "It, indeed, seems too monstrous for belief," he exclaimed, "that such gross violations of the laws, both of God and man, should be suffered in the very heart of a community professing to be Christian."

Clarkson T. Collins also published an editorial on "Madame Restell, and Some of Her Dupes" in the *New York Medical and Surgical Reporter* that year. Collins denounced Madame Restell as a "notorious fiend in human form," and excoriated abortionists generally for "practicing their charlatanism upon the unwary, and becoming millionaires from the fruits of their wickedness."

It was not until 1847, however, that Madame Restell's opponents could bring her to court. That year a physician informed the magistrates that one of his patients had obtained medicine for an abortion from Madame Restell. Officials arrested the patient, Maria Bodine, for seeking an abortion, but they dropped the charges against her when she agreed to testify against Madame Restell.

That November, Madame Restell stood trial before the Court of General Sessions. The district attorney charged that the defendant did "wilfully kill and slay" Maria Bodine's "child," while the defense counsel contended that his client had treated the woman for venereal disease. The trial did not go smoothly for the "notorious fiend in human form." The district attorney interrogated Maria Bodine about her private life. "I had sexual intercourse with a man named Cook," she stated. "I became pregnant in the latter part of April, 1845." The defense counsel also questioned the witness about her private life. "Did you," he inquired, "have sexual intercourse with any other person than Cook prior to April, 1845?" But the judge disallowed the question. "The witness," he declared, "cannot be compelled to give an answer which would have a tendency to degrade her character." The defense counsel proceeded to interrogate Maria Bodine about Madame Restell's medical treatment. "Did you not," he asked, "have the venereal disease during the fall of 1845?" The judge disallowed this question for the same reason.

The defense counsel surrendered, the jury found Madame Restell guilty of a misdemeanor, and the judge imposed the maximum penalty of imprisonment for one year. The defense counsel duly appealed the decision on the ground that the judge unlawfully disallowed cross-examination of the chief witness for the prosecution, and the New York Supreme Court reviewed the writ of error in January 1848. "The witness in this case had voluntarily proclaimed her own infamy for the purpose of fixing a criminal charge upon the defendant," the judges observed. "She thereby precluded herself from claiming the privilege of not answering questions of a similar character, if they related to the same point." They found the judge in error. The Supreme Court judges nevertheless deemed the error inconsequential in this case. "[S]o far as we can discern," they mused, "it could not have led to any thing material to the defense." They sustained the decision against Madame Restell.

The defense counsel then filed a writ of error with the New York Court of Appeals. Although they granted a stay of proceedings in February 1848, the magistrates refused to release Madame Restell on bail. So, the defense counsel filed a writ of habeas corpus with the New York Supreme Court. Here, Judge Elisha P. Hurlbut conceded that the judiciary customarily granted bail in cases involving only a misdemeanor, but he denied the request in this case. "[T]he offense," he explained, "involves deep moral turpitude."

Judge Hurlbut admonished the defense counsel for contending that the authorities had "punished" Madame Restell. "She suffers no privation but that of her liberty," he stated. "She is under no discipline with a view to her reformation. . . . [N]o punishment can be inflicted on her," he concluded, "until her case shall have been reviewed by the court of last resort." In June 1848, that court summarily sustained the decision against Madame Restell.

Even in jail, however, Madame Restell seemed to escape her proper punishment. Officials eventually discovered that she received special treatment on Blackwell's Island. "Her husband was allowed to visit her alone," a newsman later noted, "her victuals were of a far superior kind to the regular prison fare, she was allowed a feather bed to sleep on, had a light in her cell and was not locked up at the same time as the other convicts." The magistrates dismissed the warden who provided such humane treatment to such a notorious evildoer. But her enemies had not foreseen Madame Restell's resiliency. Released from prison in 1849, she once again pursued her occupation.

Officials meanwhile reported prosecuting eight other medical entrepreneurs for performing abortions around the country during the 1840s, five of whom they convicted and imprisoned. Arrested too was Dr. Walter Scott Tarbox, the Boston leafleteer. The district attorney charged that the defendant "did print, publish, and distribute a certain printed paper containing obscene language and descriptions, manifestly tending to the corruption of the morals of youth, which was left at the door of the dwelling houses of one hundred of the Citizens of Boston." A jury found Tarbox guilty of a misdemeanor under the state obscenity law, but the Massachusetts Supreme Court reversed the decision in 1848 on a technicality.

The effect of the 1840s crackdown on planned parenthood was not to be measured by these court cases. Although government officials failed to intimidate medical entrepreneurs like Restell, they apparently did discourage most reputable physicians from openly dispensing the relatively safe methods of controlling fertility known to them.[6]

THE MEDICAL CRUSADE

During the 1850s medical men launched a crusade against planned parenthood. Their impetus was the recognition of an unexpectedly low native birthrate that threatened a decline of their people. In 1851 Jesse Chickering presented an astounding discovery in a report on the population of Boston. "American births," he observed, "hardly equalled American deaths in 1850." Chickering found that native fertility approached zero population growth in Boston at mid-century. By 1853 other investigators had confirmed Chickering's findings for the entire state of Massachusetts. Two years later D. Humphreys Storer, Professor of Obstetrics at Harvard University, proposed a concerted campaign against planned parenthood.

Storer initially assailed planned parenthood in a lecture to his students in 1855. "[V]ariations in tables relating to population," he explained, "must force this subject upon the mind of the physician." He admonished medical men to exert a greater influence against "the means so extensively employed to prevent impregnation," as well as "criminal abortion." Although Storer admittedly viewed planned parenthood as a

6 New York *Herald*, March 23, 1841, and April 2, 1878; *People* v. *Restell*, 3 Hill (N.Y.) 291 (1842); *People* v. *Lohman*, 2 Barb. (N.Y.) 216 (1848); *Lohman* v. *People*, 1 Comst. (N.Y. App.) 379 (1848); *Commonwealth* v. *Tarbox*, 55 Mass. 72 (1848); Clarkson T. Collins, "Madame Restell and Some of Her Dupes," *New York Medical and Surgical Reporter*, 1 (1846), 158–162.

social problem, he raised the specter of danger to justify legal restrictions on such medical practices. He contended that "the functions of no organ" —including the reproductive organs—"can be interfered with without suffering being induced." Even though he was "without sufficient data to warrant me in stating positively the fact," he would "nevertheless, venture the belief that numberless cases of induration, and finally organic disease, must be the inevitable consequences." Thus, Storer charged that planned parenthood inherently involved extreme danger.

Edward H. Clarke, Professor of Materia Medica at Harvard, strenuously objected to Storer's radical allegations. Physicians had discovered relatively safe methods of controlling fertility; they realized that danger arose not from these methods but from improper techniques. An angry Clarke prevented Storer from publishing his allegations in 1856.

Storer, ordinarily a leading proponent of the scientific method in medical research, admitted that he lacked sufficient data to substantiate his allegations, but he subsequently conducted no investigation to produce such evidence. He conceded, by default, that he doubted the validity of his own hypothesis. He did, however, sponsor research on a related question. He persuaded his son to investigate his hypothesis about planned parenthood reducing native fertility.

Storer finally admitted that he knew about relatively safe methods of controlling fertility. "[W]e may be called upon to destroy the foetus in utero," he mentioned in passing, "[t]o save the life of the mother." He was left, then, with this hypothesis: Abortion involved extreme danger only when performed with intent to restrict family size. He indicated that he only "reluctantly" raised this issue of danger when he found that other arguments had failed to deter the populace from controlling fertility.

Although Storer was restrained from publishing his lecture in 1856, he nevertheless circulated the manuscript privately to his colleagues, and persuaded two medical editors to publicize his views. That year, W. W. Morland and Francis Minot endorsed Storer's ideas in the *Boston Medical and Surgical Journal.* The editors praised the doctor's "bold and manly appeal" against "the *crime of procuring abortion* and the scarcely less heinous offense of *preventing impregnation,*" and they exhorted other physicians to emulate his stand against such behavior, which "lessens our population, at the same time it lays the foundation of many uterine diseases." "In silence and by sufferance," they warned, "these mighty evils are feeding on the life-blood of the nation itself." Not content with this warning alone, the editors then proceeded to elaborate their own theory about the dangers of contraception. "If impregnation be prevented by the well-known means so widely used, or in any way, why," they speculated, "should we not look for the termination of the naturally aroused uterine excitement, which fails of its legitimate end, in congestion, inflammation and final disorganization?" Morland and Minot thus used their resources to advance Storer's line of argument, and called for legal restrictions on the use of the known medical expertise.

Storer again expressed his concern about declining fertility, this time at the annual convention of the American Medical Association (AMA) in 1857. He suggested that his colleagues form a committee "to investigate the subject of Criminal Abortion, *with a view to its general suppression,*" and he recommended his son, Horatio R. Storer, as chairman.

From this point, the younger Storer rapidly emerged as the leading spokesman in the medical crusade against planned parenthood. In 1857, as chairman of a "Committee on Criminal Abortion" for the local Suffolk District Medical Society in Massachusetts, he attempted to have contraception as well as abortion condemned. However, Henry I. Bowditch, a member of the committee, objected. "We are asked to report on Criminal Abortion," Bowditch explained. "Prevention of conception may be equally criminal, but we are not called at present to discuss it, and we should have hard work enough, I fear, to persuade the Society, *as a Society,* to act on the subject of abortion." Storer deleted his statements on contraception, but the "Report on Criminal Abortion" that he submitted to the Suffolk Medical Society in April 1857 was strong and clear.

It has clearly become the duty of the medical profession as the guardians of public health, if for no higher reason, and as those who, of all others, sooner or later in almost every instance become cognizant of the crime, to declare its true nature, its prevalence, and its deplorable consequences; to denounce it in unmeasured terms, and where possible, to point out and to enforce efficient means for its suppression.

A similar report followed to the Massachusetts Medical Society in February 1858. Storer's next step was to present a definitive study "On the Decrease of the Rate of Increase in Population" to the American Academy of Arts and Sciences in December 1858. He observed:

In the state of Massachusetts it has been found of late years that the natural increase of population, or the excess of births over deaths, has been wholly of those of recent foreign origin. . . . [I]n the absence of immigration from abroad, the population of Massachusetts is stationary or decreasing. . . . [T]his annual lessing of the population must be owing . . . almost wholly . . . to "prudence" on the part of the community, not as a State, which ever encourages population, but as individuals.

The younger physician readily reiterated his father's allegations about the extreme danger inherent in planned parenthood. "[C]onjugal habits, existing extensively among the French, and by no means rarely imitated in this country, are," he charged, "as unnatural and degrading as they are detrimental to the physical health of both male and female."

Storer then presented his "Report on Criminal Abortion" to the AMA in May 1859. "We are the physical guardians of women; we, alone, thus far, of their offspring in utero," he stated. "The case is here of life and death—the life or death of thousands—and it depends, almost wholly, upon ourselves. If, by any act, we can effect ought towards the suppression of this crime, it must be done." Storer must have struck a chord with his argument, for the AMA convention unanimously adopted "an earnest and solemn protest against such unwarranted destruction of human life."

Storer capped his efforts in 1860 with the publication of *Criminal Abortion in America.* He dedicated the volume—in what may have been a descending order of authority and responsibility—to "those whom it may concern, physician, attorney, juror, judge,—and parent."

If Storer was the most devoted, he was not the only medical figure to warn against the dangers of planned parenthood. In 1860, in the *Knickerbocker Magazine,* Augustus K. Gardner, Professor of Clinical Midwifery at New York Medical College, wrote: "The laws of nature and the necessities of our existence implanted by an over-ruling providence cannot be contravened without detriment to the system." In Gardner's view:

Local congestions, nervous afflictions and debilities are the direct and indisputable results. Inquiry of any gynecologist will convince the most skeptical that the general employment of any means for the prevention of conception, is fraught with injury to the female certainly, if not to the other sex also. Exactly how these evils are effected are not fully known but of this fact there is no mistake, and reasonably enough, for sexual congress is thus rendered but a species of self-abuse.

Seven other physicians assailed "Criminal Abortion" in professional journals before the Civil War, each emphasizing and echoing the new medical line about the extreme danger inherent in planned parenthood, a danger that would justify legal restrictions on such medical expertise.

Even as physicians raised the specter of danger in their propaganda against planned parenthood, the same men continued producing abortions when women incurred medical complications with pregnancy. Obstetricians discussed *these* operations under the rubric of "inducing premature labor." None other than Horatio R. Storer himself published such a study "On the Induction of Premature Labor—Modes of Effecting It" in the *Boston Medical and Surgical Journal* in 1855. He emphasized the safety of several methods of producing abortion in this technical monograph. His colleague, Hugh L. Hodge, also examined advanced techniques for "inducing premature labor" in *Principles and Practices of*

Obstetrics in 1866. He observed: "[I]f the child must perish, it ought to be in the early stages of pregnancy when the mother would not be much endangered." Thus did these men refute their own propaganda in their scientific work.[7]

The call by men like Storer and Hodge for legal action against planned parenthood was largely eclipsed during the next six years by national preoccupation with the Civil War. Still, the advocates of legal restrictions could point to one victory. In 1862, in a unique mix of the two professions, Dr. Thaddeus A. Reamy, noted obstetrician and Ohio legislative representative, introduced and saw passed "An Act to prevent the advertisement, sale, or gratuitous distribution of any drug, medicine, instrument or apparatus intended to prevent conception or procure abortion." Thus, it was a physician who instigated the first statute banning contraception as well as abortion.

Reamy's medical colleagues renewed their general crusade against planned parenthood when the war ended. The AMA leaders prodded their phalanx into battle by conducting an essay-writing contest on "criminal abortion." In 1865 a special committee, chaired by D. Humphreys Storer, awarded the prize to the chairman's son, Horatio R. Storer, for his treatise, "The Criminality and Physical Evils of Forced Abortion." In 1866 the younger Storer reproduced his prize-winning essay as *Why Not? A Book for Every Woman*. This piece, and its mate, *Is It I? A Book for Every Man*, raised the old themes: the need to prevent depopulation by legislative interference, if necessary, and the danger of both abortion and contraception. In the six years between his *Criminal Abortion in America* and the *Why Not/Is It I?* volumes, these dangers in planned parenthood appear to have grown even more extensive. Storer now warned abortion seekers and contraceptive users that by such practices "the tendency to serious and fatal organic disease, as cancer, is rendered greater at the so-called turn of life." His certainty of the connection between planned parenthood and serious and incurable disease arose, he said, from general

---

[7] Jesse Chickering, *Report of the Committee Appointed by the City Council,* Boston, 1851, p. 36; D. Humphreys Storer, *Two Frequent Causes of Uterine Disease,* James Campbell, Boston, 1872, pp. 3–11; [W. W. Morland and Francis Minot], "Bibliographical Notes," *Boston Medical and Surgical Journal,* 53 (1856), 410–411; Henry I. Bowditch to Horatio R. Storer, April 20, 1857, Storer MSS, Countway Library; Storer, *Report of the Committee on Criminal Abortion,* Boston, 1857, pp. 4–5; Storer, "On the Decrease of the Rate of Increase of Population," *American Journal of Science and Arts,* 43 (1867), 145–148; Storer, "Report on Criminal Abortion," *Transactions of the American Medical Association,* 12 (1859), 75–78; Storer, *Criminal Abortion in America,* J. B. Lippincott, Philadelphia, 1860, p. iii; Augustus K. Gardner, "Physical Decline of American Women," *Knickerbocker Magazine,* 55 (1860), 47–49; Storer, "On the Induction of Premature Labor—Modes of Effecting It," *Boston Medical and Surgical Journal,* 52 (1855), 329–335; Hodge, *Principles and Practices of Obstetrics,* Henry C. Lea, Philadelphia, 1866, p. 301.

observation. "From a constantly increasing practice devoted to the specialized diseases of women," he explained, "I have been led to recognize certain general laws." But after a decade of writing on the subject, he had still presented no evidence to substantiate his hypotheses.

The same concern over the decline of native population so evident in all of Storer's works led other physicians to call for drastic legislative action. To stamp out the advertisement of contraceptives, E. P. LeProhon urged an end to the "unlimited freedom of the press in the United States." And, like LeProhon, L. C. Butler was eager to see the government suppress any information that threatened his people with "utter annihilation." By 1870 the professional organization of which these men were a part, the AMA, revived its official interest in the matter.

The Executive Council of the AMA formed a committee in 1870 "whose duty it shall be to represent the evil of criminal abortion in its proper light, and to take into consideration the best course to be pursued by the profession in arresting its progress, and in forcing from our ranks all who now, or may hereafter, pursue this iniquitous course." By the following year, the committee's report was ready. When D. A. O'Donnell presented the report, he discussed "God's first commandment to Adam and Eve . . . to increase and multiply," and made several other references to human reproduction in the Bible. As it turned out, only religious matters appeared to have been examined in this medical report. The AMA convention must have been satisfied, however, for it unanimously adopted a resolution reaffirming opposition to abortion.[8]

THE GREAT OFFENSIVE AGAINST ABORTION

It was in New York City, home of Madame Restell and Dr. Gunning Bedford, that the great legal offensive against abortion was at last launched. The campaign began with a spate of arrests. Starting in 1867, with the arrest of Dr. Peter J. Harrison, the city magistrates arrested six medical entrepreneurs over the next two years. All were charged with performing surgical abortions. Although the magistrates failed to convict

[8] *Ohio House Journal*, 55th Gen. Assem., 1st Sess., 333 (1862); Ohio Acts (1862); Storer, "The Criminality and Physical Evils of Forced Abortions," *Transactions of the American Medical Association*, 16 (1865), 711–743; Storer, "The Abetment of Criminal Abortion by Medical Men," *New York Medical Journal*, 3 (1866), 423–424; L. C. Butler, "The Decadence of the American Race," *Boston Medical and Surgical Journal*, 77 (1867), 89–98; E. P. LeProhon, *Voluntary Abortion*, Thurston & Co., Portland, 1867, pp. 4–13; H. L. Hodge, *Foeticide*, Lindsay & Blakiston, Philadelphia, 1869, p. 3; D. A. O'Donnell, "Report of the Committee on Criminal Abortion," *Transactions of the American Medical Association*, 22 (1870), 240; Augustus Gardner, *Conjugal Sins Against the Laws of Life and Health*, J. S. Redford, New York, 1870, pp. 107–126.

any of these alleged lawbreakers, they had reintroduced the issue of abortion into the political process.

In January 1871 the first conviction was handed down. Dr. Michael Wolff stood trial for an abortion fatality. The jury deliberated for several hours, but they could not reach any agreement. The foreman reported the deadlock, but Judge Gunning S. Bedford, the son of the physician propagandist of the same name, admonished the jurors for returning without a verdict. He instructed them to continue deliberating until they reached agreement. Eventually the jurors found the suspect guilty of "manslaughter in the second degree, with a recommendation for mercy."

The district attorney immediately arose to address the jury. "Madame Restell, Dr. Evans and Dr. Wolff are the most notorious and well known abortionists on this island, constituting a detestable trio," he cried. "No mercy ought to be extended to him." Judge Bedford then turned to the jury. "Gentlemen," he said, "I now ask you, do you still recommend this man to mercy?" "No," all twelve jurors answered in unison. "I thank your honor on behalf of the jury for your courtesy," the foreman added. Judge Bedford then addressed the defendant.

Wolff, you are a well known abortionist. The authorities have declared war to the bitter end against the fraternity which you, today, so guiltily represent. Let every abortionist—male and female, rich or poor, in this City—take warning, for on conviction their fate shall be the same as yours, namely, confinement in the State Prison for the period of seven years, the longest term allowed under the statute.

A second success followed in the court of Gunning Bedford. In May 1871 the district attorney prosecuted Dr. Thomas Lookup Evans for selling abortifacient medicine. As in the Wolff case, the jury deliberated for several hours without reaching agreement, and the foreman reported a deadlock. Judge Bedford once again acted. He ordered the bailiff to "lock" the jurors in their chamber "for the night." The next morning, the jury found the defendant guilty. The judge ceremoniously thanked the jurors for their verdict. Then he quipped: "I am surprised that twelve intelligent men could have remained out all night before deciding to agree upon a verdict in such a case." Having reprimanded the jurors, Bedford next turned his wrath on Evans. "I now sentence you," he stated, "to confinement in the State Prison, at hard labor, for three years and six months, the longest term allowed under the law."

New Jersey officials proved even more zealous than their New York counterparts. In May 1871, Dr. James B. Cutter, head surgeon at the Newark City Hospital, found himself before a jury. He was accused of successfully inducing an abortion. Cutter pleaded guilty to the charge of a misdemeanor. The New Jersey judge took the opportunity to lecture the doctor. He expressed especially strong misgivings about a prominent physician committing such a "heinous" crime. "[H]is special position and known skill," the judge declared, "only made his crime the more deserving of punishment." Cutter was fined 500 dollars and costs.

Then, on August 27, 1871, only three months after the Evans decision, New York City newspapers printed a sensational headline: "The Dead Body of a Woman Found in a Trunk at the Hudson River Railroad." The coroner ruled that this death had been caused by a surgical abortion, and the day after they had discovered the trunk, officials arrested Dr. Jacob Rosenzweig for allegedly committing this crime. The district attorney prosecuted Rosenzweig before Recorder John K. Hackett in October 1871. A man testified that he had seen the defendant load a trunk into a wagon on the day that officials had discovered the dead woman. His recollections constituted the only evidence connecting the suspect to the crime.

The prosecutor's most compelling evidence against the defendant was the defendant himself, for Rosenzweig *looked* the part of a criminal abortionist. A *New York Times* reporter described him as "a fat, coarse, and sensual-looking fellow, without any traces of refinement or manners, and does not bear the faintest appearance of the educated physician." The jury found Rosenzweig guilty of "manslaughter in the second degree, with a recommendation to mercy." Recorder Hackett was not satisfied. "Ordinarily I would mind the recommendation of the jury to mercy," he explained to Rosenzweig, "but in this case I must ignore it, for you deserve no mercy. You sent two human beings to their last account deliberately, willfully, murderously. I sentence you to seven years imprisonment, with hard labor."

Like Rosenzweig, Cutter, and Evans, 40 other medical entrepreneurs and doctors were arrested and prosecuted during the decade of the seventies. The arrests, begun in New York City, spread across the country; the 20 convicted men and women bore witness to the fact that the offensive against planned parenthood was a national effort.[9]

THE COMSTOCK LAWS

Even as officials cracked down on abortion, Protestant businessmen in New York City's Young Men's Christian Association (YMCA) were organizing their own campaign to suppress all trade in goods and services for planned parenthood. The YMCA leaders in this era included Cephas Brainerd, a corporation lawyer; Morris K. Jesup, a manufacturer; J. Pier-

[9] *New York Times*, May 28, 1867, and May 28, 1871; New York *Herald*, January 27, May 18 and May 19, August 27, and October 29, 1871; *Evans* v. *People*, 49 N.Y. 86 (1872).

pont Morgan, the financier; Charles E. Whitehead, a corporation lawyer; and Jacob F. Wyckoff, a merchant. These capitalists provided the "means," as Brainerd's son put it, to implement an unpopular social policy.

In 1866 the YMCA leaders commissioned Brainerd and Whitehead to draft legislation "for the suppression of the traffic in obscene literature and immoral articles." They inserted a provision, similar to Reamy's Ohio act of 1862, that expressly banned contraception as well as abortion. New York lawmakers adopted the YMCA bill in 1868.

Although the YMCA leaders faced little difficulty in enacting their statute, they found that officials seldom enforced it. Unhappy with this, they decided to enforce the law themselves. Thus, in March 1872, at the crest of the magistrates' crackdown on abortion, the YMCA leaders formed a Committee for the Suppression of Vice to, as they put it, "prosecute, in all legal forms, the traffic in bad books, prints, and instruments." The committee included Wyckoff as chairman, Brainerd, Jesup, and Whitehead. These men hired an agent, Anthony Comstock, to execute their program.

Comstock proved a true enthusiast and pounded the pavements of New York in pursuit of evildoers. He found them. In 1872 he filed complaints against eight medical entrepreneurs for selling contraceptives. Officials failed, however, to convict any of Comstock's catch. Agent Comstock saw forces at work against him, and suggested that the culprits "fixed" their cases through the use of "strong political influence."

Even as he made his complaint, Comstock's own employers were setting about to use *their* political influence to see that a *federal* law be enacted to ban planned parenthood information and devices from the U.S. mails. Brainerd and Whitehead drafted legislation adding such a provision to the already existing postal obscenity act of 1865. With agent Comstock, Whitehead presented the YMCA bill to Republican party leaders in Washington.

In March 1783, Congress adopted "An Act for the suppression of trade in, and circulation of, obscene literature and articles of immoral use." The legislation banned "any article or thing designed or intended for the prevention of conception or procuring of abortion," as well as any "advertisement" or "information" about this contraband.

Although the YMCA leaders had secured enactment of this law, they renounced credit for the legislation in order to protect their association from adverse publicity. They proclaimed that the federal statute had been enacted solely "through the instrumentality of Mr. Comstock." In this way, the YMCA bill became known as "the Comstock law." The YMCA leaders next secured Comstock an appointment as a Special Agent of the Post Office Department. By this arrangement, the YMCA committee continued to pay his salary, and the federal government only had to subsidize his travel expenses. Comstock attacked his new duties with vigor. Traveling around the country in 1873, he arrested 35 medical entrepreneurs. Twenty-three of these men and women were convicted under the new federal law.

While Comstock tracked down evildoers, the YMCA leaders decided to institutionalize their Committee for the Suppression of Vice. Brainerd and Whitehead drafted a charter for an independent corporation, and New York lawmakers adopted "An Act to Incorporate the New York Society for the Suppression of Vice" in May 1873.

By January 1874, the New York Society for the Suppression of Vice was a functioning body, with an executive committee that included Charles Whitehead, the corporation lawyer, as president; A. S. Barnes, a publisher; Samuel Colgate, a manufacturer; J. M. Cornell, a manufacturer; and Jacob Wyckoff, the merchant. These men agreed to retain Comstock as their functionary.

During the first nine months of 1874, Comstock was both busy and successful. Of 20 arrests, 14 resulted in conviction. But in October, agent Comstock seized Charles Conroy, a "smut dealer," in Newark, New Jersey. "As Mr. Comstock opened the carriage-door for his prisoner to alight at the jail," a newsman reported, "Conroy stabbed him in the head twice, inflicting frightful wounds, the last stab cutting a gash from the temple to the chin, laying open the flesh to the bone, and severing four of the facial arteries." A jail guard subdued the assailant before he killed the agent. Despite the assault, Comstock was back on the job within six months. Resuming his "still-hunt campaign," as he called it, he arrested seven medical entrepreneurs in 1875. To his satisfaction, officials convicted all of these suspects.

Not everyone was as satisfied as agent Anthony Comstock. In 1875 Dr. Edward Bliss Foote challenged the Comstock Law in *A Step Backward*. "It is my conscientious conviction," Foote stated, "that every married woman should have it within her power to decide for herself just when and just how often she will receive the germ of a new offspring."

Foote himself had been advertising contraceptives for many years in his medical encyclopedia, *Plain Home Talk*. Through this medium he offered "womb veils" and "envelopes," as well as an "electro-magnetic preventive machine." In January 1876, Comstock arrested his critic Foote for "mailing advertisements of articles for prevention of conception." "Foote bitterly opposed the Act of Congress," Comstock noted. "He tried to amend the law of the state, as well." Judge Charles L. Benedict fined the physician the considerable sum of 3,500 dollars.

Foote's defense counsel immediately filed an appeal explaining that the defendant had received a doctorate in medicine from the University of Pennsylvania in 1860. He contended that a certified physician should be exempt from the law. But when Judge Benedict reviewed the writ of error in July 1876, he argued that "any attempt to exclude information given by medical men from the operation of the statute would afford an easy way of nullifying the law. If the intention had been to exclude the communications of physicians from the operation of this act, it was, certainly, easy to say so." On the basis of this argument, Judge Benedict sustained his previous decision against Foote.

Foote's had been an individual protest against the Comstock Law; the only collective protest against federal policy during the 1870s came from the Freethinkers. Forming the National Liberal League in 1876, they gathered an impressive 70,000 signatures on a petition to repeal the Comstock Law. Robert G. Ingersoll, an outspoken Freethinker and a prominent Republican party orator, sponsored the appeal. His political influence apparently won the protesters a hearing in Congress.

In February 1878, Representative Benjamin F. Butler of Massachusetts introduced the Freethinkers' petition in the House. When the speaker instructed him to place it in a box on the clerk's desk, Butler replied: "The petition is too large." The clerk reported "laughter" in the chamber.

The House Judiciary Committee conducted hearings on the postal obscenity law in April 1878. Freethinkers charged that the legislation abridged "freedom of the press" as well as "personal rights of privacy." But Samuel Colgate, then President of the New York Society for the Suppression of Vice, testified in defense of the statute. And Anthony Comstock also insisted on testifying at the hearings. "As I entered the Committee room," he later observed, "I found it crowded with long-haired men and short-haired women, there to defend, obscene publications, abortion implements, and other incentives to crime, by repealing the laws." Consider the source, Comstock was saying; he then vigorously endorsed the legislation that had come to bear his name.

Representative George A. Bicknell of Indiana presented the committee report in May 1878. "[T]he post-office was not established to carry instruments of vice, obscene writings, indecent pictures, or lewd books," he stated. "Your Committee believe that the statutes in question do not violate the Constitution of the United States, and ought not be changed." With that, the House tabled the petition indefinitely.

In 1879 A. L. Rawson, a leading Freethinker, requested that congressmen reconsider the Ingersoll petition. "I understand that statements were made by Mr. Anthony Comstock before the Committee on the Judiciary to the effect that many names on the petition were forgeries," he stated. "To answer that charge I hand you the affidavits of E. B. Foote, Editor of the 'Health Monthly,' of D. M. Bennett, Editor of the 'Truth Seeker'." The gesture was dramatic but perhaps naive. Rawson's intent was to show the Congress the extent of legitimate widespread opposition to the law. But congressmen already knew that many Americans favored contraception. It was exactly because such practices had, in their judgment, become too popular that the Comstock Law was enacted. Ingersoll's petition was left on the table permanently.

Comstock and Comstockery were in the ascendancy. In the very month that the Freethinkers first placed their petition before the Congress, Anthony Comstock arrested the legendary Madame Restell. "I effected entrance to her establishment," he explained, "under the pretense of obtaining professional advice." Once inside, he confiscated "10 dozen condoms" and "2 quarts of pills for abortion." "I think I have a good case," he boasted. "I am so advised by my counsel and the District Attorney to whom I submitted the case before arrest." But Madame Restell was never brought to justice. In April 1878, on the evening before her trial was to begin, Madame Restell committed suicide. "[S]he came to a violent end," a newsman reported, "by cutting her throat from ear to ear."

The *New York Times* editors praised her final act. "The death of 'Mme. Restell' by her own hand," they proclaimed, "is a fit ending to an odious career." Anthony Comstock, too, found poetic justice in her death. "A bloody ending to a bloody life," he mused.

The agent's next arrest went less smoothly. In May 1878, he apprehended Dr. Sara Blakesly Chase for selling a vaginal syringe in New York City. "I first learned of this woman through a prominent physician," he noted. "She is an infamous offender." But the trial jury was not sympathetic to Comstock's cause; when Comstock appeared to testify, a juror inquired if the agent wanted the defendant to commit suicide like Madame Restell. The jurymen then unanimously rejected a motion to indict Dr. Chase. Now Comstock got a taste of his own medicine, for Chase duly filed a complaint against Comstock for false arrest. Policemen apprehended the agent at his office on Nassau Street in June, but his patrons persuaded officials to drop the charges without a formal hearing. Comstock in turn re-arrested Chase for selling a vaginal syringe in July.

While Comstock and Chase waged their legal duels, other federal agents busied themselves in the field. Thirty-one suspects were brought in for mailing illicit matter during the 1870s by agents other than Comstock. Although these men did not specify the nature of the contraband in their official register of arrests, they indubitably enforced the provisions against planned parenthood as well as obscene literature.[10]

[10] New York City YMCA, *Report of the Committee for the Suppression of Vice*, New York, 1874, pp. 2–3; "Reports of Persons Arrested," 1 (1872–1880), New York Society for the Suppression of Vice MSS, Library of Congress; Anthony Comstock to David B. Parker, February 13, 1878, Comstock MSS, Post Office Department Library; *New York Times*, November 3, 1874, April 2 and April 11, and July 11, 1878; Edward Bliss Foote, *A Step Backward*, Murray Hill, New York, 1875, pp. 10–11; Foote, *Plain Home Talk*, Murray Hill, New York, 1870, p. 911; "Register of Arrests for Mail Depredations," 3–4 (1872–1880), Post Office Department MSS, National Archives; *Congressional Record*, 45th Cong., 2nd sess., 1340, 3960 (1878); Anthony Comstock, *Frauds Exposed*, John Howard Brown, New York, 1880, p. 424; A. L. Rawson to S. S. Cox, March 18, 1879, Congressional MSS, National Archives; N.Y. Laws (1868); U.S. Laws (1873); *U.S. v. Foote*, 25 Fed. Cas., 1141 (1876); *U.S. v. Kelly*, 26 Fed. Cas., 695 (1876).

CONCLUSION

During the last two decades of the nineteenth century, government officials in the field, in the courts, and in the legislatures continued to enforce the legal restrictions on abortion and contraception that were the legacies of the Storers, Brainerds, and Comstocks. Although these men failed to abolish planned parenthood completely, they did prevent medical experts from openly dispensing those relatively safe methods of controlling fertility known in their century. As a result, many women needlessly perished from inferior medical treatment. But far more women bore unwanted children in order to avoid bodily harm. The danger of planned parenthood thus reduced declining fertility. But it was public leaders who had consciously increased that danger, and had used their influence and power to admonish the American women: "Be fruitful, and multiply, and replenish the earth."

Documents

An Essay on the Principle of Population, by Thomas R. Malthus, 1817

. . . I should always particularly reprobate any artificial and unnatural modes of checking population, both on account of their immorality and their tendency to remove a necessary stimulus to industry.* If it were possible for each married couple to limit by a wish the number of their children, there is certainly reason to fear that the indolence of the human race would be very greatly increased; and that neither the population of individual countries, nor of the whole earth, would ever reach its natural and proper extent. . . .

Law Against Contraception and Abortion, Ohio Acts, 1862

Be it enacted by the General Assembly of the State of Ohio,† That if any person shall, by printing, writing, or in any other way, publish an account or description of any drug, medicine, instrument, or apparatus, for the purpose of preventing conception, procuring abortion, or miscarriage, or shall, by writing or printing, in any circular, newspaper, pamphlet, or book, or in any other

---

* Reprinted from Thomas R. Malthus, *Additions to the Fourth and Former Editions of an Essay on the Principle of Populations,* John Murray, London, 1817, p. 292.
† From Acts of a General Nature and Local Laws and Joint Resolutions passed by the Fifty-fifth General Assembly of the State of Ohio, 1862. Richard Nevins, State Printer, Columbus, 1862, pp. 63–64.

way publish or circulate any obscene notice, or shall within the state of Ohio keep for sale or for gratuitous distribution, any newspaper, circular, pamphlet, or book, containing such notice of such drugs, medicines, instruments, or apparatus, or shall keep for sale any secret nostrum, drug, or medicine, for the purpose of preventing conception, procuring abortion, or miscarriage, such person so violating any of the provisions of this act shall be deemed guilty of a misdemeanor, and shall, upon conviction thereof, be fined in any sum not exceeding one thousand dollars, or imprisoned in the county jail not exceeding six months, or both, at the discretion of the court: Provided, that nothing in this act shall be so construed as to affect teaching in regularly chartered medical colleges, or the publication of standard medical books.

A Circular Advertising a Contraceptive Device, 1847

STRICTLY CONFIDENTIAL
DR. CAMERON'S PATENT FAMILY REGULATOR
OR, WIFE'S PROTECTOR

A new invention, at once safe, sure and easy application.*

In introducing this novel invention, the writer feels he is broaching a delicate subject. These few explanatory remarks are not therefore, designed for the public eye, but addressed to those only, who have entered the married state, whom, I trust would not be likely to misconstrue the motives of the author, or convert his invention to an evil purpose; and but for that class of females is this invention particularly designed, who have entered the married state, with such enfeebled constitutions, inherited either from their ancestors, by sickness, or by having indulged so far in the fashionable follies of our age, as to render them incapable of becoming mothers, without endangering their own lives, or imparting to their offspring, imbecility of mind, or sickly constitution, which would render existence anything but a blessing.

There are those also, whose families are already too numerous for their means of support, and to this class the writer thinks his invention cannot but prove a welcome agent in exonerating them from some of the most cruel sufferings of life, and thus smooth the future pathway of their present existence.

Besides these, there are too, those in the bloom of womanhood, the very picture of health, who having just entered the married state, tremble in constant fear of the awful wreck so often produced by the first born, when,

If not her life upon the altar sacrifice expire,
The rosy cheek, the ruby lip it will require.

* From Dr. Walter Scott Tarbox's circular, Tarbox File, Suffolk County Courthouse Archives, Boston, Mass.

To such, therefore, I trust this invention will prove a welcome minister of mercy.

This novel, though important subject, having engaged the attention for several centuries, of some of the most learned physiologists and physicians, still continued to elude their grasp. And though many theories were advanced, and methods proposed, still most of them were either injurious to health, uncertain in their effects, or extremely difficult to use, or what was considered still worse, detracted much from the sexual enjoyment, and seems to have been reserved alone for our day to witness it brought to the highest state of perfection.

This instrument now recommended is entirely free from any of the above objections. It is easily introduced by the female, and does not diminish in the least the enjoyment, and would not be discovered by the male, were he not apprised of it. It is as easily withdrawn, bringing with it every particle of semen, rendering its effects positive; and as it absorbs nothing, can be cleansed in a moment, without even wetting the fingers—can never get out of order, and will last for life.

The above instrument is for sale by Dr. W. Scott, Agent for the inventor, at No. 6 Endicott Street, Boston. Price, $5.00. Any one wishing for one of these instruments, by addressing a letter, post paid, through the Post Office, to Dr. Scott, and enclosing $5.00 in it, the instrument will be immediately forwarded.

Newspaper Advertisement, 1870

A CERTAIN CURE FOR MARRIED LADIES, with or without medicines, by Madame RESTELL, Professor of Midwifery; over 30 years practice.* Her infallible French Female Pills, No. 1, price $1, or No. 2, specially prepared for married ladies, price $5, which can never fail, are safe and healthy. Sold only at her office, No. 1 Fifty-second street, first door from Fifth Avenue, and at druggists, 152 Greenwich street, or sent by mail. Caution—All others are counterfeit.

Report of Arrest of a Contraceptive Distributor, 1878

I have the honor to report that on the 9th inst. I caused the arrest of Sarah B. Chase . . . for selling articles to prevent conception.†

This person has been for about two years privately lecturing in the public halls and lecture-rooms of the churches—separate lectures for ladies and gentlemen. . . .

---

* Reprinted from the New York *Herald,* May 16, 1870.

† Reprinted from report of Anthony Comstock to David B. Parker, June 1, 1878, Post Office Department Library, Washington, D.C.

I first learned of this woman through a prominent physician. . . . She sold a sponge swab, and syringe, to be used by the woman immediately after copulation. . . . She is an infamous offender.

Discussion of the Prevention of Conception Held at the Detroit Medical Association, 1890

Dr. Gilbert opened the discussion.* It seemed to him to be purely a private affair . . . a question of utilitarianism. It was regrettable that these matters were not taught in our schools.

Dr. Brown said . . . that in the majority of cases some means will be employed, perhaps more harmful than those recommended by a physician.

Dr. McGraw. It seemed to him that the medical press had taken a mistaken line. . . . He could not see any wrong in the prevention of conception.

Dr. Mulheron . . . was surprised to hear this called an individual matter. He regarded it as a society matter. When a man and a woman entered the marital relation, they assumed certain duties to society. . . . He considered the practice to be wrong.

Dr. Gibson . . . regarded it as homicide.

Dr. Webber. It was a well known fact that through sin sickness and disease came into the world. It is through breach of moral laws that we have, as physicians, obtained our employment.

Dr. Davendorf was delighted at the high morality of his friend, Dr. Mulheron; the angelic purity of the gentleman who had last spoken was beyond criticism, and as for the gentleman who described the practice as homicide, he would doubtless go in mourning after an erotic dream. He thought it for the good of humanity to limit the number of children.

Dr. Gilbert thought that it was a shame that these matters should not be known; it was absurd and ridiculous.

Death Resulting from an Attempt at Abortion, 1881

. . . She was in the ninth month of her pregnancy, and for some paltry reason endeavored to kill the foetus, and so produce abortion by firing a pistol shot at the abdomen.† The ball, instead of going into the womb, and killing the child

---

* Reprinted from "The Prevention of Conception: From the Proceedings of the Detroit Medical Association," *Cincinnati Medical News*, 19 (1890): 303–308.
† Reprinted from R. J. Levis, "Suicide, the Result of an Attempt at Abortion," *Medical Bulletin*, 3 (1881): 170.

as she intended, entered the abdomen, near the margin of the seventh rib upon the left side. . . .

During the night . . . labor came on, and she succeeded in delivering herself of a living child. . . .

The mother died almost immediately after the delivery of the child. . . .

Part Four
Twentieth-Century America

Not Separate, Not Equal

Carol Ruth Berkin

If the movement for suffrage has always excited the interest of historians, the apparent disintegration of the women's movement after the passage of the Nineteenth Amendment has disturbed and puzzled them. In dozens of different ways, historians have echoed the sentiments of reformers like Jane Addams and Charlotte Perkins Gilman, asking, "What happened to feminism in the 1920s?"

WHAT HAPPENED TO FEMINISM?

The question is both legitimate and vital. Yet strangely, even historians who view themselves as sympathetic to feminism have sought to answer it by a sometimes merciless dissection of the movement itself. The result has been the isolation of a social movement from the larger context in which, perforce, it operated, and an internal exploration that seriously distorts the complex relationship between the women's movement and American society.

   The approach does have its ironies. It is surely an ironic compliment to the feminist minority that, in laying the blame for the unfinished revolution on their shoulders, historians have invested these women with the very control over events and over their own destinies that they had long been seeking. But we must take care to look for cause and effect in their proper place, even if it diminishes our confidence in the power of a determined minority.

   It was true that suffrage marked a watershed for the women's movement—if not for women. It is also true that there were many clear signs that feminism, in its most heralded victory, had somehow gone astray. Suffrage, once a practical goal among many, had come to be seen as the struggle itself. Perhaps this was inevitable, for the efforts and energies involved in the campaign tended to escalate and elevate the importance of the vote. Perhaps, in this insistence that the vote would be the universal panacea, we see the wishful thinking of women who were themselves in conflict over their personal and social identities. Yet the ballot, and the campaign for it, should not be dismissed as a symbol become an albatross. The vote could be a powerful tool for social change if wielded with skill and precision and with excellent timing.

But it was the *ifs* that proved overwhelming: if American women could be organized, quickly, into a conscious voting bloc; if a structure could be created for and by women so that they could communicate, debate, and resolve political questions as a first step toward united political action; if effective mechanisms could be found to influence the existing major party structures; and finally, if the political atmosphere in the nation was such that the political agenda could be turned to women's issues in order to bring them to a vote at all. Not surprisingly, the loose coalition known as the women's movement was no more successful in turning suffrage into a force for social change than labor or the blacks would prove to be.

This does not deny that there were also major internal weaknesses in the feminist movement. Participating women's groups—varying from pacifists to radical feminists to social reformers—could not agree on new priorities. The coalition around suffrage crumbled as old, suppressed, and unresolved differences reemerged; what, after all, did women want?

Unfortunately, the confusion of choices they faced were largely negative, not positive, choices. The question was what to struggle for next: economic equality, psychological liberation, educational reform, unionization, an end to legal discrimination? Should the priorities be women's issues or social reform in general? And, which women did the activists now represent? Womanhood was woven into the complex fabric of class, region, religion, race—a common strand that could not be pulled with the ease it occasionally seemed to promise.

The leadership was divided and uncertain about what feminism even meant. After so many years, feminism could not be defined in ways that satisfied all. The radical interpretation, an inheritance from nineteenth-century thinkers like Gilman, challenged home and family structure in ways that many reformist women could not accept. Yet no new definition was forthcoming. These women could not provide models for the mass of middle- and working-class white women, for they were themselves without a clear vision of what the modern woman and her movement should be. The consequence of this confusion was a decentralization, a return by many to discrete arenas of struggle, and a new generation of younger women who could respond to the multiple image before them by selecting bits and pieces from it to build their own identities. The middle-class flapper was, in that sense, a true child of feminism. For one thread of the women's movement had stressed acceptance as an individual as a measure of equality. The boundaries between individuality and self-absorption could be hazy; the sexual self could be viewed as the individual self; and the pursuit of individual happiness was, after all, part of America's most cherished ideological baggage.

But the inability of women activists to select and define new goals was not the major problem they faced. Even had they been able to repeat the extraordinary and difficult task of coalition they had just seen end in victory, there were concrete signs that the social and political milieu in which they operated as a minority was hostile to further reform. Historians of the 1920s give abundant evidence that this was not a decade hospitable to reform. In 1919 the Palmer raids disrupted and frightened radical labor and socialist organizations. In the twenties, a conservative Supreme Court threatened to reverse the few gains made by women and other workers toward minimum wages and maximum hours. A decade of presidents without obligations to reform factions meant that no White House support (with its legitimation of issues) could be expected. Open hostility to reform groups grew during the postwar era, and feminism, like labor organizations, was labeled foreign, dangerous, un-American. Jane Addams, it was rumored, was a Communist.

THE SUCCESSFUL WOMAN'S REVOLUTION: MYTHS AND REALITIES

Perhaps most frustrating for those who remained feminists was the public insistence, by means of the media, that equality had, after all, been achieved. The popular media treated liberation as a fait accompli, and, with a style both self-congratulatory and breathless, heralded the flapper as living proof of the revolution completed. Modern women were no longer restricted by archaic codes of dress or behavior; they smoked in public, exposed their knees, and spoke openly of sex and sexuality. They could now choose freely between a career or marriage. And, though it was conceded that the two options could not be integrated, either choice was sure to prove exciting and fulfilling. The new marriage and the new motherhood, detailed in guides like John Watson's *Psychological Care of Infant and Child,* had transformed the domestic world into a challenging life career. The woman question had, in short, been answered to every sensible American's satisfaction.

The realities of the 1920s and 1930s did not confirm this view. Mere jobs, rather than exciting careers, were not so easy to find. Access on any level to the job market, which had risen so dramatically in the first decade of the century, now seemed frozen; 23 percent of the labor force were women in 1920; 24 percent were women a decade later. The apparent employment gains won in World War I proved more illusory than real. War mobilization had not provided new workers with jobs, but new jobs for old workers; women in menial and unskilled factory jobs had been promoted to better positions during the war emergency. But their wages remained discriminatory and their promotions proved temporary.

With the armistice, women were driven out of these slots in order to restore men to their civilian occupations. The discrimination was entirely egalitarian: Women streetcar conductors and women judges were removed with the same dispatch. The same equality of treatment appeared for those who managed to remain employed; for them all, wage differentials were a constant. Among middle-class teachers, women performed their classroom tasks for 1,394 dollars a year in 1939, while men earned 1,953 dollars for the same duties. Among the working class, the differential in wages for men and women actually rose from 6.3 cents an hour in 1923 to 10.2 cents in 1929.

Those women who did find jobs in the peacetime era were clustered in the ranks of unskilled labor. Fifty-seven percent of all working women were black and foreign-born and worked as domestic servants or garment industry laborers. And, middle-class women soon discovered that training for a career and actually having one were not equally attainable goals. The doors of academia had opened wide to female students but not to female professors: One-third of all graduate degrees were awarded to women in the 1930s, but women constituted only 4 percent of the full professors at American universities. Even acquiring the skills of prestigious professions proved difficult, for medical schools and law schools established quotas as rigid as 5 percent until 1945.[1]

Few, if any, of these depressing realities were susceptible to

---

[1] The figures used above are drawn from two secondary sources, William Chafe, *The American Woman: Her Changing Social, Economic and Political Role, 1920–1970*, Oxford University Press, New York, 1972, pp. 48–65; Lois Banner, *Women in Modern America: A Brief History*, Harcourt Brace Jovanovich, New York, 1974, pp. 155–161.

modification by the ballot just won. The battlefields were too diverse, ranging from the courts to the conference rooms of the American Federation of Labor, where leaders decided women were not worth the effort to organize. Without unionization, without favorable new government policy or enforcement of old policy, without a political machine to force change, and with a diffused consciousness among their own ranks, women remained during these decades the cheapest, most flexible, and least demanding labor force in the country.

Even the sexual revolution of the postsuffrage era was more doubtful than real. The acceptance of a notion that women too had sexual drives was surely important, but a woman defined by her sexuality remained a woman defined by her sex. And, somehow, the new search for sexual satisfaction seemed to lead where the old denials of sexual drives had also led: to marriage, a family, and total responsibility for child and home care. An old set of obligations was now presented to women as a new profession; women's colleges like Barnard and Bryn Mawr rededicated themselves to producing the educated wife and the educated mother.

The Depression decade brought an end to the romantic imagery of flapper and bowdlerized Freudianism. As jobs grew scarce, complaints against working women grew frequent. The old, persistent notion that women worked for "pin money" while men worked to support their families led many to argue that one more unemployed woman meant one more working man. In 26 states, bills were introduced to prohibit married women from working. In fact, because women were confined largely to domestic service and menial factory jobs, their employment was never competitive with men.

The new Democratic administration of 1933 did seem, however, to promise improved circumstances for American working women. Women became visible in the federal government, called to Washington as members of a bureaucracy once closed to them by rule and custom. The reversal of fortune was a logical product of Roosevelt's reform agenda, with its many relief and welfare agencies. The male agency heads needed experienced social workers to implement their programs, and social work, from the earliest pioneer days of Jane Addams, was a woman's profession.

More important than this sudden visibility were the legislative gains made during the New Deal period. Reforms like the Social Security Act of 1935, which provided federal money for programs in maternal and pediatric care, and the Fair Labor

Standards Act of 1938, which established at last a maximum hour–minimum wage standard for all workers in interstate commerce, benefitted a broad spectrum of American women. For working-class women in the unskilled labor force, the New Deal's nurturing of labor organizations meant the first welcoming into the union structure through the Congress of Industrial Organizations' (CIO) activities.

These gains, important as they were, were limited; enforcement often fell short of pronouncement. Wherever industries could negotiate terms on an individual basis, they seemed able to win government approval for differential wage scales. The New Deal was willing to give women an old deal when the Friday paychecks came around.

The depth and durability of an automatic discrimination by sex in treatment and in expectation seemed best illustrated in the New Deal Youth Programs. Young men in Franklin D. Roosevelt's Civilian Conservation Corps received a regular salary; young women in Eleanor Roosevelt's retraining program received maintenance and a small allowance.

In the popular and prescriptive literature of the 1920s and even in the 1930s, the potential contradictions of the two dominant images, career woman and professional wife and mother, went largely unnoticed. The tensions did not become apparent because, in reality, the experience of work and of marriage rarely coincided. Neither experience conformed to the exaggerated idealized models, but women did live out the two options in their imperfect forms sequentially rather than simultaneously, if they experienced both at all. The fact was that women with genuine professional careers remained unmarried; only 12.2 percent of all professional women were married in 1920, and 75 percent of all women earning the Ph.D. degree were single in 1924.

The average middle-class woman worked only when she was young and single. As a wife and mother she lived within the domestic circle. Only among the poor whites and the black population did the problems of integrating the demands of the domestic role and the worker's role emerge. And, whatever their resolution to the conflicting roles and the accommodations made in family structure, they were not likely to be trendsetters in a society whose idealizations and legitimized norms filtered downward, never up. The isolation of these immigrant and black women, physically and emotionally, from the middle classes further assured that they would have no impact on American models of womanhood. Until the majority of white American women experienced a conflict between traditional sex-role expectations and the new demands of work outside the house, the "woman problem" would remain officially solved.

THE IMPACT OF WORLD WAR II

Seen in this light, World War II acquires a new primacy in the history of women. As several recent historians have pointed out, the mobilization of women in the war effort changed American reality, even if American sex-role definitions lagged far behind. This very gap between reality and the available interpretation of it may have spurred the social consciousness we associate with the rebirth of feminism in the 1960s.

The war mobilization brought six million women into the labor force—women working outside the home for the first time. The government, now seeking to overcome the very traditional prejudices against working married women that it had long supported, tapped the nation's greatest reserve labor source by propaganda campaigns, by the suspension of protective legislation that had locked women out of skilled work and its higher salaries, and by the establishment of federally funded day care centers. Within five years the percentage of women in the work force rose from 25 percent (1940) to 36 percent (1945). And these women were to be found in heavy industry; "Rosie the Riveter" was a factory worker, not a clerk or a domestic. But a peacetime economy shifted government priorities once again. The problem was to avoid massive unemployment after the war, and to government policy makers, unemployed was a male adjective. Women had to be taken off the job so soldiers could return to their rightful places in the civilian economy.

Women, however, proved resistant. An overwhelming majority wanted to remain in the labor force not the labor reserve. Eighty percent of these working women, especially those black women for whom factory work meant upward mobility from domestic service, tried to keep their jobs. Most were unsuccessful: Layoffs, demotions in rank and pay, outright firings, all eliminated women from their wartime positions. Within less than two years, women were reduced from 25 percent to 7.5 percent of American auto workers.[2] The government assisted women's early retirement by cutting off federal funds for day care in 1946.

But a return to a nostalgic prewar "normalcy" was not to be effected. Although Rosies no longer riveted, many did continue

[2] Chafe, *The American Woman*, p. 180.

to bring home a paycheck. Increasing bureaucracies shifted labor needs after the war, and the new worker—the office worker—was an excellent slot for the middle-class white woman. What seemed to trouble most of their critics was that these postwar working women included many wives and mothers. In the literature of the day a new reinterpretation of American social ills began to focus on this entrance of housewives into the job market. Philip Wylie's *Generation of Vipers* was typical, and virulent; his analysis pointed the finger at working wives as emasculating, life-sapping vipers, wrecking American morals and culture, rather than as life-giving women. The unnatural woman who deserted her home and family was the new American villain.

Soon all the problems of the modern society—war, economic depression, juvenile delinquency—were attributed to women's absence from the home. These new women were self-wreckers as well as home-wreckers, for movement into the masculine sphere was creating a new, neurotic woman. The fury of this attack by popular Jeremiahs and academic doomsayers may bespeak the certainty of the social change they abhorred. But if the literature did not alter women's steady integration into the work force, it must surely have added a conscious biting edge to the doubts of women fearful that adding new roles might well make them unable to fulfill the old.

If anything, young women of the postwar era seemed more firmly committed to marriage and family. They did not need glossy magazines to extol the virtues of suburban life and large families; the reality was that 60 percent of young women were dropping out of college to marry and start a family.[3] At no time in the twentieth century were the contradictions in the American woman's life more striking than in the 1950s: An invisible black and immigrant minority continued to work without critics showing any concern over their femininity; white middle-class girls were marrying younger than their grandmothers had done; feminism as a conscious ideology was moribund; yet, more women were working outside the home than ever before.

The pattern was not so crazy-quilt, however. Early marriage and a longer life expectancy for middle-class women were the ironic contributing factors to an increase in working wives. Married at 20, finished with childbearing at 26, these women could expect 20 years of adult life without child-rearing duties. Such women were perfectly suited to the job market demands. What employers wanted—now that the once vast immigrant labor

[3] Banner, *Women in Modern America*, p. 218.

pool was a thing of the past and young single women were growing ever rarer—was a supply of cheap, undemanding white-collar labor, with no career ambitions, willing to work part-time at wages kept low by the absence of unions and the low expectations of the workers themselves.

The jobs were there, in short. But what motivated these women to take them? It has been argued that the steady rise of married women who entered the job market was a definitive sign of trouble in suburban paradise and the sexual division of spheres it symbolized. This hypothesis, most dramatically put forward by feminist Betty Friedan, has been sympathetically received by many, but not yet subjected to historical study.[4] A second motivation could be suggested: income. The standard of living the middle-class family sought required dual earnings; amid the inflation and rising expectations of the postwar era, a woman's income was not pin money, but the necessary contribution to sustaining middle-class existence. Providing education, social opportunities, superior medical care for the children became a mothering duty best fulfilled at the typewriter or file-clerk desk.

Was the suburb a trap? On this point, feminist desires to legitimate their demands for new opportunities in the masculine sphere may have misled us. Surely the variety of responses to any role, and the creative ways in which it is given depth and dimension, are evident in women's lives as well as men's in the twentieth century. Volunteer work, participation in a network of women's clubs and organizations, the satisfaction of a familiar life—these may well be realities on a par with the social isolation of the suburb, the pleasures of adult companionship in the work situation, and the sense of emptiness Friedan found in the women she studied. This much is sure: The percentage of married women in the work force rose from 15 percent in 1940 to 30 percent in 1960. And this, despite the fact that ideology lagged behind social change: The increase in married women in the work force preceded the social imprimatur that granted wives the right to work once their mothering chores had ended.

That more women worked does not imply that their place in the competitive job market improved. They met with discriminatory wages, segregation into sex-defined occupations, and little opportunity for advancement. Further, the women of this transitional era were subject to a double jeopardy: Exploited in a job market they needed to enter and whose conditions they

[4] Betty Friedan, *The Feminine Mystique*, Norton, New York, 1963.

could not control, they were also operating in a system that had made no adjustments in the traditional monopoly of duties women faced in the home. Women could, it seemed, enter the male sphere and be women; but the role definition for men held no such reciprocal flexibility. Nothing symbolized the circumstances of the postwar woman more, perhaps, than the evolution of the secretarial position. Here the family homemaker could be the office homemaker as well. A threat to neither boss nor husband, the wife-secretary was welcome to their worlds.

THE SECOND FEMINIST MOVEMENT

In the 1960s a new feminist movement emerged. Room for the feminist movement to develop was provided by a decade of political leadership either personally liberal or dependent in some degree on liberal coalitions within the parties or voting constituencies. The sophisticated concentration on the legal system by other reform coalitions had created a social atmosphere in which feminism could again organize itself. As a movement, its roots lay in that reform cluster of the 1960s—civil rights, student radicalism, the antiwar protest. From participation in these, young women acquired the organizational skills and experience needed to lobby for their own interests.

Many middle-class young women claimed to have discovered their feminism in the sexist atmosphere of these reform movements. This awareness requires our further examination; its relationship to activism may be more, or less, than it has appeared superficially to be. The mothers of these younger activists were not lacking in organizational skills; church-related organizations, work experience as well, made available to at least a sizable minority of American middle-class women the skills needed to operate organizations like those emerging in the late sixties. What prevented them from organizing?

An awareness that the job market was discriminatory could not have been lacking. But a translation of awareness of discrimination into activism was missing. That their daughters made that step, not in relation to their real economic circumstances, but in political activities reminiscent of social feminism—in the struggle for peace, black rights, and the transformation of society—must be reckoned with. The need for an examination of mother-daughter relationships during the 1950s and 1960s presents itself for feminist scholars and the scholars of feminism.

What seemed to be true is that, if the origins of the movement as a movement lay in the reforms of the 1960s, the changed world of women in which it found itself was at least equally important to its growth and sustenance. By the 1960s a generation with working mothers had role models, no matter how modest, for self-reliance and self-esteem; better and more education had created an articulate, overtrained, and underemployed pool of talents; effective and legal birth control and a widespread belief in a population crisis made motherhood a choice rather than an inevitable product of marriage; and an increasing number of single and divorced women found their middle-class sense of rights and privileges contrasting sharply with their poverty-level economic options. Thus the women's movement was anchored even in the lives of women who refused to identify with it.

THE FUTURE OF AMERICAN WOMEN

Today, because the majority of white women have left the exclusivity of the domestic sphere, the "woman problem" has become a pervasive one. Its definition is still not entirely clear, but, like the feminism of Gilman and Stanton, its core seems to be egalitarianism. Whether it will be resolved in an egalitarian manner is, however, not known. This is not the only outcome; other options and forms of accommodation do exist.

Modern feminism struggles in three arenas: the job market and the likelihood of equal access and mobility within it, the private sphere of home and family and the redistribution of roles in it, and the psychosocial sphere, in which the image and self-image of both sexes require major readjustments before equality is a possibility. Logically the arenas overlap. But the problem for feminists is that progress or setback can be uneven in each or in any combination; social policy makers may choose to see these arenas as discrete, each with its own degree of egalitarian or non-egalitarian accommodation. Feminist goals, in short, may be granted legitimacy in one arena but not in another.

Legal victories for egalitarianism were won in the early 1960s, when civil rights legislation laid a new basis for feminist demands, and in 1972, when the Federal Education Act banned sex discrimination in higher education. In 1973 the Supreme Court ruled abortion a private decision; that same year Congress submitted the Equal Rights Amendment (ERA) for ratification. But enforcement is not always vigorous enough to transform the models *de jure* into conditions *de facto*. Significantly, the necessary apparatus to allow freedom from child care to women who wish it does not yet exist. A rational system of day-care centers is resisted by policy makers who still insist on maintenance of conservative notions of the family. Public support—male and female—for the transformation of family chores and family organization is far from unanimous.

Politically, the seventies seem less promising than the sixties. The vitality of a women's movement capable of articulating, and pressuring for, reforms is uncertain. Within the movement there remain the difficulties of forging strong political alliances across class lines and racial-ethnic divisions. The growth in the last decades of a new female labor pool composed of legal and illegal immigrants from racial and ethnic groups outside the traditional European-African identifications presents old problems with new faces. These Oriental and Hispanic women workers in the garment industry and in our factories cannot be "invisible" to the eye of the women's movement. Externally, the recessions of the 1970s, the clear shift to the center of liberal factions within the major parties, and the rise of organized antifeminist forces suggest an antireform atmosphere similar to that of the 1920s.

The high morale and the spirit of cooperation shown at the Houston Convention in 1977 must be balanced by the fact that the ERA has not yet been ratified and is in danger of failing, and by the likelihood that abortion may become a ballot-box decision. The insistence that full equality is not a priority or a necessity because many women do not want to exercise it has had an impact even upon historians writing in the field. The notion that equality should be resolved by an appeal to numbers is all too much a part of American tradition; oddly, few defenders of feminist goals have pointed out that should the same criteria apply to other rights, American suffrage itself would have been repealed years ago in the face of repeated voter apathy.

Finally, the fact is that even if the integration of women into the work force continues, this need not mean economic equality. Thus far, it has not. The percentage of women in the professions has actually decreased since 1940 and the differential between male and female wages has increased 8 percent since 1959. In 1970, the average woman college graduate could still expect a smaller annual income than the man with an elementary school education. Poverty among women has increased; in 1959, 26 percent of the total poor were female, but in 1968, that figure was 41 percent.[5]

The future of American women is not yet clear. Modern feminism has increased women's consciousness of inequality and

[5] Banner, *Women in Modern America*, pp. 237–238.

has indicated the areas in which that inequality is buttressed by law, custom, and sexual stereotyping. But because more women know what they want, this does not mean they will get it.

The essays in Part IV give point and counterpoint to this introduction's suggestion of the complexities of women's experience in modern American society. They also reveal, through the variety of methodologies, subject matter, and sources of evidence, what readers of this volume must have noted earlier: the sometimes bewildering wealth of data and issues historians must incorporate if they are to understand a group that exists within, yet above, the categories of class, race, ethnicity, region, and religion. No artificial effort has been made in these essays to simplify the difficulties of the historian's task.

That womanhood is often only one part of an identity is made clear in Susan Reverby's portrait of Lillian Roberts. Here, through the oral-history technique, we see a woman who perceives herself in a multiplicity of vital identities: as a woman, as an American of economically marginal origins, as a member of a newly forged profession, as a professional labor organizer, and as a black. In Roberts's life we can see the levels of simultaneous struggle in the three arenas we have discussed: the failure of her marriage, the success of her campaign to organize and professionalize the nurses' aides, and her growing consciousness that, even as a representative of labor at the bargaining table, she must deal with implicit sexual as well as explicit class issues.

Despite their differences of time and place, Inman, Gilman, and Roberts share the experience of being anomalies in their society, women who consciously sought to test the social norms and expectations of their era. They share, too, a consciousness that they will serve as role models for younger women. In this their womanhood finds its centrality.

Roberts's autobiography suggests a feminist consciousness that evolved from experience, but Rosalind Rosenberg's "The Academic Prism" provides a look at a systematic and intellectualized feminism. In this study of university women and their concern to test the validity of sex-based assumptions of feminists and antifeminists alike, we once again see, as we did in the Gordon and Sklar essays, the importance of educational institutions in the history of American women. The access to modern professions and the modern university proves to be a radical step, not simply because it challenges masculine monopoly on science and the social sciences, but because, as Rosenberg shows, the tools of these intellectual trades can now be turned upon the woman question by women themselves.

In the twentieth century, women may at last direct the examination of the nature of women. Yet as Rosenberg shows, no easy synthesis should be expected to emerge from the academic prism. The question of whether women have a unique nature remains moot and finds expression in such political disagreements among women as those on the ERA and on protective legislation. Further, Rosenberg shows us that women do not escape role conflict even in the most privileged positions of academe. Sisterhood can conflict with professional loyalties, and the traditional support networks among women have not often survived the transition from outsider to insider status within once-masculine domains. Finally, Rosenberg shows us that gains for women can never be considered final: As in so many instances, women were edged out of university positions in the 1920s once those positions were firmly established as prestigious.

The ability of women to function effectively within an ambiguous self-definition is shown in Jacquelyn Hall's study of the southern women's antilynching campaign. Here social feminism reveals its durability and vitality as a movement and as an explanatory model for women acting outside the domestic sphere. Buttressed like Dunn's Quaker women by religious precepts and by the practical leadership experience religious settings so often provide, women like Jessie Ames successfully did battle in a sensitive political and social arena. Here, we can see once more the importance of female support systems and the absence of identity conflict in the activism of the social feminist. Unlike working women fighting for economic equality or social egalitarianism, Ames and her southern reform coalition could successfully rechannel their personal dissatisfactions with the shrinking duties of the home into an energetic mobilization for racial reform. Perhaps it is the absence of any sense of incongruity between the role they played as civil rights reformists and their own subordinate status as women that accounted for their immediate successes— and for their ultimate failure to evolve a women's rights movement.

Hall shows us women successful in their efforts to influence other people's destinies. But the sense that women have not yet been able to control their own public destinies is reinforced by Leila Rupp's study of the mobilization of women for wartime production. Here we can see policy and opinion makers determinedly pulling the strings of women's lives, first one way, then the next, a circumstance reminiscent of John Harper's look at the history of family planning. Rupp traces two governments' propaganda efforts to make women in the work force a palatable concept to a middle-class society officially wedded to the separate spheres' doctrine.

Both the Nazi and American governments faced a delicate problem: how to suspend sex-role stereotypes without destroying them, how to bring rapid change yet ensure it a temporary status. As Rupp shows, both governments had considerable success, for the war left traditional attitudes intact and thus made the actual change in the sex composition of the postwar labor force politically and legally invisible for a decade. Rupp's conclusions raise those very questions about the relationship of ideology to actual motivation we have tried to suggest. Women, it seemed, responded to employment in wartime America for income and the economic gains it promised, less troubled than their men by the immediate implications for identity.

The final essay of this volume deals with the complex origins and nature of the feminist movement of the 1960s and 1970s. In this history of the movement, the central themes of the previous essays seem to reverberate: The reality of demographic changes traced by Wells is here, as is evidence of a desire to control one's personal and public destinies, shown implicitly and explicitly in the struggles of women like Elizabeth Inman, Charlotte Gilman, and the anonymous women of the nineteenth century who sought out abortion and contraceptive devices despite the illegality and the dangers involved. The essay shows the development of a coherent movement and a feminist ideology based on the contacts provided at work, in educational institutions, in religious and political organizations—contacts that had provided support networks and practical experience to women throughout American history, as Dunn, Sklar, Hall, Rosenberg, and Turbin have shown us, but that only rarely could be merged to create the promising consciousness modern feminists seem to be molding.

The problems of identity voiced by young women of different backgrounds throughout Evans's essay echo the persistent problem of women born into a world of separate spheres and sex-role stereotypes and a confusion of what, after all, masculine and feminine do and should mean. Like Gilman, the women of "Tomorrow's Yesterday" re-examine the nature of femininity, the future of the family structure, and the division of labor in the home and in the public sphere. And, as Reverby's portrait of Lillian Roberts shows, these women too are subject to multiple identifications; their ability to operate within a feminist context requires recognition of, and space for their differences of class, race, region, and religion.

Evans is optimistic for the future, but it is not an optimism naively held. She is aware that women do not often control the arena of their struggle, and that, like Hirata's Chinese prostitutes, today's women must operate within the context of American capitalism, its constitutional politics, and the still deeply ingrained traditional notions of sex roles. The skill is not in denying these realities but in finding room to maneuver within them and in recognizing real options when and where they present themselves.

11 *From Aide to Organizer:*
The Oral History of Lillian Roberts

Susan Reverby

Lillian Roberts as she left court after being sentenced in December 1968.
Courtesy of Public Employee Press, District Council 37, AFSCME.

Introduction

Historians usually turn to novels, biographies, autobiographies, or diaries to obtain a sense of how individuals actually *felt* about historical events and experiences; for the historian who is trying to interpret the consciousness of working-class and minority men and women, these sources often do not exist. Thus, in the last ten years, oral history—the taped recollections of people's lives—has become an increasingly important source of data.

Such tapes do give us a glimpse of otherwise invisible historical moments or new perceptions on well-known events. But oral histories are no more a total picture than histories based only on published government sources or dry statistical compilations. Oral history places its subjects in the center of historical events and refracts events through their eyes. Historian Michael Frisch has suggested that oral history helps us to understand *historical memory patterns,* the way in which a set of cultural experiences shapes how we remember, order, and make sense of the experiences of our lives.[1] Oral history may, however, neglect to give us an understanding of the institutional context and social forces that shape those perceptions.

By the very process of asking certain questions and not others, or by juxtaposing certain answers in an edited manuscript, the historian-interviewer is shaping the responses of the subject. Thus, an oral history interview is no more value-free, no more a simple set of facts, than is any other form of historical evidence. Nevertheless, even with these limitations, oral histories do give us an opening into a world view whose existence is obscured by the use of other types of sources. The following oral history gives us a way to understand the struggle of a twentieth-century black woman for dignity and justice.

Lillian Roberts's history is in many ways similar to that of other black women of her generation. Her parents left the agricultural South during the second great black migration in the 1920s for the mecca of Chicago. Her father was unable to work, and her mother had to turn to welfare during the Depression to support her five children. Lillian Roberts had to work, even after she was married, to survive. She became a nurse's aide in a hospital in the mid-1940s, a time when minority women and men were increasingly becoming the nonprofessional and low-paid workers of the growing health sector. As hospital unionism slowly began to grow in the late 1950s and early 1960s as a part of the expansion of public employment and in conjunction with the civil rights movement, she became an active trade unionist in the American Federation of State, County, and Municipal Employees (AFSCME). She climbed

[1] "Oral History and *Hard Times,* A Review Essay," *Red Buffalo,* Oral history issue, No. 2–3, n.d., pp. 217–231.

up the union hierarchy: shop steward, local official, representative, organizer, international union staffer, to her current position as associate director for organization of New York City's 100,000-member District Council 37 of AFSCME.

But in other ways, Lillian Roberts's experience is unique. Sexual, racial, and class boundaries on jobs make it almost impossible for minority women to move out of poorly paying, dead-end jobs. Most women workers are neither union members nor union leaders. In 1972 only 16.6 percent of all women workers were union members, as compared to 33.3 percent of all male workers. Similarly, less than one-fifth of all hospital workers are in unions. Women's segregation into service, white-collar, and low-wage industries, in addition to their familial responsibilities, has made them less likely to be either organized by a union or able to participate in one. Other women, unlike Lillian Roberts, have found the labor movement unconcerned and unwilling to deal with the particular problems of women and blacks or to support their demands.[2] Few women, white or black, have reached so high a position in a large union. Only 7 percent of elected governing board members of unions and employee associations are women. In appointed positions, women were more likely to be research directors or editors than director of organization as is Lillian Roberts.

Despite her uniqueness, or perhaps because of it, through her recollections we begin to understand the inhumanity and self-perpetuating structure of the welfare system, the search for dignity on the job, the struggle through the labor movement for justice and equality. The following oral history was edited both in length (the original transcript is nearly 200 pages) and in content to remove the interviewer's questions.[3]

[2] Florence Rice, "It Takes a While to Realize That It Is Discrimination," *Black Women in White America,* ed. Gerda Lerner, Vintage, New York, 1972, pp. 275–284; Sumner M. Rosen, "The CIO Era, 1935–55," and Herbert Hill, "The Racial Practices of Organized Labor: The Contemporary Record," *The Negro and the American Labor Movement,* ed. Julius Jacobson, Anchor, New York, 1968, pp. 188–208 and pp. 286–357; Annemarie Troger, "The Coalition of Labor Union Women," *America's Working Women,* ed. Rosalyn Baxandall, Linda Gordon, and Susan Reverby, Vintage, New York, 1976, pp. 390–400.

[3] As any oral historian knows, this process is made up of contradictory tasks: of selecting passages that reflect the subject's perceptions and forms of expression but do not damage the readability or the interviewer's own sense of "what really happened" from other sources. I most gratefully acknowledge the support and advice given me by: Lydia Kleiner, Joyce Kornbluh, Amy Lang, Marsha Love, Tim Sieber, and Lise Vogel. Above all I wish to thank Lillian Roberts for her openness and generosity of both spirit and time. The longer oral history was made possible through the generous support of "The 20th Century Trade Union Woman: Vehicle for Social Change" project at the University of Michigan—Wayne State University, and the tape and transcribed manuscript are available from them. Their address is: c/o Institute of Labor and Industrial Relations, Museums Annex, University of Michigan, Ann Arbor, Mich. 48104.

GROWING UP IN CHICAGO

I was born the second of five children in Chicago, Illinois, January 2, 1928. My father's name is Henry Davis, and he was born in Dublin, Mississippi, May 12, 1901. And he died July 10, 1971. My mother's maiden name was Lillian Henry, and she was born August 3, 1903, in Edward, Mississippi, and she's still alive.

My father's childhood was—I guess I can talk about it now—pretty secretive, because I think that he was involved in some crime in the South. And he had to go through some woods to escape, and I could remember that when people would come to the house how careful he was about who they were.

My mother was one of, I think there were nine of them, and a couple of them died in their youth. She would talk about the chores each one of them had. I got the sense that they came from a very large farm and that they were not necessarily poor as defined in those days. It was probably considered middle class at that time, because they seemed to have food to eat, enough clothes to look respectable, and they dated, picnicked, went to dances, and did little things as the average middle class would do, it seemed to me. They moved from Mississippi to Missouri and that's where the family is now, the rest of them. I think she was about 20, 21 when she got married, and then she started to have children two years after, then every year thereafter or every year and a half until she had five of us. I was the second child and the oldest daughter.

My parents came to Chicago together about two years before I was born. That was probably about 1926. They were seeking employment. My mother's brother was here, and he had a wife, and they came and stayed with them until my dad was able to find a job. And then they moved out on their own. I think my dad probably worked all of about two years, and then he never had another job. My mother never worked. She had five children, and so she was home with us. And of course we were on welfare. And my father had terrible varicose veins and he was semi-invalid. He had about a third grade education. He could count very well, very well, but he wasn't able to do a lot of reading, but he had an awful lot of innate intelligence.

I never really had a childhood, like the way people have it, you know? I guess I had to be an old lady at a very young age. And my mother had no time to bother herself, because she had all of us and absolutely just herself, and we were on welfare and it was a struggle trying to see that we had at least one meal a day and something to wear, things of that kind.

And I think the biggest thing she enjoyed was prayer service. And maybe that was the sanity for her—that there was a group that had prayer once a week, and she would take us to church on Sundays. I'll never forget that. We'd stay in church from early in the morning to late at night without a meal. I'd always have a headache. I would be so disgusted with that until I thought I would die. But she enjoyed it so thoroughly. She had to take us with her, obviously, because she had nobody to watch us. But I remember that the neighbors had a lot of respect for my mother because she really was a God-fearing woman and I guess that that established principles within us. But I don't think any of us kids go to church today, we had enough church going, but we do have principles, and we do believe in what's right. I think that's what the church is all about—is to reinforce those things in you.

So we are very grateful for that. But that was not very pleasant for me. I used to be bored, very bored, as a child. I had a lot of chores because I had the family wash, and I washed on a washing board until my knuckles were raw. Every week, religiously. Then I did the ironing. And I'd get up early in the morning because I liked to finish my chores early. And I started ironing and I'd iron for about two days. I can remember having varicosity at the age of 12 because I'd stand for so many hours.

I enjoyed love story magazines, that we used to consider dirty magazines, or something to read so that I could view other forms of life. I would find them because somebody would throw them out, in the area, you know. I would sneak 'em in the house and would read 'em—True Love, love stories, things like that.

Of course we were plagued by gangs—all of the things that come with poverty and boredom, prostitution, and just everything, robberies. There was always a knifing, fighting, something going on all the time.

So my mother isolated us with her prayers. She kept us in the house because she didn't want us to get involved in these things. I think the only child that she began to let out much earlier was my oldest brother. He worked for the grocer downstairs. Even though he was sneaking drinking and all—we would tell her and she would act like she didn't hear us. I mean he would get away with murder. But out of the five of us I think two were lost to that ghetto. The brother that was two years younger than I was a drug addict and he died at the age of 27. The sister who was four years younger than I was killed by the baby's father at the age of 32. He came out of the ghetto, one of the worst, and he would gamble. And he didn't want to work. There was a whole series of things, and she decided she was going to leave him, and so he killed her. I had to take, of course, her three children, but that was later after I married.

Well, my mother was pretty much for a lot of causes . . . for instance, the schools were—it's like the same fight—they were not good. . . . And so, she knew that we were not getting a well-rounded education because of not having history and all the other things. She'd go up and speak to the principal, which was unheard of at that time. And I guess they would try to get her off their backs by talking to the politicians who would want to appease and try to explain to her that, "you're wrong," and so on. So they got to see her.

And then of course at one time they wanted to sell the building that we were in. At that time they didn't have such things as relocating individuals, and there were over . . . close to 2,000 people in the building in which we lived. And these people had no place to go. They had to stand up and fight, and she was quite a leader in that struggle. So they hung on to the building for a very, very long time. I must have been a bit proud of her.

But my mother and father fought because my dad was a drinker. And he was very abusive and he didn't want her to go to church, didn't want her to go anywhere. And he would stay out all night gambling sometimes in the building, you know. Imagine them fighting over 15 cents, big deal. And then he'd come home in the middle of the night and want her to get up and fix some food and she would refuse to do it and there would be fights.

My father loved me very much. I was the oldest girl, and I guess girls love their fathers. And I knew all his shortcomings, but he was my father. And so, I would go to school frequently worrying when they'd go through these fighting things. I would be very worried about what was happening at home, sort of, to the degree preoccupied.

Once I got in the middle of the fights to stop him. I seem to have been the one with a little more courage than the others and the others were just screaming and trembling. I would always be in the middle of these fights, it's amazing that I didn't get killed, and push them apart and try to talk to them. But finally, she put him out and never had him back in the house anymore.

I kind of wanted them back together, and then I didn't because he fought her so that I was wondering how long she'd live. She would fight back, of course, but that was a hell of a way to live. And I always said that my criteria for a husband was that he didn't fight. It's sad, but that was my only frame of reference.

And of course the men around me, the young men, the boys around me that I could date when I got old enough were not the kind of fellas that I wanted because they were similar to my dad. And so it was a, I don't know, empty kind of a childhood. Boy, I never really felt that I lived; I always felt that I existed throughout that whole age. And it had its toll certainly on me and my sister and my brothers because, surely, they had their own feelings but they didn't share them. We never shared how we felt, because we really couldn't examine that, you know, at that point. So it was a whole thing of climbing up out of that whole mess that haunted me, practically all of my life.

I guess I was sort of a child that observed other people because I loved people a lot. And I saw so much misery. I was seeing people a lot. I was seeing the people around me who wanted very much to have welfare, but they didn't have children, so they couldn't get welfare. So, some of the women to survive were prostitutes. And they were forced into that kind of thing.

My mother would share her [welfare] box. I remember getting prunes and beans and things like that—that's how the welfare came—in a big box, soap and stuff that was supposed to last you for a month. Everybody sort of tried to share it. And I can remember writing letters of these people and crying inside that you know, you wanted to help, and you couldn't. And it was terrible, really. I always said that if I ever got an opportunity to do something, I would do something for those people.

Becoming a Hospital Worker

I really didn't know what I wanted to do. And I finally decided that maybe I would like to be a teacher. But none of those things appeared to be fulfilling to me. My aspirations as a nurse, I didn't see that. I certainly didn't see becoming a doctor. Or any of those things, because you see, another thing is, I didn't have any heroes. That's very important. It's almost like you don't belong, you know? It was just a very strange feeling. I used to look at my mother and wonder why she would live in a society without almost saying, "Well, this is terrible. I'd rather be dead than to be alive. Because what is there for me? This ho-hum, am I just to exist?"

And finally, in high school, I had to come right home because there were gangs and all. My mother was very strict about you getting home on time and all these other things. And I didn't enjoy it, because I couldn't go to the dances; I didn't have dresses and things like other kids. I felt very inferior, inferior to other black kids, because I didn't have, you know, things. We were on welfare and had to wear welfare clothes. You're earmarked. You're on welfare so you're less than somebody else. So even if other kids' parents had something that was not from welfare that they wore, it gave them a certain amount of prestige within that ghetto. These are things that impact upon a child, and they don't say anything, but they take their mark.

I always wanted to work, but I never could find a job. When I was about 14 I was going to high school, and I got a job as an aide in a Catholic hospital. And I went down, and kept going down and finally they hired me. They had a good meal there, that was one nice thing. They fed you very well. You had what the patients had and the food was good. Well, the hospital would hire someone that said they were

15, so I just took up my age because they were paying nothing anyway. You worked eight hours, and you probably got paid like 11 dollars for two weeks' work. I was really exploited. That must have been about 1940.

Even if it was a small amount of money, it gave me something, because I had nothing. I couldn't even buy lipstick and things like that. And I was getting to the age where I would want to date, where I wanted to look attractive to boys. And so when I began to work I would give my mother probably half of that, and then the rest of that I managed after several months to get a dress, a couple of little dresses.

In spite of the ghetto, because of my mother, we all finished high school. I was an honor student, so she insisted on trying to get me a scholarship—which she did. I was approaching 18 then, and she managed through a black politician to get the scholarship to the University of Illinois in Champaign-Urbana. But then she couldn't get the room and board. And so my brother then was able to get himself a paper route which paid him a little bit more than the grocery store. He said that he would send the money for my room and board. So I then gathered my little belongings. I had accumulated a few things, a trunk full, that I could take off to school.

And I went to school. I stayed with a family, because I couldn't stay on campus. It was too much money, so I stayed with a black family. My brother would send his money in order to pay for room and board. It was like 40 dollars a month. And they would all be doing the best they could, plus the neighbors who I used to write the letters for would send quarters and 50 cents, and things like that. It was just the warmest feeling.

There were some other black students, mostly boys. I could only see about two or three other black girls. We were truly isolated. And then not to have the proper clothing, I don't need to tell you that I never went near the sororities, I stayed the hell away from it. And I would walk to school, which was a long distance, and I had breakfast, but I couldn't eat until I came back, because we didn't have lunch money or anything like that. I was taking liberal arts. And I, I just felt so alone because I couldn't share with people the embarrassment of the poverty that I suffered. And they did better because their parents had more, you know, to offer.

Well, after about a term and a half, my brother was drafted into the service, and I no longer had the room and board and the woman would ask me for it, and I would do chores at the house to be helpful, but I just felt so bad because I couldn't help it. And I said, "Well, I guess I just have to go home." So I then picked up near the end of that term and went home, and they told me that when I was ready that I could come back. But it was just so many ugly memories, and I said, "I have to get a job now, obviously." And I was so angry at society that here I was on welfare, I did not want welfare, I was humiliated by it, and they were doing absolutely nothing to help me to get out of that situation. They wouldn't pay the room and board or anything, in spite of the fact that there was a scholarship.

But at any rate, I went home in 1946 and I started looking for a job. I'd heard about this hospital job at the University of Chicago, Lying-In Clinics. So I decided to go over there, and there was a nursing supervisor who came from New York. And while they never had any black nurse's aides, she was going to hire her first one. That was me.

I don't think she had too much of a choice because the war had taken most of the whites away from those menial jobs into jobs that were paying a lot more in defense plants. And so they were really uptight about help at that point.

I realized I could make more in another kind of job, but I wanted to do something that I felt . . . I really needed something at that time to feel that it was necessary for me to even go on living. So I took that job.

And right away some of the people in the kitchen told me that they didn't have black nurse's aides. I didn't think anything of that. I was about 18, 19 then. And so I proceeded to do my job, and I loved it. I never wanted to be bossed a lot, so what I did was find out what is it I'm responsible for, and I did that. And I would do more than that, because I didn't want to be ruled all the time. I remember being very lonely. While there were blacks in the kitchen, there were no black aides, and the white aides didn't want to talk to me. So I sort of ignored them. I mean, at that point, who cares?

They were older than I. I was very young, too, you know, compared to them. And they just looked at me with curiosity, and I never bothered. And finally they got to the place to kind of like me, 'cause I didn't bother anybody. They would be knitting and all, and I started learning during my breaks as well as they did, and we'd talk and we got to be very, very good friends.

I worked in the nursery, that was the first job. And that was diapering and feeding the babies. I did a lot more there. Cleaning, first of all. I did a lot of cleaning, and I kept things sterile and got the formula ready for the babies, and all. It was, of course, glass around the nursery. And you would think that I was some monkey on display. The doctors and everybody were looking in the window. And just constantly watching me. And this one doctor, it was the kind of watch, that he was looking for some reason to say, "Get her out of there," because you had to wash your hands in between babies and all, so he wanted to know whether I was observing the techniques and all.

I was working with a white southern nurse, Mrs. Montique. It was just she and I. So we got along very well. And I was able to relate to her, asking her every day I wanted to learn something new. And so I would

ask her about all kinds of deformities that we would see in the nursery:
the color of a baby, and why this was happening and why the other thing
was happening. And then I explored with her using my own analysis of
things. Sometimes I'd be right just in observing and putting some
common sense into it. Before long, when the interns would come to
examine the babies I could tell them what was wrong with every baby.
I'd have them lined up for them. And they got so that they depended
upon me, because I really got to know.

So the doctors, they get to know that you know your job and you
can tell them certain things: "I think it would be wise if you did this."
But you'd always have to do it in such a discreet way not to step on their
pride, because they're supposed to be the expert, you know.

I had gotten so good at it, with so many compliments from so many
people going down to the office—I didn't realize it—that they scheduled
me when Mrs. Montique was off—to be in charge. And they didn't tell
you you were in charge, but I'd get a whole mess of new students in there
who didn't know what to do. I would very diplomatically have to direct
them, although they resented to hell that I was both black and a nurse's
aide. But I had to do it in such a way that they didn't feel that I was
claiming to know more than they did. And I realized that. Because they
said, "Well, you're just an aide, and blah." I said, "I know that." I said,
"I'm not concerned about that, but we do have feeding times here." And
I would go on to talk about what we had to do and how would they
suggest we go about doing it, as if they knew anything, they never
had worked there. But that was the kind of thing that I found I had
to do.

And they would never allow me to sit in on the report to the changing guard of nurses. They never dignify you with that. Even though it
would help you give better care. There were limitations on what I could
do. But there was variety. And then you get to the point where you
conquer that and you want to go on to something else. I mean that was
my feeling. I wanted to learn something else. So when I got to a boredom
stage, I wanted to move on because it was important. I looked forward
to the job when I thought there was something in it. I did my job and
all, it was something I loved, because I loved people.

They never had any formalized training for me. I learned by experience and I would ask questions. We didn't have enough formalized education. It was nice for me to learn in the nursery because I would ask—
and to learn wherever I would go. But the "why you do certain things"
is very important to a nonprofessional person. And I thought we should
have had a lot more formal education and a lot more excitement brought
to the job and be part of the team, which means that you should be
there when reports are given about a patient. All you're saying is that
you are a human being and what you do is very important, is part of a

team, and it's not taking a doggone thing away from you—it's enhancing you, and making you so proud of yourself and more attentive to the job. Because it has more meaning to you.

It was pretty hard to hear the shift report. Because here everybody's crowding around the desk and you come up there, they ask you: "What do you want?" You know, like "Who are you?" I mean, that's the way it was. And I always, and today, I still feel that way. There's something very small about and something very insecure about people who claim to be educated, that feel so threatened by those who don't have the academic standing, who just simply want to learn how they can do more. I mean, when you examine it, you see how ridiculous it is.

After I had been there for a while . . . I really didn't think about getting a different job. I was hoping to make that a better job, and I, I was a little angry that they were always crying about not having nurses, and there was never an opportunity for a person like myself to be one. And when I loved it, and would have been a very good one, I thought. I always felt that I was cheated out of that opportunity.

I couldn't have afforded to go to nursing school. I needed the income, and you can't just quit the job and go to school. I was caught in a box, and the salary wasn't big enough to save to go to school. And getting into the nursing schools was a real racist problem as well. So there was a combination of many things. And I used to say, "Why does this country have to go elsewhere and get people when people like myself want to do something? We really want to do it, and we're not forced into it." And that was always a dream of mine. So I guess that when I went on to organizing, that was one of the first things that I saw was done. I set up a program in New York so that aides could be trained on the job to become licensed practical nurses.

About two years after I started working in that hospital, I got married. When I went away to school, I met my husband. He was a serviceman who had come home because of his mother. And he was quite a bit older than I but a very nice person, a good family; it was the family I stayed with. They had a family life I never had. They were sort of like middle class in a way. The mother and father were in the house. That was a big bonus, I thought. They didn't fight each other, and I thought that was an extra bonus. The sister was there, and she was dating, and doing all the things that I wish I had had an opportunity to do. And finally he got out of the services and he came to Chicago looking for me.

I liked him because he was the most decent thing that I had met. And he was a hard-working man, pretty stable and so on. He was a silkscreen operator. And so, although he had to pay heavy alimony because he was divorced, he was the hand that really helped me out of the ghetto. I wanted to have a man. I was at the stage where I wanted to be loved. And I wanted a little house, a little apartment, a room, something of my own, because I never had that.

I was about 20, 20½ when we got married. And so we saved our little money, and we had about 400, 500 dollars. That's a lot of money for us. And we both worked hard and we didn't have much to save. If it was 50 cents a week, I saved it. You know, I, I really learned that I had to do that, to have something. I felt like . . . there was nobody for me to depend on. I had to depend upon myself. His salary was very small, very small. And when he finished giving his little 11 dollars, 12 dollars a week to his wife who had two kids by him, there was very little left. So that it was never a question about my working.

And finally, we got enough money. I remember the first thousand dollars to put down on a car. We were, we were like kids, we were on the floor throwing those bills up and down, and just, just. . . . It was the happiest moment, you know, because we were going to have something that we could go to visit his family with—and I could see, being on the road, other things, you know?

Learning to Organize

So to keep us going, I kept on working. I always worked the days, because I had an opportunity because of the seniority I built up. I stayed there 13 years. I also worked in the emergency room, central supply, and the operating room.

After ten years there, I got involved in the union, our union AFSCME [American Federation of State, County, Municipal Employees] which was already in the hospital but it didn't do too much. It was the pressures that got me involved.

That was when ten of the nurse's aides had left. And because I had the ability to work in many places, I was being exploited—myself and a few others who had the skills to walk into a situation and get it in order. And we were very proud of our work. Because once I would do something, I would want not to be questioned. I mean, if I had to prepare instruments for an operation, I would do that very thoroughly. And when you got a pack with my name on it, you knew it was in order.

What I did was I went to the shop steward, who had been there a long time, about this extra work. And to her the union was just picking up the dues and, you know, "don't rock the boat." She did nothing. So I called the union office, and I said: "Look, we been paying our dues for years now. We need the union. We don't have help here, and it's killing all of us. And the best people are going to have to quit. So what's the union going to do about it?" So I called them very angry. They said,

"Yes, that's an over workload grievance." I said, "Well, who's going to handle it?" They said, "The steward. Then if you don't want her you'll have to get a new steward elected," which was not a good answer for us—"and to handle it yourself."

So then I came back, and I told the girls what was said. They said, "Well, let's get rid of her. Let's get another steward, and *you* be it." I said, "No, I don't want to be it." And they said, "Well, you have to. Either we quit or we stand up and fight."

And so then I decided and went home and told my husband, "If I'm going to take this stewardship, then I've got to go to meetings, because I really have to know what I'm doing. I'm going up against some heavies." So he said, "All right. Go ahead and take it." I told him how many meetings it involved—one or two a month. He really didn't want me to get involved. But I told him I had to. It was either that or quit, which meant the rent wasn't going to be paid.

So then I started. I got the union contract, and I heard what the woman had told me that it was an over workload grievance. And I began to document the people who had left and what we were doing. Then the election was held and I won the election. So then I asked the ex–shop steward who was also the secretary of the union if she'd be kind enough to introduce me to the nursing supervisor in my new role. I really didn't get that much leadership. She took me and then I pulled out my little contract book, and I told the nursing supervisor I was there on behalf of all the young ladies who worked at Lying-In Hospital, that we enjoyed working there very much, but we felt we had been exploited and that ten people had left and they had not replaced them. And we certainly didn't mind working when there was an emergency of any kind, but we felt that to be scheduled every day to do three people's jobs was just too much. She screamed at me and told me that no ten had left, and who was I to come into her office telling her. And I told her I was the shop steward. And I don't know what she was accustomed to, but she and I were going to have a very different relationship. Because by then it was either fight or quit. I said, "Here's a contract book. Our union and the university had felt that these were the fair rules—name of the game. And I'm going to go according to them, and I hope that you're going to do the same. You have five days in order to respond to my grievance." And she started screaming and yelling. And then I got up and told her she had the grievance, and I'd see her in five days. And I left.

So she went up to my boss the next day when I was off and wanted to know what kind of worker I was, because she wanted to fire me. And my boss said, "You can't do that. She's the best worker we have. I, I don't have any reason—nothing to bring her up on charges for." So she said, "When she comes tomorrow, you have her come downstairs."

When I came in, I went downstairs. So the nursing supervisor said,

"I want you to apologize." And I told her I was not apologizing. I had nothing to apologize for. I said, "Either you hire the people—you've got three days to do it—or I am going to appeal it. That's all. There's nothing to argue about." And so I left her again with her mouth open. And she hung around very upset. But at the end of the five days she brought ten girls up and introduced them to us. I was on my way, you know.

We also used the union to keep good people working there. I don't know whether we were straitlaced, or what, but we were kind of dedicated to the job. And we were embarrassed by people who didn't come to work, because they'd leave us running all over the place. So we had our own way of discipline. And that was surely sooner or later the nursing supervisor would bring 'em up on charges. And I would go in and make a plea for them, and I would talk to them afterwards very strongly. And then she would call me in again with them; I'd go in and make a second plea for them and talk to them again very strongly. In the meantime, all the other young ladies knew that this person was a lemon. And then the third time I'd go in and I'd say, "Well, I really don't know what we can do about it." And then, of course, she would fire them, and then I would not make any appeals, and I would refuse to let our mechanism be used for an appeal for a person who obviously didn't want the job. And that way we kept very good people there.

I continued to do organizing. I was a little different. I would go into the dining rooms and sit down and talk to the different workers. In fact, they tried to put me out a couple of times, because I would just sit at the table with a group and tell them I was from the union. And it was always pretty negative for a while—until they got to know that I was there. And then it was a sense of security for them. And they would just greet me, and everybody knew that here I was. I knew that if the union ever was to be strong, and I ever was to gain things for them, I needed their support.

I had certain scheduled times that I would go see people, sign up people who didn't belong, and talk to them about the union, and take up their problems. To the point that I had a lot of problems coming, because the more active the union is, the more people then want you to relieve them of injustices that they have been living with for a long time.

I was anxious to take those things on, and I guess I was pretty effective. And I began to get some pretty big increases for them as a result of being on the negotiating team. And it was a very good experience, a growing experience for me, probably one of the most essential experiences in teaching me, you know, what to do, how to do it, and when to do it.

Well, Vic Gotbaum [an AFSCME organizer, now Executive Director of District Council 37 of AFSCME in New York] came in during the time I was steward and noticed that I was aggressive, that I was responsible. When I would talk to him about a grievance, I would tell him what I thought we ought to do. And then, you know, he would tell me whether it needed to be changed. Then I started bothering him and saying we need to be educated because this is a very responsible position, and you're going to represent people—it's like being a lawyer—you got to know the rules of the game. And I hounded him. Roosevelt University had an educational program, so he put me into that program, and then he noticed that I had something to offer. So he asked me to come out of the hospital and work for the union. He really was the person who gave me my start.

One of my first jobs was to organize state hospital workers in southern Illinois, mainly southern whites. There were some black workers, but they didn't want them in their union. They knew I was a black woman before I came down there, and they called Vic every day telling him to take me out, they wouldn't join a union, that I was black, and people didn't respond to that. It was during the days of Martin Luther King in the early '60s when I got started in that, so the feeling was very high. And Vic never would tell me what they said, but I could feel this. And it was very hard. They looked at me as if I was something out of space. I had to be tolerant and I had to show them that I really loved them. I would go out there once a week. And it got so I would make it a point of being on time, you know, and being there. And I started working on their problems that they had and I was able to accomplish a lot of things.

And I used to service the problems of the black members, but I would go down and see them in a different section of town. I would tell them not to say anything about what I was doing for their problems or anything, because the whites kept thinking that the blacks would take over. That was a feeling of theirs. And even in meetings I would tell the blacks, "Don't try to monopolize my time. I will always come to the train station and see you, but I want to be able to talk to the whites and let them feel free, and you have to understand that we're in a process." And they understood very well. They were southerners, too.

And so they all [blacks and whites] began to see that I was a help. And then they began to help me. And I have never had such a beautiful, loyal group of people as those. In fact, they had me then elected as vice president of this union. They carried that campaign themselves.

I have always seen the union as a protector of the working class's rights that transcend all the other things. When you get into things that border on color, you lose part of your support right away. But when you can get a class of people to see that their interests are basically the same, you got far more clout. Because I happen to think that this society works very hard at keeping the classes divided by means of color. And therefore, they really don't truly express themselves in a very democratic way, for their own well-being. This is where democracy is working; yet it's not working. Now, I mean, that's my analysis of it. And therefore I have always seen the labor movement as a beautiful instrument. If I work in the labor movement with people who have one common thing, that is, their labor, their work, being paid for their work and getting the most out of their work, well then I have a larger group. And they began to understand that we do have a common interest in making this whole society.

When I've been organizing I had people who wanted to go on strike when we didn't think it was wise to go on strike. And I could always pull out my credentials and stand up before them and tell them that there's not a person in that room more militant than I am. I said, "But I also don't practice committing suicide. You don't do that, but once."

And then I explain to them what the issues are and that we have to be adults about it. And I'm willing to yield with the majority, but I as a person who is supposed to be one of their leaders have a responsibility to tell 'em what I see. And I'm telling 'em what I see. And if they vote it down, fine. "I'll go with you, reluctant certainly, but I'll go with you. But, 'don't say I didn't tell you.'" And they vote your way.

My husband didn't like all the time it took. I was being taken away by the members, and he didn't like that. Well, it was really hard for me because I still would try to do the cooking and things like that. But, I would be in the middle of a meal and the phone would ring or something like that. And I had to do that to build up the relationships that I needed, but he was never too happy about it. So we didn't fight too much. At the end we did, a lot. It became too much of a strain. I couldn't maintain fights with the bosses and concerns for the members, and fighting at home. It was too much for me. The kind of recognition I was beginning to get and the kind of job I was doing was kind of a threat to him, and he just couldn't resist putting me down in front of people, because he felt that that made him look good.

I, I put up with it and ignored it for a long time, until I felt like, "I don't need this. I don't need it anymore; I just can't take it." He never understood it, you see. I think he does now, certainly . . . understand it.

We separated after 19, 20 years of marriage. He just couldn't come around to it. And I felt that it was giving up my entire life. It was something I had always wanted to do, and that is, to be of service to people. I couldn't see abandoning them, because in many ways the plight for workers is the plight for me as well, you see. If things get better for me, they got to get better for me, then they got to get better for everybody.

But I find that it's happening with women. I guess it happened to me back then, but it's happening to women now who want fulfillment. Well, I wanted both fulfillment and I had to work. I had no choice. So it wasn't a luxury to me. But it was just the niche that I thought I needed to be in.

LEADING NEW YORK STRIKES

After I had been working in Illinois for several years, Vic had moved back to New York and he called me in 1965 to help with the social service workers' strike. I was also going to take a look at the 19 municipal hospitals and see what could be done about organizing them. But then the Teamsters filed with the labor board for an election in the hospitals for a union for all the nonprofessional workers. We had to organize in a very short time. And I had to direct that campaign.

The Teamsters already had the supervisors and they outnumbered us. Everything was going against us. The supervisors were bringing up our people on charges to fire them. And, of course, they were part of the Teamsters. And I would have to use everything that I knew to try to force the head of the hospital department at that time to be fair with us. We really didn't have that many teeth, it was just what I could muster. The hospital department knew that if the Teamsters won they would not have to bother with grievances. And the Labor Department was tight with the Teamsters too. But people felt that we were a union that could represent them for the better because we had a positive program. So they voted for us.

The Teamsters would appear at the meetings, and they would get into fights to try to keep the people out of the meetings. They stabbed a couple of staff people. They turned the lights out while we were sitting and meeting. And they would follow me around, to harass me. And all kinds of threats and things like that. I could of swore that somebody shot at my window one day. And so it was a frightening experience, but it only made me angry and more determined. And I remember, I used to have a brick in my pocket. Some of their people who wanted to come over to us, who were in their higher positions . . . they would threaten 'em. And I would have to send people out to stay with 'em all night long to let them know they should not be bullied. Then women would attack the men, try to kick them in the privates. They had no program but they thought that they had it in the bag, because they had two members for every one that we had.

They held the election. I could see we were winning, because I had lived so close to it. I could tell almost exact how many votes I expected from each hospital. And at one hospital, they stood up and they marched the people in and out, and I had to send forces over there. I mean it was really Gestapo tactics. Management permitted them to let all their shop stewards off to run up on the floors, and to get other workers off the floors and bringing 'em down to vote.

And when they counted the votes . . . the last group to come in —we had won the election—was Welfare Island. And we had to have police and everybody to go get our people. The Teamsters had burst in, and they wanted to take the ballots away and throw 'em in the river, so that the election would be null and void. And they couldn't get away with it. And they were, they were really paralyzed, because they didn't expect us to win. We were ten months before we ever got certified [as the bargaining agent], but we won.

I had a different kind of trouble three years later when we were trying to organize the state hospital workers all over New York state, you know, hundreds of miles apart. We had to have a strike to force the governor, Governor Rockefeller, to abide by this new law allowing an election and certification of a union for state workers.

We struck the hospitals one by one. We didn't really want the strike. We weren't organized enough to strike all the hospitals at once. And I had to skip around. Part of my package was to try to drive them crazy, to hit and for them not to know where you were going. And if they didn't know where you were going, then they would move patients one place and they may find out that there's a strike there. And they'd have to move 'em out again, you see? That was the only way that we forced an election, and they have been having elections ever since.

The spirits were very high. The first hospital we took was Creedmoor, then Bronx State, then Buffalo. And then we were just about to take on Pilgrim State, and Rockefeller succumbed. And, we really should have gone further, because we should have forced the conditions and the hours of the election, but we didn't. We permitted him to have a mail ballot, of which there were more ballots than workers. And some people never got ballots. It was terrible. They divided all the state workers into four bargaining units and we only won one unit.

Our international union didn't want to go any further than that. And I was finished with my assignment. I had done my share of it, and I must say I felt bad, because the workers deserved a union. Although we won the strike to force the election, we should have opposed the mail ballot decision in court. Perhaps we would have won the entire election, but the mail ballot left a lot of room for manipulation. I think I would have handled it differently if I had been calling the shots, but I wasn't.

For the first time, I had a good look at the laws and people who make laws, who make them to control you but not to live up to them themselves—who force you then to break the law and then blame you for the whole thing. That was what happened with Rockefeller, who was responsible for the law allowing elections and bargaining for state workers. And then after the law was set, he refused to abide by the law, which forced me to then ignore the law. And then I went to jail because the law said you couldn't strike. And nothing happened to him.

I think that was really an awakening for me—a very painful, painful thing to me. And all we wanted was the right to decide. That's all we were asking for. And he, because he was a Rockefeller, he felt that after all you don't challenge him. And nobody was really able to take him on, so he had to be taken on.

Through the judge he had me sentenced for a month, which was the longest sentence they had given anyone under this law. But I was in jail for two weeks because of the people in New York who were very outraged by it. I'm very grateful to them. They took it a lot harder than I did. People made it very clear to him, you know, that this was a terrible thing. So then he began to blame the male leadership of the union for what happened to me. I was so insulted by that remark. And I had to tell him that I was a woman who was an organizer. And I did all the things that the men did, and if I violated a law, it was me who wanted to pay that price. I didn't need anybody to pay it for me. And that was it. Because, it was like I didn't have any sense, and I would permit myself to be used. And what he didn't understand is—not he or anyone else would use me. I was the one organizing out there, and I wasn't going to step aside and let somebody else take it because I'm a big girl. I can take whatever I put out, you know.

REFLECTIONS

One of the problems in the union is getting more participation from young women. You don't have a lot of very young women, unless they're not married. If they're married young, chances are they're not going to be too active. They got their youngsters at home, and their husband doesn't quite understand, unless he's a union man. The only way we get to see the young women is when the young men are active in the union. And we are getting a lot more youth now.

Women play a much more important role in our union now than they used to. We have a large number of women representatives in the field, and several of our departments and divisions have women number one and number two. I think it's the structure of the union which makes it possible. Each local union can elect their own president, executive board, and so on. And so that gives them a freedom of expression in small areas which brings out leadership.

Many times women were more involved in the union, because when I got into strikes and fights they were really there. But they felt their role should be more played down a bit because they wanted the men to surface. Maybe it had to do with the strength that is supposed to be brought to the table or something. But they were willing to take a lot of subordinate roles.

But I always felt that if I had a job to do, it transcends whether I am male or female; I had to do the job. I never thought about not doing the job and not being aggressive. But I also wanted to be feminine, a woman, at the same time. And I think the name of the game is not to try to mimic a man, just be yourself. And each time I won I grew stronger in my determination to continue to fight for what I thought was right. I was also very fortunate that I could talk to Vic when I was uptight.

I never think about it, but I think I am a role model for younger women. I tried to encourage them. In fact, I think my very existence is encouraging to them. Their reaction to me tells me that I'm sort of like being observed by them, which is quite a responsibility. Because I like to be myself, and I like to have fun. You know, everything you do is supposed to be so stereotyped, I guess. But I don't let it bother me. I'm just me.

Every waking moment in a union you are sort of in a fish bowl. And I really don't enjoy taking a fellow that I like around to be scrutinized. And I wouldn't want to subject the best man to it. It's a tough life, and I like being cuddled like any woman likes to be cuddled. Everybody likes to be loved; that's a very normal thing, particularly after I get beat up so much during the day, and I beat up a few people. But it's nice to be able to share some warm moments with somebody you care about, very nice, you know. But I don't think that I'm as tolerant. I don't think that I want to hear any bullshit, you know what I mean? I don't want him bothering me or fencing me and all that. That's selfish probably, because I just want to be more relaxed and want him to understand what I'm going through. And sometimes he's going through the same thing, so I have to always be sort of aware of that. I'm not going to be selfish in my personal life although I have such a struggle.

And I think being a woman in this job is much harder than a man, because almost everybody I meet in the business world sooner or later takes me to the mat, because I am a woman—because they don't want to take me serious. So then I got to go and let them know I can handle myself as well as they can, and "Don't play with me. I'm not here to be played with." And that's tough. I have to be almost ready to fight more than the average man. And that's a tragedy. And I think it is far more difficult since the women's awareness of themselves than it's ever been, because men feel so threatened.

So if I come in, I'm just a threat by being there, you know. And being a black woman hasn't been easy either. And many times I know what they're thinking, because it's impolite to do it. Maybe he wants to hide it, maybe he'll learn a little something after he gets to know me. And so you have all these different pieces that you got to put in place in the whole process.

I get a little uptight sometimes, because there are so many pressures on me. You want to relax. You know, you must remember, I have a lot of responsibility at home, too. And it's not like somebody's there to grab my shoes. I'm very ordinary because I carry a lot of responsibility for my family, which was poor, still poor, and depends upon me a lot. I have a sick brother that I take care of who is older than I, and my mother, and my sister's boys now, and no husband. So, where I might make an adequate income, it's like two people working, and things to do, and so a lot of things I'm not able to do that would relieve me of a lot of pressures. So I share some of the work in the house with my mother as well. In many ways it doesn't bother me, because it keeps me in touch with what I have to do for the kinds of people that I represent. It's kind of a relief that I'm doing something at home that's quite different.

But there are times when I feel that the union has sapped, like, all my life, because it takes so much. It takes almost every waking hour. But it has been a very beautiful experience for me. I don't think I'd have it any other way.

Documents

Two Leaders of Hospital Strike Enter Jail as Hundreds Protest, 1968

Two leaders of the recent strike at state mental hospitals entered Civil Jail yesterday to serve sentences for criminal contempt as hundreds of union officials and rank-and-file members protested outside.*

Earlier, the two leaders, Mrs. Lillian Roberts, an organizing director for District 50 of the State, County and Municipal Employees, and Robert Fuller, president of Local 69 of the union, walked up and down long lines of union members and greeted many of them personally as they marched in front of the jail at 437 West 37th Street.

Then the two strike leaders stood quietly in the crowd while some of the city's top labor leaders climbed to the roof of a truck and criticized the impending imprisonment of Mrs. Roberts and Mr. Fuller for leading a strike in violation of the Taylor Law. This law forbids walkouts by public employees.

"Rocky In, Roberts Out"

At 5:30 P.M. Mrs. Roberts and Mr. Fuller, led by Jerry Wurf, president of the union, and Victor Gotbaum, executive director of District 37 of the union,

* From Damon Stetson, "Two Leaders of Hospital Strike Enter Jail as Hundreds Protest," December 14, 1968. © 1968 by The New York Times Company. Reprinted by permission.

pushed their way through the crowd and walked up the steps of the grimy, red-brick jail, built in 1870.

Mrs. Roberts was joined on the steps by her three sons, Carl, 13 years old; Rolongzo, 12, and Donzell, 6, by the union attorney Julius Topol, and by other friends.

An elderly woman with tears in her eyes, said sadly, "Those children need her at home." A man near her swore. Members of the crowd began to chant, "Rocky in, Roberts out," and they waved signs lighted by flashlights strapped to the sticks with which they held them aloft.

Some of the signs said: "Jailing leaders won't stop public workers," "Laborers say jail Rocky not Roberts," "All labor says Lillian Roberts out of jail for Christmas," "Fuller and Roberts—our heroes," and "Lock up the Rock."

After standing a few minutes on the steps under bright television lights, Mrs. Roberts waved a farewell to the crowd and said good-by to her boys. Several friends embraced her. Then, led by Mr. Topol, she and Mr. Fuller walked through the door to serve their sentences. Hers is for 30 days plus a fine of $250, and his, 20 days plus a fine of $125.

Both union leaders, who are Negroes, spent a few hours in the jail on Dec. 2 before they were released pending an appeal. Last Tuesday, however, the Appellate Division in Brooklyn unanimously upheld their convictions. They had been found guilty of criminal contempt by State Supreme Court Justice J. Irwin Shapiro for violating an order against the strike at Creedmore State Hospital in Queens.

Mrs. Roberts received the stiffest sentence imposed to date for violation of the Taylor Law ban against public employee strikes.

Her sentence of 30 days was the maximum under the law, but Mr. Fuller's was also greater than the 15-day sentences imposed on two prior offenders, Albert Shanker, president of the United Federation of Teachers, and John J. DeLury, president of the Uniformed Sanitationmen's Association.

In a statement last night Roy Wilkins, executive director of the National Association of [sic] the Advancement of Colored People, noted that Mrs. Roberts, although an employee rather than an elected leader of the union, had received the harshest penalty permitted under the law.

He said that she had received a sentence double in length for leading a union composed largely of black and Puerto Rican workers who were seeking to obtain "their legally guaranteed right to elect their own union."

"It is difficult to square the severity of the Roberts sentence with the sentences meted out, or perhaps to be meted out, against other public employ union leaders who happen to be white," Mr. Wilkins said. "We of the NAACP deplore the unprecedentedly harsh sentence . . . and call upon Governor Rockefeller to use his good offices to obtain a reduction in her sentence."

Among those who spoke up in defense of Mrs. Roberts and Mr. Fuller at Civil Jail yesterday were Harry Van Arsdale, Jr., president of the New York

City Central-Labor Council; Assemblyman Stanley Steingut, Democrat of Brooklyn, and James Farmer, former director of the Congress for Racial Equality.

Mr. DeLury, who was also there, said he felt sick about the imprisonment of the two labor leaders, but added that it would strengthen the labor movement.

Mrs. Roberts, speaking from the truck before entering the jail, said:

"You make me feel so great. As long as there are public employees that don't make an adequate salary and have the right to vote [for the union of their choice] there'll be people like me who don't mind spending 30 days in jail."

Standardized Training Course for Ward Aids, 1938

In the end "ward aid" was decided upon as being suitable and consistent with the functions of the position.* The ward aid was defined as: "a ward worker who will relieve the nurse of many nonprofessional routine tasks and assist the nurse in the performance of other duties, under the supervision of the professional group and responsible to the head nurse." . . .

No certificate is given at the end of the training period. Continuance of their employment, the granting of a slight increase in pay and a notation on the permanent personnel record are the only recognition given to their successful completion of the course.

. . . Considerable time has been spent in discussion with nursing leaders to obtain the benefit of their guidance and also to prevent misconceptions of our activities based upon erroneous fact or rumor. Although nursing groups on the whole have been receptive to the need of a well-trained employee, such as the aid, individuals within this group have feared that formal classroom instruction and ward practice would develop a class of pseudo-nurses whose status would always be a menace to the profession.

. . . There was some apprehension on the part of the nursing supervisors who anticipated friction between the ward aids and the other lay help, such as the orderly, the kitchen maid and the cleaning force. Many of these older employees who had been accustomed to assist the nurse with certain semitechnical tasks and had derived great satisfaction from the prestige to which they felt these duties entitled them resented the newcomers.

Gradually, however, when they realized that the aid had a definite routine assigned to her without any authority or supervisory power over the other

---

* Reprinted from Winifred McL. Shepler, Estelle C. Koch, and James Alexander Hamilton, "Standardized Training Course for Ward Aids," *Modern Hospital*, 51, No. 6 (December 1938), 65–72. *Modern Hospital* became *Modern Healthcare* in 1974, Copyright, Crain Communications, Inc. All rights reserved.

lay workers, she was accepted, even welcomed, into the ward family by most of the other employees. Occasionally we hear of some tension arising from over-bearance on the part of an older ward maid but of no serious quarrels.

Patients testify they have been able to receive many more comforts and prompter service since the introduction of the ward aids.

The reaction of the ward aids themselves has been of absorbing interest. Many of these young women had the ambition to enter nursing and would no doubt have attempted to enter training had circumstances, usually financial, permitted. Many of them are using the course as a stepping stone to nurse training.

A few have indicated that there is keen resentment on the part of several students because they feel that there is too much class distinction in a hospital. Probably it is inevitable that in so large a group a few would lose perspective regarding their place. On the other hand, perhaps, we, in our enthusiasm for the experiment, painted too glowing a picture of the joys of domestic work on our wards. After all, there is not much glamour to cleaning and bed making, even if they are an expression of devotion. Undoubtedly the continuance of their interest will be one of our perplexing situations.

. . . Eager, docile and pliable during the exciting training period, these young people have to assume responsibility for a round of routine tasks which may in time become unbearably monotonous to a few. Protected by their student status and interpreted by their instructor during their initiation on the wards, they are learning now to stand on their own feet in the difficult give-and-take of ward life.

It is natural for the ambitious young women, trained in certain skills, to want to use them until the novelty wears off and then to attempt to acquire new skills. By the very nature of her position, the ward aid must curb such tendencies and be satisfied to continue to try to perfect herself in the skills that her assignments permit, rather than to forge ahead to new accomplishments. For this reason we believe that the ultimate test of the young aid's stamina and the final demonstration of her worth to the hospital are yet to come.

Of this first class 20 have planned to enter nursing training. Several of them have been accepted. If it were not for financial responsibilities at home a number of others would also plan to go into professional training. It has been gratifying to observe how these young people have been determined and willing to forego immediate pleasures in their drive toward the higher goal. . . .

Guidelines for the Interviewer Seeking Oral History

These questions were developed by "The Twentieth Century Trade Union Woman: Vehicle for Social Change" project at the Institute of Labor and Industrial Relations, University of Michigan-Wayne State.* The questions reflect an attempt to elicit the subject's personal, work, and trade union history. The questions were used as guidelines for the interviewer but, as in all oral history interviews, were not followed rigidly. An oral history interview is very much an interactional process. Adherence to a strict list of questions would ruin the dynamic of the interview and would keep the history from being told in a person's own style.

I. FAMILY BACKGROUND

Do you remember your grandparents?
> Do you remember your mother talking about her parents? Do you remember things your father said about his parents?

What did your father tell you about his boyhood? Where was he born? At what age did he begin to work?

What did your mother tell you about her childhood? Where was she born?
> Did she work outside the home as a child? as a young woman? What kinds of responsibilities or chores did she do around the house as a child?

What did you like to do with your mother?

What did you like to do with your father?

What did your mother do most of her life?
> Did she work outside the home after she married? Was she working at any time when you were growing up? What were her hopes for herself? What were her hopes for her children? For you in particular? How much schooling did she have? Did she take an interest in her community? in politics? What were her views?

Was your father's background similar to your mother's? How much schooling did he have? What did he do for a living? How did his job affect the family? Did he take an interest in politics? What were his views? Did he talk with your mother about these things? What were his hopes for himself? for his children? for you?

Were you closer to one parent than the other? Which parent did you admire more? As a child, did you want to live a life like your parents' when you grew up?

How many years did you live in the house/apartment where you were born? What was that house like? the neighborhood? the town? How did you feel about the place? Who lived with you when you were growing up? (grandparents? boarders? how many people?)

* From the Rockefeller Foundation funded oral history project, "The Twentieth Century Trade Union Woman: Vehicle for Social Change," sponsored by the Institute for Labor and Industrial Relations, The University of Michigan, under the direction of Joyce L. Kornbluh, Lydia Kleiner, and Christine Miller. Reprinted with permission.

Who were your companions as a child? Did you have brothers and sisters? (birth order, spacing) What was your relationship to your brothers and sisters? To whom were you closest?

What chores or responsibilities did you have as a child? Did you ever think boys had an easier time?

What did you daydream about becoming when you grew up?

Was religion important to you as a child? In what way?

What kinds of arguments were there in your family? Was your family any different than the neighbors in your community? How did you feel about that?

II. EDUCATION

What did you think of school? What subjects did you like? Did you have any favorite teachers?

What did your family think about school? Did they have different ideas for boys than for girls?

Were your classmates from the same background as you? (ethnic, socio-economic, religious) What about the teachers?

When did you stop going to formal school? Why? Did you ever wish you had gone further?

Were you ever involved in other kinds of school such as settlement house classes, union, YWCA or other workers' education classes? What did you think of those experiences? What did you think of the teachers?

Did students ever talk about political events of the times among themselves? Often? Did you participate in this?

Is there anything special about your early schooling that may have contributed to your later union activism?

III. COMMUNITY/POLITICAL BACKGROUND

Describe the community in which you first lived. Did neighbors get together informally? Were you ever active in community organizations?

Did you belong to any religious, social or political groups as a young girl? In later life? (construct history of involvement)

What was the first political group you ever joined? Were you aware of any splits in that group over different positions? Did you take sides?

How did your political views change over the years?

IV. WORK EXPERIENCE

How did you get your first job? What did the work involve? How old were you?
Did you expect to keep it a long time? How much did you earn? What
did you do with the money? Did you work among women or mixed
sexes? Were your bosses women or men? What did you think of your
co-workers? of your boss? Did you make friends on that job? Did you
socialize with them outside of work? Why did you stop working there?
What was the worst thing about that job?

Did you have a plan about future jobs? Did you think you would stop working when you got married? How did you get your next job?

Did you ever have a job where it was possible to move up to more money or
more interesting work? What was the best job you ever had? What was the
worst job? (construct job history)

Have you ever stopped working since you began? For what reasons?

What did you usually do when you came home from work? (chores as a young
girl? domestic responsibilities later?)

(If applicable) How did your husband feel about your working? What kinds of
child care arrangements did you make through the years? Was this an
important part of your responsibilities?

During wars, women were often encouraged to work and then discouraged after
the soldiers came home. Did you ever feel that pressure?

How do you think your work experiences would have been different if you were
a man?

Have you ever been refused a job or a promotion because you weren't friendly
enough to a male boss?

If you had a choice of all the jobs in the world and could get the right training,
looking back, what kind of work would you choose to do?

V. START OF UNION ACTIVISM

Where were you working when you got involved in union activities? How did
you first get involved?

Was going to union meetings a source of conflict in your family? When you first
got involved, were there many other women active?

Who was your first union connection, the first person you knew who was involved? What did you think of him/her?

How popular were unions in your neighborhood, in the newspapers when you
first got started?

Were you active right from the beginning? What was your first official position
in the union? Appointed or elected? Who encouraged you to become more
active?

How did being part of the union affect your private life at first? Did you go to
any other union activities, such as schools or conventions?

When you had your first union position, what were your responsibilities? Were
there many women in similar positions? Did women go to meetings?

(If first position was steward:) What kinds of problems tended to come up?
What were most of the grievances that you remember? Were there any
particular to women? How did they get settled?

(If first position was organizer:) What were your approaches in getting women
involved? What kinds of problems did you encounter? Did you get support from ministers, community leaders? How did you relate to women
in other unions? Were they ever helpful? From whom did you learn
specific things about organizing skills?

Did you expect to continue active union work? Were there any other things that
competed for your time? (social, political, religious activities, private life)

VI. WOMEN'S PARTICIPATION IN THE LIFE OF THEIR UNION

When you first got involved in the union, did you think you would ever have a
leadership role? Did you think being a woman made any difference?

Have you ever been discouraged from running for union office?

Did you ever do much travelling in your union work? (If so) did you travel
alone or with groups? Was travelling with men a problem? Did hotels ever
refuse to put you on the same floor with the men you worked with? Was
your personal life ever criticized?

Think back to women in your local who were active and then dropped out—
why did they, and why did you remain?

How was your union structured? How did you fit into that? Were there informal
lines of power that differed from the formal positions? Did you ever feel
left out of informal caucusing or decision-making over beers?

At what periods in your life was union responsibility heaviest? How did you
juggle the rest of your life at those times? Did you have any energy left
for non-work and non-union interests? What are some of the sacrifices
you made in order to be active?

What is the highest position a woman ever reached in your union?

When you were most active, did you ever devote much energy to "women's"
issues? Were you particularly interested in planning any special programs for women workers? What was the support and opposition like in
these cases? Were you involved with protective legislation concerns?

How was your union and industry affected by national issues such as price and
wage control? What happened to your industry during and after the
wars? What stand did your union take on workers being laid off? Did you
agree with them?

What was the effect of the depression, the New Deal on your industry/union?

What type of community support did you receive (in the 1920s, 30s, 40s) from groups such as National Consumers League, Y's, churches, settlement houses? Which was most effective?

While you were active in the union, were you ever active in any community or political groups? How did the two relate?

Was there a special kind of camaraderie that developed among union activists? Was it especially strong during certain time periods? Was this usually mixed or same sex groups? Have you stayed in touch with some of these people? Who were you closest to during your active union years?

What was involved in being a steward/organizer/local recording secretary? (all positions she has had; probe for autonomy, policy making power)

How many of the employees in the plants you worked with were women?

What were the lifestyles of the women you (organized/served as steward)? Were you asked, or did you ever help with community and family related problems? How different was your life from the lives of the women you worked with? (marriage/children/living alone/with roommates)

How did various strikes and organizing campaigns affect the women workers? Were there special barriers to their participation? Were there any issues in particular campaigns of interest to women?

VII. General

What was the most exciting part of your life? If you could relive any part of your life, when would it be?

(If you had) a daughter, would you want her to live through your experiences? What parts would you want her to avoid?

Have you been generally more comfortable working with women or men? Which have you worked with most? (in what ways)

Were you active in getting women the vote (or other non-union feminist issues)?

Do you remember reading anything, or seeing a movie, or meeting someone special that influenced your life dramatically?

Do you support ERA? Do you think organized labor responds to women's needs?

Do you think women working within the labor movement were generally more or less effective because they were female?

What was the most frustrating part of your work within unions? most satisfying? When did you feel that it wasn't worth it?

If you could be 16 years old again, how would you relive your life? Would you still be involved with unions? (marry/change number of children/education/travel)

Rosalind Rosenberg

Marion Talbot. Courtesy of University of Chicago Library.

At the turn of the century a small number of American women cut themselves off from the mainstream of feminist thought.[1] Though committed to the feminist goal of greater freedom for women and often active in the woman's movement, they objected to the claim of female distinctiveness so often used to support that goal. They suggested instead that women could lay no special claim to unique traits and that the character of any particular female or male owed far more to the accidents of external circumstances and relationships than to internal secretions or physiological structures.

The views of these dissident women were not fostered in the suffrage movement, or in the women's reform movements, or in the women's colleges of the turn of the century. While in each of these places women struggled for independence and affirmed their equality with men, at the same time they maintained that they were innately different, that they possessed unique natures and made distinctive contributions. Most feminists in the Progressive years believed that they were separate but equal.

The women who broke with the separate but equal doctrine worked not in the traditional centers of female activity, but primarily in a new place: the university. Beginning around 1900 and continuing through the Progressive generation, women academics, especially those in the infant social sciences, developed an increasingly critical view of conventional assumptions about women's nature. In a period when the women's movement was emphasizing political activity and social reform, the academics' preoccupation with psychological theory made them marginal figures. Yet, despite their initial obscurity, they were vanguards, in their personal as well as their intellectual life, in what may be the fundamental movement of the twentieth century: the abolition of the separate male and female worlds that characterized nineteenth-century America. Furthermore, their impact on the generation that came of age in the 1920s helped inspire a new brand of feminism based on a fundamentally altered conception of womanhood.

To most historians the winning of the vote in 1920 represents a watershed separating a period of feminist achievement from an era of conservative reaction. Bereft of social purpose, disillusioned by war, and preoccupied with sex and personal gratification, women, the historians say, abandoned their role as social reformers and embarked on a period of antifeminism.

For the academic woman, however, whose interest in psychological and social theory paralleled but remained separate from the development of the suffrage campaign, the winning of the vote did not represent the

[1] Research for this essay was made possible by grants from the Council for Research in the Social Sciences. Earlier versions of the essay were delivered at the Berkshire Conference, 1976, and the Radcliffe Institute Conference on "Changing Commitments of Educated Women," 1976.

crisis of purpose it posed for political women. Indeed, the ideas growing out of their scholarly work appealed more strongly to the younger women of the 1920s than did the feminist ideology of the suffrage era. If one focuses not on social reform and politics but on the university and on how women came to be a part of it, a new view of the twenties emerges. It is a view in which the twenties represent the continuation of an attempt to define fundamentally modern attitudes toward women and sex roles rather than as a period of social reaction.

THE FEMINIZATION OF ACADEME

American colleges once devoted themselves almost exclusively to the preparation of young men for the ministry and teaching. By the middle of the nineteenth century this practice appeared to be placing colleges in ever greater financial trouble. As commercial growth agitated a country in the midst of rapid industrial expansion, the country's young men sought business success and shunned both the ministry and teaching. With declining enrollments, colleges faced three alternatives: They could go bankrupt, they could open their doors to women, or they could revise their curricula to cater to the needs of youth determined to exploit the possibilities of an industrial society.

Turning to women seemed natural enough to many, though there was little precedent for it. As men focused their attention on commercial success, women came increasingly to be seen as the guardians of culture. Because colleges had long been the repositories of culture in America, women and colleges seemed ideally suited to one another. When schools opened their doors, women flocked to them, some seeking training for careers as teachers, a very few hoping to break the barrier of such traditionally male domains as the ministry or medicine, and many more searching for literary and artistic fulfillment. It seemed a happy marriage.

But at the same time that the colleges were encouraging the enrollment of young women, they were revamping their curricula in the hope of recapturing their male audience. Through courses in political science, economics, sociology, engineering, medicine, law, and business administration, college administrators sought to convince the public of the colleges' utilitarian character. Many colleges, emulating the example of European institutions, transformed themselves into universities with graduate departments and professional schools and began to argue that science could speed economic and social development. At the turn of the century these schools were often available to women; because of overexpansion, some had little choice. But it was assumed from the beginning that they would appeal primarily to men.

These curricular and institutional innovations proved tremendously successful, but the success was tinged with irony. By welcoming young women at the same time that they were altering their curricula to appeal to young men, universities found themselves with a growing female student body dedicated to an educational ideal that the university was trying to abandon. The danger, as many saw it, was that women would overrun the university and jeopardize the reform effort.

In 1902 fear gripped many at the University of Chicago, who foresaw the imminent feminization of their school. One professor, economist J. Lawrence Laughlin, sought to reassure his colleagues. He was aware that in the ten years since the university's opening the female enrollment had increased from 25 percent to 50 percent of the student body, but he predicted that once the university's scientific programs and professional schools became firmly established the trend would be reversed.

The congestion of numbers [of women students] is now due largely to the fact that the undergraduate courses are practically used by women as an advanced normal school to prepare for teaching, the one profession easiest to enter by them. At present, this part of the university is the main part. The best men are going less and less into teaching. Just so soon as proper support and endowments are given to the work which offers training for careers in engineering, railways, banking, trade and industry, law, medicine, etc. the disproportion of men will doubtless remedy itself.[2]

On one level the concern over female enrollment at Chicago, as well as Laughlin's reassurances, reflected the new university's parochial desire for status; but on another level it reflected the pervasive fear of feminization that plagued American society in the early twentieth century. As the economic change of a rapidly industrializing society brought social dislocation, Americans clung ever more tenaciously to their most basic assumptions about sexual identity and fought any changes in accepted sex-role divisions.

Education played a singularly important role in this drama, because the special circumstances of the development of the university placed American higher education at the fulcrum of social change. No sooner had higher education been opened to women as a relatively unnecessary pursuit in a commercial, industrializing society, than it became clear to many that education could make a significant contribution to that industrialization. But by the time education's potential value was perceived, women had flooded the schools, filling 50 percent of the student body at many schools by 1900. Society was faced with two alternatives. It could acquiesce in the surrender of education to women and thereby

[2] J. Lawrence Laughlin to A. K. Parker, July 25, 1902, the President's Papers, University of Chicago Archives.

protect the separation of sexual spheres, but suffer the loss of a valuable institution for male training, or it could continue trying to make higher education more attractive to men and risk the danger to sex-role divisions posed by sexual integration. Apprehensively, society chose the latter alternative and accepted coeducation.

Many historians have noted the importance of professionalization in the late nineteenth and early twentieth centuries in assuring middle-class status through exclusionary rules; but professionalization was as important to the Progressives' fears about sex as it was to their fears about class. The effort on the part of many schools to alter their curricula to attract male students suggests that professionalization was, at least in part, an effort to give modern definition to the male sphere and thereby to protect the traditional division of sex roles. To continue to emphasize the college's role in religion, teaching, and the arts was not simply to risk irrelevance in an industrial age but to surrender to a feminine constituency. Even as women brought fiscal health to much of American higher education, administrative officials met the threat their presence posed to male enrollments and sex-role divisions by fostering a dual purpose within a single educational system: a liberal arts education open to men and women alike, which would prepare women for teaching and the volunteer work of the wife and mother but equip men for later professional training. Men and women received their undergraduate training together, but they were encouraged to expect that their paths would diverge following graduation.

As part of this accommodation, college officials sought to emphasize the worth of a college education in enhancing feminine values while minimizing the corrosive effect on those values of the increasingly popular professional and scientific ideals. For most members of the Progressive generation this differentiation of sexual spheres succeeded. Indeed, historians might find it easier to sort out the disparate strands of the Progressive movement if they were to see it as a movement in which men and women engaged in two separate campaigns.

There was first of all the movement for social reform, dominated by women educated in the humanism of the American liberal arts curriculum. These women sought to temper the strident individualism that characterized American public life. Through their support of the arts they tried to preserve America's tenuous claims to culture. Through charitable efforts, they attempted to help the needy and to soften class antagonism. Women like Jane Addams, Julia Lathrop, and Florence Kelly of Hull House used higher education to advance the social vision, the zeal, and the humanitarianism that marked a significant dimension of the Progressive movement.

On the other hand, there was the segment of the Progressive movement that was more concerned with professionalization than with moral uplift, with efficiency and expertise than with social concern. This segment was dominated by the men who were the most recent products of the modernized universities.

This sexual division within the ranks of reformers suggests that Progressivism was more than the movement to tame private enterprise that it has long been portrayed as being; it was also an effort to work out a new *modus vivendi* between middle-class men and women. Women were finally granted the acceptance within the public sphere that they had fought so long to attain, through admission to education and reform activity; however, the cost of that acceptance was the establishment of sex roles within the public sphere that protected conventional notions of sexual difference. Social reform and teaching became the special domains of women, and professionalism was the sphere of men.

As Progressive society accommodated itself to the changes being wrought in higher education by redefining sex roles in such a way as to concede as little change as possible on the more fundamental question of sex differences, many within the university resisted this conservative effort. Even in the university's earliest years there were women, as well as some men, who responded to the crisis over feminization in American society by rejecting conventional assumptions rather than by trying to protect them. For these deviant scholars, academics became a prism through which sexual differences could never again be seen in quite the same way as they had been seen before.

WOMAN'S NATURE BECOMES AN ISSUE

Curricular reform and coeducation rescued higher education from financial collapse, but their influence extended beyond institutional salvaging to affect the intellectual life of American universities. Schools that undertook reform, and especially those that sponsored graduate research, fostered a heretical spirit in their faculty and students. Schools established new disciplines and downgraded others. Classics departments watched Greek become an elective as departments of sociology made their first appearance, usually with only a vague idea of what sociology should be. American universities imitated the European university and then used that model to develop critiques of European doctrines in psychology, anthropology, and sociology, just to mention the social sciences.

While intellectual ferment pervaded the new schools, concern with the specific issues of personality formation and sex roles was centered in only a few places. In universities where women were either refused admission or admitted as tokens there was little interest in finding new ways to think about sex. At Harvard, where Mary Whiton Calkins completed all of the work for a doctorate in psychology under William

James, only to be denied a degree by the trustees, the subject of personality formation in the sexes attracted little interest. At Columbia, where Margaret Floy Washburn suffered similar difficulties, interest in sex differences was also restricted to only a few people until after work on this issue had started elsewhere. For the most part the work of social scientists like Calkins and Washburn followed the pattern established by their mentors. Having struggled against great prejudice to be accepted as scholars, most women strove to prove themselves within the accepted confines of their disciplines and did not risk questioning the prevailing views about women's psychology and sex roles.

Even the newly established women's colleges showed little interest in the issue of women's psychology. Determined to establish the legitimacy of their fledgling institutions, the leaders of the women's colleges sought to emulate the hallowed traditions of the male colleges, just as men's colleges were beginning to question the classical course. As President John H. Raymond of Vassar put it:

My own faith on this subject is briefly this: that while the education for men has outgrown the old college system, and is demanding room for expansion and free development in various directions, that for women has but just grown up to it, and needs for a season the bracing support of its somewhat narrow forms. And I think we shall commit a serious, if not fatal, mistake in our policy for the College if we overlook this important distinction.[3]

Ironically, the very effort of educators like Raymond to adopt the male pattern of education ended in women being trained differently from men. In following a narrow, classical program the women's colleges stifled the creative activity that was just then beginning to characterize some of the men's schools. As a result, schools like Vassar and Bryn Mawr tended unwittingly to reinforce conventional assumptions about women, both because their very establishment as women's schools buttressed a belief in female separateness and because the curriculum they adopted discouraged innovative thinking.

For new thinking to take place about sex it was necessary to have both a creative atmosphere and significant numbers of women. In addition, a university needed to have at least a few women who thought of themselves as advocates of the women's movement for a school to develop a dialogue on the subject when sexual tensions arose. Few schools could lay claim to the rare mix of conditions needed to create the atmosphere conducive to initiating a challenge to conventional ideas about men's and women's natures. Several schools could claim one or more of these

[3] Mabel Newcomer, *A Century of Higher Education for American Women*, Harper, New York, 1959, p. 82.

conditions (coeducation, innovative research, or committed women), but only one school, at the turn of the century, claimed them all: the University of Chicago. And it was there, despite J. Lawrence Laughlin's confident prediction that women posed no threat to conventional educational patterns, that the most dramatic alteration of American social thought in general and thought about women in particular took place.

COEDUCATION EMBATTLED

When Marion Talbot left her position as an instructor of domestic economy at Wellesley College in September 1892 to become dean of women and assistant professor of sociology at the newly established University of Chicago, a friend pressed a little box into her hand. "It holds," said the friend, "a fragment of Plymouth Rock." This gesture symbolized the attitude of many Bostonians toward the new educational venture in Chicago. It was something built, literally, on the sands.[4]

The University of Chicago had been preceded by a school of the same name, whose financial problems had forced it to close despite efforts to increase enrollment by admitting women. The financial support of John D. Rockefeller put the new University of Chicago on a sound economic footing, but the person who made Chicago unique was its new president, William Rainey Harper. Armed with Rockefeller's money and his own vision of what a university of the 1890s should look like, Harper raided the major schools of the country, creating in a matter of months a faculty that some argued was the strongest in the country. Money had a lot to do with it, for Harper offered the highest salaries then given (up to 7,000 dollars). But he offered more. He offered a break with tradition, and he offered autonomy and a chance to build new disciplines.

Most extraordinary of all, Harper included women in his raids. From Wellesley he took ex-President Alice Freeman Palmer and Marion Talbot. He brought them to Chicago as deans, but true to his conviction that the university should be primarily a place of research and scholarship, he appointed Palmer to an assistant professorship in history and Talbot to an assistant professorship in sociology. Chicago was to be a new departure, yet Harper was ambivalent toward coeducation, as he was to prove later. Marion Talbot and other young members of the

[4] Quoted in Marion Talbot, "The Challenge of Retrospect," *The University Record,* 11 (April 1925), 87. The following account of Marion Talbot's experience at Chicago is drawn from the correspondence and other materials in the Marion Talbot Papers, University of Chicago Archives, and *One in Spirit, A Retrospective View of the University of Chicago Based on the Records of the University Archives,* the Joseph Regenstein Library, University of Chicago, 1973.

sociology, psychology, and philosophy departments pushed the university on the question of women in a way that Harper did not intend.

Marion Talbot set the tone of the women's community at Chicago from the beginning. Alice Freeman Palmer might have done so, but she was commuting from Boston, where her husband taught at Harvard, and after two years of spending part of the year in Chicago and part in Boston, she resigned. Though Talbot had only occupied the rank of instructor of domestic economy at Wellesley, she wrote Harper before accepting her new appointment that she would like to see Chicago establish a department of sanitary science under her direction in which students would be expected to have training in chemistry, physics, physiology, political economy, and modern languages. Sanitary science was not to be instruction for girls in how to run a home; it was to be a social science that would train experts to deal with the problems of urbanization. Talbot asked for money for laboratories and an assistant; indeed, she suggested that an associate professorship would be in keeping with her dual responsibilities as both department head and dean.

Harper wrote back that many department heads were only assistant professors, so Talbot would have to be satisfied with that rank in the beginning; although he supported her plan for a department of sanitary science, her work would have to be subsumed under the department of sociology for the moment.

Talbot split her time between trying to develop her new discipline and trying to advance the position of women within the university and the society at large. As dean she decided to play the role of women's advocate. When Harper started the practice of issuing a president's report, Talbot insisted that she be given space to report on the condition of women at the university. She also acted as a one-person employment agency for university women looking for suitable jobs after graduation. Through her friends in the Association of Collegiate Alumnae, of which she was a founder, and in the social reform movement, she placed many Chicago women.

When Josephine Shaw Lowell enquired through the ACA for recommendations to fill the position of head of the Bedford Hills Reformatory, Talbot saw to it that graduate student Katherine Bement Davis was hired. She took Sophinisba Breckenridge as her assistant and carried on a lengthy argument with Harper about whether Breckenridge was being paid enough. For 30 years Talbot was a thorn in the side of successive administrations, which she faulted for not advancing women and for not giving them fellowships. Chicago never kept pace with her demands, but her achievements, when compared with those made elsewhere, were impressive. In 1900 when the national percentage of women earning doctorates was 6 percent, it was 20 percent at Chicago.

Talbot represented the cutting edge of a new kind of feminism.

While she made the most of the opportunities available to her students in the female reform societies, she devoted the major part of her efforts to trying to break down the artificial divisions that separated the sexes in American society. She demonstrated this concern most strikingly in 1902, when the university exploded over the issue of coeducation.

Concerned by the precipitous rise in Chicago's female enrollment and the deleterious effect that it might have on male enrollment, President Harper suggested that Chicago use the new funds that a generous benefactor had recently put at his disposal to establish a separate junior college for women. Though Chicago already had strong science departments and was developing professional schools, Harper feared that segregation would be necessary to stem the tide of feminization.

Marion Talbot met the challenge of Harper's proposal by mounting a campaign against segregation. Marshaling the support of both the female faculty and the alumnae, she convinced a large number of faculty men to join the opposition to segregation. A surprised President Harper soon found himself in the midst of a major battle.

Those who favored Harper's scheme emphasized that coeducation had its origins in economic necessity. "It was reluctantly accepted as simply a lesser evil than exclusion of women from college privileges altogether," remembered one professor. Harper's supporters went on to stress the different needs and goals of men and women students. As one professor wrote, "Had they [women students] been allowed to follow their own instincts and preferences in all respects, I have no doubt that they would have chosen from the beginning separate instruction . . . but economic considerations have hitherto prevented this development." [5]

Many of the prosegregation writers argued that coeducation at Chicago discouraged men from coming there. In other parts of the country, one professor wrote:

The strongest of the colleges for men admit men only. These colleges most strongly attract prospective college men who are wholly at liberty to choose. There is a growing disinclination on the part of such prospective college men to seek a coeducational college. . . . The steady increase in the proportion of girls enrolled operates more and more to divert from coeducational colleges a large number of the best class of college men.

Leading the antisegregation forces, Marion Talbot disputed the segregationists' assertion that women had different interests or capacities from men. "If the trustees could know," she wrote, "how eager girls and

---

[5] The letters from which comments relating to the coeducation fight have been taken are collected under the heading "Segregation of Men and Women in Junior Colleges" in the President's Papers, University of Chicago Archives.

women are to study as thinking beings and not as females, they would hesitate in justice to women to adopt this measure."

A number of professors supported Talbot's position. John Dewey, in particular, wrote Harper at great length opposing segregation. "The argument that the separation will give opportunity for the growth of a more distinctively feminine and more distinctively masculine college life," he wrote, "implies, in my judgment, the most profound, because the most subtle, of all the attacks upon the coeducational principle." The very policy of separation, he suggested, would produce feelings of difference that had not existed before. "The scheme is sure to accomplish what it is supposed to obviate—the fixing of attention upon sex matters."

It at once draws the attention of the students coming to the university to the matter of sex as a fundamental consideration in determining the instruction they are to receive. . . . There is no point upon which public sentiment is so deeply and extensively sensitive as upon the question of sex.

If the university wanted to attract male students, it should direct its attention to improving the university, Dewey suggested, not to creating segregated conditions. The "kind of man that will be kept from the University simply because he will have to associate upon equal terms with his equals is not the kind the University wants or needs."

Despite Dewey's arguments, and those of many others both inside and out of the university, the prosegregation forces won the fight over coeducation and succeeded in building a separate junior college for women. But in a sense they had only won a battle; ultimately, they were to lose the war over protecting traditional conceptions of sex. For the fight over coeducation fueled a movement at Chicago that would, within the next decade, challenge the most basic assumptions about personality formation and sex roles.

Principally within the social sciences, scholars undertook research to discover the nature of sex differences, even as the university debated the merits of coeducation. Were women really as different from men as foes of coeducation insisted and the public generally assumed? Were women specially suited, by mental capacity and temperament, to certain kinds of activity? These were questions that lingered on among the social scientists long after the new women's college was built.

THE NEW PSYCHOLOGY THROUGH WOMEN'S EYES

Skeptical of the conventional belief in sex differences defended both in public debate and scholarly literature, one of Dewey's graduate students,

Helen Thompson, commenced a study of the mental differences between men and women that was to become a landmark in psychological research. At the turn of the century most educated people, including feminists, accepted the following beliefs about human nature:

First, human psychology was a product of human physiology, and differences in physiology could be shown to correlate with differences in mental capacity.

Second, men possessed a highly active metabolism, which manifested itself in an analytical mind, while women possessed a more quiescent metabolism, which manifested itself in an emotional and irrational mind.

Third, these differing psychologies suited men and women to different roles within society. Men were particularly well adapted to a life of science and commerce, while women were best fitted to a life of family care and social activity.

Even the feminist theoretician Charlotte Perkins Gilman adhered to these views, arguing in *The Man-Made World:*

The feminine attitude in life is wholly different [from the male]. As a female she had merely to be herself and passively attract—neither to compete nor pursue; as a mother her whole process is one of growth— first the development of the live child within her, and then the wonderful nourishment from her own body, and then all the later cultivation to make the child grow, all the watching, teaching, guarding, feeding. In none of these capacities is there desire, combat, or self-expression. The feminine attitude, as expressed in religion, makes of it a patient, practical fulfillment of law; a process of large, sure improvements, a limitless, comforting love and care.[6]

The physiological assumptions that underlay Gilman's description of the female personality were spelled out in the work of one of Chicago's sociologists, William I. Thomas, shortly before Thompson began her research.

The superior physiological irritability of woman, were we to call it sensibility, feeling, emotionality, or affectability, is due to the fact of the larger development of her abdominal zone, and the activity of the physiological changes located there in connection with the process of reproduction. . . . Both social feeling and social organization are thus primarily feminine in origin—functions of the anabolism [i.e., the nurturant metabolism] of women.[7]

[6] Charlotte Perkins Gilman, *The Man-Made World; or, Our Androcentric Culture,* Charlton, New York, 1911, pp. 260–262.
[7] William I. Thomas, "On a Difference in the Metabolism of the Sexes," *American Journal of Sociology,* 3 (July 1897), 61.

Encouraged by her psychology professors John Dewey and James Angell, Thompson proposed to examine this "anabolic" view of woman's nature. For her research she chose 50 Chicago undergraduates of the same age and background and devised a series of experiments to test motor skills, hearing, vision, intellectual faculties, and even emotion and values. The scientific study of mental traits was still a novelty in 1900; laboratory techniques were primitive and IQ tests as yet undeveloped, but the little work that had been done on sex differences had confirmed existing prejudices. While Thompson did find some sex differences in her study, the extent of the similarity that she observed contrasted sharply with the findings in earlier work.[8]

Because Thompson assumed, along with other psychologists, that mental function was based in physiology, many of the tests she administered were aimed at measuring motor skills, perception, sensory capacity, precision discrimination, and reaction time. Yet the results of these tests showed little difference between the sexes, belying the conventional belief that women possessed greater sensibility than men. In the area of simple mental activity, as measured by sense perception, sex differences appeared to be inconsequentially small. But what, she wondered, of complex mental function?

Thompson sought a more direct examination of intellectual ability with puzzles to test ingenuity and with general information exams. She found sex differences far more pronounced in the puzzle tests than they had been in her sensory tests, but she believed that this sex difference could be traced to the emphasis placed on mechanical training for boys. In evaluating the results of her general information exams, she found no difference at all between the men and women "who had taken the same course of education."

Thompson gave her tests before Chicago started segregating the sexes, and she found differences in general knowledge only where she also found differences in the selection of courses. "Many of the women were preparing to be teachers and had, therefore, from practical considerations, devoted themselves primarily to those subjects in which the openings for women are most numerous, viz. literary subjects." Except where women students chose courses for practical reasons, they studied the same subjects as the men and demonstrated the same proficiency in learning. Nowhere did Thompson suggest that the women might have had a greater aptitude for literary subjects.

To argue that women and men shared a common level of intelligence was astonishing, but most experts believed that the critical difference between the sexes was that women were far more emotional than

[8] Helen Thompson (Woolley), *Psychological Norms in Men and Women,* University of Chicago Press, Chicago, 1903, *passim.*

men. Emotional differences between the sexes seemed undeniably pronounced in the popular imagination; indeed, the general conception of emotion as a visceral impulse seemed to many to make it a distinctively feminine attribute.

As Thompson admitted, the methods she used to examine emotion were crude. Besides measuring circulation and respiratory changes under different conditions, she asked each subject for an introspective account of his or her emotional processes and personality. Her dependence on the self-analysis of each individual troubled her, for as she conceded, "many individuals will not be, or cannot be, perfectly honest in answering questions on personality." Despite this grave limitation on her research, she offered a few tentative conclusions. Although those who believed that there were important psychological differences of sex had always pointed to emotion as the most telling example, Thompson found "a series of men and a series of women reacting towards questions about the life of feeling in wonderfully similar ways."

The similarities that Thompson observed extended to "the strength of the emotional nature, the form of its expression, and the degree of impulsiveness in action." The only differences she discovered related to inhibition. "Women seem to have a greater tendency to inhibit the expression of emotion and to act from reason rather than from impulse. . . . Men are more frank than women and are more easily embarrassed." While women remained visibly more reticent than men, in general, it was difficult to discriminate between the sexes on the basis of emotional characteristics.

Given the prevailing biological view of the mental differences between the sexes, Thompson's findings of marked similarity represent a major departure in psychological work. Her results can be traced to several factors. First, Thompson had the benefit of the most sophisticated psychological training available at that time. Where most researchers selected subjects at random, Thompson carefully matched her subjects according to social, economic, and educational background. While most researchers averaged the results of their tests and emphasized the differences in the averages between the male group and the female group, Thompson graphed her results and emphasized the high degree of overlap in all of the tests.

Also, Thompson's subjects probably resembled one another more than most men and women of the time because of their peculiar educational experience. Coeducation was still considered a novelty in 1902, as many of the faculty tried to emphasize that spring in their letters to President Harper opposing coeducation. These students were pioneers in social change. Most young people of their age were either in single-sex schools or under the close supervision of their parents. Much of the concern over coeducation at Chicago was based on the fear that young people away from home, thrown into daily intimate contact with the opposite sex, would abandon the code of conduct that governed civilized relations between the sexes. Men might become less manly and women might become less womanly if thrown together so completely at such an impressionable age.

As one member of the Chicago faculty put it:

[E]xperience has shown that, where men and women share the same quadrangle, sit side by side in the class-room, jostle each other in the halls and on the walks, cultivate interest in the same sports, form as far as possible a solid community, each sex loses something. . . . This opinion is based on the belief that there are certain virtues, traits, matters of deportment, and the like, more or less distinct for either sex, which should be cultivated in an educational institution during the formative years.[9]

The opponents of coeducation agreed in one important way with Thompson's conclusions: Men and women at Chicago resembled one another more in their behavior than either scientists or popular writers had ever thought possible.

Even Marion Talbot, who insisted that female students be referred to as neither coeds nor girls but as women, worried about the breakdown in conventional mores when the independence made possible by boardinghouse living at Chicago resulted in students entertaining one another in their rooms. She insisted that no rooms be advertised at the university except those "in houses or flats where a reception room is provided." If necessary, she was prepared to exercise "close scrutiny" over the living arrangements of the students. Talbot found herself walking an ideological tightrope, determined to treat women students as independent adults and to abolish artificial sex distinctions, but still constrained by Victorian conceptions of female virtue.[10]

Even though frankness, as Thompson observed, still seemed a typically male attribute in 1902, students at Chicago already enjoyed the economic security and the freedom from parental control that would spur a sexual revolution among American youth within a decade. With the coming of this revolution, frankness would increasingly dominate the relations of both sexes and the differences between male and female behavior would diminish even further.

The third factor that set Thompson's study apart from others of

[9] Edward Capps to the University Recorder, July 21, 1902, the President's Papers, University of Chicago Archives.
[10] Marion Talbot to William R. Harper, April 7, 1903, Marion Talbot Papers, University of Chicago Archives.

the time, besides her technical skill and the unusual qualities of her subjects, was her egalitarian bias. Thompson had studied at Chicago as an undergraduate and had shared in the pioneering feeling of being among the first women to have both a college and a graduate education at a school in which a significant number of the faculty and administration believed strongly that women, if given the opportunity, could accomplish all that the male students could accomplish. As her daughter later recalled, Thompson would have followed the conventional path to becoming a teacher rather than a psychologist if it had not been for the unusual opportunity she found at Chicago. Faculty like John Dewey and James Angell were iconoclasts; they were critical, in general, of the received wisdom of their day, and the conventional ideas about women seemed as suspicious to them as conventional ideas about Hegel and Darwin.

Inspired by skeptical teachers, Thompson in turn influenced others at Chicago. Professor William I. Thomas, the sociologist who had so recently described the visceral roots of the female personality, quickly noted the significance of her research. "Her findings are probably the most important contribution in this field, and her general conclusions on differences of sex will I think, hold also for differences of race."

Crediting Thompson with laying to rest the old notion that a heavy brain was evidence of a mighty intellect, Thomas developed in his own work an environmentalist view of mental and personality formation. The mental processes of women differed from those of men, he declared in 1907, only to the extent that women's attention is usually focused on a narrower range of activity than is men's.

The direction of attention and the simplicity or complexity of mental processes depend on the character of the external situation which the mind has to manipulate. If the activities were nil, the mind would be nil. The mind is nothing but a means of manipulating the outside world.

Thomas's emphasis on the role of experience and habit prompted psychology graduate student Jesse Taft to analyze more fully the psychological origins of female reticence. Her 1912 dissertation on the social psychology of women raised the discussion of personality formation to a new level in the social sciences. Believing that men and women shared the same basic mental and emotional capacities, Taft explained sex differences by suggesting that behavior was learned in the process of social interaction. Women and men, she argued, learned to deal with their common psychological impulses differently in order to satisfy the expectations of those around them and to function most profitably within the constraints of the social system in which they lived. Observing that modesty was approved in them, little girls strove to be modest, and they succeeded. Women were not born female; femininity had to be learned.[11]

Taft's ideas set her at odds with the ideology of the women's movement. Feminists like Charlotte Perkins Gilman were right, Taft believed, that women could not be expected to exhibit independence while restricted to the individual kitchen. But Taft did not believe that economic self-sufficiency would emancipate women until the traditional ideals of womanhood were abandoned. It would not profit the woman to get out of the kitchen until she was surrounded from babyhood by people who did not expect her to be uniquely devoted, in Gilman's words, to "comforting love and care."

Much less could one expect the granting of the vote, or any other right or privilege, to alter women's lives. The suffrage campaign, which was reaching a crescendo as Taft wrote, premised its demands on an older theory of personality, to the degree that it appealed to any theory at all. Suffragists argued that women, being superior because of their maternal traits, were potentially better citizens than men and only needed the vote to prove it. Taft argued that emancipation was not simply an economic or a political problem; it was a psychological one as well. The very claim of maternal superiority in the suffrage campaign belied the claim of emancipation. No fundamental change in women's social position was likely until rationality was no longer regarded as a hallmark of masculinity and until the maternal virtues were no longer regarded as exclusively maternal.

THE SECOND GENERATION OF WOMEN SOCIAL SCIENTISTS

By the 1920s an increasing number of young men and women were going to college and coming under the influence of the new social sciences, which by then had replaced biology as the queen of American intellectual life. Furthermore, the belief that men and women, as well as members of different races, possessed the same basic mental apparatus and emotional impulses and that they differed in their behavior only because of differing social contexts gained wide acceptance in the social scientific literature.

As William Allen White put it, those who were exposed to the new social scientific literature, or popular accounts of it, were discovering:

that the Hottentot obeys impulses similar to those which activate the pastor of the First Baptist Church, and is probably already better adapted

[11] Jesse Taft, *The Woman Movement from the Point of View of Social Consciousness,* University of Chicago Press, Chicago, 1916, *passim.*

to his Hottentot environment than he would be if he followed the Baptist code; that sex is the most important thing in life, that inhibitions are not to be tolerated, that sin is an out of date term, that most untoward behavior is the result of complexes acquired at an early age and that men and women are mere bundles of behavior-patterns anyhow.[12]

The power of physiology was by no means discounted; in fact, sex drives assumed an importance in determining behavior they had never enjoyed before. But where the study of sex differences was concerned even this new emphasis on sex drives served to highlight the similarities between the sexes: Women as well as men had sexual needs that could be ignored only at their peril.

No longer could a professor argue, as W. I. Thomas had in the 1890s, that the physiological differences of sex produced clearly distinguishable male and female mental types: an analytical male and an irrational female. The supposed connection between physiological structure and mental capacity had been severed by a generation of research, centered at Chicago but quickly spreading elsewhere. Indeed, by the 1920s social science textbooks were recognizing and supporting female intelligence, companionship within marriage, equality of privilege and responsibility, and mutuality in sexual gratification; in addition, they were disseminating the environmental theory of personality development that the first generation of social scientists had developed.[13]

Novel though these textbook judgments seemed when compared with traditional views of family life and sexual place, they were rooted in the observation of actual social behavior. The twenties saw the culmination of the social change fostered by a generation of student life. The critics of coeducation had been right in one respect—the university, especially the residential, coeducational university, did undermine the old patterns of behavior and the divisions between sexual spheres. As young people enjoyed the freedom from parental control provided by college, they fumbled toward new codes of behavior and new attitudes toward sexual roles. Taught in the classroom to think critically about the conventional wisdom in intellectual life, students carried this message into their private lives.

In Marion Talbot's day women simply wore more tailored clothes to enable them to engage in sports and to ride bicycles, but by 1920 they were bobbing their hair, wearing short skirts, and discarding undergarments. Many argued that the change in dress came for practical reasons, to enable young women to live in a male world, but the new

[12] William Allen White, *Only Yesterday: An Informal History of the 1920s,* Perennial Library Edition, 1964, Harper and Brothers, New York, 1931, p. 165.
[13] Paula Fass, *The Damned and the Beautiful: American Youth in the 1920s,* Oxford University Press, New York, 1977, Ch. 2.

dress enhanced young women's sense of sexual freedom as well. The young developed an insatiable interest in sex and contraception, and sex studies conducted in the twenties suggest that the large majority of college students engaged in petting and approved of contraception, though premarital intercourse remained largely confined to those who were engaged.

The difference that a generation of university life made in the experience and views of social scientists can be seen perhaps most vividly in the life of Margaret Mead, whose work on sex and temperament represented one of the most important contributions to her generation's understanding of human nature. Both her mother and father had been trained in social science at Chicago at the turn of the century, her mother, Emily, as a sociologist, her father, Edward, as an economist. While Emily Mead worked as a social scientist only in her spare time, devoting herself primarily to her family and social reform, she had a profound influence on her daughter. As a child Margaret Mead absorbed "many of the premises of anthropology," learning "to regard all the races of man as equal," "to look at all human cultures as comparable," and to believe that "the mind is not sex-typed." At Barnard she studied with social scientists who shared the views of the Chicago School.[14]

After graduation Mead married her girlhood sweetheart, a divinity student. She planned a large family and a life as a minister's wife, a goal very much in keeping with the ideal of her mother's generation: the life of social concern and family nurturance. But only part of Mead wanted this life. The other part wanted to be an anthropologist, and the second side prevailed. For one thing, she had a much clearer sense than her mother could have had about what being a social scientist meant, and she had been preceded by a whole generation of women who had paved the way. Furthermore, changes that had taken place in attitudes toward sexuality and contraception made a tremendous difference.

It was not necessary for her, as it had been for her mother, to choose between a total commitment to motherhood and a career. Unlike her mother, Mead approved of contraception and used it to postpone children. "Luther and my marriage was an ideal student marriage," she later wrote, "unclouded by the fear of pregnancy. The pressure to have children was not great enough to make those who wavered in their determination careless." Moreover, her acceptance and enthusiasm about sexuality made the tension of being a woman in a man's world less disturbing than it must have been for her mother and for her mother's fellow student, Helen Thompson. Helen Thompson, like Emily Mead, married and suffered tremendous emotional strain in trying to combine the conventional life of motherhood with the demands of a scholarly life.

14 Margaret Mead, *Blackberry Winter: My Earlier Years,* Touchstone edition, Simon and Schuster, New York, pp. 111, 54, and *passim.*

Freed from much of the practical burden of family life as well as much of the psychological burden that her mother's generation had shouldered in trying to achieve a greater sense of equality and autonomy, Margaret Mead enjoyed an unprecedentedly rich career. This career might not have been possible without the institutional and intellectual precedents set by her parents' generation, but of course not all women who came of age in the twenties achieved the personal fulfillment or made the kind of contribution that she made. For all of the social change that had taken place by the twenties, one cannot discuss the development of the university and women's place within it without making due note of the limits that the university placed on women's acceptance.

As the university gained prestige in America, it began attracting more young men, and by the twenties the sheer magnitude of male enrollment was already confining women to a marginal position in the graduate and professional schools. At Chicago, where women in 1900 represented 50 percent of the graduate students, only 40 percent of the graduate students were women by the 1920s and the percentage was declining. In 1924 Marion Talbot resigned and protested to the president and the board of trustees that, among other things, "although women comprise over 40% of the graduate students and show by the grades accompanying the doctorates they receive that they reach a very high place of achievement, they receive only about 20% of the fellowships, including special fellowships designated for women." [15]

But more than male hegemony discouraged women from fighting their exclusion from university life as higher education achieved success within American society. Women's success in winning a place in higher education served to dissolve the bonds among women that had given courage to those who first fought for that place. In the early years of college education the distinctive culture of womanhood in which nine-teenth-century women had been reared shaped students' relationships, producing strong personal attachments among students and women teachers and administrators. As long as these close, affective relationships among women persisted they gave courage and conviction to those who sought fuller expression, whether it be in medicine, literature, art, or sociology.

Through organizations like the Association of Collegiate Alumnae, women fought to expand the horizons of their sisters, to give womanhood a fuller meaning. But there was a self-destructive mechanism in their efforts. To take advantage of the opportunities opening up in the professional and academic world, women had to renounce many of the values

[15] Edith Flint, Marion Talbot, and Elizabeth Wallace to the President of the University and the President of the Board of Trustees of the University of Chicago, Marion Talbot Papers, University of Chicago Archives.

that had defined them as women. A scientist is by definition coolly, dispassionately objective and rational. Professionals devote themselves completely to a particular area of competence. Affiliation with professional societies assumed greater importance than membership in women's organizations. Success as a scientist or professional was won at the cost of much that women had considered distinctively female.

Success isolated women from their culture of origin and placed them in an alien and often hostile community. Consequently, the achievements of the first generation proved difficult to build on. The values of science and professionalism undercut the very culture and political climate that had given women strength to expand their lives and to look critically at conventional assumptions about their basic personalities. Women lost their old feminine supports but had no other supports to replace them. As America entered the third decade of the twentieth century, there were fewer male champions of dissent, like the early John Dewey, willing to speak up on women's role in a university in which success discouraged iconoclasm.

The triumph of higher education in America had a major impact on feminism, an impact producing gains but also losses for women. The ideological change fostered by work in the social sciences freed women from the restrictions imposed by old prejudices about female inferiority, but at the same time undermined the sense of support women had enjoyed as members of a distinctive and self-consciously separate community. Having won a place within higher education, women suffered the strain of no longer feeling secure in the old, separate world of womanhood and maternal nurture, without being fully accepted or feeling comfortable within the new world of professionalism and science.

The long battle between feminists fighting for protective laws for women and those fighting for the ERA provides striking illustration of this tension. If our understanding of woman's nature remains confused and tentative, perhaps it is because women remain, despite great change, aliens in a society that champions science and professionalization but continues to fear, as it did in 1900, the threat to sex-role divisions that full acceptance of women would entail.

Documents

On a Difference in the Metabolism of the Sexes, 1897

It is increasingly apparent that all sociological manifestations proceed from physiological conditions.* The variables entering into social consciousness and activity—technology, ceremonial, religion, jurisprudence, politics, the arts and

* Reprinted from William I. Thomas, "On a Difference in the Metabolism of the Sexes," *The American Journal of Sociology*, 3 (July 1897), 31–32, 60–62.

professions, trade and commerce—have confessedly either a primary or a secondary connection with the struggle for food, and the evidence here detailed is designed to show that the determination of sex is a chemical matter, maleness and femaleness being solely expressions of a difference of attitude toward food. If such a connection can be traced between sex and nutrition it will afford a starting point for a study of the comparative psychology of the two sexes and for the investigation of the social meaning of sex.

A grand difference between plant and animal life lies in the fact that the plant is concerned chiefly with storing energy, and the animal with consuming it. . . . Expressed in biological formula, the habit of the plant is predominantly anabolic, that of the animal predominantly katabolic. Certain biologists, limiting their attention in the main to the lower forms of life, have maintained very plausibly that males are more katabolic than females, and that maleness is the product of influence tending to produce a katabolic habit of body. If this assumption is correct, maleness and femaleness are merely a repetition of the contrast existing between the animal and the plant. The katabolic animal form, through its rapid destruction of energy, has been carried developmentally away from the anabolic plant form; and of the two sexes the male has been carried farther than the female from the plant process. The body of morphological, physiological, ethnological, and demographic data which follows becomes coherent indeed, only on the assumption that woman stands nearer to the plant process than man, representing the constructive as opposed to the disruptive metabolic tendency. . . .

Social feeling, as such, originates in the association connected with reproduction, and its physical basis in the anabolic nature of the female . . . culminating among the mammals in the intra-uterine development of the young and the disposition in the female to care for the young after bringing them forth. The expansion of the abdominal zone in the female in connection with this modification of her reproductive system is the physical basis of the altruistic sentiments. . . .

This physiological predisposition of woman to feeling expresses itself primarily in love of offspring, and secondarily in ties of blood. Subsequent to the conversion of her surplus energy into offspring there follows a period in which her surplus energy is converted into milk for the sustentation of the offspring, and the time during which the child draws its life from the breast of the mother is a moment of supreme importance for the development of the race, since it is in connection with this quasi-physiological association that the first altruistic sentiments are knit. . . . Both social feeling and social organization are thus primarily feminine in origin—functions of the anabolism of woman. . . .

The striking historical contrast and parallelism of the militant and industrial activities of society is a social expression of this sexual contrast [between the nurturant anabolism of women and the disruptive, militant, katabolism of man]. Man's katabolism predisposed him to activity and violence; woman's anabolism predisposed her to a stationary life. The first division of labor was, therefore, an expression of the characteristic contrast of the sexes. War and the chase were suitable to man, because his somatic development fitted him for bursts of energy, and agriculture and the primitive industries were the natural occupation of woman. This allotment of tasks was not made by the tyranny of man, but exists almost uniformly in primitive communities because it utilizes most advantageously the energies of both sexes. The struggle is so fierce and constant that the primitive community which should let any energy go to waste would not long survive.

The Mental Traits of Men and Women, 1903

The suggestion that the observed psychological differences of sex may be due to difference in environment has often been met with derision, but it seems at least worthy of unbiased consideration.* The fact that very genuine and important differences of environment do exist can be denied only by the most superficial observer. Even in our own country, where boys and girls are allowed to go to the same schools and to play together to some extent, the social atmosphere is different from the cradle. Different toys are given them, different occupations and games are taught them, different ideals of conduct are held up to them. The question for the moment is not at all whether or not these differences in education are right and proper and necessary, but merely whether or not, as a matter of fact, they exist, and, if so, what effect they have on the individuals who are subjected to them.

The difference in physical training is very evident. Boys are encouraged in all forms of exercise and in out-of-door life, while girls are restricted in physical exercise at a very early age. Only a few forms of exercise are considered ladylike. Rough games and violent exercise of all sorts are discouraged. Girls are kept in the house and taught household occupations. The development in physical strength is not held up to girls as an ideal, while it is made one of the chief ambitions of boys. . . .

When we consider the other important respect in which men are supposed to be superior to women—ingenuity and inventiveness—we find equally important differences in social surroundings which would tend to bring about this result. Boys are encouraged to individuality. They are trained to be independent in thought and action. This is the ideal of manliness held up before them. . . . Girls are taught obedience, dependence, and deference. They are made to feel that too much independence of opinion or action is a drawback to them—not becoming or womanly. A boy is made to feel that his success in

* Excerpted from Helen Thompson (Woolley), *The Mental Traits of Men and Women,* The University of Chicago Press, Chicago, 1903, pp. 177–179.

life, his place in the world, will depend upon his ability to go ahead with his chosen occupation on his own responsibility, and to accomplish something new and valuable. No such social spur is given to girls.

Sex and Temperament, 1935

We have now considered in detail the approved personalities of each sex among three primitive peoples.* We found the Arapesh—both men and women—displaying a personality that, out of our historically limited preoccupations, we would call maternal in its parental aspects, and feminine in its sexual aspects. We found men, as well as women, trained to be co-operative, unaggressive, responsive to the needs and demands of others. We found no idea that sex was a powerful driving force either for men or for women. In marked contrast to these attributes, we found among the Mundugumor that both men and women developed as ruthless, aggressive, positively sexed individuals, with the maternal cherishing aspects of personality at a minimum. Both men and women approximated to a personality type that we in our culture would find only in an undisciplined and very violent male. Neither the Arapesh nor the Mundugumor ideal profits by a contrast between the sexes; the Arapesh ideal is the mild, responsive man married to the mild, responsive woman; the Mundugumor ideal is the violent aggressive man married to the violent aggressive woman. In the third tribe, the Tchambuli, we found a genuine reversal of the sex-attitudes of our own culture, with the woman the dominant, impersonal, managing partner, the man the less responsible and emotionally dependent person. These three situations suggest, then, a very definite conclusion. If those temperamental attitudes which we have traditionally regarded as feminine—such as passivity, responsiveness, and a willingness to cherish children—can so easily be set up as the masculine pattern in one tribe, and in another be outlawed for the majority of women as well as for the majority of men, we no longer have any basis for regarding such aspects of behavior as sex-linked. And this conclusion becomes even stronger when we consider the actual reversal in Tchambuli of the position of dominance of the two sexes, in spite of the existence of formal patrilineal institutions.

The material suggests that we may say that many, if not all, of the personality traits which we have called masculine or feminine are as lightly linked to sex as are the clothing, the manners, and the form of head-dress that a society at a given period assigns to either sex.

* Reprinted by permission of William Morrow & Company, Inc., from *Sex and Temperament in Three Primitive Societies* by Margaret Mead, pp. 279–280. Copyright © 1935, 1950, 1963 by Margaret Mead.

13 Woman's Place Is in the War: Propaganda and Public Opinion in the United States and Germany, 1939-1945

Leila J. Rupp

World War II poster.

"[M]en are apt to wake up some day and stop wars on the ground that women win them," editor Anne O'Hare McCormick wrote optimistically in 1943.[1] She expressed a conviction as widely held in our time as in hers, that women benefit from wars because they are drawn into areas of activity previously closed to them. The Second World War, in particular, brought an unprecedented number of women into such areas, including heavy industry and the armed forces.

But the temporary lowering of barriers made no permanent impact on women's opportunities or status in society. In both the United States and Nazi Germany, recruitment propaganda urged women to participate in the war effort but did not challenge traditional conceptions of women's nature and roles. The appeals addressed to women in both countries reveal an insistence that women function primarily as wives and mothers. Despite public opinion data collected by both governments indicating that women responded to economic motivation, recruitment campaigns never appealed to women on this basis. An examination of the content of propaganda directed at women and of women's attitudes toward employment indicate that women could be and were mobilized in wartime without challenging traditional ideas or bringing about permanent changes in the status of women. This essay concentrates on the American experience during the war and considers briefly the similarities of the German case in order to suggest that women do not necessarily "win" modern wars regardless of the political or economic system under which they live.

AMERICAN AND GERMAN PROPAGANDA FOR THE MOBILIZATION OF WOMEN

The government of Franklin Roosevelt and the Nazi regime of Adolf Hitler differed in ideological foundations, ultimate objectives, and methods of social control.[2] Nevertheless, both faced the problem of mobilizing women in similar ways, a fact that suggests that women have been assigned similar roles in modern Western societies and that these roles are subject to manipulation in response to the needs of highly industrialized economies in wartime. Women constituted the largest available labor reserve in both countries. The American government debated but did not institute labor conscription, choosing to rely instead on intensive

---

[1] I would like to thank Harriet Lightman and Marylynn Salmon for reading and commenting extensively on this article. The quote is from the *New York Times,* March 8, 1943, p. 8.

[2] This section and the concluding section are based on my book, *Mobilizing Women for War: German and American Propaganda, 1939–1945,* forthcoming from Princeton University Press. Full documentation is available in the book.

propaganda campaigns designed to sell war work to women. The Nazis, hampered by a chaotic bureaucratic structure and Hitler's conviction until mid-war that Germany could win in a state of partial mobilization, passed but did not enforce the registration of women for civilian labor. In lieu of effective conscription, Nazi propaganda urged women to participate in the war effort. Although the Nazi effort pales beside the massive American campaigns, both governments relied on propaganda rather than conscription to mobilize women for war.

The United States succeeded in mobilizing women, but Germany did not. The American female labor force increased by 32 percent from 1941 to 1945; the German increased by only 1 percent from 1939 to 1944. In spite of the fact that preparations for war began in Germany before 1939, the insignificant increase in the German female labor force does not reflect an advanced stage of mobilization. American women assumed the places of men called into military service, but German women did not respond to the increasingly serious labor shortages that even the importation of foreign workers and prisoners of war could not solve.

The Office of War Information, in conjunction with the War Manpower Commission, took responsibility in the United States for, in its own words, "selling" the war to women. Even after a congressional attack on the Domestic Branch of the OWI in 1943 resulted in a severe budget cut, the office continued to act as a coordinating agency for promotional campaigns. It sent out monthly guides to magazine and newspaper writers and editors, as well as to radio commentators, suggesting approaches to war topics and allocating time and space so that the various media would emphasize the same themes at the same time; supervised and distributed films; maintained a close relationship with the advertising industry through the War Advertising Council; and planned major national campaigns designed to recruit women for war work.[3] Four campaigns—launched in December 1942, March 1943, September 1943, and March 1944—combined national informational efforts with intensive local campaigns in areas of labor shortage to actually recruit women.

All of these campaigns used similar media techniques. Newspapers and magazines publicized the need for women workers and featured stories of women already at work. The OWI urged magazines to picture women workers on their front covers in September 1943 and arranged a competition for the best cover, with prizes awarded at a special exhibition at the Museum of Modern Art in New York. Posters and billboards appealed to women to take war jobs. Encouraged by the OWI's distribution of professionally prepared announcements and recordings made by famous radio personalities, radio stations devoted entire shows, spot

[3] Copies of OWI publications and information about its activities can be found in the Records of the OWI (RG 208), Washington National Records Center, Suitland, Maryland.

announcements, and special features to the campaigns. Theaters across the country showed special womanpower shorts, such as *Glamour Girls* of 1943. A Retailers War Campaign Committee published a calendar for retailers with suggested advertising techniques, including displays of work clothes and a schedule to coordinate war advertising. The War Advertising Council encouraged advertisers of all kinds of products to tie in war themes with their ads. The War Manpower Commission prompted Boy Scouts to paint recruitment slogans on sidewalks and suggested that officials in labor shortage areas set up a roster of women war workers in the city hall and ceremoniously inscribe the names of new workers.

In contrast to American campaigns, the German propaganda effort seems minor.[4] Propaganda emanating from both a Nazi party and a state propaganda agency spread throughout Germany by means of the regional and local offices. Newspapers, pamphlets, posters, films, slide shows, exhibitions, and community bulletin boards reached the most isolated areas. But, unlike the United States, a Nazi women's organization had responsibility for much of the propaganda addressed to women, indicating the low priority attached to such propaganda, for the organization was neither important nor powerful in the Nazi hierarchy. There seems to have been just one major campaign, similar to the American ones, aimed at recruiting women for the war effort. Despite the lack of concerted campaigns, however, German propaganda continued to call for sacrifice for the good of the state, a theme much in evidence in prewar propaganda aimed at both women and men.

THE PATRIOTIC APPROACH

The appeals to American women recommended by the OWI campaign plans and those actually used in the recruitment efforts reveal a great deal about the attitudes toward women in the United States. Although some of the campaign plans suggested an appeal to women on the basis of high wages—"There's a good job, at war wages, that are the same as men's wages, waiting"—this was never the major thrust of a campaign plan and was rarely mentioned in actual recruitment. Even as the government recommended such an appeal, it cautioned that wages should not be stressed too much or increased spending and inflation would result. But more complex, though perhaps subconscious, reasons underlay American reluctance to appeal to women as economic beings interested

---

[4] Information on the dissemination of propaganda urging women to participate in the war effort can be found in the Records of the NSDAP (T-81), National Archives Microcopy, Washington, D.C. T-81 includes directives from the Propaganda Ministry (Roll 24), the Party propaganda agency (Roll 117), and the women's organization (Roll 75).

in earning good money. Most of the campaign plans emphasized the importance of reaching women through emotion rather than reason: "The copy should be pitched on a *highly emotional, patriotic appeal*." The cherished notion that women are ruled by their emotions set the tone and determined the content of most of the recruitment efforts.

American propaganda developed a special form of emotional appeal in addressing women. Assuming that women responded to personalized patriotism rather than any abstract ideal, the government noted: "The 'shorten-the-war' theme is obviously the one which appeals most deeply to women. Mothers, grandmothers, sisters, wives, sweethearts—there isn't one who doesn't want her man back as fast as possible. Working will speed the day—and will help make the waiting easier."

Such personalized patriotism took two forms. Women were promised that their contributions could help to bring their men back sooner, or were threatened with responsibility for the death of a soldier if they refused to cooperate. One plan stated: "It should be made clear that by working on a war job (war production or civilian) a woman is protecting her own loved ones from death on the battlefield. . . ." An announcer in one radio spot told women: "You *can* do something—you can shorten the war, make your son or husband's chances of coming home better!" A second spot illustrates the guilt approach: "Certain women in [city] are unintentionally prolonging the war. They have *not* taken war jobs. The need for them is critical. *Are you one?*" Likewise, a special booklet for critical labor shortage areas warned: "Unless local women like yourself apply for war jobs now, our soldiers on the war fronts may die needlessly."

This appeal to personalized patriotism dominated actual mobilization propaganda. A War Manpower Commission recruitment poster pictured an obviously nonemployed woman sadly clutching a letter from her husband in the service. The caption read: "Longing won't bring him back sooner . . . GET A WAR JOB!" Another poster, taking up the government's suggestion that men needed to be persuaded to let their wives take jobs, showed a woman worker and her husband in front of an American flag, and proclaimed: "I'm proud . . . my husband *wants* me to do my part." An advertisement for DuBarry Beauty Preparations promised that "One woman can shorten this war!" Making perfectly explicit the personalized appeal, a newspaperwoman wrote of the "deep satisfaction which a woman of today knows who has made a rubber boat which may save the life of her aviator husband, or helped to fashion a bullet which may avenge her son!" [5]

These examples of personalized patriotism are typical of the primary appeal used in propaganda addressed to women, although recruitment efforts used other approaches as well, including the glamorization and

[5] Mrs. William Brown Meloney, Foreword, in *American Women at War, by 7 Newspaper Women*, National Association of Manufacturers, New York, 1942, p. 6.

the domestication of factory work. One woman newspaper-reporter-turned-factory-worker complained that there were "too many pictures of beautiful girls posed on the wings of planes with a glowing caption to make you think that war is glamorous." [6]

Glamour became an integral part of much of the propaganda. *Life* featured a two-page spread of models in work clothes, entitled "Flying Fortress Fashions." *Woman's Home Companion* proved that women war workers could be beautiful by taking four of them to Hollywood to be dressed and made up as starlets. An advertisement for Woodbury Facial soap enticed women with the caption: "She turned her back on the Social Scene and is finding Romance at work!" Such propaganda promised women that they could be glamorous and desirable as war workers in industry, despite overalls and smudged noses.

The appeal to glamour revealed an underlying assumption that women are frivolous and concerned with their appearance above all else. Another secondary appeal assumed that women are naturally suited to housework but not other types of work. Campaign plans constantly recommended that recruitment liken war work to "women's work": "Millions of women find war work pleasant and as easy as running a sewing machine, or using a vacuum cleaner." Following this suggestion, one writer reported that women took to industrial machines "as easily as to electric cake-mixers and vacuum cleaners." [7] A top official at the Aberdeen Proving Grounds found that women workers "justified his hunch that a determined gal can be just as handy on a firing range as over the kitchen stove." [8]

The similarities in German propaganda suggest that the concept of the woman as wife and mother is pervasive in Western societies. Because Nazi ideology had called on women as well as men to sacrifice their individual interests to the good of the state even before the war, the Nazi image of women (as opposed to Nazi policy toward women) had to change less than the American image. Despite the emphasis on abstract patriotism in Germany, the Nazis also utilized a concept of extended motherhood.

The American woman who avenged her son by producing a bullet had her counterpart in Germany in the woman who reportedly worked in a factory while her son fought and who summed up her function in this way: "Earlier I buttered bread for him, now I paint grenades and think, this is for him." [9] Nazi propaganda did not glamorize war work, but at

---

[6] Nell Giles, *Punch In, Susie! A Woman's War Factory Diary*, Harper, New York, 1943, pp. 1–2.
[7] Mary Hornaday, "Factory Housekeeping," in *American Women at War*, p. 35.
[8] Quoted in Peggy McEvoy, "Gun Molls," *Reader's Digest*, 42 (March 1943), 48.
[9] "Munition für die Söhne," in Magda Menzerath, *Kampffeld Heimat: Deutsche Frauenleistung im Kriege*, Allemannen Verlag Albert Jauss, Stuttgart, 1944, p. 49.

least one writer used an approach identical to the American domestication of factory work, arguing that women could master industrial jobs because they were experienced at running sewing machines and using typewriters.

These various appeals reveal the way in which propaganda in both countries exhorted women to take up jobs in areas previously reserved for men without challenging traditional ideas about women's nature and roles. War work for women threatened to upset the social order by breaking down sex roles, a threat symbolized by the furor, especially in the United States, over women appearing in public in pants. But the danger could be neutralized by presenting war work as an extension of a woman's traditional role as wife and mother. The concept of personalized patriotism assumed that women took war jobs in order to bring their men home sooner. The glamorization of war work and women workers in the United States assured the public that the wearing of overalls wrought no permanent changes, while the domestication of factory work, intended to persuade women that they could handle industrial jobs, also convinced the public that such jobs would not transform women.

In the United States and Germany, contrary to the intentions of its disseminators, propaganda was more important in adapting public images to the wartime situation without disrupting the social order than it was in mobilizing women.

The relationship between propaganda and the success or failure of mobilization is a complex one. Propaganda may operate in conjunction with a number of objective factors, such as financial incentive, by stressing or ignoring appeals that touch on women's actual concerns. This relationship does not assume that women are simply manipulated into and out of the labor force. Although it may be impossible to recover women's motivations in seeking or not seeking employment during the war, even with exhaustive interview data, both the American and German governments collected information on public attitudes toward the employment of women. This material sheds some light on the question of women's motives and sets in perspective the propaganda campaigns in both countries.

Governmental Neglect of Public Attitudes

Recruitment propaganda in both countries assumed that women would be motivated by patriotism to take war jobs and, by implication, that women accepted the current idea of their "place." The information on public attitudes collected by the governments suggests that both assumptions were wrong. While the German material is somewhat sketchy on these points, the information gathered by the United States government gives a good indication of public attitudes.

The idea that woman's "place" was in the home except in the war emergency maintained a strong following in the United States during the war, but among men more than women. Real obstacles such as child-care and domestic responsibilities, rather than their own attitudes, kept most nonemployed American women from seeking employment. Despite the lack of material on the motives of individual women who entered employment during the war years, the American public believed that financial incentive, rather than patriotism, brought women into the labor force. The American and German governments collected information on public opinion in order to improve their recruitment efforts, yet failed to act on their knowledge. This seeming paradox strengthens the argument that a major function of propaganda was the adaptation of public images of women in a nonthreatening way.

In the United States, the Office of War Information collected two basic types of information. The first included surveys of representative samples of the population, undertaken in conjunction with the National Opinion Research Center at the University of Denver, and weekly intelligence reports on public attitudes.[10] The second, more interesting type of information, consists of letters solicited from volunteer correspondents.[11]

The OWI compiled lists of possible "able and unbiased observers" in several major categories: editors, labor editors, clergymen, businessmen, social workers, and housewives. The head of the Correspondence Panels Section asked these individuals to write a confidential monthly report on public opinion among the people with whom they came into contact. The records of the Correspondence Panels Section include the letters of hundreds of individuals from urban and rural locations throughout the country who agreed to take the assignment. While the panels are in no sense a representative sample, they do represent a fairly wide range of middle-class respondents in the selected occupational categories. The choice of categories precluded women war workers; most of the 139 women correspondents were housewives (51.8 percent) or social workers (36.7 percent). This material cannot reconstruct the motivations of individual women who chose to take up war work, but the letters of the women correspondents, and especially their responses to a March 1944 questionnaire on the employment of women, provide impressionistic evidence of the responses of women to mobilization and propaganda. After all, these women, especially the housewives, were the ones at whom the recruitment propaganda was aimed.

The OWI surveys and reports, designed to guide the officials in

10 The OWI reports of poll data and weekly intelligence reports can be found in the Records of the Office of Government Reports (RG 44), Boxes 1798, 1802, 1803, 1805, 1806, Washington National Records Center, Suitland, Maryland.

11 The Correspondence Panels materials can be found in the Records of the Office of Government Reports (RG 44), Boxes 1733–1761, WNRC, Suitland, Maryland.

charge of the recruitment campaigns, tended to stress the reluctance of nonemployed women to take up war work. A report dated May 6, 1942, noted that two-thirds of the country's women had "given little thought as yet to undertaking such employment." In August of the same year, a special report indicated that the most important obstacle to the employment of women was their reluctance to enter the labor market. Asked in January 1943 how they felt they could best contribute to the war effort, a large majority (77 percent) of nonemployed women replied that they could continue to do just what they were doing. By June 1943, the OWI still reported widespread resistance among nonemployed women to taking up war work. A survey undertaken late in 1943 showed that a majority of American women were aware of the need for labor and thought more women should enter the labor force, but that 73 percent of the nonemployed women were unwilling to take a full-time war job. The OWI continued to report resistance among nonemployed women into 1944.

Such results spurred the OWI to investigate the reasons why women avoided employment. Most women, when asked, expressed concern over home responsibilities. A June 1943 survey reported that women with children overwhelmingly opposed the idea of employment, and noted that this fact had serious consequences for the recruitment effort, since five out of six nonemployed young women were mothers.

Women with young children often faced real problems in taking a job, and many of the intelligence reports took seriously the obstacles women felt prevented them from participating in the war effort. While some of these reports called for the provision of services, especially child care, which would make possible the employment of women, the OWI concluded that the attitudes of the women themselves were extremely important in keeping women out of the labor force. One report commented: "Not all of these reasons [i.e., domestic responsibilities] are to be taken at face value. . . . There are strong prejudices in some social groups against married women working, and the feeling that woman's place is in the home has a deep appeal for most women." This statement, however, reflects attitudes of government officials more faithfully than those of women themselves.

A poll taken in 1944 on the idea of the registration of women found that of the 36 percent of the women surveyed who opposed registration, only 27 percent gave as a reason their belief that "woman's place is in the home." Despite the fact that this was the reason women gave most often, it still represents less than 10 percent of all the women surveyed, hardly the basis for the statement that most women believed that their place is in the home. Another 1944 survey reported that only 1 percent of the women and men who thought that the demand for women workers had decreased in the last months believed that women should stay at home and take care of their children.

MALE FEARS AND FEMALE ATTITUDES

If attitudes did in fact stop women from seeking employment, the OWI's information suggests that men's attitudes, rather than women's, were responsible. Men often expressed fears that women might replace them in the labor force or depress wages or that the employment of women might destroy family life. Such fears prompted the OWI to address men specifically in the campaigns designed to recruit women. One survey investigated the attitudes of both women and men and reported: "Women are more prone than men to favor the use of married women in war industries; and, as might be expected, women who are now working approve the idea more frequently than housewives and unemployed women."

   The letters of male correspondents strengthen the impression created by the surveys and polls that men, rather than women, believed in the old adage about woman's place. An OWI report based on letters written in September and October 1943 expressed fear that women would want to remain in the labor force after the war. One man summed up this attitude well: "We should immediately start planning to get these women back where they belong, amid the environment of homelife, where they can raise their children in normal, healthy happy conditions, free from demoralizing influences." Women correspondents, too, reported male fears that women would not be satisfied to return to housekeeping after the war. An Ohio farm woman warned: "And be very careful about how many women you men push into industry. Post-war days will come bye and bye and women in industry will be a head-ache for someone." Several women reported that husbands prevented their wives from taking jobs.

   A social worker with personal experience saw the problem as more subtle than overcoming the objections of men who flatly refused to permit their wives to work:

Here is the difference between a man working & a woman as seen in our home—while I prepare the evening meal, my husband reads the evening paper. We then do the dishes together after which he reads his medical journals or cogitates over some lecture he is to give or some problem at his lab. I have to make up grocery lists, mend, straighten up a drawer, clean out the ice box, press clothes, put away anthing strewn about the house, wash bric a brac, or do several of hundreds of small "woman's work is never done stuff." . . . All this while my husband is relaxing & resting. When I worked full time, we tried doing the house-cleaning together but it just didn't click.

This woman put into words the classic problem: how women can manage paid employment and their domestic responsibilities at the same time.

Her dismissal of full sharing of household duties with her husband as an attempt that "just didn't click" indicates the difficulties of changing long-established patterns in the sexual distribution of labor.

Significantly, the women correspondents, and even the housewives, did not express the conviction that women belonged at home. Yet of all the housewife correspondents, not one seems to have taken a job in the course of the war. Only two women even noticed the irony of their reporting on the effectiveness of recruitment campaigns. An Indiana housewife wrote: "My own personal suggestion is that woman power (especially me) be drafted before breaking up any more families." Yet she appeared to be waiting to be drafted rather than voluntarily taking a war job. An Iowa woman wrote: "I would be pleased to have employment as I have to be away from my husband, but I have 2 adorable small children—Like many other young mothers I do not feel that I can be away from them." A marginal note penned by the OWI staff remarked that she was "about the only HW [housewife] who seems to have considered taking a job." That seems to be true.

In fact, a number of correspondents actually quit jobs, or reported that women were leaving employment, because of increased household responsibilities. A Philadelphia woman with the Amalgated Clothing Workers Union, recruited as a member of the Labor Editors panel in 1943, married and quit her job, resulting in a transfer to the Housewives panel. She noted:

Too bad you didn't want a comment on manpower this week because I am a victim of the m-p-shortage, and have had to give up my own job in order to come home and keep house for lack of an adequate house-keeper at any price. I think I detect a trend in this direction with a majority of my married friends caught in the same predicament.

Other correspondents complained about the "servant problem" or reported that many women were doing their own housework for the first time. Statistics show that most women did not leave their jobs for lack of domestic help, but the letters indicate the social confusion that must have resulted as women employed in domestic service responded to the opportunity of better employment.

The letters of the correspondents show that the OWI was wrong in assuming that women avoided employment out of a belief that they belonged at home. They were also wrong in believing that women sought jobs out of personalized patriotism. The attitudes of the women correspondents on the issue of women's motives in taking up war work are extremely interesting in light of the government's insistence on using an emotional patriotic approach in recruitment propaganda. Although many correspondents mentioned patriotism as a factor influencing women to seek employment, most believed that money was the primary motive. One housewife summed up what many others expressed:

The main inducement is money! So-called patriotism plays a minor part. It's only in news-reels and in write-ups or on propaganda radio programs that a noble femme takes over a grease-monkey's job, or rivets or welds because her husband or sweetheart is a Jap prisoner—or something! I've never met up with any such noble motive. It's more apt to be a fur coat.

Only one correspondent supported the government's interpretation of why women worked, reporting that women took jobs out of a "[f]eeling of identification with beloved member of family attached to fighting forces and personal stake in each additional shell manufactured."

More surprising than the correspondents' belief that women, like men, took employment for the income is the frequent expression of the idea that women sought jobs out of dissatisfaction with housewifery. A social worker in Utah wrote: "Many women thoroughly enjoy working & getting away from the home. They seem to get much more satisfaction out of it than out of housework or bringing up children." A Baltimore housewife agreed: "Women like to be out taking a part in the world. They feel a grateful sense of freedom, an aliveness, a personal satisfaction. They forget their own small lives." An unusually articulate correspondent, a social worker from Houston, summed up the feelings of several of the women:

To many, it affords an opportunity to escape the responsibilities of house-keeping and caring for children which was never really accepted in the first place. Employment, particularly at a job ordinarily filled by a man, is to some a legitimate channel for the expression of aggressive drives in women. I have talked with quite a number of women who seemed to me to be rather obviously competing with their husbands and at least one who was watching her husband who was employed in the same plant.

Such opinions suggest that the war may have provided an eagerly awaited opportunity for some women to take up paid employment in a socially approved fashion. One letter makes this point explicitly: "For some women the war situation has made work acceptable whereas heretofore they were inhibited against paid employment." A glimpse of the women the government ignored, women who had worked before the war, is provided in the comments of a Pittsburgh housewife:

I have talked to women that are working in big plants doing men's work that say "Boy, have the men been getting away with murder all these years. Why I worked twice as hard selling in a department store

and got half the pay.["] Grandmothers are working out in the real heavy
stuff and are jolly and like it.

Thus, the letters of the women correspondents offer an extraordinary
opportunity to examine the views of ordinary mostly white middle-class
women on the issue of wartime employment. These letters provide the
first indication in the OWI records that women might enjoy the economic
independence and satisfaction of a job. That the correspondents, most
of them housewives, believed that women sought employment for financial gain and often preferred employment to full-time housework suggests
that the OWI staff overemphasized the reluctance of women to take
employment.

Public opinion generally accepted the wartime employment of
women, yet fears that women might want to linger on in the labor force
after the war indicate little change in basic attitudes. Home responsibilities and lack of institutional arrangements to lighten women's load kept
some women out of the labor force, but the government failed to act on
this information that would make possible the employment of more
women. The OWI continued to attempt to persuade women that their
place was in the war, despite indications that men's attitudes were more
significant in erecting barriers to women's participation.

WOMEN IN THE LABOR FORCE

Despite the obstacles, however, millions of American women moved into
war industry or took jobs for the first time. Germany presents a sharp
contrast, even though the Nazi government, like the American, anxiously
kept an eye on public opinion. The Security Service of the SS collected
and compiled reports on the attitudes of the population, circulating these
reports to government agencies every few days.[12] But the Nazi régime
failed to make use of this information to improve the recruitment effort.
As the war continued, German women complained about low wages,
suggesting that they too were interested in working for money. Their
complaints about receiving less pay than men doing the same work led
the Security Service to recommend an equal-pay policy to encourage
women to seek employment, but the policy was never implemented. And
so, as in the United States, heavy household responsibilities and lack of
institutional arrangements to alleviate the burden combined to keep
women out of the labor force.

The German government, like the American, viewed women's
participation in the labor force as a temporary arrangement. One report
stressed that "the main task of every woman lies in the performance of

[12] The Security Service reports on the German population can be found in the Records
of the Reich Leader of the SS and Chief of the German Police (T-175), Rolls 258–266,
National Archives Microcopy, Washington, D.C.

her domestic and maternal duties, and that if in exceptional times the woman must to a great extent be brought into industry for reasons of state, her nature should be taken into account as much as possible." It then went on to emphasize the importance of suiting the conditions of work to woman's nature and of convincing "the woman through propaganda of the necessity of her voluntary participation in the labor force."

One important factor in explaining the reluctance of German women to take employment was unique to the Nazi state. The Security Service reports make clear that German women feared the imposition of controls by the regime should they take jobs. This led to enormous resentment on the part of employed women, who were subject to such controls, against nonemployed women who avoided registering with the employment offices. Women often criticized the "so-called better circles" and the wives and daughters of party leaders for avoiding employment. Employed women could not understand why the government did not conscript the nonemployed for war work. Since women already in the labor force could be punished by law for infractions of work discipline, they believed that other women too should be subject to legal sanctions. A February 1942 report noted that employed women were willing to make sacrifices but could not understand why the burden of war should be so unequally distributed. In particular, workers in armaments industries favored the conscription of women in the interests of social justice.

When a registration decree ordering women to report to the employment offices went into effect in January 1943, the working population greeted it enthusiastically, wondering only why it had not been passed earlier. In the weeks that followed, the Security Service noted first that women were reporting to employment offices that were often unprepared to place them, later that the willingness of women to take war work had not increased. The population believed that not all women covered by the order had registered. The complaint that leading personalities used their influence to keep women out of the labor force surfaced in a December 1943 report. In April 1944, women were still complaining that many had not registered, that those who had registered had not been employed, and that the women of the "so-called better circles" were not cooperating.

The fear of German women that employment would subject them to greater control by the government indicates that women were not the fanatical supporters of the regime pictured in Nazi propaganda. They avoided registering with the employment offices, complained about wages and conditions, and criticized party measures and even party leaders, although the Security Service reported that women stood resolutely behind Hitler. For purposes of comparison, however, the indications that women were not moved by appeals to patriotism are most important. The German government, like the American, paid little attention to its own information about public opinion when designing recruitment campaigns.

CONCLUSION

The divergence between Nazi propaganda and the realities of the Third Reich is clear. Although the American case was less extreme, it also shows propaganda diverging from reality. Nazi propaganda portrayed the German woman joyfully sacrificing her personal interests for the good of her people, but in reality German women avoided employment. The American woman, according to propaganda, took a war job in order to bring her man home sooner, but the OWI's own survey material suggested that women in fact responded predominantly to the high wages offered in war industry.

In light of the OWI's information on the importance of financial incentive to American women, one would expect propaganda that emphasized wages to succeed in encouraging women to enter the labor force. The Nazi government, in a situation of low wages for women, could not use such an appeal and would not raise wages. But the United States faced no such difficulties. Wages were attractively high and the OWI's correspondents indicated that they believed that women took employment because of high wages.

Early on in the propaganda effort, the OWI recommended an appeal based on high wages, but only hesitantly, fearful of encouraging inflation. But the appeal based on wages was never central or even prominent in the campaign plans, and rarely if ever appeared at all in actual mobilization propaganda. The OWI concentrated on an emotional patriotic appeal in disregard of both women's motives and the very real obstacles preventing women from seeking employment. The lack of appeals to women's needs or desires to earn money, in spite of available information that women would respond to such an appeal, strengthens the impression that wartime propaganda avoided challenging traditional assumptions about women. With economic motivation ignored or downplayed, women could be viewed as wives and mothers responding to the needs of the country or of their men rather than as workers.

An examination of propaganda and public opinion shows that both the United States and Germany urged women to move into new areas of activity without changing basic attitudes about women. The wartime changes expanded the options of women in a way intended by the propagandists and understood by the population as temporary. The way in which public images of women adapted to the needs of recruitment propaganda—by presenting women's participation in the war effort as an extension of traditional maternal roles, particularly in the American case—helped to assure that the wartime range of options would contract once again in peacetime. The German experience was complicated by defeat and occupation, but the postwar situation in the United States shows that the image of women did not have to make tremendous adjustments after the war. The American public perceived the war as an extraordinary situation and accepted many temporary changes it would not tolerate in peacetime.

The OWI material on public opinion suggests that the public accepted the employment of women in war industry without revising traditional attitudes. Many men feared permanent changes, but the post-war situation assured them that little had changed. The proportion of employed women in the female population continued to increase after the immediate postwar layoffs, as it had throughout the twentieth century, but the war itself had no permanent impact on this trend. Women who had found their first opportunity to work during the war were no doubt affected by the experience, yet the impact of the war on public attitudes toward women was negligible. The seeming paradox of the intensely domestic 1950s following on the heels of a supposedly liberating war dissolves if one considers the form in which war participation was presented to the public.

Thus, in two very different but highly industrialized societies women were recruited for war work without challenging traditional attitudes or bringing about permanent changes. The form of recruitment propaganda reveals how tenacious the image of woman as wife and mother is, even in crisis situations. Such evidence indicates that modern war is a factor of dubious value in the struggle of women for status and power in society. Despite the fact that millions of women experienced the male world of heavy industry and high wages for the first time, Anne O'Hare McCormick was wrong. The case of the Second World War suggests that in wartime women are not necessarily the winners.

Documents

Letter from Mrs. Norma Yerger Queen to Clyde Hart, 1944

c/o Lt. Col. F. B. Queen
Bushnell Hospital
Brigham City, Utah
3-26-44

My dear Mr. Hart,*

In reply to your questions about women working I should like to say that from March 1, 1943 to July 31, 1943 I was the Day Care Worker for our county and as such tried to learn the needs of day care for children of working mothers and to make possible the employment of women. Since then as child welfare worker

* From letter from Mrs. Norma Yerger Queen to Clyde Hart, head of the Correspondence Panels Section of the Office of War Information, May 26, 1944; document in the National Archives of the United States in the custody of the General Archives Division.

for our county, I have continued to keep in touch with the need for women
working, their problems & the attitudes of the community about it. We opened
a day nursery for preschool children June 15th & closed Oct. 31st because it was
never sufficiently used. It was more than well publicized but we finaly decided
that really not enough women with preschool children were employed to warrant keeping it open.

1. The people of this community all respect women who work regardless of
the type of work. Women from the best families & many officers wives work at
our hospital. It is not at all uncommon to meet at evening parties in town
women who work in the kitchens or offices of our hospital (Army-Bushnell-large
general). The city mayor's wife too works there.

The church disaproves of women working who have small children. The
church (L.D.S.) has a strong influence in our county.

For the canning season in our county men's & women's clubs & the church
all recruited vigorously for women for the canneries. It was "the thing to do" to
work so many hrs. a week at the canneries.

I personaly have encouraged officer's wives who have no children to get
out and work. Those of us who have done so have been highly respected by the
others and we have not lost social standing. In fact many of the social affairs are
arranged at our convenience.

Some husbands do not approve of wives working & this has kept home
some who do not have small children. Some of the women just do not wish to
put forth the effort.

The financial incentive has been the strongest influence among most economic groups but especialy among those families who were on relief for many
years. Patriotic motivation is sometimes present but sometimes it really is a
front for the financial one. A few women work to keep their minds from worrying about sons or husbands in the service.

In this county, the hospital is the chief employer of women. A few go to
Ogden (20 miles away) to work in an arsenal, the depot, or the air field. When
these Ogden plants first opened quite a few women started to work there, but the
long commuting plus the labor at the plants plus their housework proved too
much.

Many women thoroughly enjoy working & getting away from the home.
They seem to get much more satisfaction out of it than out of housework or
bringing up children. Those who quit have done so because of lack of good care
for their children, or of inability to do the housework & the job.

We definitely found that having facilities for the care of children did not
increase the number of women who worked. In 1942, the women kept saying they
couldn't go to the canneries because they had no place to leave their children.
In 1943 everyone knew we had the day nursery & private homes available & still
there was difficulty in recruiting. One of the big reasons we got the nursery was
to help in our canning & poultry seasons.

Most all jobs are secured thro our U.S.E.S. so I assume people know about
it. It runs frequent stories in our local paper.

I am convinced that if women could work 4 days a week instead of 5½ or 6 that more could take jobs. I found it impossible to work 5½ days & do my housework but when I arranged for 4 days I could manage both. These days one has to do everything—one cannot buy services as formerly. For instance—laundry. I'm lucky. I can send out much of our laundry to the hospital but even so there is a goodly amount that must be done at home—all the ironing of summer dresses is very tiring. I even have to press my husband's trousers—a thing I never did in all my married life. The weekly housecleaning—shoe shining—all things we formerly had done by others. Now we also do home canning. I never in the 14 yrs. of my married life canned one 1 jar. Last summer I put up dozens of quarts per instructions of Uncle Sam. I'm only one among many who is now doing a lot of manual labor foreign to our usual custom. I just could not take on all that & an outside job too. It is no fun to eat out—you wait so long for service & the resturants cannot be immaculately kept—therefore it is more pleasant & quicker to cook & eat at home even after a long day's work. I've talked with the personnel manager at the hospital & he agrees that fewer days a week would be better. The canneries finaly took women for as little as 3 hrs. a day.

This is a farming area & many farm wives could not under any arrangements take a war job. They have too much to do at their farm jobs & many now have to go into the fields, run tractors & do other jobs formerly done by men. I marvel at all these women are able to do & feel very inadequate next to them. Some do work in Ogden or Brigham during the winter months.

Here is the difference between a man working & a woman as seen in our home—while I prepare the evening meal, my husband reads the evening paper. We then do the dishes together after which he reads his medical journal or cogitates over some lecture he is to give or some problem at his lab. I have to make up grocery lists, mend, straighten up a drawer, clean out the ice box, press clothes, put away anthing strewn about the house, wash bric a brac, or do several of hundreds of small "woman's work is never done stuff." This consumes from 1 to 2 hrs. each evening after which I'm too weary to read any professional social work literature & think I'm lucky if I can keep up with the daily paper, Time Life or Reader's Digest. All this while my husband is relaxing & resting. When I worked full time, we tried doing the housecleaning together but it just didn't click. He is responsible for introducing penicillin into Bushnell & thus into the army & there were so many visiting brass hats & night conferences he couldn't give even one night a week to the house. Then came a mess of lectures at all kinds of medical meetings—he had to prepare those at home. I got so worn out it was either quit work or do it part time.

This has been a lot of personal experience but I'm sure we are no exception. I thought I was thro working in 1938. My husband urged me to help out for the war effort—he's all out for getting the war work done & he agreed to do his share of the housework. He is not lazy but he found we could not do it. I hope this personal experience will help to give you an idea of some of the problems.

[*Norma Yerger Queen*]

14 "A Truly Subversive Affair": Women Against Lynching in the Twentieth-Century South

Jacquelyn Dowd Hall

Jessie Daniel Ames.

On May 9, 1930, a Sherman, Texas, mob lynched a black farm laborer named George Hughes. Hughes was accused of raping his employer's wife in revenge against "the white folks who hated him and his race." But the story told in the black community, and whispered in the white, was both chilling and prosaic: an altercation over wages had ended in mob violence.

Once Hughes had been arrested and indicted, lurid rumors had begun to circulate through the county: The defendant had raped the woman three times in succession, mutilated her, and infected her with venereal disease. Hughes, reported the local county attorney, was "a beast who knew what he wanted and meant to have it, hell and hanging notwithstanding." By the time the trial began, white farmers from the surrounding countryside were converging on the town. Although the governor sent four Texas Rangers in a halfhearted attempt to forestall violence, the crowd, enraged at the sight of the woman carried into the courtroom on a stretcher, set fire to the building. Left in a second-floor vault, Hughes died in the flames. The police directed traffic, while men dragged the corpse to a cottonwood tree in the Negro business section. There it was hanged and burned; afterward the crowd looted and destroyed most of the black-owned property in town. In the months that followed, employers were warned to dismiss their black laborers, and many black families left the area altogether. The size of the crowd, the complicity of a moderate governor, the burning of the courthouse—all brought the Sherman lynching a special notoriety. But in its origins, development, and aftermath, it typified a long and deeply rooted tradition of extralegal racial violence.[1]

Unlike other incidents in this bloody record, the Sherman lynching called forth a significant white response. Moved by Hughes's death and fearing an upsurge of violence with the onset of the Great Depression, a Texas suffragist named Jessie Daniel Ames founded a unique women's voluntary organization, the Association of Southern Women for the Prevention of Lynching (ASWPL). The goals of the group were ambitious indeed: It sought to devise practical means for preventing threatened lynchings in the rural and small-town South. More broadly, it hoped to persuade southern white women that lynching posed a threat to their own interests and to use such women as a medium of crystallizing public sentiment against the crime. Jessie Daniel Ames self-consciously assumed the task of guiding her constituency toward a complex view of the origins of mob violence; under her leadership, the Anti-Lynching Association endeavored not only to bring the region into line with national norms of law observance and social order but also to modify the definition of

[1] Arthur Raper, *The Tragedy of Lynching,* 2nd. ed., Dover Publications, New York, 1970, pp. 319–355.

womanhood in southern society. As a result, the group's internal discussions and public pronouncements provide a rare and instructive view of the self-images and attitudes of a cross-section of middle-class white women in the twentieth-century South.

A Different Kind of Suffragist

Jessie Daniel Ames was born in East Texas in 1883, the daughter of a railroad station master and a dedicated Methodist church worker.[2] After a lonely childhood, dominated by a father who, she believed, preferred her older sister to herself, Jessie graduated from a private coeducational college and married an army surgeon named Roger Post Ames. Her marriage was an unhappy one, marked by frequent separations and financial and family conflicts. In 1914 Roger died, leaving Jessie, at 31, a widow with three children to support.

In the years after her husband's death, Ames began her journey out of obscurity and into a new role as a social reformer. Operating a local telephone company with her widowed mother, she gained the autonomy and self-confidence that made possible her emergence as an advocate of women's rights. As an organizer and treasurer of the Texas Equal Suffrage Association, she helped make Texas the first state in the South to ratify the Nineteenth Amendment; in the following decade, she worked indefatigably to mobilize female support for the goals of the social-justice wing of southern progressivism. Unlike most suffragists, however, Jessie Daniel Ames also began, in the early twenties, to sense the limitations of a women's movement for whites only. As the Ku Klux Klan rose to power in the state, she saw her efforts at progressive reform undercut by racism and by her constituency's refusal to recognize the plight of women doubly oppressed by sex and race. Consequently, she joined the Woman's Committee of the Texas Commission on Interracial Cooperation and turned to the task of forging a bond of common womanhood across the color line.

The Atlanta-based Commission on Interracial Cooperation (CIC) had been formed in response to the race riots that erupted in the wake of World War I; seeking to accommodate black grievances within a segregated caste system, the commission had become the major biracial reform organization in the South. At first, however, women had been excluded from the group. Bringing "white women and colored men into interrela-

---

[2] The following essay is drawn from a larger study of Jessie Daniel Ames and the movement she led. Jacquelyn Dowd Hall, *Revolt Against Chivalry: Jessie Daniel Ames and the Women's Campaign Against Chivalry*, forthcoming from Columbia University Press. See also the author's unpublished Ph.D. dissertation of the same title, Columbia University, 1974.

tionships that symbolize equality," its founders feared, would open a
Pandora's box of sexual fears and taboos. Delicacy would forbid an open
discussion of lynching, as it was supposedly related to sexual attacks on
white women. Moreover, the social and political attitudes of white women
could not be predicted. Some argued that women were "the Hindenburg
line" in race relations; more conservative and timid than men, they would
remain the last holdouts for the status quo. On the contrary, others maintained that women were emotional and sentimental and would become
"wild-eyed fanatics" on the race question. What women thought and did
in their own sphere mystified the CIC's founders as much as the endlessly
puzzling matter of "What the Negro thinks" and "What the Negro wants."

In fact, southern women had already provided abundant evidence
of their approach to social problems, as Jessie Daniel Ames's own formative years in Texas politics make clear. The predominant channels for
these concerns, however, were not the secular organizations through
which Ames entered public life but the Protestant, and especially the
Methodist, missionary societies that appeared throughout the South in
the 1870s and the Young Women's Christian Associations that spread
slowly into the region after the turn of the century. For most middle-class
southern women, the institutional structure of the church provided a
basis for female solidarity, and evangelical religion created a rationale
for seeking a female alliance across racial lines.

In October 1920, these strands converged in a historic meeting of
black and white southern women in Memphis, Tennessee. Jointly initiated
by the Methodist Woman's Missionary Council and black YWCA members who had come to believe that "the time was ripe [to] go beyond the
YWCA and any other organization and reach a few outstanding white
and Negro women, Christian and with well-balanced judgement and not
afraid," the Memphis Conference marked the beginning of interracial
women's activities in the region.[3] By 1929, however, when Jessie Daniel
Ames moved to Atlanta, Georgia, to assume the position of regional director of the CIC Woman's Committee, the interracial gatherings that were
the major achievement of the group had begun to lose their symbolic
impact; white leaders as well as blacks were searching for a more effective
mode of operation, for more realizable goals. Ames brought to the movement an instrumentalist approach to social issues that set her apart from

[3] Reminiscences of Will W. Alexander, Oral History Research Office, Columbia Uni-
versity; Wilma Dykeman and James Stokely, *Seeds of Southern Change*, University of
Chicago Press, Chicago, 1962, p. 88; "Background" of Memphis Conference, Jessie
Daniel Ames Papers, Southern Historical Collection, University of North Carolina at
Chapel Hill; Continuation Committee Meeting, November 16, 1920, Commission on In-
terracial Cooperation Papers, Trevor Arnett Library, Atlanta University, Atlanta,
Georgia; Mary J. McCrorey to Lugenia Hope, July 6, 1931, Neighborhood Union Papers,
Trevor Arnett Library, Atlanta University.

her more religiously oriented coworkers. Spurred by the rise in racial violence at the onset of the Depression, she channeled the Woman's Committee away from interracialism and into an elaborately organized, single-issue campaign against lynching. In doing so, she linked the language and assumptions of evangelical reform with the pragmatic, issue-oriented style of the secular movement for women's rights. In the 1930s she, and the antilynching organization she founded, served as a vital bridge between a tradition of social feminism and the twentieth-century struggle for black civil rights.

THE FOUNDING OF THE ANTI-LYNCHING ASSOCIATION

On November 1, 1930, 26 white women from 6 southeastern states answered Jessie Daniel Ames's call to a meeting in Atlanta. Will Alexander, director of the Interracial Commission, opened the conference with a review of the history of lynching and of the efforts of the CIC to combat it. Jessie Daniel Ames presented more precise information: in the 204 lynchings of the previous 8 years, she told the assembled women, only 29 percent of the victims were even accused of crimes against white women. This statistical fact would form the cornerstone of the women's antilynching campaign. As the program of the new organization evolved over time, its leaders developed a variety of strategies to combat racial violence and to link it with other issues. But throughout the history of the group, its main purpose would be to hammer home the argument that black men did not provoke lynching by raping white women.

"Convinced by the consideration of facts," Ames reported, the women resolved "no longer to remain silent in the face of this crime done in their name." Constituting themselves the Association of Southern Women for the Prevention of Lynching, they issued a statement to the press, putting themselves "definitely on record as opposed to this crime in every form and under all circumstances." "Public opinion has accepted too easily the claim of lynchers and mobsters that they were acting *solely in the defense of womanhood*," they announced. "Women dare no longer permit the claim to pass unchallenged nor allow themselves to be the cloak behind which those bent upon personal revenge and savagery commit acts of violence and lawlessness." Six days later a similar group of southwestern women meeting in Dallas adopted an antilynching resolution and agreed to join in a regionwide women's movement against vigilante justice.

Both the white and the Afro-American press greeted the founding of the ASWPL with enthusiasm. "The greatest gain of the anti-lynching [fight]," editorialized the Atlanta *World*, "is to be found in the support now being given by the white women of the South." Such a positive evaluation was by no means unjustified. Yet it must be stressed that Jessie Daniel Ames did not organize the first extensive female resistance to mob violence, nor did her campaign exist in the historical vacuum implied by many of the Anti-Lynching Association's contemporary supporters and critics. For decades black women had filled the front ranks of the fight against lynching. They had developed an analysis of the relationship between racial violence and sexual exploitation that the white ASWPL adopted only haltingly and ambiguously. Indeed, years of black struggle against lynching deeply shaped the social and political climate that made the founding of the Anti-Lynching Association possible.

In 1892 a black Memphis woman, Ida B. Wells-Barnett, had initiated a one-woman antilynching crusade; after 1910, the NAACP had expanded Wells's campaign into a multifaceted offensive against mob violence. Twelve years later, the NAACP formed a women's group called the Anti-Lynching Crusaders to mobilize support for the Dyer Anti-Lynching Bill. Led by Mary B. Talbert, President of the National Association of Colored Women, the Crusaders made a concerted though largely futile attempt to bring white women into its ranks. "This is the first time in the history of the colored women that they have turned to their sister white organizations and asked for moral and financial support," Mary Talbert declared, "and as we have never failed you in any cause that has come to US, we do not believe that YOU will fail us now." Talbert sent 1,850 letters to white women known to be sympathetic to social reform. She sought to make contact with the CIC state women's committees in Arkansas, Texas, and Alabama. Approximately 900 white members enrolled, and individual CIC women indicated their support. But the hoped-for response from southern white women never materialized.

By 1930, when the ASWPL was founded, years of black-led publicity and agitation had made inroads on the consciousness of the nation. No aspect of regional life contributed more to the galling image of the benighted South, and during the decade of the twenties, a number of southern journalists began to condemn lynching in general, though most newspapers continued to justify specific instances close at hand. Partly in an effort to undercut the NAACP campaign for federal legislation, southern governors increasingly took steps to prevent lynchings, and southern legislatures passed antilynching laws, which, while virtually never enforced, did indicate a pro-forma disavowal of mob violence upon which the women of the Anti-Lynching Association could draw.

To say that the way had been prepared for the ASWPL, however, is not to deny the importance of its campaign. Even though most southern leaders had ceased to defend the practice with the assurance and virulence of earlier generations, lynching had by no means been extirpated from southern society, and a strong current of public opinion still condoned vigilante action for the crime of rape. Moreover, while Jessie Daniel Ames and her coworkers were not the first to attack the sexual rationalization of lynching, no one could drive home the point with the dramatic force of a group of white southern women. Repeatedly, the black women of the Interracial Commission had emphasized that lynching was carried on for the protection of white women and "that when Southern white women get ready to stop lynching, it will be stopped and not before." The formation of the ASWPL signified an acceptance of this responsibility. The construction of a regionwide women's group to transmit the antilynching message into the rural South and take concrete steps to prevent mob violence would be a feat requiring extraordinary organizational genius, courage, and commitment. At the same time, the willingness of a group of middle-class white women to involve themselves in an issue with such profound psychosocial implications in itself constituted a sign of social change: a rebellion, as Jessie Daniel Ames eloquently put it, against "the crown of chivalry which has been pressed like a crown of thorns on our heads." [4]

The Organization and Its Members

The structure and constituency of the ASWPL were predicated on a tradition of middle-class voluntarism and a belief in the potential power of enfranchised women. As in the suffrage and prohibition movements, Jessie Daniel Ames sought to mobilize an existing network of women's church and civic groups with their own program budgets around an issue consistent with their preoccupations and concerns. From the ranks of these organizations, she hoped to attract leaders, like herself, who had "fought for political freedom" or "younger women . . . educated in the increasing numbers of co-educational schools, [who] did not accept the dictum of the man-made society." These women—whom Ames viewed as strategic elites within the female subculture—would be predisposed against lynching and ideally placed to wage an educational campaign aimed first at southern white women in general and then at the larger society.

The institutional structure Ames designed was quite well suited to these ends. A Central Council of dedicated leaders met annually in Atlanta to set policy and issue resolutions. State councils were charged

4 "History of the Movement" and "Resolutions, Conference of Southern White Women, Atlanta, Georgia, November 1, 1930," ASWPL Papers, Trevor Arnett Library, Atlanta University; ASWPL, *A New Public Opinion on Lynching: A Declaration and a Pledge,* ASWPL, Atlanta, 1941; Atlanta *World,* December 12, 1932; Mary B. Talbert to Mary White Ovington, October 21, 1922; Jessie Daniel Ames to Mary McLeod Bethune, March 9, 1938, ASWPL Papers; Dykeman and Stokely, *Seeds of Southern Change,* p. 143.

with recruiting local supporters by presenting the ASWPL program to women's clubs and missionary societies, outlining concrete steps women could take to prevent lynchings, and asking everyone present to sign pledges indicating their commitment to take those steps. Finally, ASWPL leaders solicited endorsements from every major women's group in the region, and they relied on these organizations to disseminate a steady stream of antilynching literature to their broader membership.

The ASWPL's endorsing organizations included the women's auxiliaries of the major Protestant denominations, national and regional federations of Jewish women, the YWCA, and the business and professional women's clubs. Such endorsements did not necessarily signify a commitment to make an antilynching campaign part of an ongoing organizational program. But the ASWPL's staunchest supporters—church women's groups—not only passed resolutions of support, thus lending their names to ASWPL publicity, but also actively incorporated the issue of racial violence into educational materials used by a network of women's missionary societies that reached into the most remote of rural counties.

Predictably, the 250,000-member Methodist Woman's Missionary Council served as the Anti-Lynching Association's most important endorsing group. In the name of foreign missions, Methodist women had created the first regionwide women's organization in the South. After the turn of the century they had begun to graft onto the evangelical idiom the language of the social gospel and to use both to expand women's roles in the church and the social order. Their pioneering work in the settlement house movement and their successful struggle for laity rights had spawned an articulate and highly visible leadership. Moreover, organizational autonomy, together with traditional cultural assumptions that channeled feminine assertiveness and ambition into benevolent action, encouraged these leaders to take a stance toward social issues that was often in advance of that of the general church. At the outset of the ASWPL effort, Woman's Missionary Council officers notified conference presidents to give all the assistance in their power to Jessie Daniel Ames's organizational work in the states; under their direction, the lynching issue was routinely incorporated into the programs of local missionary societies throughout the region. By 1934, Bertha Payne Newell, superintendent of the Methodist Bureau of Christian Social Relations and secretary of the ASWPL, could report that "thousands and thousands of women all over the South" had signed the ASWPL antilynching pledge presented to them in Methodist zone, district, and conference meetings. In addition, over half the association's numerous pamphlets, posters, and flyers were distributed throughout this Methodist network.

By working through these local women and pre-existing organizations, the ASWPL hoped to avoid the stigma of outside interference. "With a knowledge of the psychology of State's rights and to what extent it is used as an alibi," Jessie Daniel Ames explained, the ASWPL "has developed a method of procedure which makes it possible for us at head-quarters to encourage State women to act when their particular State [or county unit] is involved." Moreover, by garnering support in this way, the Anti-Lynching Association enlisted a strategic constituency: small-town church women, schooled for decades in running their own affairs within women's clubs and missionary societies, familiar with the social gospel, and sensitized by the prohibition and suffrage movements to issues of law enforcement and social order.[5]

The social origins of the women who became official members of the ASWPL's central or state councils reflected the rise of an urban middle class convinced that capitalist development in the region de-manded the orderly administration of the law. Most of those who at-tended the founding meetings in 1930 and returned to set state organiza-tions in motion lived in large population centers. In a survey of 122 active members, 49 percent came from metropolitan areas of over 100,000 persons; a total of 72 percent lived in cities of over 25,000. The organi-zation was headquartered in Atlanta, the region's major transportation and commercial center and the capital of an aggressive new middle-class spirit. Nashville, boasting of the largest proportion of college students of any city in the country and vying for the position of southern financial center, supplied the ASWPL with its coterie of strong Methodist church leaders.

It would, however, be a mistake to exaggerate the modernity of ASWPL members. Almost all of those whose ages are known were born before the turn of the century; their average age was 48 in 1930, and a small but significant group was born in the 1860s. Thus many of these dwellers in newly expanding cities probably shared with Jessie Daniel Ames origins in the countryside. Such women came of age as sexual tensions and racial violence wracked the region; their political con-sciousness was shaped by the search for order of the Progressive era. Their deepest premises were informed by moral conviction rather than cosmo politan rationalism, and their concern with the dynamics of chivalry and the consequences of interracial sex betrayed their roots in the Victorian past.

Moreover, a number of active leaders did in fact live in rural counties. Thirteen of these 122 women were from towns of less than 2,500; 21 from towns with a population between 2,500 and 25,000. In

---

[5] Jessie Daniel Ames, *Toward Lynchless America*, ASWPL, Atlanta, December 1940, p. 60; *Twenty-Third Annual Report, Woman's Missionary Council, Methodist Episcopal Church, South, 1933*, Publishing House of the Methodist Episcopal Church, South, Nashville, 1933; Jessie Daniel Ames to Margaret Prescott Montague, December 16, 1931, ASWPL Papers.

Mississippi, for example, the most rural of southern states, ASWPL leadership was drawn almost exclusively from small communities. Bessie Alford, chairman of the Mississippi council throughout the life of the organization, lived in McComb, population 10,000. Montie B. Greer, who, as chairwoman of Christian Social Relations for the Mississippi Conference of the Southern Methodist Church, played a major role in the antilynching movement in the state, resided in the tiny town of Potts Camp. In addition, the ASWPL's broader constituency—the 43,000 individuals who eventually signed the antilynching pledge—consisted mainly of women in small towns, recruited through the Protestant women's missionary societies. Thus, even though the ASWPL's leaders tended to be members of an urban bourgeoisie, they evinced a steady commitment to organize at the grass-roots level, where lynching actually took place, rather than limiting themselves to disavowals of mob violence from the safety of the cities.

The high incidence of city and town dwellers among the association's leaders is mirrored in educational and occupational backgrounds that set them apart from southern women in general. An unusually high percentage worked outside the home for at least some portion of their adult lives. Of the 122 women surveyed, almost one-half were gainfully employed, all of these in clerical or professional positions. Of these 61 employed women, 13 were salaried church executives; others were social workers, journalists, college instructors, librarians, or businesswomen; one was a state legislator, two were lawyers, one a Quaker minister. A smaller proportion were clerks, bank tellers, or WPA employees. Of the 53 women whose educational background is known, all had attended a college or female academy; of these, 19 had taken graduate courses or attained professional degrees.[6] The ASWPL thus drew its major leaders from a group of women who had already, to some extent, stepped outside the domestic sphere. Like Jessie Daniel Ames, they had been among the first generation of women college graduates in the region, and had acquired the altered self-perceptions associated with economic autonomy.

It should be noted, however, that whether or not they held jobs, most ASWPL members were married women with children; few maintained long-term careers, and doubtless their primary identity lay not in their occupations but in their roles as wives and mothers and as leaders of women's voluntary organizations. Of the 79 husbands whose occupations are known, most were managerial or professional workers. Professional men and politicians made up 42 percent of this group, businessmen 32 percent, and ministers 18 percent. Although their positions ranged

---

[6] In contrast, in 1940, 30.5 percent of the employed women in the South Atlantic region were engaged in white-collar occupations.

from postman, deputy sheriff, pharmacist, and railroad inspector to bishop, governor, and company owner, all were white-collar workers who could supply their wives with a degree of leisure, domestic help, and opportunity for travel. The wives of such men, of course, derived their status in the society at large from that of their husbands. Yet, unless their husbands were very prominent, ASWPL leaders acquired their importance within the association from their own positions within organized women's groups, or, to a lesser extent, from their personal accomplishments, not from their husbands' occupations or activities.

THE CENTRAL IDEAS

Through pamphlets, articles, resolutions, and speeches—what Jessie Daniel Ames termed a "word of mouth" campaign—these ASWPL leaders sought to undermine public approbation of lynching in the white South. The first, and central, argument employed in this effort at public education pivoted on the identity of the southern lady and the notion of southern chivalry. The major justification for lynching held that only the threat of immediate retribution stood between the white women of the "lonely, isolated farmsteads of the South" and the lust of the black rapist. As creatures absolutely inaccessible to the men of the subordinate race, white women served as the most potent symbol of white male supremacy. Thus rape of a white woman was *"The Most Terrible Crime on the Face of This Earth"* for which legal punishment was inadequate and too uncertain. Only ritual murder—arbitrary and exemplary—could adequately assert white caste solidarity against such a loaded form of social deviance.

This "Southern rape complex," as W. J. Cash pointed out, was never based on objective reality. Every study of the crime down to the present has underlined the fact that despite the persistent mythology of black attacks on white women, in fact rape has been an overwhelmingly intraracial event, and the victims of rape have been predominantly black women. Accordingly, a major strategy of antilynching reformers, beginning with Ida B. Wells-Barnett in the 1880s and carried on by the NAACP and the ASWPL, used facts and figures to undermine the sexual rationalization for mob violence.

Yet the fear of rape, like the practice of lynching, was embedded far beyond the reach of factual refutation—in the heart not only of American racism, but of American attitudes toward women as well. Rape and rumors of rape became a kind of acceptable folk pornography in the Bible Belt. As stories spread, the attacker became not just a black man but a ravenous brute, the victim a beautiful, frail, young virgin. The experience and condition of the woman (who could not be put on the witness stand to suffer the "glare and stare of public curiosity") were described in minute and progressively embellished detail: a public fantasy that implies a kind of group participation in the rape of the woman almost as cathartic as the subsequent lynching of the alleged attacker.[7]

The small percentage of lynchings that revolved around charges of sexual assault gripped the southern imagination far out of proportion to their statistical significance. In these scenes, described in the popular press in strikingly conventionalized words and phrases, the themes of masculinity, rage, and sexual envy were woven into a ritual of death and desire. The story such rituals told about the place of white women in southern society was subtle, contradictory, and demeaning. The frail victim, leaning on the arms of her male relatives, might be brought to the scene of the crime, there to identify her assailant and perhaps to witness his execution. Humiliation mingled with heightened worth, as she played for a moment the role of the Fair Maiden violated and avenged. For this privilege—if the alleged assault had in fact taken place—she might pay with physical and psychological suffering in the extreme. In any case, she would pay with a lifetime of subjugation to the men gathered in her behalf.

The lynch mob in pursuit of the black rapist thus represented the trade-off implicit in the code of chivalry, for the right of the southern lady to protection presupposed her obligation to obey. The role of the lady demanded chastity, frailty, vulnerability. "A lady," noted one social psychologist, "is always in a state of becoming: one acts like a lady, one attempts to be a lady, but one never *is* a lady." Internalized by the individual, this ideal regulated behavior and restricted interaction with the world. If a woman passed the tests of ladyhood, she could tap into the reservoir of protectiveness and shelter known as southern chivalry. Women unable or unwilling to comply with such normative demands forfeited the claim to personal security. Together, the practice of ladyhood and the etiquette of chivalry functioned as highly effective strategies of control over women's behavior as well as powerful safeguards of caste restrictions.[8]

Ironically, the symbolism of southern womanhood may have created an objective basis for the fear of black attacks on white women. "When men sow the wind," warned the abolitionist Frederick Douglass in 1892,

---

[7] Report of the Committee on Methods, January 10–11, 1938; Mrs. E. S. Cook to Frederick Sullens, Editor, Jackson *Daily News,* May 25, 1937, ASWPL Papers; Conyers (Ga.) *Times,* Nov. 27, 1931, quoted in Jessie Daniel Ames, "The Lynchers' View on Lynching," typescript of speech, 1937, Ames Papers; W. J. Cash, *The Mind of the South,* Vintage Books, New York, 1941, p. 117.

[8] Greer Litton Fox, " 'Nice Girl': Social Control of Women Through a Value Construct," *Signs,* 2 (Summer 1977), 805–817.

"they will reap the whirlwind." Twentieth-century writers like Eldridge Cleaver, Calvin Hernton, LeRoi Jones, and Frantz Fanon asserted that the assault of a white woman, the taking of the forbidden fruit, could indeed be seen as an act of political retribution. Whether or not George Hughes—victim of the Sherman, Texas, lynching of 1930—actually explained his motives for attacking his employer's wife in the words attributed to him, the white community's ready belief that he acted in protest against white racism reveals a significant and deeply felt tension in southern society.

Neither Jessie Daniel Ames nor the women she led rejected the norms of ladyhood outright; indeed, the antilynching campaign relied for its impact precisely on its members' exemplification of this ideal. Nevertheless, ASWPL members sought to undermine the rationalizations for lynching by dissociating the image of the lady from its connotations of female vulnerability and retaliatory violence. With even fewer reservations, they attacked the paternalism of chivalry. The claim that lynching was necessary as a protection of white women, they argued, served to mask the self-interest and sadism out of which mob violence really sprang. The mythology of lynching cast white women in the humiliating position of sexual objects—ever threatened by black lust, ever in need of rescue by their white protectors. Asserting their identity as autonomous citizens, secure in their own rectitude and their confidence in the established agents of law enforcement, the women of the ASWPL dramatically refused to play the role assigned to them.

Response to the ASWPL campaign indicated the effectiveness of this persistent reiteration of a simple, dramatic motif. To be sure, here and there the women's efforts were greeted with ridicule. A newspaper in a small town in Georgia, for example, published an editorial characterizing the delegates to the annual meeting of 1931 as "all fat and forty. . . . We cannot imagine an association of twenty prize fighters and wrestlers more independent or able to protect themselves than the group picture indicates these women to be. But they forget that all women are not endowed with such a formidable line and, if attacked, would be helpless." Even such condescension, however, indicated that the ASWPL's message had hit home, and most southern papers that covered the campaign at all conveyed to their readers a favorable interpretation of its meaning. The formation of the ASWPL, editorialized the Hattiesburg *American,* indicated that white women would no longer allow the "perpetrators of such atrocities to hide behind their skirts." Women have now, noted the Macon *Evening News,* "announced to their red-handed 'protectors' that they want no more of this rope-and-faggot courtesy." Nor was the significance of this argument lost on later commentators. Looking back from the vantage point of 1949, Lillian Smith, an eloquent critic of the racial and sexual status quo, placed herself in a tradition begun by the ASWPL. By 1930, she wrote, white women had ceased to believe the lies of men who

went on with their race-economic exploitation, protecting themselves behind rusty shields of as phony a moral cause as the Anglo-Saxon world has ever witnessed. . . . The lady insurrectionists gathered together in one of our southern cities. . . . They said calmly that they were not afraid of being raped; as for their sacredness, they would take care of it themselves; they did not need the chivalry of lynching to protect them and did not want it.

It was, Smith concluded, "a truly subversive affair." [9]

The ASWPL's second argument, like its first, reflected the special concerns of a feminine constituency. It suggested that lynching "brings contempt upon America as the only country where such crimes occur, discredits our civilization and discounts the Christian religion around the globe." To women schooled in the idiom of evangelicalism, no appeal could strike a surer chord; in order to reach a larger audience, however, this argument shaded into a secular defense of United States interests abroad. Lists of lynchings, one ASWPL pamphlet read, are published throughout the Orient and in Africa and "presented as a reason why [foreign peoples] should not be deceived by American missionaries and exploited by American business men." By the mid-thirties the contention that lynching gave Christianity a bad name included a warning that the practice created "a fertile field for . . . communistic doctrines subversive of American democracy at home."

A third claim appearing from the beginning in ASWPL literature insisted that lynching discredited legal processes and undermined respect for officers of the law. Thus, instead of providing protection against black aggression, it actually lessened the ability of the established authorities to maintain social control. According to the original ASWPL anti-lynching resolution, lynching was "a menace to private and public safety, and a deadly blow at our most sacred institutions. Instead of deterring irresponsible and criminal classes from further crime, as it is argued, lynching tends inevitably to destroy all respect for law and order."

Designed to appeal to the interests of women in domestic peace and of the middle class in orderly administration and internalized self-discipline, this analysis could be dangerously double-edged, for it reinforced

[9] Frederick Douglass, "Lynch Law in the South," *North American Review,* 155 (July 1892), 22; Dykeman and Stokely, *Seeds of Southern Change,* p. 148; Hattiesburg *American,* November 11 and January 22, 1931; Macon *Evening News,* December 4, 1930; Lillian Smith, *Killers of the Dream,* 2nd. ed., Anchor Books, Garden City, N.Y., 1963, pp. 126–127.

the racial attitudes that Ames and other ASWPL leaders, in their more insightful moments, saw as the deeper causes of lynching. Usually implicitly, but sometimes openly, the demand for law enforcement promised that blacks could be kept in their place more efficiently, more permanently, and with less social disorganization by a legal system firmly under the control of whites than by the extralegal practice of lynching. As one black critic pointed out: "Your argument that 'the courts will convict Negroes' and that therefore Negroes need not be lynched, is a cold-blooded proposal to regularize lynching under legal forms." [10]

A New Dilemma

Almost immediately after the women's campaign began, the infamous Scottsboro case pushed the issue of "legal lynching" into the forefront of the struggle for black rights and challenged the adequacy of the ASWPL's law-and-order argument. In March 1931, four months after the association's founding, nine young blacks hopped a boxcar at Stevenson, Alabama. A group of white youths, including two women, Ruby Bates and Victoria Price, were also aboard the train. A fight ensued and when the train arrived in Paint Rock, the nine blacks found themselves charged with rape. Although Ruby Bates repudiated her claim that the two women had been sexually assaulted, all of the accused were convicted in a hasty trial at Scottsboro, the county seat, and all but the youngest were sentenced to the electric chair.

The Scottsboro case posed a new dilemma for antilynching reformers, for it focused worldwide attention on the court system and demanded that white southern liberals take a stand on more fundamental questions than whether legal formalities had been observed. "Just as we adjust our thinking and action to one line of cooperation and justice something new comes up," wrote one Alabama ASWPL member. As soon as she heard of the arrest of the Scottsboro boys, the Alabama ASWPL chairman, Mary McCoy, instructed a supporter in Scottsboro to "quiet intemperate talk" and prevent a lynching. But when the defendants had been convicted and the International Labor Defense (ILD) entered an appeal in the case, McCoy was reluctant to attempt any further action that might "connect the Interracial Movement with Communism." None of the Alabama women Jessie Daniel Ames contacted believed that the Scottsboro defendants deserved to die, but the only solution they could offer was a quiet appeal to the governor or an effort to have the sentences

[10] Atlanta *Constitution*, November 22, 1931; ASWPL, *New Public Opinion;* "Suggested Points in Presenting the Purpose of the Association of Southern Women for the Prevention of Lynching," n.d.; "Resolutions," ASWPL Papers; D. Amis to George Fort Milton, November 13, 1931, CIC Papers.

commuted to life imprisonment. Nor were they willing to try even these measures, believing that "if any action was taken by them to protest the verdict that it would cut the ground from under their feet in their campaign to prevent lynching."

Like Will Alexander and other southern interracialists, Ames came to believe that the Scottsboro case had assumed spectacular proportions primarily because of the intervention of the radical ILD. What concerned her most, however, was that Scottsboro had given lynchers a new rationalization for their crimes. The ASWPL, she argued, was accomplishing one of its major goals: Southern apologists were becoming less willing to "lay themselves open to ridicule" by defending mob violence on the grounds of gallantry or by maintaining that white supremacy could be preserved only by "force, coercion, and lynching." But now the Scottsboro case provided a new justification: Loopholes in the law and clever radical lawyers made legal procedures against blacks too slow and uncertain. Lynching, a law enforcement club explained to Jessie Daniel Ames, "is a warning to the Courts from the public" that black defendants are no longer being punished quickly and harshly enough under the law.

However much she might deplore the use of the Scottsboro case by the left on the one hand and by the defenders of lynching on the other, Jessie Daniel Ames perceived that the questions raised by this cause célèbre could not be damped. Indeed, she herself took advantage of the opportunity it offered to "deepen the thinking" of the women of the ASWPL. "Picture the courthouse under guard by several thousand men down from the hills to join the mob to see that justice is done," she admonished.

The jury sitting within the court room hearing the evidence but listening to the noise of the rioters, trying to render a "fair and impartial" verdict guaranteed by the Constitution to every American citizen regardless of race, yet sensing the restive stirring of the human mass gone mad, knowing that the shouts of gratified passion greeting each sentence of death will be turned into snarls of rage against them if they interpret the evidence contrary to the verdict of the mob.

Such "legal lynchings," she concluded, rocked the foundations of American democracy.

Throughout the period, the ASWPL probed the implications of the court's treatment of blacks. "Which is Better—A Lynching or the Prostitution of the Courts and a Prevented Lynching?" became a recurring discussion topic at ASWPL meetings. Beneath the symptom of lynching, Jessie Daniel Ames argued, lay the disease of a legal system that punished blacks with disproportionate severity but allowed mob members to escape unscathed. Far from slipping through legal loopholes, blacks uniformly received perfunctory trials and maximum sentences. The public's low estimate of the black man's worth, she pointed out in a report to ASWPL members, "the ready assumption of his guilt, his ignorance of court procedures, his lack of money and friends and political influence, all make his arrest and conviction easier than that of a white man."

By the late thirties most participants in ASWPL meetings seem to have agreed that the legal system was weighted against blacks. But rather than act on this realization, ASWPL leaders continued to reassure whites that legal processes could be as "swift and sure" as lynch mobs and gave tacit support to critics of the Scottsboro defense by campaigning for legal reforms to ensure speedy trials. An executive committee meeting in 1936 condemned legal lynchings vigorously but finally concluded that such corruption of the courts was a lesser "danger to social institutions" than mob violence.[11]

THE ISSUE OF RAPE

Just as the Scottsboro case raised the question of legal justice in a manner the ASWPL could not ignore, so it challenged the organization to confront the issues of rape and interracial sex. In the beginning, ASWPL discussions revealed a distressing ambivalence about what participants could bring themselves to refer to only as "the unspeakable crime." While the women gathered for the founding meeting were united in their opposition to extralegal violence, they did not necessarily assume that white women had nothing to fear from sexual assault. Ames tried to close the subject with statistical proof that only a small proportion of lynch victims were accused of rape. But however conscientiously she might steer the discussion toward what she regarded as the main topic— "lynching as a lawless act"—other participants kept turning to the subject of rape itself. "The white women are afraid," asserted Mary McCoy of Alabama. "What program should be carried on by Negro women to educate their people?" asked Ames. Teach their sons "that rape is a worse crime than murder," answered an ASWPL member. "Doing away with rape would do away with lynching."

Such preoccupations were aired only in private discussions, never

11 Mrs. J. F. Hooper to Jessie Daniel Ames, April 16, 1931; Mary M. McCoy to Jessie Daniel Ames, April 21, 1931; Jessie Daniel Ames to Louise Young, May 22, 1931; Jessie Daniel Ames, "Editorial Treatment of Lynching," *Public Opinion Quarterly*, 2 (January 1938), 77–84; Law Enforcement Club to Jessie Daniel Ames, November 30, 1933, ASWPL Papers; Jessie Daniel Ames, *Whither Leads the Mob?* Commission on Interracial Cooperation, Atlanta, 1932; Jessie Daniel Ames, *The Changing Character of Lynching,* Commission on Interracial Cooperation, Atlanta, 1942, pp. 12–14; ASWPL Semi-Annual Report, January–June 1936, ASWPL Papers.

in public pronouncements, and after the first few years they were seldom voiced at all. Nevertheless, the fact remained that many of the women whom the ASWPL education campaign hoped to reach had thoroughly internalized the racial and sexual mythology surrounding them. "Whether their own minds perceive danger where none exists," commented Jessie Daniel Ames, "or whether the fears have been put in their minds by men's fears," the terror of sexual assault was deeply embedded in the feminine psyche. "Someday someone is going to be bold enough to write fully and completely about the Southern white women through slavery up to the present," she concluded, "but that day is far off." Meanwhile she held to her task of convincing women as well as men that the way to prevent the crime of rape did not lie in extralegal violence.

The Scottsboro case, however, provided Ames with another dilemma, for it posed the disturbing possibility that behind many accusations of rape might lie clandestine interracial affairs. The virtue of Ruby Bates and Victoria Price quickly became a central issue in the controversy. Convinced by the efforts of the defense and by her own investigations that the Scottsboro women were "common prostitutes," Jessie Daniel Ames began delving beneath the surface of lynchings in which a white woman was involved. As she did so she was "shocked" to find that white women did indeed voluntarily "cohabit with Negro men." By the end of the decade, most ASWPL leaders were thoroughly disabused of the notion that, as one Mississippi editor claimed, there had never been a southern white woman so totally depraved as to "bestow her favors on a black man."

In contrast to its private discussions, the organization's literature usually shied away from a direct confrontation with this issue. For one thing, as the Scottsboro defense had learned, an attack on the virtue of white southern womanhood could be extremely unpopular. The jury did not even discuss, let alone consider, Ruby Bates's testimony denying her earlier story. Victoria Price "might be a fallen woman," commented a spectator, "but by God she is a white woman." In his charge to the jury, Judge William W. Callahan remarked that when a white woman had intercourse with a black man, the presumption must be that she had been raped. At a district meeting of the Methodist Women's Missionary Society in Scottsboro, reported an ASWPL supporter, "All were agreed that the punishment fitted the crime, since the assailants were *black*. No white women would be safe if such crimes were not punishable by death. Regardless of the status of the girls justice must be meted out and quickly, since they were *white* girls." [12]

[12] "Minutes, Anti-Lynching Conference of Southern White Women, Atlanta, Georgia, November 1, 1930," Ames Papers; "Report of Activities of 1933"; Ames, "Lynchers' View on Lynching"; Minutes, ASWPL Annual Meeting, January 13, 1936, ASWPL

Certainly the ASWPL's admission that intercourse between white women and black men was not prima facie evidence of rape was, in the context of the times, an important step. But the reaction of some members to this insight typified the more repressive impulses of white interracialism. Jessie Daniel Ames, for example, wrote to ASWPL members in Alabama that "we women must consider . . . some kind of action against loose white women who do cohabit with Negroes." And in 1935, South Carolina ASWPL chairman, Kate Davis, indicated just what such action might entail. A lynching, she reported, had been narrowly averted when a white woman in Orangeburg gave birth to a black man's child. The grand jury considering the case suggested that the city council adopt a segregation ordinance to prevent the "racial intermingling" that gave rise to such affairs, and Davis played an important role in seeing that the law was finally enacted. Five years later, she was still working to enforce and extend housing segregation in South Carolina.

The ASWPL's urge to control sexual mores also led, more positively, to a process of internal education about the exploitation of black women. In the winter of 1931, Jessie Daniel Ames organized a meeting with black women leaders for what she hoped would be a "free and frank" discussion of their mutual grievances against masculine behavior. The women, she felt, should gather in closed session with no men present "because there are some vices of Southern life which contribute subtly to [lynching] that we want to face by ourselves, and we Southern white women still have a feeling that many things we know we should not know. Consequently, when there are . . . men present we feign ignorant [sic] because of our traditional training." The black leader Nannie Burroughs agreed: "All meetings with white and colored women on this question should be held behind closed doors and men should not be admitted."

Ames opened the discussion with the question, "Have slavery and reconstruction in the South produced a *Double Standard of Ethical and Moral Conduct* based upon race? If so, does this *Double Standard* contribute to the phenomenon of lynching in the South?" The conversation that followed touched on the ways in which legal, political, and economic discrimination against blacks created a climate of opinion conducive to violence. But the group's most impassioned exchanges focused on the status of women. White male attitudes, they concluded, originated in a slave system in which black women "did not belong to themselves but were in effect the property of white men." To rationalize sexual exploitation, the myth arose that "Negro women invited and preferred promiscuous relationships with white men. . . . Negro women were looked

Papers; John Dollard, *Caste and Class in a Southern Town,* 3rd. ed., Anchor Books, Garden City, N.Y., 1957, pp. 169–170; Jackson *Daily News,* Feb. [n.d.], 1931, ASWPL Papers; Dan T. Carter, *Scottsboro: An American Tragedy,* Louisiana University Press, Baton Rouge, 1969, p. 36; Daisy T. Morris to Jessie Daniel Ames, April 27, 1931, ASWPL Papers.

upon as degraded creatures, quite without instincts of personal decency and self-respect. As a corollary to this conception of Negro women in terms of animal wantonness, white public opinion conceived all white women in terms of angelic purity." This double standard had resulted in a society that "considers an assault by a white man as a moral lapse upon his part, better ignored and forgotten, while an assault by a Negro against a white woman is a hideous crime punishable with death by law or lynching."

Like legal justice, opposition to the sexual exploitation of black women never surfaced as a major argument in the ASWPL campaign. Confronting this problem, Jessie Daniel Ames felt, "is logically the next step in our whole program." She urged ASWPL members to encourage respect for black women by personal example and to build community institutions providing "moral and spiritual safeguards for adolescent girls." "The relationship of the Negro woman to the white woman here in the South," she commented, "is so very close, and such immense power rests in the hands of the white women to establish the status of the Negro woman that I have taken every opportunity which has come my way to open the minds of the southern white women in regard to their . . . responsibility in this matter." [13] Nevertheless, for the most part, the issue of rape remained a latent theme rather than an integral part of the antilynching campaign.

THE ROOTS OF LYNCHING

The ASWPL's final argument attempted to grapple with the class nature of lynching and with the relation of racial violence to the operations of the plantation economy. Lynching occurred most often, a typical ASWPL analysis ran, in sparsely populated rural counties during the summer months; it was brought on by idleness, pent-up emotions awakened by revivals and "competition between lower class whites and blacks." Blacks guilty of raping white women were "illiterate and feeble-minded" and thus themselves victims of society. Lynchers were often "mentally defective" unskilled laborers. Lynching was, then, a manifestation of social pathology, a "reversion to barbarism" by the deprived poor whites of the countryside. And Ames sought to convince her constituency that "fairer treatment, better schools . . . certain human considerations will do more [to preserve racial peace] than a lynching." By placing blame on the

---

[13] Jessie Daniel Ames to Mrs. W. J. Adams, May 1, 1931; Mrs. George E. Davis to Jessie Daniel Ames, May 11, 1935; Jessie Daniel Ames to Nannie Burroughs, October 24, 1931; Burroughs to Ames, October 30, 1931, ASWPL Papers; "Appendix F, Digest of Discussion," n.d. [Nov. 20, 1931], Ames Papers; Jessie Daniel Ames to Jane Cornell, July 16, 1935, ASWPL Papers; Jessie Daniel Ames to Charlotte Hawkins Brown, March 20, 1930, CIC Papers.

rural poor, this interpretation of racial violence could absolve middle-class whites of responsibility. But it also enabled the ASWPL to link the anti-lynching campaign with an issue increasingly in the spotlight of national attention: the plight of the southern tenant farmer. New Deal agencies, Jessie Daniel Ames emphasized, were making an important contribution to the fight against lynching by giving "debt-ridden, bankrupt, and poverty-depressed families of both races . . . a new lease on life." Most important, as ASWPL women inquired more closely into the economic causes of racial violence, they began to stress not the racism of poor whites but the roots of lynching in white supremacy itself.

This focus on the deeper implications of lynching increased through the decade of the thirties as mob murders gave way to new, less spectacular forms of violence against blacks. By 1933, ASWPL leaders were discussing the "changing character of lynching," and Ames began to suggest that lynchings were being carried out with greater frequency by small groups of upper-class men acting with quiet premeditation. In fact, she claimed, "prominent people," especially in deep South plantation areas, engineered over 50 percent of the lynchings. Moreover, whether ruling elites actually participated or not, ASWPL literature pointed out, lynching survived only because it was condoned by the whole white community. "What group benefits most by the cheap and subservient labor guaranteed by a system of white supremacy and enforced in the final analysis by lynching?" Ames asked participants in an ASWPL annual meeting. "We ourselves profit most by cheap labor," she replied.

At the annual meeting of 1934, the ASWPL adopted a resolution that Ames regarded as a landmark in the development of ASWPL thought:

We declare as our deliberate conclusion that the crime of lynching is a logical result in every community that pursues the policy of humiliation and degradation of a part of its citizenship because of accident of birth; that exploits and intimidates the weaker element . . . for economic gain; that refuses equal educational opportunity to one portion of its children; that segregates arbitrarily a whole race in unsanitary, ugly sections; . . . and finally that denies a voice in the control of government to any fit and proper citizen because of race.

"The women," Jessie Daniel Ames reported proudly, "traced lynching directly to its roots in white supremacy."

Conclusion

The message of the women's antilynching campaign reached its widest audience just as the ASWPL's viability as an organization was coming to an end. In 1939, for example, a *Reader's Digest* condensation of an article entitled "Ladies and Lynchings," written by Texas journalist Lewis T. Nordyke, was featured in newspapers across the country. The ASWPL had evolved from a small band of church women pledged to "stand under fire" to a socially acceptable expression of an emerging consensus. At first, Jessie Daniel Ames told an ASWPL gathering, they had been called "sob sisters" and worse; now they had become thoroughly respectable.

At the same time, the accomplishment of the ASWPL's goals seemed almost in sight. In 1930, lynch mobs had claimed 22 victims; two years later the number climbed to 28. But since 1933, mob violence had steadily declined. In May 1940, Ames released to the press a statement that, for the first time in her career, the South could boast of a "lynchless year." Ames harbored no illusions that the decline of lynching signaled the end of covert racial violence. But by the end of the decade, she was convinced that community-sanctioned ritual murders were becoming a thing of the past. Most important, she maintained that lynching, when it did occur, had ceased to be justified as a necessity for the protection of white women. In 1942, believing that the purpose of the women's campaign had been fulfilled, she allowed the Association of Southern Women for the Prevention of Lynching to pass quietly from the scene.[14]

Writing about the ASWPL six years after its dissolution, Lillian Smith commented that few of these antilynching reformers "had disciplined intellects or giant imaginations and probably no one of them grasped the full implications of this sex-race-religion-economics tangle." Indeed, none of the leaders of the women's campaign against lynching, including Jessie Daniel Ames, was an original thinker, and their attitudes toward social questions ranged across a broad political spectrum. The lowest common denominator of their crusade was an impulse toward social order, and many of the women whose names appear on ASWPL membership lists probably shared the white supremacist views of their contemporaries. Nevertheless, the ASWPL provided a forum in which women drawn from the entire range of middle-class women's organizations in the region confronted issues whose implications went far beyond the substitution of legal for extralegal forms of social control. In ASWPL discussions, black and white women explored together their position in southern society, and Jessie Daniel Ames took every opportunity to use the prism of lynching for exploring sexual as well as racial oppression.

Many of the arguments employed in the ASWPL educational campaign could also be found in the research of sociologists and of the

14 "The Ladies and the Lynchers," *Reader's Digest*, 35 (November 1939), 110–113; Jessie Daniel Ames, *Southern Women Look at Lynching*, Association of Southern Women for the Prevention of Lynching, Atlanta, 1937; Minutes, ASWPL, Annual Meeting, January 26–27, 1939, ASWPL Papers.

NAACP. But the ASWPL conveyed this information to men and women who would be unlikely to read such scholarly works and who viewed the northern-based black protest group as a threat to their most keenly felt values. Association literature simplified and reiterated the claims of other antilynching reformers and translated social research into palatable and comprehensible forms. Most significantly, it shaped its rhetoric in accord with specifically feminine interests and assumptions. Through the decade of the thirties, the leaders of the women's campaign against lynching succeeded in disseminating their central message—if not their more complex ideas—to an ever widening audience in the white South.

The women of the Anti-Lynching Association had opened their educational campaign with three primary arguments: Lynching, they maintained, far from offering white women an indispensable shield against sexual assault, in fact made them pawns in a deadly masculine conflict and hedged them about with an exaggerated myth of female vulnerability and dependence. Also, mob violence crippled the missionary efforts of evangelical church women, undermined the political and economic interests of the United States abroad, and provided propaganda for radical movements in the black community at home. Finally, lynching discredited legal authorities and undermined social order.

As ASWPL women went into local communities where mob violence had recently erupted and pursued a course of internal education that exposed them to the growing literature of regional self-criticism and the thinking of black scholars and activists, their ideas and arguments evolved. Lynching, they came to see, was rooted in the deprivation of the black and white rural poor, and beyond that, in the whole system of white supremacy. Middle- and upper-class southerners like themselves benefited from the economic exploitation it enforced and were directly or indirectly responsible for its persistence. While the infamous bloodthirsty mob itself might be restrained, the threat of violence and coercion would continue as long as the caste system remained unaltered.

For the women who participated in it, the antilynching campaign offered what Jessie Daniel Ames called a journey "along a disillusioning road of hard reality." [15] At the same time, it represented a step toward emancipation from the prison of sexual stereotypes and from the confining role of the southern lady. Like earlier feminine reform efforts, the crusade against lynching was conducted within the framework of women's

[15] Minutes, ASWPL Meeting, November 19, 1932, Ames Papers; "Report," Jessie Daniel Ames, Executive Director, January 10, 1935, ASWPL Papers; Ames, *Changing Character*, p. 16; Minutes, ASWPL Annual Meeting, January 13–14, 1936, ASWPL Papers; Norfolk (Va.) *Journal and Guide*, January 20, 1934; Jessie Daniel Ames to Miss Doris Loraine, March 5, 1935, ASWPL Papers; Smith, *Killers of the Dream*, p. 128; Ames, *Southern Women Look at Lynching*.

traditional religious and domestic concerns. But the antilynching movement served as a declaration of independence and a search for social
leverage as well. ASWPL women debunked the folklore of black sexual
aggressiveness, seeking to free themselves and others from the fear of
assault that circumscribed their physical and psychic autonomy. By
curbing interracial sex, they hoped to impose their own standards of
domestic morality on the larger society. They asserted the values of the
middle class against the corrupt mores of an agricultural elite by ex-
posing the genesis of lynching in the self-interest of plantation owners.
In the context of a period and a region profoundly inhospitable to
feminist protest, they articulated and acted upon a sense of group
identity, registering a significant, if muted protest against the cultural
shibboleths of their time. Through all these endeavors, ASWPL members
held proudly to the image of the southern lady, while at the same time
seeking to remake that image according to their own definition of
responsible womanhood. In this sense, Jessie Daniel Ames led a revolt
against chivalry that was part of a long process of both sexual and racial
emancipation.

Documents

Newspaper Report of a Lynching, 1915

LYNCHING OF _____, BLACK FIEND,
RAPIST AND MURDERER OF THREE
INNOCENT LITTLE CHILDREN

————, confessed rapist and murderer, paid the price of his crime at the stake
on the public square shortly after midnight this morning.*

Five thousand people witnessed the execution of the coal black fiend whose
three dead victims lie in a local morgue while two others linger at the gates
of death.

From 5 o'clock until midnight the streets adjacent to the justice court
were filled with people—not a mob, but a judicial body of good citizens determined that swift and terrible justice should be rendered once the guilty man
was found.

The negro, ————, was brought to the city after an exciting effort on the
part of the officers to get him to the county jail at Belton. Three hundred people
accompanied the officers from the Little River bottoms to Temple.

A few of the more impetuous members of the crowd were for immediate

* Reprinted from the Williamson County *Sun*, Georgetown, Texas, August 5, 1915,
with permission.

action, but cooler counsel prevailed and the time was given to thoroughly investigate all the evidence at hand. From time to time reports were made to the waiting thousands by the officers and the cooler headed citizens, and more time was asked, and in every case granted.

At 11 o'clock last night the officers and citizens conducting the investigation asked for one hour more and stated that of the three negroes in custody one was assuredly guilty.

At 11:55 peace officers began to mass in the stairway leading to the justice court room on the second floor of the Wilkerson building, there and then to make their last desperate stand as the hour of midnight approached.

On the stroke of twelve, determined citizens moved up the stairway to take justice into their own hands.

Gallant as it was, the resistance of Sheriff Smith and his officers could not prevail against the thousands who were convinced that there could be no doubt of the guilt of the negro. The evidence was conclusive: the crowd was convinced.

The guilty negro was found in the inner office of the justice court. No attempt was made to molest the other two negroes who were being held.

The journey from the court room to the plaza was as orderly as a circus parade. The crowd had been orderly, quiet and patient all day. It was orderly until the gruesome task was finished.

———— Confesses

Standing upon the threshold of eternity, when all hope was gone, ———— confessed that he was guilty.

At 1 o'clock very few people remained abroad in Temple. The will of the people had prevailed. A terrible warning had been given those whose brutal lust might lead them to a similar crime.

Letter from Mrs. S. L. Hollingsworth to Mrs. Greer, 1933

September 27, 1933

My dear Mrs. Greer:*

I enclose my meagre report for 3rd quarter.

Regarding the lynching you asked me to investigate, . . . I am perfectly sure that no *innocent* person could be lynched without resentment or prosecution against the lynchers. But as long as there are certain crimes committed by Negro men against white women and there is a drop of southern manhood left, there will be lynching. . . .

---

* Three letters from the Association of Southern Women for the Prevention of Lynching Papers, Trevor Arnett Library, Atlanta University, reprinted by permission of the Library and of the Southern Regional Council, successor to the Commission on Interracial Cooperation.

I am quite sure our leaders [of the Methodist Woman's Missionary Coun-
cil] are overdoing this phase of our church work, they seem to have a Negro
complex, and I am not at all alone in my objection to such over emphasis on this
point. I know that holding the office you do you must pass on whatever is recommended by Council and I do not censure you for so doing. I am merely passing
on to you our ideas and hope the Council will find out that they are losing some
members and many subscriptions to the World Outlook on this account.

With best wishes, I am
Sincerely,

Mrs. S. L. Hollingsworth(s)

Letter from Mrs. L. Greer to Mrs. Hollingsworth, 1933

Potts Camp, Miss.
Sept. 29, 1933

My dear Mrs. Hollingsworth: *

. . . In this anti-lynching work, I think you are doing what I did, what
others over the South are doing, namely, refusing to look an unpleasant fact in
the face. I am all Southern and fully understand. The Council did not change
me; it cannot change you. I had a conference with God about this thing and
came out a changed woman. And I warn you and all of the women with convictions like yours, that if you want to hold these convictions, do NOT hold a
conference with God, for He has some very plain things to say about giving one
man a trial and refusing another.

The Council must not be a shield for me. I do remain true to it, for so far
they have suggested nothing beyond plans for aiding humanity. . . . I do not
believe they have a "complex"; they simply urge these activities along with many
others. . . . However, I suspect a complex would be beneficial for them and all
other church societies. It might in part make amends for their looking over the
dark skin at their door to dark skins far away. . . . If they are losing members
because they stand for Law and Right, it is well. These members belong elsewhere. . . .

Now, my dear, of course your men are fine and they think they are doing
right in lynching, for they have not given it serious thought. I never censure
men; I censure women. Men think we want them to do it; when they find we do
not they will stop. . . .

If you do not mind, I wish you would read my letters to your Auxiliary,
for I know these things are discussed among women. I want them to know what
I stand for as you do, so that when election comes around, a little more than a

* See footnote, page 384.

year hence, they will know whether to elect me again as their Supt. Social Relations. . . . Perhaps they want a woman who thinks "trays and flowers" truly represent the Master's dealings with Society. If they do, the Conference has many of them, and such may be had easily. In the meantime, I appreciate the faith, the love, the cooperation of my women. I love them all and if the parting of the ways has to come, I shall still call them MINE.

Thanks again,

Mrs. L. Greer

Letter from Mrs. C. C. Alford to Mrs. Lester Greer, 1935

Sept. 9, 1935
Mrs. Lester Greer,
Potts Camp, Mississippi

My dear Mrs. Greer,*

Your letter of August 30 received and I appreciate very much the fact that you consider me enough of a leader for good to want me to be one of your ten key women in the state to fight lynching and I wish it were possible for me to accept the office. . . . I am married to a man who does not see things as I do and I have enough opposition to meet from him where my work with the negros is concerned that I do not feel like undertaking any thing else that he is not in sympathy with and like a great many other southern men, he thinks we women should keep our mouths out of this and let the men take care of it as they think best. Now of course that isn't right but unfortunately for us there are too many men who feel exactly that way about it. However I do not and I deplore the fact that Mississippi leads in this horrible thing but under the circumstances I cannot afford to be militant about it and trust that you will see and understand my position. . . .

Yours truly,

[Mrs. C. C. Alford]

* See footnote, page 384.

Organizations Committed to a Program of Education to Prevent Lynching, 1942

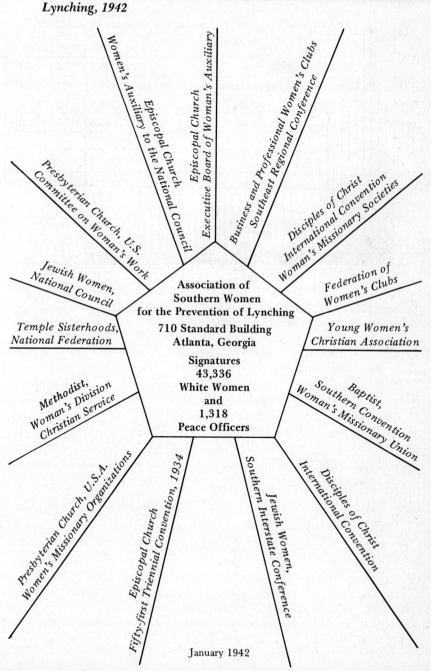

Women's Auxiliary to the National Council

Episcopal Church Executive Board of Woman's Auxiliary

Business and Professional Women's Clubs Southeast Regional Conference

Presbyterian Church, U.S. Committee on Woman's Work

Disciples of Christ International Convention Woman's Missionary Societies

Jewish Women, National Council

Federation of Women's Clubs

Temple Sisterhoods, National Federation

Association of Southern Women for the Prevention of Lynching

710 Standard Building Atlanta, Georgia

Signatures 43,336 White Women and 1,318 Peace Officers

Young Women's Christian Association

Methodist, Woman's Division Christian Service

Baptist, Southern Convention Woman's Missionary Union

Presbyterian Church, U.S.A. Women's Missionary Organizations

Disciples of Christ International Convention

Episcopal Church Fifty-first Triennial Convention, 1934

Jewish Women, Southern Interstate Conference

January 1942

SOURCE: Jessie Daniel Ames, *The Changing Character of Lynching*, Commission on Interracial Cooperation, Atlanta, July 1942, p. 20.

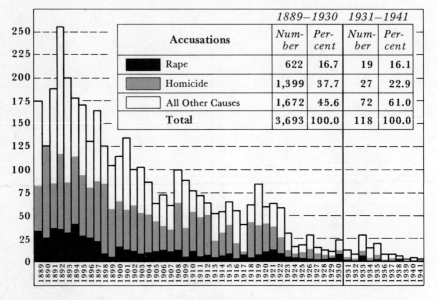

Accusations Against Persons Lynched, 1889–1941

Accusations	1889–1930 Number	1889–1930 Percent	1931–1941 Number	1931–1941 Percent
Rape	622	16.7	19	16.1
Homicide	1,399	37.7	27	22.9
All Other Causes	1,672	45.6	72	61.0
Total	3,693	100.0	118	100.0

SOURCE: Jessie Daniel Ames, *The Changing Character of Lynching*, Commission on Interracial Cooperation, Atlanta, July 1942, p. 6.

15 Tomorrow's Yesterday:
Feminist Consciousness and the Future of Women

Sara M. Evans

"Women on the move." Courtesy of April Saul/Minnesota Daily.

In the final quarter of the twentieth century the prospects for women encompass a wider range of possibility and promise than could have been imagined at earlier points in American history. A new wave of feminism has raised the basic issue of women's place in society. Young women participants in the civil rights and student movements of the 1960s appropriated for themselves the egalitarian ethos of those movements with its emphasis on the personal and moral dimensions of political action. In so doing, they created a radically transformed feminist movement and ideology demanding equality of results, not simply of opportunity, and analyzing the intricate subtleties of interpersonal power.

The insights of this younger generation joined with an emerging movement for women's rights (more narrowly and legalistically defined) to generate a torrential demand for change. In its insistence that "the personal is political," contemporary feminism has moved beyond a focus on public or legal inequities to the broader questions of sex roles, socialization, and the economic function of women's work in the home. The issue is not simply discrimination. It penetrates to the underlying cultural definitions of *femaleness* and *maleness*. The sources of this renewed examination of basic meanings lie both in social changes that render patriarchal tradition less and less tenable and in particular experiences that precipitate a new consciousness.

CRACKS IN THE MOLD

At a number of points in United States history, particular groups of women have chafed under the restrictions of their assigned roles, frequently because changes in the broader society offered glimpses of wider possibilities. By the mid-1960s, at least two groups of American women had reached this point to challenge tradition. The first were professional women, whose abilities and commitment to their work coexisted most uneasily with the domestic ideology of the feminine mystique. Widespread access to higher education generated a growing number of such professionals whose experiences of discrimination drew them into contact with one another and led to the creation in 1966 of an organization specifically to lobby for public, civil equality for women, the National Organization for Women (NOW).

For most American women, however, the problems were more complex and the solutions less obvious. The feminine mystique of the 1940s and 1950s had blinded American women. It had depicted happiness where there was frustration, and pleasant housework that for many women was an additional job after they got home from work. The mystique drew on the power of centuries of tradition, defining women as uniquely suited to domesticity and deviant in any other role. Yet women's supposed devotion to suburban togetherness grew at the same time that they were leaving the home, not for fulfilling professional jobs but for secretarial and clerical work, unskilled factory jobs, service occupations such as waitressing, and paraprofessional work in the expanding fields of education, medicine, and social work.

The old models of male and female roles had been designed around the separation of home (female) and work (male) in the urban setting. Suddenly the booming postwar consumer economy assaulted this division by creating a wide range of new jobs in expanding bureaucracies, services, and social services. These occupations were quickly labeled women's work, and the women who flocked to them found themselves performing housewifelike tasks. They received in the public sphere, as they had in the private, a low evaluation of their work and their worth—this time expressed in the form of low pay and job discrimination. As public and private spheres interpenetrated with women at the nexus, inherited sex roles proved less and less adequate sources of identity and self-esteem. Traditional definitions could not encompass, explain, or help women to cope with the new realities of their lives. Thus, only a movement that challenged their roles in the home as well as in the workplace could have tapped the pain and anger of most women and moved them to action.

A New Catalyst

The catalyst for a more thoroughgoing critique of sex roles and a mass mobilization of American women developed among young female participants in the social movements of the 1960s. These women were younger counterparts of the professional women who organized the women's rights branch of the new feminism. Unlike their older sisters, younger women had neither a stake in defending or furthering particular positions in the public realm, nor clarity about what their future roles should be. These college-educated daughters of the middle class had received mixed, paradoxical messages about what it meant to grow up female. The cultural idea—held up by media, parents, and schools—informed them that their only true happiness lay in the twin roles of wife and mother. At the same time they could observe the reality that housewifery was distinctly unsatisfactory for millions of suburban women and, furthermore, that despite the best efforts of the *Ladies' Home Journal*, most American women could expect to work outside the home during a substantial part of their lives. Such contradictions made young educated women in the 1960s dry tinder for the spark of revolt. When such a revolt appeared in the black and student uprisings, large numbers of women responded and found their own confusions strangely transformed.

By the late 1960s, most American women's lives were dramatically unlike the happy-housewife image of the 1950s. And like the proverbial child who pointed out that the king had no clothes, America's youth first heralded the discrepancy between myth and reality. While professional women in NOW challenged the widespread inequities facing women in law and civil rights, young participants in the social movements of the 1960s—civil rights, the new left, the antiwar movement— tore away the shrouds of ambiguity and mystification surrounding women's roles with intrepid zeal and directness. When they asserted that the personal was political, they set out to trace all aspects of women's lives—work, sexuality, family roles, self-image—back to their social and political roots. Women's liberation meant not only civil equality but also a rethinking of the most fundamental assumptions from the perspective of women's actual experience. Kathie Sarachild compared their examination of personal experience with the seventeenth-century struggle against scholastics and dogmatists who clung to ancient texts on anatomy despite the very different facts revealed by dissection: "So they'd deny what they saw in front of their eyes, because Galen didn't say it was there." [1]

Thus, the women's liberation movement was initiated by women in the civil rights movement and the new left who dared to test the old assumptions and myths about female nature against their own experience, and discovered that something was drastically wrong. They dared because within these movements they had learned to respect themselves and to know their own strength. They could dare because the new left provided an egalitarian ideology stressing the personal nature of political action, the importance of community and cooperation, and the necessity to struggle for freedom for the oppressed. They had to dare because within the same movement that gave them so much they were simultaneously thrust into subservient sex roles—secretary, sex object, dumb chick. Their experience was in some ways an intensified version of that of millions of American women. But in the process they developed a collective consciousness of the need to create unity among women (sisterhood) that could function as an insurgent force in American culture. It is this process of awakening consciousness that we must examine further.

VISIONS AND PURPOSES

The youthful insurgency known as the new left represented a moral revolt of middle-class youth in the 1960s against the evils of poverty,

[1] Interview with Kathie Sarachild, July 1973. Much of this article is based on interviews conducted in the summer of 1973 with the following women: Mary King, Cathy Cade, Mimi Feingold, Sharon Jeffrey, Marya Levenson, Dorothy Burlage, Fay Bellamy, Ella Baker, Nan Grogan, Jean Wiley, Betty Garman, Gwen Patton, Vivian Rothstein, and Naomi Weisstein; and upon one with Sandra Cason (Casey Hayden) conducted in July 1977. All interview tapes, including those conducted by Harry Boyte, are in the author's possession.

racism, and war. Beginning with the civil rights movement in the South and antinuclear protests on northern campuses, it grew in size, locations (campuses, urban slums, rural cooperatives), and tactics (sit-ins, freedom rides, voter registration, block organizing, draft-card burning, mass marches). New left ideology reflected the combined visions of rural southern blacks and a generation of middle-class youth who had absorbed the idealism implicit in the cold-war rhetoric of the 1950s only to discover evils of poverty and discrimination in the midst of the good society. As cold-war liberals, students had accepted the view defining the world as divided between the free and democratic nations of the West and the monolithic evils of communism. The rhetoric of the cold war throughout the fifties was that of a moral crusade. Students took their inherited values literally. They believed in freedom, equality, love, and hope. But their world failed to match up. Within the university they eventually came to perceive themselves as cogs in an expanding system geared to train them to join other cogs in corporate and government bureaucracies, where efficiency, forced cooperation, and mass organization won out over critical thinking and intellectual community. When black students in the South initiated a wave of sit-ins in the spring of 1960, the generation entering the sixties had the opportunity to act on their ideals and beliefs.

From the beginning, the student movement emphasized the importance of building new kinds of human relationships and the political import of personal choice. Instead of abstract ideology, the movement offered vision and purpose. The Student Nonviolent Coordinating Committee (SNCC) asserted: "Nonviolence as it grows from Judaic-Christian tradition seeks a social order of justice permeated by love." The goals of the movement described as the "redemptive community," or more often, the "beloved community," constituted both a vision of the future obtained through nonviolent action and a conception of the nature of the movement itself. Jane Stembridge, daughter of a southern Baptist minister who left her studies at Union Seminary in New York to become the first paid staff member of SNCC, expressed it in these words:

finally it all boils down to human relationship. . . . It is the question of . . . whether I shall go on living in isolation or whether there shall be a we. The student movement is not a cause . . . it is a collision between this one person and that one person. It is a I am going to sit beside you. . . . Love alone is radical.[2]

Northern activists developed more analytical and abstract versions of the southern movement's concepts like beloved community. Tom Hayden argued in 1962 that "the essential challenge is . . . to quiet the

---

[2] SNCC founding statement, quoted in Cleveland Sellers, *The River of No Return: The Autobiography of a Black Militant and the Life and Death of SNCC*, William Morrow, New York, 1973, p. 39; Stembridge, quoted in Howard Zinn, *SNCC: The New Abolitionists*, Beacon Press, Boston, 1965, p. 7.

acquiescence to political fate, cut the confidence in business-as-usual futures, and realize that . . . the time has come for a re-assertion of the personal." Three years later the Students for a Democratic Society (SDS) University Committee reported: "The free university is not defined by a particular structural arrangement, but by the questions the participants ask. . . . The central question of the free university seems to be 'what kind of inter-personal relations allow people to treat each other as human beings?' " [3]

Within the student movement, the intensely personal nature of social action and the commitment to equality resulted in a kind of anarchic democracy and a general questioning of all the socially accepted rules. "Let the people decide" and "participatory democracy" were the ideological passwords of SNCC and SDS. This new left politics nourished the seeds of a new feminism whose central assertion would be "the personal is political." The ideals for the revolt of women were: the importance of the personal; the need to change the quality of human relationships; participatory democracy; equality. What was necessary was the experiential basis within the new left from which women could initiate a new self-assertion.

Women who shared these ideals did not at first believe they could or should apply them to themselves. The parallels were obvious: beloved community/participatory democracy/sisterhood; freedom now/third world liberation/women's liberation. By 1965–1966 the watchword had become "look to your own oppression," but few women noticed the feminist implications. When they began to do so, however, they pointed out bitterly that the movement vision of participatory democracy had rarely applied to them. Yet on closer examination the challenge to women's roles in the new left occurred not where the ideology was clearest—such arenas tended to be dominated by male intellectuals—but in the places where women were strongest. More important, then, than the fact that the new left exhibited the same sexism characteristic of American society was the fact that it provided women with a particular kind of social space within which they could grow in self-confidence. This occurred particularly within the southern civil rights movement and the new left community organizing projects in northern cities.

SOCIAL SPACES

Within the southern civil rights movement, the daily realities of hard work and responsibility admitted few sexual limitations. Young women's sense of purpose was reinforced by the knowledge that the work they did

[3] Tom Hayden, "Student Social Action," March 1962, mimeo, New York, SDS; "Report of the SDS University Committee," June 28–30, 1963, SDS Papers, series 3, State Historical Society of Wisconsin.

and the responsibilities they assumed were central to the movement. In the beginning, black and white alike agreed that whites should work primarily in the white community. They had an appropriate role in urban direct-action movements where the goal was integration, but their principal job was generating support for civil rights within the white population. The handful of white women involved in the early sixties either worked in the SNCC office—gathering news, writing pamphlets, facilitating communications—or organized campus support through such agencies as the YWCA.

In direct-action demonstrations, many women discovered untapped reservoirs of courage. Cathy Cade attended Spelman College as an exchange student in the spring of 1962. She had been there only two days when she joined Howard Zinn in a sit-in in the black section of the Georgia legislature. Never before had she so much as joined a picket line. Years later she testified: "To this day I am amazed. I just did it." Though she understood the risks involved, she does not remember being afraid. Rather she was exhilarated, for with one stroke she undid much of the fear of blacks that she had developed as a high school student in Tennessee.

Others, like Mimi Feingold, jumped eagerly at the chance to join the freedom rides but then found the experience more harrowing than they had expected. Her group had a bomb scare in Montgomery and knew that the last freedom bus in Alabama had been blown up. They never left the bus from Atlanta to Jackson, Mississippi. The arrest in Jackson was anticlimactic. Then there was a month in jail, where she could hear women screaming as they were subjected to humiliating vaginal "searches."

When SNCC moved into voter registration projects in the Deep South, the experiences of white women acquired a new dimension. The years of enduring the brutality of intransigent racism finally convinced SNCC to invite several hundred white students into Mississippi for the 1964 "freedom summer." For the first time, large numbers of white women would be allowed into the field, to work in the rural South.

White women had previously been excluded because in rural communities they were highly visible; their presence, violating both racial and sexual taboos, often provoked repression. According to Mary King, "the start of violence in a community was often tied to the point at which white women appeared to be in the civil-rights movement." However, the presence of whites also brought the attention of the national media, and, in the face of the apparent impotence of the federal law-enforcement apparatus, the media became the chief weapon of the movement against violence and brutality. Thus, with considerable ambivalence, SNCC began to include whites—men and women—in certain voter-registration projects.

The freedom summer brought hundreds of northern white women

into the southern movement. They taught in freedom schools, ran libraries, canvassed for voter registration, and endured constant harassment from the local whites. Many reached well beyond their previously assumed limits: "I was overwhelmed at the idea of setting up a library all by myself," wrote one woman. "Then can you imagine how I felt when at Oxford, while I was learning how to drop on the ground to protect my face, my ears, and my breasts, I was asked to coordinate the libraries in the entire project's community centers? I wanted to cry 'HELP' in a number of ways." While they tested themselves and questioned their own courage, they also experienced poverty, oppression, and discrimination in raw form. As one volunteer wrote: "For the first time in my life, I am seeing what it is like to be poor, oppressed and hated. And what I see here does not apply only to Gulfport or to Mississippi or even to the South. . . . This summer is only the briefest beginning of this experience."

Some women virtually ran the projects they participated in. They learned to live with an intensity of fear that they had never known before. By October 1964 there had been 15 murders, 4 woundings, 37 churches bombed or burned, and over 1,000 arrests in Mississippi. Every project set up elaborate security precautions—regular communication by two-way radio, rules against going out at night or walking downtown in interracial groups. One woman summed up the experience of hundreds when she explained, "I learned a lot of respect for myself for having gone through all that." [4]

The community organizing projects in northern urban centers represented an attempt to translate into the northern context the sense of engagement, community, and identity with the very poor that SNCC had achieved in the South, and also to respond to the expressed wishes of black civil rights leaders that whites create allies for the civil rights community within the poor white community. Women in these projects, like their immediate predecessors in civil rights, discovered in the concrete realities of day-to-day work a newfound strength and a sense of self that could make sexual oppression seem increasingly burdensome and unacceptable. The reality of community organizing shaped a new sense of identity—a vocation as an "organizer." Participation brought risk and, for most, achievement and growth.

The most influential single group of projects resulted from a decision on the part of SDS to build an "interracial movement of the poor." The experiences of women in the SDS Economic Research and Action Project (ERAP) paralleled those in numerous similar groups established by other organizations on a local level. In these SDS projects a few men

[4] Elizabeth Sutherland, ed., *Letters from Mississippi*, McGraw-Hill, New York, 1965, pp. 111–112, 229–230; Len Holt, *The Summer That Didn't End*, William Morrow, New York, 1965, p. 12.

functioned as effective organizers. Most good organizers, however, were women. Women were generally better trained in the interpersonal skills good organizing required—empathy, listening, warmth, and noncompetitiveness in interpersonal relationships.

The original analysis of the SDS-ERAP projects specified that the key strategic population would be the unemployed, probably youths. Implicit in this calculus was the cultural assumption that unemployed people are male. A mother on welfare is not considered, and does not consider herself, unemployed. So in the beginning projects passed out leaflets at unemployment centers and went door-to-door looking for unemployed men. But the analysis was wrong. The Vietnam War intervened to heat up the economy, and the unemployment rate did not rise. It fell. The only unemployed men left to organize were the unstable and unskilled, winos and street youth.

As a result ERAP projects were forced to shift their focus. For a while the issues were posed as a conflict between JOIN (jobs or income now) and GROIN (garbage removal or income now—that is, the nitty-gritty issues of daily life in the ghetto). Reality, however, soon forced all of the projects that survived for any time to work on the more mundane concerns of community life among the very poor—recreation, day care, schools, street lights, housing, and welfare. In cultural terms the GROIN approach focused on women's issues, that is, issues that sprang from the woman's sphere of home and community life. It is a general rule, but one to which ERAP was blind, that women provide the backbone of most community organizing attempts, though not necessarily the publicly known leadership. Not only do community issues touch women more directly, but also women are most likely to be at home during the day when the organizer comes around to talk.

As the most effective organizers in ERAP, women had for the first time within SDS an independent ground from which to draw their self-respect and to command the respect of others. SDS was never fully able to face this reality, but it nevertheless created unwittingly the experiential basis for female revolt: an arena in which women could start with the skills they already had and build a new sense of potential and self-respect. Though ERAP failed in its attempt to organize an "interracial movement of the poor," its most important legacy in the community may have been the groundwork it helped lay for a national welfare rights movement. While men futilely tried to organize unemployed men, street youth, and winos, women quietly set about creating stable organizations of welfare mothers. Marya Levenson described the impact on women in her project: "What happened in Boston was that a group of us who were women became much stronger. We learned how to deal with a lot of situations. We learned how to fight. . . . And so when it came to appearing in SDS national things I had no question I could talk." A generation of female leadership like Carol McEldowney and Sharon Jeffrey, key leaders in the Cleveland project, emerged from such experiences into positions of influence.

ROLE MODELS

As women tested themselves, in North and South, discovering capabilities they never imagined, their new self-images were reinforced by the examples of strong and assertive women in the communities they organized. Southern black women inspired middle-class participants as they shattered cultural images of appropriate female behavior. "For the first time," according to Dorothy Burlage, a white southern woman, "I had role models I could respect."

Within the movement many of the legendary figures were black women around whom circulated stories of exemplary courage and audacity. Rarely did women expect or receive any special protection in demonstrations or jails. Frequently, direct-action teams were equally divided between women and men, on the theory that the presence of women in sit-in demonstrations might lessen the violent reaction. In 1960, slender Diane Nash had been transformed overnight from a Fisk University beauty queen to a principal leader of the direct-action movement in Nashville, Tennessee. Within SNCC she argued strenuously for direct action—sit-ins and demonstrations—over voter registration and community organization. By 1962, when she was 22 years old and four months pregnant, she confronted a Mississippi judge, refusing to cooperate with the court system by appealing her two-year sentence or posting bond:

This will be a black baby born in Mississippi, and thus wherever he is born he will be born in prison. I believe that if I go to jail now it may help hasten that day when my child and all children will be free—not only on the day of their birth but for all their lives.

Perhaps even more important than the daring of younger activists was the towering strength of older black women. There is no doubt that these women were key figures in organizing the black community. In 1962, SNCC staff member Charles Sherrod wrote the office that in every southwest Georgia county "there is always a 'mama.' She is usually a militant woman in the community, outspoken, understanding, and willing to catch hell, having already caught her share." [5]

[5] "News from SCEF," by Anne Braden, April 30, 1962; and "Statement by Diane Nash Bevel," issued April 20, 1962, both in Carl and Anne Braden Papers, Box 47, State Historical Society of Wisconsin; Sherrod quoted in James Forman, *The Making of Black Revolutionaries: A Personal Account,* Macmillan, New York, 1972, p. 276.

Stories of such women abound. For providing housing, food, and active support to SNCC workers, their homes were fired upon and bombed. Fannie Lou Hamer, the Sunflower County sharecropper who forfeited her livelihood to emerge as one of the most courageous and eloquent leaders of the Mississippi Freedom Democratic Party, was the most famous but by no means the only outstanding leader.

Similarly, in northern community projects, as young women organized the poor they also learned from them, thereby developing powerful female role models. Some of the women they met impressed upon them the strength necessary simply for survival. Others visibly overcame deeply entrenched fear and passivity to stand up for themselves against landlords and welfare bureaucrats. In Newark, New Jersey, Mrs. Ira Brown joined a rent strike protesting building-code violations. When others in her building became frightened and began to pay their rent, she carried on a solitary strike for five months.

Since virtually all local leaders in most projects were women, they provided the most positive images available to the young organizers. But the powerful image of the southern mamas also penetrated the northern movement. Most community organizers had worked in civil rights at some time and therefore identified with SNCC. When ERAP held a "Conference of the Poor" in Cleveland in February 1965, organizers gathered constituents of ERAP projects in Baltimore, Boston, Newark, Chester, Hazard (Kentucky), Chicago, and Detroit. They also invited a number of blacks from the Mississippi freedom movement, including Fannie Lou Hamer and Mrs. Unita Blackwell. Connie Brown of the Newark project wrote, "Four Negroes from rural Mississippi were at the conference. Perhaps because of the extreme youth of the Northern organizations, the personal strength of these Mississippi Negroes, their experience in organizing, their dramatic tales of oppression and brutality in many ways dominated the conference." She admired the way that the "people from Mississippi were able to cut through again and again" to the contradictions behind making adjustments to "the system." [6]

Thus, community organizing in North and South offered young women new role models: the image of a woman who recognizes and names her own oppression and then learns to stand up for herself, breaking through patterns of passivity and learning new self-respect in the process. Inevitably these models carried with them important lessons, which were bound to be absorbed in some measure by the young women who spent weeks and months going from door to door exhorting people to stand up for themselves.

[6] Connie Brown, "Cleveland: Conference of the Poor," *Studies on the Left*, 5 (Spring 1965), 72–73.

UNDERTOW OF OPPRESSION

By 1965 some organizers had begun to recognize that many of the problems facing these powerful women derived from their sex. Newer, younger women did not have the life experiences with which to empathize with family-related troubles—fights with husbands, hassles with children. But they soon would. Many would undergo the stress of personally oppressive relationships within the movement. All experienced the contradiction of doing most of the concrete long-range organizing work but remaining largely invisible. Women were effective, but men were the stars.

Eventually new models bumped up against old ones; self-assertion generated anxiety; new expectations existed alongside traditional ones. Women found it difficult to appropriate their potential strength as the effort to create a beloved community of equality, either racially or sexually, foundered in a movement deeply enmeshed in the culture it set out to challenge. Feminism was born out of this contradiction: The same movement that permitted women to grow and to develop self-esteem, energy, and skills generally kept them out of public leadership roles and reinforced expectations that women would conform to tradition as houseworkers, nurturers, sex objects.

Within movement offices black and white women took on important administrative tasks, but they also performed virtually all typing and clerical work. Very few women assumed the public roles of national leadership. In 1964 black women held a half-serious, half-joking sit-in in the SNCC office to protest these conditions. By 1965 the situation had changed enough that a quarrel over who would take notes at staff meetings was settled by buying a tape recorder.

In community work there was a tendency to assume that women would perform the housework around the "freedom house." As early as 1963 Joni Rabinowitz, a white volunteer in the southwest Georgia project, submitted a stinging series of reports on the woman's role. "The attitude around here toward keeping the house neat (as well as the general attitude toward the inferiority and 'proper place' of women)," she asserted, "is disgusting and also terribly depressing." Similarly, in urban community projects women usually made the peanut butter sandwiches (a dietary staple). Furthermore, their primary organizing work—with women, welfare mothers, and teenage girls—rarely received its due. Work that men did with street youth was considered "exciting" and "daring" while women were assigned the more routine door-to-door work. Because their constituents were not "tough," women's organizing received little status or recognition.

Furthermore, women experienced sexual exploitation and ambiguity within the new left. Their generation reached sexual maturity simultaneously with the widespread introduction of oral contraceptives. This technological divorce of female sexuality and procreation thus enhanced the possibilities of cultural revolt. But it was not a possibility for which young women's upbringing had prepared them.

In the southern movement, the stresses of changing sexuality were further complicated by the issue of race. White women's presence inevitably heightened the sexual tension that runs as a constant current through racist culture. Southern women understood that in the struggle against racial discrimination they were at war with their culture. They reacted to the label "southern lady" as though it were an obscene epithet, for they had emerged from a society that used the symbol of southern white womanhood to justify an insidious pattern of racial discrimination and brutal repression. They had, of necessity, to forge a new sense of self—a new definition of femininity apart from the one they had inherited. Gradually they came to understand the struggle against racism as, Dorothy Burlage said, "a key to pulling down all the . . . fascist notions and mythologies and institutions in the South," including "notions about white women and repression."

Thus, for southern women this tension was a key to their incipient feminism, but it also became a disruptive force within the civil rights movement itself. The entrance of hundreds of white women, most of them from northern campuses, into the southern movement could hardly have been anything but explosive. Interracial sex was the most potent social taboo in the South. And the struggle against racism brought together young, naive, sometimes insensitive, rebellious, and idealistic white women with young, angry black men, some of whom had hardly been allowed to speak to white women before. They sat-in together. If they really believed in equality, why shouldn't they sleep together?

Such tensions in the southern movement contributed to a growing rift between black and white women and to the rise of black nationalism. Black women angrily charged that they could not develop relationships with black men because the men did not have to be responsible to them as long as they could turn to involvement with white women. Their anger and demands constituted one part of an intricate maze of tensions and struggles that were in the process of transforming the civil rights movement. SNCC had grown from a small band of 16 to a swollen staff of 180, of whom 50 percent were white. The earlier dream of a beloved community was dead. The vision of freedom lay crushed under the weight of intransigent racism, disillusion with electoral politics and non-violence, and differences of race, class, and culture within the movement itself. Within the rising spirit of black nationalism, the anger of black women toward white women was only one element. It is in this context, however, that Ruby Doris Smith Robinson, one of the most powerful black women in SNCC, is said to have written a paper on the position of women in SNCC.

Ruby Doris Smith Robinson was a strong woman. As a teenager

she had joined the early Atlanta demonstrations during her sophomore year at Spelman College. That year, as a participant in the Rock Hill, South Carolina, sit-in, she helped initiate the "jail-no bail" policy in SNCC. A month in the Rock Hill jail bound her to the movement with a zeal born of common suffering, deepened commitment, and shared vision. Soon she was a battle-scarred veteran, respected by everyone and feared by many; she ran the SNCC office with unassailable authority.

As an early leader of the black nationalist faction, Robinson hated white women for a number of years because white women represented a cultural ideal of beauty and femininity that by inference defined black women as ugly and unwomanly. But she was also aware that women must from time to time assert their rights as women. In 1964 she participated in and perhaps led the sit-in at the SNCC office protesting the relegation of women to typing and clerical work. Thus, when an anonymous paper entitled "The Position of Women in SNCC" circulated at the tension-filled Waveland conference in the fall of 1964, most of the speculation about its authorship centered on Robinson. She died of cancer in 1968, and we may never know her own assessment of her feelings and intentions in 1964. It appears that she did not go to any great lengths to refute the rumors. We do know, however, that tales of the memo generated feminist echoes in the minds of many. And Stokely Carmichael's response that "the only position for women in SNCC is prone" stirred up even more discontent. The persisting myth among white feminists that Robinson wrote and presented this first overt attack on sexism in the movement remains a testimony to the powerful image of black women and of Robinson in particular. It has become a staple in accounts of the revival of feminism. In fact, however, the anonymous authors were southern white women, Casey Hayden and Mary King.

A year later, Casey Hayden and Mary King wrote a signed memo on the same subject, but its tone was more philosophical and conciliatory. As southern white women who had devoted several years of their lives to the vision of a beloved community, they found the rejection of nonviolence and the trend toward a more ideological, centralized black nationalist movement to be bitterly disillusioning. The second memo was addressed to black women and to some of their friends in the northern new left in the vain hope of finding a common ground. In it they argued that women, like blacks,

seem to be caught in a common-law caste system that operates, sometimes subtly, forcing them to work around or outside hierarchical structures of power which may exclude them. Women seem to be placed in the same position of assumed subordination in personal situations too. It is a caste system which, at its worst, uses and exploits women.

Hayden and King set the precedent of contrasting the movement's egalitarian ideas with its replication of sex roles. They noted how women's position in society determined women's roles in the movement —like cleaning houses, doing secretarial work, and refraining from active or public leadership. At the same time, they observed:

having learned from the movement to think radically about the personal worth and abilities of people whose role in society had gone unchallenged before, a lot of women in the movement have begun trying to apply those lessons to their own relations with men. Each of us probably has her own story of the various results.

This "kind of memo" represented a flowering of women's conciousness that articulated contradictions felt most acutely by middle-class white women. The black women who received it were on a different historical trajectory. They would fight some of the same battles as white women, but in a different context and in their own way. Cynthia Washington, who had left her studies at George Washington University to join SNCC, recalled discussing the role of women in SNCC with Casey Hayden in the fall of 1964. Hayden's complaints about women's restriction to office-work roles made little sense to her

because, at the time, I had my own project in Bolivar County, Mississippi. A number of other black women also directed their own projects. What Casey and other white women seemed to want was an opportunity to prove they could do something other than office work. I assumed that if they could do something else, they'd probably be doing it. . . . It seemed to many of us . . . that white women were demanding a chance to be independent while we needed help and assistance which was not always forthcoming. We definitely started from opposite ends of the spectrum.

It is not surprising that the issues were first defined and confronted by southern white women whose consciousness developed in a context that inextricably and paradoxically linked the fate of women and black people. These spiritual daughters of Sarah and Angelina Grimké kept their expectations low in November 1965. "Objectively," Hayden and King wrote, "the chances seem nil that we could start a movement based on anything as distant to general American thought as a sex-caste system." [7] But change was in the air and youth was on the march.

In the North hundreds of women had shared in the southern

[7] Casey Hayden and Mary King, "Sex and Caste: A Kind of Memo," *Liberation*, 11 (April 1966), 35–36; Cynthia Washington, "We Started from Different Ends of the Spectrum," *Southern Exposure*, 4 (Winter 1977), 14–15.

experience for a week, a month, a year, and thousands more had participated vicariously or had worked to extend the struggle for freedom and
equality in northern communities. These women were ready to hear
what their southern sisters had to say. Sexual exploitation within the
new left had been much less ambiguous than in the South. Some men
in community projects were known for bringing in one girl friend after
another. Women were aware that when they became involved with a man
in the inner circles they were privy to many conversations and decisions
central to the project's development. Thus, at times a woman's status
could rise or fall according to the changes in her sex life.

Some of the women refused to play, either by avoiding relationships within the project altogether or by developing a single, primary,
monogamous relationship, sometimes even a marriage. Others enjoyed
their new freedom. But many women were caught somewhere in the
painful middle. They rejected many social norms concerning sexual relationships, but they were confused about what should replace them.
People talked about openness, honesty, and democracy in relationships,
but few felt sure how such values might be achieved. In the absence of
any clear understanding of the ways sex roles continued to shape behavior, the double standard collapsed into a void. Men believed that women
would simply adopt the culturally accepted norms of male behavior.
But what then should women do with the needs already socialized into
them for security, stability, and dependability in relationships?

Furthermore, from 1965 on, the northern movement as a whole
became increasingly alienating for women. The escalation in Vietnam
that year generated a massive response and a chaotic influx into SDS.
At a conference in December 1965, women organized groups to discuss
the issues raised by Hayden and King's memo. They asked:

*If SDS is the organization that envisions itself as a small-scale model of
the new society, as a living example of participatory democracy, why
has it been unable to deal creatively with the role of women? Why do
women so rarely participate in large discussions? Why does most of the
intellectual leadership in SDS consist of men? Why do many women feel
inhibited from participating in the decision-making and discussion
processes of SDS?*

Over the next year and a half conditions within the movement
increasingly threatened women's newfound strength. The social spaces
for assertive women contracted as whites lost legitimacy in southern
civil rights and as community organizing gave way to antiwar activity.
The movement became more alienating, more massive, competitive, sexually exploitative. At the same time it opened the process of radicaliza-
tion for thousands and sharpened the ideology that women would

eventually use to describe their own oppression. In an important way these years produced a mass constituency for the women's liberation movement. By 1967–1968 hundreds of thousands of young women had been to a march, a meeting, a sit-in, a rally. When a few women with longer movement histories revolted, this was the first constituency to which they turned.

The size of the movement rendered women invisible. Meetings of hundreds, rallies of thousands, marches of hundreds of thousands did not constitute arenas conducive to female leadership, except for those already exceptionally strong and self-confident. More and more women found themselves relegated to typing and coffee serving. In large meetings their words went unheard. In addition, women after 1966 found that they were auxiliaries to the central issue of the movement—the draft. Men were drafted; women were not. Men could resist the draft; they burned draft cards; they risked jail. And women's role was to support them. "Girls Say Yes to Guys Who Say No!" was the widespread slogan of the movement. Finally, the burgeoning youthful counter-culture raised sexual ambiguities to new heights. With no critique of sex roles, the counter-culture frequently left women feeling used and sexually objectified more than ever.

REBIRTH OF FEMINISM

In this context, women finally broke away in the fall of 1967. They had learned too much respect for themselves and too much organizing skill to acquiesce quietly in their eclipse. By 1967 a generation of women in the new left had built on the precedents of women like Casey Hayden and Carol McEldowney and had begun to assert their own leadership abilities. In the South, in community organizing projects and in personal struggles for self-definition, they had gained a new maturity and self-confidence as they broke through the boundaries of traditional womanhood. Yet as they did so they simultaneously experienced the increased male domination of the left and felt for the first time the full force of adult sex roles.

These, then, were the women ready to take up the banner of women's liberation when once again the new left seemed to be disintegrating in counterpoint to the theme of black power. In sharp contrast to the goals of Casey Hayden and Mary King in 1965, however, they were not interested primarily in repairing the fissures within the new left. Armed with a political rationale and the knowledge that many women within the left were raising the issue of women's roles, they set out to create something of their own. Ideologically, the new left had

moved from the notion of beloved community to the need for all oppressed groups to organize themselves. "Black power," "Chicano power,"
"student power" proliferated as movement slogans. When NOW formed
in late 1966, radical youth disdained to work in such a "reformist"
organization. But it didn't take much to force the final logical connection
and to begin a movement for "woman power." Young radicals drew on
the analogy with black oppression in defining a complex of discriminatory attitudes (sexism) comparable to racism, which were backed by an
infrastructure of discriminatory institutions and laws. They also understood quickly by analogy that women had internalized many of the
negative things attributed to them and that mutual solidarity and support were necessary to wage a struggle that was both internal and
external.

After the National Conference for New Politics in Chicago in
August 1968, where women who demanded equal representation had
been ridiculed and booed, a core of young women declared: "Women
must not make the same mistake the blacks did at first of allowing others
(whites in their case, men in ours) to define our issues, methods and
goals. Only we can and must define the terms of our struggle." As a
result, they argued, "it is incumbent on us, as women, to organize a
movement for women's liberation." [8] This new flood of self-conscious
feminism flowed into the channels left by several years of movement
activity. Through a combination of personal friendship networks, movement media, and movement events the word spread until within a year
there was hardly a major city without one or more "women's liberation
groups," as they called themselves.

Reports from these early meetings bear a remarkable similarity.
In all parts of the country, women experiencing ambiguity and strain
in their roles—whether as housewives, in jobs, or in movement activities
—and sharing a new left history suddenly discovered each other. The
private experience of oppression and the intellectual perception of sexual
inequality merged in the emotional realization that "I'm not alone."

Kathie Amatniek had spent two years in New York after leaving
the South extremely alienated from the white left. She had begun a
career in film editing and occasionally produced film strips for the
antiwar movement, but she really came alive again when the women's
meetings began: "Well, when those meetings began, I felt like it was
almost being back in the South. . . . I was very conscious that this was
a grass roots movement again, and, you know, that these were real
people, really seriously going to do something about their lives." Soon
she adopted the feminist surname, Sarachild, child of Sara.

---

[8] "To the Women of the Left," mimeo, reprinted as "Chicago Women Form Liberation
Group," *New Left Notes,* November 13, 1967.

The excitement deepened as women began to share their personal lives. In sharp contrast to new left ideological debates from which they had been excluded, women found, for the first time, that they could legitimately talk about themselves, their relationships, their hopes and angers. The vitality of these exchanges and the growing sense of collective power—the knowledge that there was a movement to back them up—allowed many women to claim for the first time the leadership capacities they had developed. Naomi Weisstein had raised the issue of women's oppression for years, had led classes at the Center for Radical Research and at the University of Chicago, but remained terrified of speaking at mass gatherings. As it gradually dawned on her that a social movement of women was emerging, she felt herself transformed. No longer afraid, because she was no longer alone, she soon became one of the most effective orators of the women's liberation movement. As she put it, "The women's movement really gave me my voice. Before I was never very good, but with the women's movement I spoke really thunderingly effectively, sometimes five-minute standing ovations." When she spoke at a women's peace march "and did all the wrong things and got booed," she was not crushed, "because I had a movement and the movement was behind me. I remember getting down and saying, 'wow, I really fucked that one up.'"

On the other hand, the vitality itself could be frightening. This was a movement without barriers. The young women had not begun with a legalistic definition of women's rights. They were radicals, used to taking on issues and getting down to their roots whatever the cost. And they began with a high level of shared cultural alienation. Personal life had already been politicized in the rebellions against parents, in the emergence of new, alternate life-styles, in life-shattering decisions about resisting the draft, leaving school, going to jail. *Freedom* and *liberation* were absolutes—to be fought for and won. But whom would they fight? Men? Their husbands and boy friends? The rest of the left? The consumer society? Maybe even themselves as well. While some women claimed their new strength joyfully, others cringed inwardly, wanting independence but insecure about their own capacity to sustain it, fearful that no one could love an independent woman, afraid to test their conviction against male ridicule and rage. As Carol Hanish, a southern woman who had worked with Southern Conference Educational Fund (SCEF) in the South, described her experience in the New York group: "I want to say this whole movement is the most exhilarating thing of my life. The last eight months have been a personal revolution. Nonetheless, I recognize there is dynamite in this and I'm scared shitless." [9]

9 "Memo: Carol Hanish to SCEF Women, Proposal for a Women's Liberation Program," August 10, 1968, Carl and Anne Braden Papers, Box 82.

The new feminist movement made its explosive debut in the Miss America demonstration in August 1968. With a sharp eye for flamboyant guerrilla theater, young women crowned a live sheep to symbolize the beauty pageant's objectification of female bodies, and filled a "freedom trashcan" with objects of female torture—girdles, bras, curlers, issues of *Ladies' Home Journal.* Peggy Dobbins, dressed as a stockbroker, auctioned off an effigy of Miss America: "Gentlemen, I offer you the 1969 model. She's better every year. She walks. She talks. She smiles on cue. *And* she does housework." [10] Even though coverage of such events was likely to be derogatory—in reports of the Miss America demonstration the media coined the term *bra-burner*—the dramatic rise in media coverage in 1969 and 1970 accompanied a massive influx of new members into all branches of the feminist movement.

Consciousness Raising

The experiences of the first few women's liberation groups were repeated many times. Young women's instinctive sharing of their personal life experiences soon became a political instrument called *consciousness raising,* evolving into a kind of phenomenological approach to women's liberation. Kathie Sarachild advocated that women should junk all the old theories and start from scratch, relying on their own experience: "In our groups, let's share our feelings and pool them. Let's let ourselves go and see where our feelings lead us. Our feelings will lead us to ideas and then to actions." Thus consciousness raising became both a method for developing theory and a strategy for building movement.

Consciousness raising exemplified both the frontal assault on sex roles and the personalized approach that soon became hallmarks of the proliferating new feminist groups. The radical democracy of the new left carried over into an unequivocal assertion of sexual equality and an impatience with any belief that women should be treated or expected to act differently from men. The notion that women were different but equal, argued by biological determinists, sounded to the new movement like the separate but equal rhetoric used by southern segregationists. And their demands led beyond equal rights, in formal terms, to a demand for equality of power. Thus, they inspired a thorough critique of personal life and of the subtleties of an oppression that was at once internal and external.

The focus on the personal experience of oppression, moreover, led to the creation of small groups within which women could share with

---

10 Susan Suthein, "Radical Women Protest Ugly Pageant," *National Guardian,* September 14, 1968.

mutual trust the intimate details of their lives. Formed almost instinc-
tively at first as radical women gathered in each others' living rooms to
discuss their needs, these small groups quickly became the primary structure of the women's revolt. They provided a place, a "free space," in
which women could examine the nature of their own oppression and
could share the growing knowledge that they were not alone. The qualities of intimacy, support, and virtual structurelessness made the small
group a brilliant tool for spreading the movement. Anyone could form
a group anywhere: an SDS women's caucus, a secretarial pool, a friendship circle, a college dorm, a coffee klatch.

BEYOND THE NEW LEFT

Each small group, and soon there were thousands, created a widening
impact among the families, friends, and coworkers of its members. Soon
the radical ideas and the cooperative forms of the women's movement
were reshaping the more conservative, more tightly structured women's
rights branch of the movement. Within a few years NOW had strengthened its positions on issues like abortion and lesbianism and had considerably changed its style. In several cities NOW became the chief
instigator of new consciousness-raising groups. Individual leaders responded as well, for the new movement awakened them to the broader
aspects of their feminism. For instance, theologian Mary Daly advocated
women's rights in the church when she wrote *The Church and the
Second Sex* in 1968. Several years later she had become a leading exponent of a feminist theology challenging patriarchal images of God.

The situation of younger women had proved parallel to that of
millions of American women far beyond the enclaves of the left. Indeed,
it represented an intensified microcosm of the dilemma of most American women, trapped in an obsolete housewife role while new realities
generated an unarticulated sense of greater potential. Though women's
liberation was shocking and alienating to many, especially as seen
through the magnifying lens of the hostile media, reactions to the out-
cry on behalf of women's equality indicated that feminism had tapped
a vein of enormous frustration and anger. The Harris Survey found in
1971 that 62 percent of American women believed that women had to
"speak up" in order to accomplish anything. Yet most of them disapproved the tactics of picketing and protest and did not support "efforts
to strengthen and change women's status in society." Nearly five years
later, after the intervening upsurge of activism, 65 percent endorsed such
efforts. Previously, women's ambivalence and fear of change had made
them even less likely than men to advocate greater sexual equality. By
1975 a new sense of rights and possibility led women to assert their belief

in equal rights and opportunities for females in greater numbers and with greater intensity than men. Similarly, on specific issues such as abortion, child care, and the Equal Rights Amendment, opinion polls recorded a steady shift in public opinion toward endorsement of feminist programs. By the bicentennial year, 1976, the *Reader's Digest* conceded: "Women's Liberation has changed the lives of many Americans and thus the way they look at family, job, and sexual equality." [11]

Thus, within a few years, the challenge to traditional sex roles had penetrated the mainstream of American society. Outrageous assaults on cultural icons like Miss America, motherhood, and marriage caught the attention of the mass media. Americans were both shocked and intrigued by the sudden questioning of fundamental assumptions. As ever-widening circles of women joined in the process, a range of institutions, from corporations to families, began to experience angry insurgency from within. The *Ladies' Home Journal,* its offices seized by female journalists, agreed to print a special section written and produced by feminists in August 1970. Soon afterward, women at *Newsweek* and *Time* staged their own rebellions. No institution, it seemed, was sacred or safe. Nuns organized within the Catholic church; female seminary students began to agitate for full equality within Protestant churches. By 1975 the Episcopal church was wracked with controversy, when 11 women defiantly joined in an unauthorized ordination service.

Women in the New University Caucus, a new left group, joined with a large constituency of professional women, many of whom were already active in NOW, to form women's caucuses within academic professions. Normally staid professional meetings began to ring with acrimony as women protested hiring, admissions, and promotion practices. Exercising the intellectual tools of their disciplines on the substance of the disciplines themselves, they criticized the male biases involved in treatment of women and sex roles. Thus, armed with new questions and with mutually supportive structures, women generated an outpouring of scholarly studies in the sociology of family and sex roles, female psychology, women's history, and literature by and about women. Whole programs on women's studies encouraged interdisciplinary cross-fertilization and provided points of intersection with the women's movement.

The dramatic growth of feminism—a term that itself signaled the blurring lines between women's liberation and women's rights—proceeded neither smoothly nor without opposition. Predictably, traditionalists organized a reaction to turn back the Equal Rights Amendment, proscribe abortion, punish homosexuality, and in general return women

---

[11] "The American Woman on the Move," *Reader's Digest,* 108 (March 1976), 54. See the Harris Survey reports for May 20, 1971, and December 8 and 11, 1975; and "The Gallup Opinion Index," report number 92, February 1973, and report number 113, November 1974.

to a subservient domesticity. For many women the feminist challenge shook their already precarious self-esteem. They experienced its critique as a personal attack. Others, enjoying the fruits of vicarious power and status, found the notion of equality profoundly threatening. Opposition among women, moreover, was often financed in the seventies by resurgent business conservatism, which sought to roll back reforms won in the turbulent sixties.

Eleanor Langer described the corporate backing of the anti-ERA movement:

The higher up you go . . . the less you hear about homosexual marriage, women in combat and unisex toilets. The major business interests splayed within both parties . . . have concluded that equality for women, coming on top of the decreasing flexibility in the hiring and firing of black people that has followed the civil rights movement, would introduce an inelasticity into the labor force that their profit margins cannot bear.[12]

But for all their vehemence and occasional victories, their arguments drew on visions of a mythic past in which women and men knew their places and the patriarchal family served as the stable foundation of a stable social order. Though there was reaction, there could be no return.

Just as predictably, the women's movement splintered as it grew. Who could say what was *the* central issue: equal pay? abortion? the nuclear family? lesbianism? welfare policies? capitalism? Groups formed around particular issues, constituencies, and political styles, and many were sure that they had found the key to women's liberation. Although some became disillusioned at the fragmentation, the movement continued to spread. Some of the more radical branches mellowed and grew self-critical of their purism. At the same time former conservatives were radicalized. NOW chapters organized consciousness-raising groups and radical feminists headed for law school. By 1973 feminist organizations addressed specifically to the needs of black women had begun to emerge.

As the women's movement dispersed, splintered, formed, and reformed, its importance lay less with the specific groups who initiated it and more with the kinds of responses it made possible. The experiences that formed a feminist's consciousness in the first place re-created themselves not only beyond the new left, but beyond the middle class as well. In thousands of consciousness-raising groups; hundreds of health clinics, rape crisis centers, shelters for battered women; in the proud assertion of lesbian community and culture; in feminist therapy collectives and growing research on female sexuality from the female point of view; in magazines and newspapers addressed to women; in feminist caucuses and women's studies programs; in feminist publishing houses;

[12] Eleanor Langer, "Why Big Business Is Trying to Defeat the ERA," *Ms.* (May 1966), 66.

in the Conference of Labor Union Women (CLUW) and the National Black Feminist Organization (NBFO)—the process repeated and renewed itself as questions and possibilities deepened and spread.

Like many suburban housewives, Jan Schakowsky felt isolated in 1968 and 1969. She had few female friends and saw little chance to find help and support from other women. "I felt real different; my kids were both in diapers; I felt totally trapped." Then she began to hear and read about the women's movement, "about the injustices, and I started reading, you know, even women's magazines, and watching the talk shows." Her days became consumed not only with diapers but also with news of feminism. "By the time my husband walked in the door all hell would break loose. He was responsible for all the evils of the world and especially responsible for keeping me trapped. What kind of person was he? Didn't he understand?"

Through this crisis in her life and her marriage Jan Schakowsky felt constant support from "all those unseen people" about whom she had read. "I knew that if I ever met Gloria Steinem we would be best friends. I felt real close. *MS* magazine, I read it totally uncritically. I didn't care what kind of bullshit articles were in there, it was my magazine." Knowing of no local groups related to the women's movement, she and her friends formed a consumer group as their own feminist gesture. "We talked about how the problems that we faced related directly to the fact that we were women, and the kind of changes as women that we had to go through in order to face those things." From that experience she went on to become a prominent leader of the Citizens Action Project in Chicago and later a staff member of Illinois Political Action Council.[13]

In sharp contrast, women whose initial refusal to participate in the prescribed life patterns had forced them to the periphery of American culture also found in the new ideas a handle on change and visibility. Lesbians entered the women's movement only to find that they had to struggle there, too, for autonomy and recognition. In the process, however, they sparked not only a movement for gay rights but also the development of a self-affirming lesbian culture. As one woman put it, "without a sense that I go back further than my literal birth, I find it difficult to feel substantial and to resist various strains on my energy and self-respect caused by attitudes toward me both as a woman and as a lesbian." Links with other lesbians "living next door or living years, even centuries before me" strengthened her ability to struggle for selfhood. The knowledge that her story follows patterns of other, older ones "lets me believe in my ability to survive and accomplish." Battling alone against the dominant culture leads to hopelessness. Hence, "to remain isolated from the

---

[13] Interview with Jan Schakowsky conducted by Harry C. Boyte, April 1977. I am indebted to Harry Boyte for sharing the research from his forthcoming study of new forms of grass-roots organizing in the 1970s. His work demonstrates concretely the widespread impact of resurgent feminism.

mainstream of contemporary culture may not be such a bad thing; to remain isolated from my own lesbian culture for one more day delays beyond all acceptable limits my coming into my own strength and power."[14]

The movement galvanized women who had always felt deviant and invisible (lesbians) as well as those who had followed "normal" paths but also felt invisible (housewives). It also reached into the lives of the mass of women in women's jobs, groups considered unorganizable by the labor unions. Darlene Stille had worked her way through college against her parents' wishes, and got a job in an insurance company in 1965. Her starting salary, lower than that of male counterparts, was 85 dollars per week. "I worked in a great bullpen with a lot of other people. It was noisy, it was uncomfortable; it was gloomy; it was depressing. I just couldn't believe that after all those years of effort, this is what it had come to." That "first great anger" grew as she was rejected for a supervisory post because of her sex, but it had nowhere to go. "The great anger I felt just sort of stuck there." It stayed on through other jobs. "I just had this notion that I could pull myself up by my bootstraps. And my bootstraps kept breaking" until April 1973.

Stille had avoided women's meetings, fearing that they would be just gripe sessions, but when some friends in NOW suggested that she come to an action protesting the differential treatment of women employees by Chicago businesses, she went. "I came away from that action feeling that something could be done. . . . That I had seen something done, that I had seen these men sign an agreement. . . . It was the first time I had seen something accomplished other than griping." Two days later she was on a picket line at the Kraft Food Plant, demanding equal treatment for women. "It was wonderful feeling that all this anger that had been backing up inside me now had a release, that I could bark back somehow. . . . That I could find my voice in a larger community of women." Subsequently Stille was elected chairperson of Women Employed, the organization of female employees in Chicago that had called these demonstrations. Women Employed built on the insights of feminism to organize women workers with an eye not only to seeking equal pay and benefits, but also to the humiliating subtleties of sexism on the job. When a legal secretary was fired for refusing to make coffee, Women Employed instigated a nationally televised demonstration to protest the stereotypic presumptions involved. The woman—who announced that she made coffee at home in the mornings and had no intention of doing it again at work—was quickly rehired.

A similar organization in Boston, 9 to 5, developed out of a YWCA workshop in which a group of women sought ways to organize women as

---

[14] Toni A. H. McNaron, "Finding and Studying Lesbian Culture," *Radical Teacher,* December 1977, p. 16.

office workers, teachers, homemakers, and students. Ellen Cassedy, one of the originators, pointed out that most of the women who joined 9 to 5 would preface their entrance with: " 'Well, listen, I'm not one of those women's libbers, but . . .' which to me meant that the women's movement was very much on their minds, and they really did see this as kind of stepping into fighting for their rights, and didn't want to have to look different or sleep around or something to be involved, but really did think of themselves as joining some kind of movement and were kind of nervous about it." [15]

THE FUTURE OF WOMEN

Such nervousness persists. Change continues to be difficult and frightening. It produces reaction and backlash, but it remains the only impelling choice. In the late twentieth century the future is more open for women than at any time in recorded history. The technology exists to liberate women from building their lives around biological rhythms. They can take control of the process of reproduction through birth control and abortion. At the same time, the place of women in society has been questioned at the broadest and the deepest levels. Not only can we begin to imagine public equality—equal pay, equal participation in the political arena and the professions—but private life has also been politicized. The future is up for grabs, and we must begin to fashion new ways of being women.

How will women live in the future? How will they define their sexuality? their parenthood? their families? their work? What seems to be evolving is a kind of pluralism within a unity that at its best can be called sisterhood. Together, women can strengthen and affirm one another. Their collective strength forces changes in employment, wages, political participation, law. They have tentatively begun to validate the variety of life options that must exist if any choice is to be a free one. Thus, if no woman can openly choose to live alone or to build her personal life around a community of other women, then the possibility of freely choosing the more traditional tracks of marriage and family are seriously diminished, because they remain the only socially approved option. If women cannot choose not to have children, then their freedom to choose motherhood is similarly circumscribed. At the same time, women have moved beyond the simple reaction against traditional roles to a reevaluation of the fundamental values and experiences that have been female: childbirth, mothering, menstruation, nurture, cooperation, emotion. These provide links to thousands of years of female experience.

[15] Interviews with Darlene Stille, Day Creamer, and Ellen Cassedy, conducted April 1977 by Harry Boyte.

In a new feminist social order they will not be secondary or deviant, but an intimate part of the social norm. Women will be valued, because they will value themselves and demand respect. And sisterhood, powerful in its infancy, will transform the future.

Documents

The Position of Women in SNCC, 1964

1. Staff was involved in crucial constitutional revisions at the Atlanta staff meeting in October.* A large committee was appointed to present revisions to the staff. The committee was all men.

2. Two organizers were working together to form a farmers league. Without asking any questions, the male organizer immediately assigned the clerical work to the female organizer although both had had equal experience in organizing campaigns.

3. Although there are women in Mississippi project who have been working as long as some of the men, the leadership group in COFO is all men.

4. A woman in a field office wondered why she was held responsible for day to day decisions, only to find out later that she had been appointed project director but not told.

5. A fall 1964 personnel and resources report on Mississippi projects lists the number of people in each project. The section on Laurel however, lists not the number of persons, but "three girls."

6. One of SNCC's main administrative officers apologizes for appointment of a woman as interim project director in a key Mississippi project area.

7. A veteran of two years work for SNCC in two states spends her day typing and doing clerical work for other people in her project.

8. Any woman in SNCC, no matter what her position or experience, has been asked to take minutes in a meeting when she and other women are outnumbered by men.

9. The names of several new attorneys entering a state project this past summer were posted in a central movement office. The first initial and last name of each lawyer was listed. Next to one name was written: (girl).

10. Capable, responsible and experienced women who are in leadership positions can expect to have to defer to a man on their project for final decision making.

11. A session at the recent October staff meeting in Atlanta was the first large meeting in the past couple of years where a woman was asked to chair.

---

* SNCC Position Paper by Sandra Cason (Casey Hayden) and Mary King; reprinted with permission.

Undoubtedly this list will seem strange to some, petty to others, laughable to most. The list could continue as far as there are women in the movement. Except that most women don't talk about these kinds of incidents, because the whole subject is not discussable—strange to some, petty to others, laughable to most. The average white person finds it difficult to understand why the Negro resents being called "boy," or being thought of as "musical" and "athletic," because the average white person doesn't realize that *he assumes he is superior*. And naturally he doesn't understand the problem of paternalism. So too the average SNCC worker finds it difficult to discuss the woman problem because of the assumption of male superiority. Assumptions of male superiority are as widespread and deep rooted and every much as crippling to the woman as the assumptions of white supremacy are to the Negro. Consider why it is in SNCC that women who are competent, qualified and experienced, are automatically assigned to the "female" kinds of jobs such as typing, desk work, telephone work, filing, library work, cooking and the assistant kind of administrative work but rarely the "executive" kind.

The woman in SNCC is often in the same position as that token Negro hired in a corporation. The management thinks that it has done its bit. Yet, every day the Negro bears an atmosphere, attitudes and actions which are tinged with condescension and paternalism, the most telling of which are when he is not promoted as the equally or less skilled whites are. This paper is anonymous. Think about the kinds of things the author, if made known, would have to suffer because of raising this kind of discussion. Nothing so final as being fired or outright exclusion, but the kinds of things which are killing to the in-sides—insinuations, ridicule, over-exaggerated compensations. This paper is presented anyway because it needs to be made known that many women in the movement are not "happy and contented" with their status. It needs to be made known that much talent and experience are being wasted by this move-ment when women are not given jobs commensurate with their abilities. It needs to be known that just as Negroes were the crucial factor in the economy of the cotton South, so too in SNCC, women are the crucial factor that keeps the movement running on a day to day basis. Yet they are not given equal say-so when it comes to day to day decision making. What can be done? Probably nothing right away. Most men in this movement are probably too threatened by the possibility of serious discussion on this subject. Perhaps this is because they have recently broken away from a matriarchal framework under which they may have grown up. Then too, many women are as unaware and insensitive to this subject as men, just as there are many Negroes who don't understand they are not free or who want to be part of white America. They don't understand that they have to give up their souls and stay in their place to be accepted. So too, many women, in order to be accepted by men, on men's terms, give themselves up to that caricature of what a woman is—unthinking, pliable, an ornament to please the man.

Maybe the only thing that can come out of this paper is discussion—amidst the laughter—but still discussion. (Those who laugh the hardest are often those who need the crutch of male supremacy the most.) And maybe some women will begin to recognize day to day discriminations. And maybe sometime in the future the whole of the women in this movement will become so alert as to force the rest of the movement to stop the discrimination and start the slow process of changing values and ideas so that all of us gradually come to understand that this is no more a man's world than it is a white world.

Women Employed: Office Workers' Bill of Rights, 1977

Women are invaluable to the smooth functioning of any office. We are proud of our skills as well as our decision making abilities. The following rights are basic to any working situation:

1. The right to recognition as professionals and individuals.

Authoritarianism must be abolished from the workplace and be replaced by the understanding that secretaries work alongside their employers in a mutually dependent relationship.

2. The right to develop our potential.

We want opportunities for responsibility and development both within and beyond the secretarial field. Work experience should be considered as equivalent to formal education. It is time that business use the untapped intelligence, creativity and dedication of its secretarial personnel.

3. The right to fair hiring and termination practices.

Secretaries must be hired on the basis of ability, experience, and skills, not by sex, age, appearance, or marital status. . . .

4. The right to clear job descriptions and reasonable work loads.

We must know what is expected of us so we can pace our work according to priorities, with an understanding of how our work relates to the function of the company.

5. The right to equitable salaries.

Our salaries should be commensurate with our contributions to the company. . . .

6. The right to adequate health care.

We insist that all companies comply with the federal guidelines relating to health care and benefits. For example, women must receive the same health and life insurance benefits as male employees.

7. The right to a secure retirement.

Equitable pension plans for all employees must be established. Whenever possible, pension benefits should be transferable from one job to another.

Suggestions for Further Reading

PART I. INTRODUCTION

Mary Beth Norton and Carol Ruth Berkin: Women and American History

Carroll, Berenice, ed. *Liberating Women's History: Theoretical and Critical Essays.* University of Illinois Press, Urbana, Ill., 1976.

Davis, Natalie Z. "Women's History in Transition: The European Case." *Feminist Studies,* 3, No. 3-4 (1976), 83–103.

Gordon, Michael, ed. *The American Family in Social and Historical Perspective.* St. Martin's Press, New York, 1978.

Hartman, Mary S., and Lois Banner, eds. *Clio's Consciousness Raised: New Perspectives on the History of Women.* Harper and Row, New York, 1974.

Lerner, Gerda. "The Lady and the Mill Girl." *American Studies,* 10, No. 1 (Spring 1969), 5–15.

Smith-Rosenberg, Carroll. "The New Woman and the New History." *Feminist Studies,* 3, No. 1-2 (1975), 185–198.

Welter, Barbara. "The Cult of True Womanhood, 1820–1860." *American Quarterly,* 18 (1966), 151–174.

1. Robert V. Wells: Women's Lives Transformed

Chafe, William H. *The American Woman: Her Changing Social, Economic, and Political Role, 1920–1970.* Oxford University Press, New York, 1972.

Fischer, David H. *Growing Old in America.* Oxford University Press, New York, 1977.

Hartman, Mary, and Lois W. Banner, eds. *Clio's Consciousness Raised: New Perspectives on the History of Women.* Harper and Row, New York, 1974.

Kennedy, David M. *Birth Control in America: The Career of Margaret Sanger.* Yale University Press, New Haven, 1970.

Morantz, Regina. "Making Women Modern: Middle Class Women and Health Reform in 19th Century America." *Journal of Social History,* 10 (June 1977), 490–507.

O'Neill, William L. *Divorce in the Progressive Era.* Franklin Watts, New York, 1973.

Pivar, David J. *Purity Crusade: Sexual Morality and Social Control, 1868–1900.* Greenwood Press, Westport, Conn., 1973.

Rabb, T. K., and Robert I. Rotberg, eds. *The Family in History: Interdisciplinary Essays.* Harper and Row, New York, 1973.

Shorter, Edward. *The Making of the Modern Family.* Basic Books, New York, 1975.

Uhlenberg, Peter R. "A Study of Cohort Life Cycles: Cohorts of Native Born Massachusetts Women, 1830–1920." *Population Studies,* 23 (1969), 407–420.

PART II. COLONIAL AMERICA TO 1800

Mary Beth Norton: The Myth of the Golden Age

Carr, Lois Green, and Lorena S. Walsh. "The Planter's Wife: The Experience of White Women in Seventeenth-Century Maryland." *William and Mary Quarterly,* 3rd. ser., 34 (1977), 542–571.

Cott, Nancy. "Divorce and the Changing Status of Women in Eighteenth-Century Massachusetts." *William and Mary Quarterly,* 3rd. ser., 33 (1976), 586–614.

Kerber, Linda. "Daughters of Columbia: Educating Women for the Republic 1787–1805." In *The Hofstadter Aegis: A Memorial,* edited by Stanley Elkins and Eric McKitrick. Alfred A. Knopf, New York, 1974.

Kulikoff, Allan. "The Beginnings of the Afro-American Family in Maryland." In *Law, Society, and Politics in Early Maryland,* edited by Lois Green Carr, Edward Papenfuse, and Aubrey C. Land. Johns Hopkins University, Baltimore, 1977, pp. 171–196.

Norton, Mary Beth. "Eighteenth-Century American Women in Peace and War: The Case of the Loyalists." *William and Mary Quarterly,* 3rd. ser., 33 (1976), 386–409.

Smith, Daniel Scott. "Parental Power and Marriage Patterns: An Analysis of Historical Trends in Hingham, Massachusetts." *Journal of Marriage and the Family,* 35 (August 1973), 419–427.

Wilson, Joan Hoff. "The Illusion of Change: Women and the American Revolution." In *The American Revolution: Explorations in the History of American Radicalism,* edited by Alfred A. Young. Northern Illinois University, DeKalb, Ill., 1976.

2. Mary Beth Norton: A Cherished Spirit of Independence

DePauw, Linda Grant, and Conover Hunt. *"Remember the Ladies": Women in America 1750–1815.* Viking Press, New York, 1976.

Dexter, Elisabeth Anthony. *Colonial Women of Affairs.* Houghton Mifflin, Boston, 1924.

Leonard, Eugenie. *The Dear-Bought Heritage.* University of Pennsylvania Press, Philadelphia, 1965.

Norton, Mary Beth. " 'My Resting Reaping Times': Sarah Osborn's Defense of Her 'Unfeminine' Activities, 1767." *Signs,* II (1976), 515–529.

Spruill, Julia Cherry. *Women's Life and Work in the Southern Colonies.* University of North Carolina Press, Chapel Hill, 1938.

3. Ann D. Gordon: The Young Ladies Academy of Philadelphia

Benson, Mary S. *Women in Eighteenth-Century America: A Study of Opinion and Social Usage.* Columbia University Press, New York, 1935.
Cott, Nancy F. *The Bonds of Womanhood: "Woman's Sphere" in New England, 1780–1835.* Yale University Press, New Haven, 1977.
Kerber, Linda. "Daughters of Columbia: Educating Women for the Republic, 1787–1805." In *The Hofstadter Aegis: A Memorial,* edited by Stanley Elkins and Eric McKitrick. Alfred A. Knopf, New York, 1974.
Rasmusson, Ethel E. "Democratic Environment—Aristocratic Aspiration." *Pennsylvania Magazine of History and Biography,* 90 (1966), 155–182.
Rowson, Susanna. *Charlotte Temple: A Tale of Truth.* College and University Press, New Haven, 1964.
Rush, Benjamin. *Thoughts upon Female Education, Accommodated to the Present State of Society, Manners, and Government in the United States.* In *Essays on Education in the Early Republic,* edited by Frederick Rudolph. Harvard University Press, Cambridge, 1965.
Stearns, Bertha Monica. "Early Philadelphia Magazines for Ladies." *Pennsylvania Magazine of History and Biography,* 64 (1940), 479–491.
Woody, Thomas. *A History of Women's Education in the United States.* 2 vols. Science Press, New York, 1929.

4. Marylynn Salmon: Equality or Submersion?

Beard, Mary R. *Woman as Force in History.* Macmillan, New York, 1946.
Flaherty, David H., ed. *Essays in the History of Early American Law.* University of North Carolina Press, Chapel Hill, 1969.
Friedman, Lawrence. *A History of American Law.* Simon and Schuster, New York, 1973.
Kent, James. *Commentaries on American Law,* Vol. 2. O. Halsted, New York, 1826.
Keyssar, Alexander. "Widowhood in Eighteenth-Century Massachusetts: A Problem in the History of the Family." *Perspectives in American History,* 8 (1974), 83–119.
Morris, Richard B. *Studies in the History of American Law,* 2nd. ed. Joseph M. Mitchell, Philadelphia, 1959. Ch. 3, "Women's Rights in Early American Law," pp. 126–200.
Reeve, Tapping. *The Law of Baron and Feme.* Oliver Steele, New Haven, 1816.

5. Mary Maples Dunn: Women of Light

Brailsford, Mabel Richmond. *Quaker Women, 1650–1690.* Duckworth & Co., London, 1915.

Cadbury, Henry J. "George Fox and Women's Liberation." *The Friends Quarterly,* 18 (October 1974), 370–376.

Frost, J. William. *The Quaker Family in Colonial America.* St. Martin's Press, New York, 1973.

Gummere, Amelia Mott. *The Quaker: A Study in Costume.* Ferris & Leach, Philadelphia, 1901.

James, Sydney V. *A People Among Peoples: Quaker Benevolence in Eighteenth-Century America.* Harvard University Press, Cambridge, 1963.

Ross, Isabel. *Margaret Fell: Mother of Quakerism.* Longmans, Green and Co., London, 1949.

Wells, Robert V. "Quaker Marriage Patterns in a Colonial Perspective," *William and Mary Quarterly,* 3rd. ser., 29 (July 1972), 415–442.

Part III. Ninteenth-Century America

Mary Beth Norton: The Paradox of "Women's Sphere"

Cott, Nancy. *The Bonds of Womanhood: "Woman's Sphere" in New England, 1780–1835.* Yale University Press, New Haven, 1977.

Dublin, Thomas. "Women, Work, and the Family: Female Operatives in the Lowell Mills, 1830–1860." *Feminist Studies,* 3, No. 1-2 (1975), 30–39.

Farragher, John, and Christine Stansell. "Women and Their Families on the Overland Trail to California and Oregon, 1842–1867." *Feminist Studies,* 2, No. 2-3 (1975), 150–166.

Gutman, Herbert. *The Black Family in Slavery and Freedom, 1750–1920.* Pantheon, New York, 1976.

Kraditor, Aileen. *Ideas of the Woman Suffrage Movement, 1890–1920.* Atheneum, New York, 1965.

Lerner, Gerda. "Early Community Work of Black Club Women." *Journal of Negro History,* 59 (1974), 158–167.

Sklar, Kathryn Kish. *Catharine Beecher: A Study in Domesticity.* Yale University Press, New Haven, 1973.

Smith, Daniel Scott. "Family Limitation, Sexual Control and Domestic Feminism in Victorian America." *Feminist Studies,* 1 (1973), 40–57.

Smith-Rosenberg, Carroll. "Beauty, the Beast, and the Militant Woman." *American Quarterly,* 23 (1971), 562–584.

———. "The Female World of Love and Ritual: Relations Between Women in Nineteenth-Century America." *Signs,* 1 (1975–1976), 1–30.

6. Carol Ruth Berkin: Private Woman, Public Woman

Degler, Carl. "Charlotte Perkins Gilman on the Theory and Practice of Feminism." *American Quarterly* (Spring 1956).

Gilman, Charlotte Perkins. *The Living of Charlotte Perkins Gilman.* D. Appleton-Century, New York, 1935.

Nies, Judith. *Seven Women: Portraits from the American Radical Tradition.*
  Viking, New York, 1977.
O'Neil, William. *Everyone Was Brave.* Quadrangle, Chicago, 1969.

7. Kathryn Kish Sklar: The Founding of Mount Holyoke College

Cott, Nancy F. *The Bonds of Womanhood: "Woman's Sphere" in New England,
  1780–1835.* Yale University Press, New Haven, 1977.
Cross, Barbara. *The Educated Woman in America.* Teachers College Press,
  New York, 1956.
Gordon, Sarah. "Smith College Students: The First Ten Classes, 1879–1888."
  History of Education Quarterly (Summer 1975), 147–167.
Kerber, Linda K. "Daughters of Columbia: Educating Women for the Republic,
  1787–1805." In *The Hofstadter Aegis: A Memorial,* edited by Stanley
  Elkins and Eric McKitrick. Alfred A. Knopf, New York, 1974, pp. 36–59.
Newcomer, Mabel. *A Century of Higher Education for American Women.*
  Harper Brothers, New York, 1959.
Noble, Jeanne L. *The Negro Woman's College.* Teachers College Press, New
  York, 1956.
Pond, Jean Sarah. *Bradford, A New England Academy.* Bradford Academy,
  Bradford, 1930.
Schulz, Louise. *Women's Education Begins: The Rise of the Women's Colleges.*
  Wheaton College Press, Wheaton, Mass., 1935; reissued, Arno Press,
  New York, 1971.
Sklar, Kathryn Kish. *Catharine Beecher: A Study in American Domesticity.*
  Yale University Press, New Haven, 1973; W. W. Norton, New York, 1976.
Swint, Henry Lee. *The Northern Teacher in the South, 1862–1870.* Vanderbilt
  University Press, Nashville, 1941.
Thompson, Eleanor Wolf. *Education for Ladies, 1830–1860, Ideas on Education
  in Magazines for Women.* King's Crown Press, New York, 1947.

8. Carole Turbin: And We Are Nothing but Women

Abbott, Edith. *Women in Industry.* D. Appleton and Company, New York, 1910.
Andrews, John B., and W. P. D. Bliss. *History of Women in Trade Unions.*
  Arno Press, New York, 1971 (reprint of 1911 ed.).
Baker, Elizabeth Faulkner. *Technology and Women's Work.* Columbia Uni-
  versity Press, New York, 1964.
Flexner, Eleanor. *Century of Struggle.* Atheneum, New York, 1970.
Montgomery, David. *Beyond Equality: Labor and the Radical Republicans,
  1862–1872.* Vintage Books, New York, 1972.
Penny, Virginia. *The Employments of Women.* Walker, Wise, and Company,
  Boston, 1863.
Sumner, Helen L. *History of Women in Industry in the United States.* Arno
  Press, New York, 1971 (reprint in 1911 ed.).

Walkowitz, Daniel J. "Statistics and the Writing of Working Class Culture: A Statistical Portrait of the Iron Workers in Troy, New York, 1860–1880." *Labor History,* Vol. 15, No. 3 (Summer 1974).

Ware, Norman. *The Industrial Worker, 1840–1860.* Quadrangle Books, Chicago, 1964, c. 1924.

Wolfson, Theresa. *The Woman Worker and the Trade Unions.* International Publishers, New York, 1926.

9. Lucie Cheng Hirata: Chinese Immigrant Women in Nineteenth-Century California

Coolidge, Mary. *Chinese Immigration.* Henry Holt, New York, 1909.

Dillon, Richard. *The Hatchet Men.* Coward-McCann, New York, 1962.

Gibson, Otis. *Chinese in America.* Hitchcock and Walden, Cincinnati, 1877, pp. 127–157; pp. 200–222.

Hirata, Lucie. "Free, Enslaved and Indentured Workers in Nineteenth Century America: The Case of Chinese Prostitution." *Signs,* 4 (1979) (forthcoming).

Liu, Bo-ji. *Mei-guo Hua-qiao shi* (A History of the Chinese in the United States of America). Li-ming, Taipei, 1976.

Loomis, A. W. "Chinese Women in California." *Overland Monthly,* 2 (1869), 343–351.

McWilliams, Carey. *California, The Great Exception.* Peregrine Smith, Santa Barbara, 1967.

Sui Seen Far. "The Chinese Women in America." *Land of Sunshine,* 6 (1897), 59–64.

U.S. Congress. Joint Special Committee to Investigate Chinese Immigration. *Report.* U.S. Government Printing Office, Washington, D.C., 1877.

10. John Paull Harper: Be Fruitful and Multiply

Barker-Benfield, G. J. *Horrors of the Half-Known Life: Male Attitudes Toward Women in Nineteenth-Century America.* Harper and Row, New York, 1976.

Gordon, Linda. *Woman's Body, Woman's Right: A Social History of Birth Control in America.* Grossman Publishers, New York, 1976.

Himes, Norman E. *Medical History of Contraception.* William and Wilkens Co., Baltimore, 1936.

Kennedy, David M. *Birth Control in America: The Career of Margaret Sanger.* Yale University Press, New Haven, 1970.

Reed, James. *From Private Vice to Public Virtue: The Birth Control Movement and American Society Since 1830.* Basic Books, New York, 1977.

Smith-Rosenberg, Carroll, and Charles Rosenberg. "The Female Animal: Medical and Biological Views of Woman and Her Role in Nineteenth-Century America." *Journal of American History,* 60 (1973), 332–356.

Part IV. Twentieth-Century America

Carol Ruth Berkin: Not Separate, Not Equal

Banner, Lois. *Women in Modern America: A Brief History*. Harcourt Brace Jovanovich, New York, 1974.

Chafe, William. *The American Woman: Her Changing Social, Economic, and Political Role, 1920–1970*. Oxford University Press, New York and London, 1974.

Lemons, Stanley. *The Female Citizen*. University of Illinois Press, Urbana, 1975.

Lerner, Gerda. *Black Women in White America*. Random House, New York, 1972.

O'Neill, William, ed. *Women Who Work*. Quadrangle Books, Chicago, 1972.

Ryan, Mary. *Womanhood in America: From Colonial Times to the Present*. New Viewpoints, New York, 1975.

11. Susan Reverby: From Aide to Organizer

Baxandall, Rosalyn, Linda Gordon, and Susan Reverby. *America's Working Women: A Documentary History 1600 to the Present*. Vintage, New York, 1976.

Drake, St. Clair, and Horace R. Cayton. *Black Metropolis: A Study of Negro Life in a Northern City*. Harcourt, Brace, New York, 1945 and 1962.

Health PAC. *American Health Empire: Power, Profits and Politics*. Prepared by John and Barbara Ehrenreich. Vintage, New York, 1970.

———. *Prognosis Negative: Crisis in the Health Care System*. Edited by David Ketelchuck. Vintage, New York, 1976.

Jacobson, Julius. *The Negro and the American Labor Movement*. Doubleday Anchor, New York, 1968.

Lerner, Gerda. *Black Women in White America: A Documentary History*. Random House, New York, 1972.

"Oral History." *Red Buffalo*, No. 2-3, no date. American Studies Program, SUNY at Buffalo, N.Y.

Shumway, Gary, and William Hartley. "Oral History Primer." The authors, Fullerton, Calif., 1973.

"Union Maids." Available from New Day Films, Franklin Lakes, N.J.

12. Rosalind Rosenberg: The Academic Prism

Bernard, Jessie. *Academic Women*. Pennsylvania State University Press, University Park, Penn., 1964.

Fass, Paula. *The Damned and the Beautiful: American Youth in the 1920s*. Oxford University Press, New York, 1977.

Freedman, Estelle. "The New Woman: Changing Views of Women in the 1920's." *Journal of American History*, 61 (September 1974), 372–393.

Mead, Margaret. *Blackberry Winter: My Earlier Years.* Simon and Schuster, New York, 1972.

Thompson (Woolley), Helen. *Psychological Norms in Men and Women.* University of Chicago Press, Chicago, 1903.

Vesey, Laurence. *The Emergence of the American University.* University of Chicago Press, Chicago, 1965.

13. Leila J. Rupp: Woman's Place Is in the War

Chafe, William H. *The American Woman: Her Changing Social, Economic, and Political Role, 1920–1970.* Oxford University Press, New York, 1972.

Koonz, Claudia. "Mothers in the Fatherland: Women in Nazi Germany." In *Becoming Visible: Women in European History,* edited by Renate Bridenthal and Claudia Koonz. Houghton Mifflin, Boston, 1977.

Mason, Tim. "Women in Germany, 1925–1940: Family, Welfare and Work." *History Workshop: Journal of Socialist Historians,* No. 1 (Spring 1976), 74–113; No. 2 (Autumn 1976), 5–32.

Quick, Paddy. "Rosie the Riveter: Myths and Realities." *Radical America,* 9 (July–October 1975), 115–131.

Rupp, Leila J. *Mobilizing Women for War: German and American Propaganda, 1939–1945.* Princeton University Press, Princeton, 1978.

Stephenson, Jill. *Women in Nazi Society.* Barnes and Noble, New York, 1976.

Straub, Eleanor F. "U.S. Government Policy Toward Civilian Women During World War II." *Prologue. Journal of the National Archives,* 5 (Winter 1973), 240–254.

Tobias, Sheila, and Lisa Anderson. "What Really Happened to Rosie the Riveter." *MSS Modular Publications,* Module 9, 1974.

Trey, J. E. "Women in the War Economy—World War II." *Review of Radical Political Economics,* 4 (July 1972), 41–57.

14. Jacquelyn Dowd Hall: "A Truly Subversive Affair"

Ames, Jessie Daniel. *The Changing Character of Lynching.* Commission on Interracial Cooperation, Atlanta, 1942.

Brownmiller, Susan. *Against Our Will: Men, Women and Rape.* Simon and Schuster, New York, 1975.

Carter, Dan T. *Scottsboro: A Tragedy of the American South,* 2nd. ed. Oxford University Press, New York, 1971.

Dollard, John. *Caste and Class in a Southern Town,* 3rd. ed. Anchor Books, Garden City, N.Y., 1957.

Dykeman, Wilma, and James Stokely. *Seeds of Southern Change: The Life of Will Alexander.* University of Chicago Press, Chicago, 1962.

Hammond, Lily H. *Race and the South: Two Studies, 1919–1922,* reprint. Arno Press, New York, 1972.

Lerner, Gerda, ed. *Black Women in White America: A Documentary History.* Random House, New York, 1972.

MacDonell, Mrs. R. W. *Belle Harris Bennett, Her Life Work.* Board of Missions, Methodist Episcopal Church, South, Nashville, 1928.

Raper, Arthur. *The Tragedy of Lynching,* 3rd. ed. Dover Publications, New York, 1970.

Scott, Anne Firor. *The Southern Lady: From Pedestal to Politics, 1830–1930,* 2nd. ed. University of Chicago Press, Chicago, 1972.

Smith, Lillian. *Killers of the Dream,* 2nd. ed. Anchor Books, Garden City, N.Y., 1963.

Wells, Ida B. *Crusade for Justice: The Autobiography of Ida B. Wells.* Edited by Alfreda Duster. University of Chicago Press, Chicago, 1970.

15. Sara M. Evans: Tomorrow's Yesterday

Cade, Toni. *The Black Woman: An Anthology.* New American Library, New York, 1970.

Chafe, William H. *Women and Equality: Changing Patterns in American Culture.* Oxford University Press, New York, 1977.

Filene, Peter G. *Him/Her Self: Sex Roles in Modern America.* New American Library, New York, 1974.

Firestone, Shulamith. *The Dialectic of Sex.* Bantam Books, New York, 1971.

Freeman, Jo. *The Politics of Women's Liberation.* McKay, New York, 1975.

"Future Visions and Fantasies." *Quest: A Feminist Quarterly,* 2 (Summer 1975).

Hole, Edith, and Ellen Levine. *Rebirth of Feminism.* Quadrangle, New York, 1971.

Morgan, Robin. *Going Too Far: The Personal Chronicle of a Feminist.* Random House, New York, 1977.

Stack, Carol. *All Our Kin.* Harper and Row, New York, 1974.

Notes on the Contributors

CAROL RUTH BERKIN is Associate Professor of History at Baruch College, City University of New York. She is the author of *Jonathan Sewall: Odyssey of an American Loyalist* and a forthcoming book, *Colonists in Crisis: The Loyalist Experience of the American Revolution.* She has also written in the field of women's history, *Within the Conjurer's Circle: Women in Colonial America,* and is currently working on a full biography of Charlotte Perkins Gilman. She has received the Bancroft Dissertation Award, 1972, and grants for her continuing research from the American Council of Learned Societies, National Endowment for the Humanities, and the CUNY Research Foundation.

MARY MAPLES DUNN, professor of history at Bryn Mawr College, is the author of a book entitled *William Penn: Politics and Conscience,* and is currently working on a study of Protestant women and religion in colonial America.

SARA M. EVANS teaches women's history at the University of Minnesota. She is the author of *Personal Politics,* a study of the origins of contemporary feminism. She has been active in a variety of feminist groups since 1967.

ANN D. GORDON coauthored "Women in American Society: An Historical Introduction" in 1971 and earned her Ph.D. in American colonial history from the University of Wisconsin. She taught in Northwestern's School of Education, worked as associate editor of the Jane Addams Papers, and is now on the staff of the Woodrow Wilson Papers at Princeton.

JACQUELYN DOWD HALL is director of the Southern Oral History Program and a member of the history department faculty at the University of North Carolina at Chapel Hill. She received her undergraduate degree from Southwestern at Memphis and her Ph.D. from Columbia University. Her dissertation, "Revolt Against Chivalry: Jessie Daniel Ames and the Women's Campaign Against Lynching," was the recipient of the 1974 Bancroft Dissertation Award. She is presently coordinating a research project on southern labor history funded by the National Endowment for the Humanities.

JOHN PAULL HARPER is director of Cornell University's Labor Liberal Arts Program in New York City. He received the Ph.D. in social history from Columbia University where he held a National Institute of Mental Health Fellowship for 1966–1970. He has contributed articles and reviews to numerous labor publications.

LUCIE CHENG HIRATA received her Ph.D. from the University of Hawaii in 1970. She is currently Associate Professor of Sociology and the Director of Asian American Studies Center at the University of California, Los Angeles. She has published numerous articles on modern Chinese society and on Chinese Americans. She is currently completing a book tentatively titled *Race, Sex and Class: A History of Chinese Women in America.*

MARY BETH NORTON is a member of the History Department, Cornell University. She is the author of *The British-Americans: The Loyalist Exiles in England, 1774–1789,* which won the Allan Nevins Prize. Her current research examines women in the era of the American Revolution, the subject of several of her recent articles and her forthcoming book.

SUSAN REVERBY is a graduate student in the American Studies Program at Boston University. Under a grant from the National Center for Health Services Research she is writing a dissertation on the work culture of American nurses. She is the coeditor of *America's Working Women, A Documentary History* and of the forthcoming *Historical Perspectives on the American Health Care System.*

ROSALIND ROSENBERG received her B.A. in 1968 and Ph.D. in 1974 from Stanford University and has taught American history since then at Columbia University. She is also working with the Columbia Center for the Social Sciences in its program on Sex Roles and Social Change, and is expanding her dissertation, "The Dissent from Darwin," into a book on the changing ideas about women's nature among American social scientists over the last century.

LEILA J. RUPP received her Ph.D. from Bryn Mawr College in 1976 and is currently assistant professor of history and women's studies at Ohio State University. She is the author of *Mobilizing Women for War: German and American Propaganda, 1939–1945* and the coeditor of *Nazi Ideology Before 1933: A Documentation.*

MARYLYNN SALMON, a graduate student at Bryn Mawr College, has been the recipient of two research scholarships and the S. Maude Kaemmerling fellowship in the department of history. She is currently at work on her dissertation, a study of equity law and its influence on the legal status of women in early America. This is her first published article.

KATHRYN KISH SKLAR received her B.A. from Radcliffe College and her Ph.D. from the University of Michigan. After having taught at the University of Michigan, she is now an Associate Professor of History at the University of California at Los Angeles where she teaches both graduate and undergraduate courses in the social history of American women from 1600 to the present, and chairs the Committee to Administer the Program in Women's Studies. She is the author of *Catharine Beecher: A Study in American Domesticity* (Norton, 1976), "American Female Historians in Context, 1775–1930," *Feminist Studies, 3* (Summer 1975), and other writings in the history of American women. She was a Fellow at the Radcliffe Institute, 1973–1974, and a Fellow at the National Humanities Institute, New Haven, 1975–1976.

CAROLE TURBIN has just completed at the New School for Social Research a dissertation that compares women's trade unions and the women's rights movements in the 1860s and 1870s in the United States. She has taught sociology at the State University of New York, Stony Brook, and other institutions. Her main teaching interests are social stratification, social movements, and sex roles.

ROBERT V. WELLS is an associate professor of history at Union College. He is the author of "Demographic Change and the Life Cycle of American Families," "Family History and Demographic Transition," and *The Population of the British Colonies in America before 1776.* He has been a fellow of the Charles Warren Center at Harvard University and the John Simon Guggenheim Foundation.

Index